Sexual Misconduct, Harassment, and Discrimination in Healthcare

History, Analysis, and Solutions with Case Studies

∞

By Matthew J. Mazurek, MD, MHA, CPE, FACHE, FASA

American Association for
PHYSICIAN
LEADERSHIP

PUBLISHER
Nancy Collins

PRODUCTION MANAGER
Jennifer Weiss

DESIGN & LAYOUT
Carter Publishing Studio

COPYEDITOR
Patricia George

TABLE OF CONTENTS

ABOUT THE AUTHOR

Matthew Mazurek, a Fresno, California, native, graduated as a valedictorian at C.L. McLane High School and *magna cum laude* from California State University, Fresno, earning a Bachelor of Arts in English literature with a focus on creative writing and poetry. For two years, he was poetry editor for *The San Joaquin Review*.

Early in his career, Mazurek taught astronomy at Fresno State and physics at Bullard High School before pursuing medicine at the University of California, San Francisco (UCSF) School of Medicine. During medical school, he was awarded a Genentech research grant to study the mechanisms of volatile anesthetics, co-authoring two papers on the discovery of a novel tandem-pore potassium channel sensitive to volatile anesthetics. This research resulted in Mazurek being selected as a finalist for the Dean's Prize for student research.

As an anesthesiology resident at UCSF, Mazurek developed a strong interest in the history of anesthesia. He won the Anesthesia History Association's resident essay contest in 2004 and presented a prize-winning paper at Cambridge University in 2005 on Chauncey Leake's development and experimental use of divinyl ether in the 1920s and 1930s at UCSF.

After completing residency, Mazurek joined Southern Arizona Anesthesia Services in Tucson, Arizona, where he served as chair of the anesthesia department at St. Mary's Hospital and later as chief of staff. His leadership experiences inspired him to pursue advanced degrees, earning a Master of Healthcare Administration as a Distinguished Scholar with a focus on information systems from Colorado State University and an Executive MBA from the Valar Institute at the Quantic School of Business and Technology. He also earned his Certified Physician Executive (CPE) certificate and was elected Fellow of the American Association for Physician Leadership (FAAPL). Additionally, he was elected as a Fellow of the American Society of Anesthesiologists (FASA).

Mazurek later became medical director with Envision Physician Services at Sanford Health in Bemidji, Minnesota, while serving as adjunct faculty teaching students for CRNA programs at the University of North Dakota and the University of Minnesota. He also provided clinical rotations in anesthesiology for medical students at the Des Moines School of Osteopathic Medicine and the University of Minnesota.

He served on the board of directors for the Minnesota chapter of the American College of Healthcare Executives and is a Fellow of the American College of Healthcare Executives (FACHE).

His passion for quality outcomes for surgical patients led him to pursue his Certified Professional in Health Quality (CPHQ) certificate through the National Association for Healthcare Quality (NAHQ).

In addition to his leadership and teaching roles, Mazurek authored *Physicians and Professional Behavior Management Strategies: A Leadership Roadmap and Guide with Case Studies*, a book informed by his experiences managing professional behavior as a former chair and chief of staff. His recent publications in the *Healthcare Administration Leadership & Management Journal* and the *Physician Leadership Journal* focus on quality of care, operations management, and professionalism.

He now serves on several workgroup committees, including one addressing sexual misconduct and harassment for the Yale School of Medicine and Yale New Haven Health.

Throughout his career, Mazurek has remained dedicated to mentoring medical students, residents, and CRNA program students, continuing his commitment to education and professional excellence.

He is an assistant professor in the Department of Anesthesiology at the Yale School of Medicine and serves as the medical director of quality and patient safety, Department of Anesthesiology, St. Raphael's Campus, Yale New Haven Health. As a faculty member of the American Association for Physician Leadership (AAPL), he facilitates courses on professionalism and behavioral management and emotional intelligence for the AAPL.

AUTHOR'S NOTE

ONE OF MY MOTIVATIONS in writing this book is my own personal experiences. As a child, I was sexually abused and exposed to domestic violence. There never was justice — only silence. I know I am not alone, and I know my experience is not unique. My own journey has been one of continued healing through personal growth and through support groups, therapy, and now, publicly acknowledging what happened.

Silence is a burden many of us carry. Breaking my own silence, I hope to reduce the stigma and empower others to come forward. I hope this book can serve as a catalyst for continued organizational change to eliminate and reduce sexual misconduct, harassment, and discrimination.

"You can recognize survivors of abuse by their courage. When silence is so very inviting, they step forward and share their truth so others know they aren't alone." — Jeanne McElvaney, author

DEDICATION

For my wife, Kari, daughter, Ariel, sister, Cheryl, and niece, Monique. I love you.

Thank You
Many thanks for years of support to Kathy, Randy, and Susie.

PREFACE

"But the issue of sexual harassment is not the end of it. There are other issues — political issues, gender issues — that people need to be educated about."
— *Anita Hill, American lawyer, author, and educator*

THE TERM "SEXUAL HARASSMENT" was first coined in the 1970s, with its legal recognition and widespread acknowledgment of the problem growing over subsequent decades. The recent #MeToo movement, which gained significant momentum in 2017, marked a turning point in societal awareness and discourse surrounding sexual harassment, misconduct, assault, and discrimination. This movement empowered individuals, particularly women, to speak out about their experiences and hold perpetrators accountable for their actions. It shed light on the pervasiveness of such behavior across various industries, highlighting the need for systemic change. Efforts to introduce new legislation addressing both old and new issues continue.

Legal cases stemming from the #MeToo movement have played a crucial role in setting new precedents, shaping expectations, and prompting the reevaluation of existing laws and policies. Additionally, these cases have contributed to the development of new legislation aimed at addressing gaps in protection and improving avenues for victims to take recourse.

The number of programs providing training and institutions conducting research on sexual harassment and related issues has expanded significantly over the past three decades. These initiatives aim to educate individuals and organizations about appropriate conduct, prevention strategies, and the importance of fostering a safe, respectful, and inclusive workplace. The evolution of the discourse surrounding sexual harassment underscores the ongoing efforts to combat such behavior and create safer environments for all individuals.

UNIQUE CHALLENGES IN HEALTHCARE

The intersection and complex nature of sexual misconduct and harassment within the healthcare industry presents unique challenges and considerations. Healthcare settings involve intimate interactions between patients and healthcare providers, which can create vulnerabilities and opportunities for misconduct. Physicians and nurses are entrusted with their patients' care, which often involves performing sensitive physical examinations, asking personal questions, and providing support during emotionally charged situations. These interactions require a delicate balance between providing necessary care and respecting a patient's dignity and boundaries.

Despite efforts to maintain professionalism, instances of misconduct still occur, whether through inappropriate touching, comments, or behaviors. Patients, too, may sometimes engage in misconduct, complicating the dynamics of the provider-patient relationship. The inherent power dynamics in healthcare settings can further exacerbate the risk of misconduct. Patients may feel compelled to comply with providers' requests or may fear reprisal if they speak out against inappropriate behavior. Similarly, healthcare providers may abuse their authority to exploit patients' vulnerabilities.

Addressing sexual misconduct and harassment in healthcare requires a multifaceted approach. This includes robust policies and procedures for reporting and addressing misconduct, comprehensive training for healthcare providers on appropriate conduct and boundaries, and mechanisms for supporting and advocating for patients and staff who experience misconduct.

Promoting a culture of respect, professionalism, and accountability within healthcare organizations is essential in preventing and addressing misconduct. This involves fostering open communication, promoting a zero-tolerance stance toward harassment, and ensuring that all members of the healthcare team understand their roles and responsibilities in maintaining a safe and respectful environment for all patients and staff.

The psychological, social, emotional, and economic impact of continued sexual misconduct and harassment cannot be understated or underestimated. Victims pay a high price personally and professionally. Providing support and investigating claims of misconduct sensitively while adhering to legal requirements and moral and ethical obligations is not an easy task for anyone involved in the process. Investigating claims is an uncomfortable, emotionally charged process for all parties, and investigating these incidents is one of the most difficult responsibilities leaders and managers face.

An additional problem is the fact there is no universally recognized definition of sexual misconduct and harassment, nor are there standardized programs and approaches to mitigate the problem. The anti-harassment training industry is a billion-dollar enterprise, and one of the shortcomings of the training is that it has not stopped the behaviors.

Additionally, discrimination based on sex, gender, gender identity, and sexual orientation continues to affect employment and advancement opportunities. Continued discrimination hampers efforts toward building a supportive, inclusive community and reinforces the status quo. It is unacceptable, and efforts to reduce discrimination must continue.

A CONTENT NOTE

The subject matter and cases presented in this book can be triggering for some individuals, and some of the language and terms used might offend some readers. *It is not my intention to use terms or language readers may find offensive.* Navigating language and terminology in discussions about sexual misconduct is challenging due to the complexities and nuances of the subject matter. Different terms may carry different connotations or interpretations for various individuals, and what is considered acceptable or appropriate language can vary depending on cultural, social, and personal contexts. The material and cases can evoke strong emotional responses in individuals who have experienced or been affected by sexual misconduct or harassment behaviors.

The case discussions presented provide an opportunity to learn from and approach the problem. Names are altered, and many cases are based on real cases with no other identifying information to protect everyone involved. More notable cases, well known in the media, including names and other identifying information, also serve as examples for discussion — especially as examples of how organizations can improve the investigation process and response.

This book is the first to comprehensively address a gap in this important subject and serves as a guide for all organizations and individuals to understand the problem and create more effective strategies to reduce the incidence and harmful consequences of sexual misconduct, harassment, and discrimination.

The content is applicable to all industries but is specifically tailored to address the unique needs of healthcare organizations. Collectively, we can and must build better cultures that not only are intolerant of the behaviors but supportive of an inclusive, respectful culture and environment free from misconduct, harassment, and discrimination. It is a moral and ethical imperative.

> *"Responsible and respectful reporting on sexual harassment has an important role to play in shifting power by shining a light on the way in which our systems have served to silence and protect perpetrators." —Somali Cerise, chair, National Women's Safety Alliance*

REFERENCE

1. McDonald P. Workplace Sexual Harassment 30 Years On: A Review of the Literature. *Internat J Manage Rev.* 2012;14(1): 1–17.

AUTHOR'S APPROACH

"Your word is your wand. The words you speak create your own destiny." — Florence Scovil Shinn, early 20th century spiritual leader, author, and artist

IN A BOOK AS COMPREHENSIVE IN SCOPE AS THIS, it is nearly impossible to address all of the issues and concerns about this important topic. As much as possible, the research conducted on the topics includes the history of legal, social, and medical changes as our understanding has evolved. It is important to remember that a lot of progress was made possible only through the efforts of marginalized groups demanding justice and change by protesting, pressing for changes in legislation, and creating awareness in a variety of different forms of media. It has been and continues to be an evolving process that requires continued efforts despite past, present, and future resistance to change the status quo.

Progress has been achieved through *punctuated equilibrium,* a process borrowed from an evolutionary theory in biology. Punctuated equilibrium is the concept that change happens both quickly and slowly. Landmark cases, social movements, and legislation have propelled progress forward quickly, only to be followed by slowly adopting and adapting to new norms and expectations. As a result, progress can seem painfully slow and unpredictable.

To give a voice and perspective to victims and complainants, I specifically searched for qualitative studies containing verbatim quotes and statements from interviews, surveys, or questionnaires. This is a book about how people treat each other. It is a book about humanity and what it means to be human. Those directly affected by these issues must have their collective voices heard and recognized. Without these narratives and stories, the emotional impact and the importance of what this book addresses would seem sterile and have less impact and urgency.

Our lives are a complex tapestry of our identity, relationships, experiences, emotions, behaviors, actions, reactions, and words. No one lives in a vacuum. Written words, like art or music, are the only unique, tangible thing we leave behind. They transcend time. They capture and preserve our thoughts and feelings. By sharing the stories, narratives, emotions, and experiences, I hope to convey that all of us have a lot more in common than we realize. Our humanness is what bonds us. *Namaste.*

Historical Development of Awareness of Sexual Harassment and Misconduct

*"We are not makers of history. We are made by
history."* — *Rev. Martin Luther King Jr.*

*"People talk to me all the time about sexual harassment. This
sort of behavior did not only happen in the past. And it's not in
just the working class. It's in every industry. It's in the military.
It's in politics."* —*Niki Caro, film director and screenwriter*

U NDERSTANDING THE HISTORICAL CONTEXT of sexual misconduct, harassment, and discrimination is crucial in comprehending the complexity of these issues and the evolution of our modern awareness and definitions. *How* and *why* did awareness evolve? *Who* continues to engage in misconduct? *What* strategies are used to mitigate and reduce sexual misconduct? *Why* does it continue? *How* can changing culture create a supportive environment free from misconduct and harassment?

Awareness of sexual harassment and misconduct has evolved over time, shaped by cultural norms and societal movements. One of the first known attempts to reduce the incidence of what we now call sexual harassment in the healthcare setting was a preventative approach by Florence Nightengale in the 1800s.[1] During a time when women were considered partially to blame for their own victimization, Nightengale believed nurses should have high moral character. She required them to live in separate quarters away from the physicians, abide by a curfew, dress in restrictive, modest clothing, and behave in a modest manner.

Nightengale believed the rules helped the nurses cope with the stress of being subjected to harassment and insults by male physicians and soldiers. Responsibility and accountability from the predominantly male physician workforce to not engage in the behavior were not addressed or enforced. The social and gender role norms of that era reinforced the injustice.

Sexual misconduct and harassment are behavioral and social practices. Social practices have institutional and semiotic lives, and lives have histories. The historical perspective allows us to examine the fundamental nature of misconduct and harassment. What are the rules and rhetoric by which law constrains — or enables — the sexual misconduct in question?[2]

Additionally, it is important to break down barriers in understanding these behaviors and explore sexual misconduct outside the traditional stereotype often attached to the subject—that of a male toward a female. Still, it is important to appreciate that this traditional "stereotype" gave rise to our modern social consciousness and awareness of this issue. Women are, by far, the most frequent victims of these behaviors.

The movement to address sexual misconduct parallels the women's rights movement and the increased presence of women in the workforce beginning in the late 19th century. The decades-long progress and impact of changing and evolving social, economic, and political factors affecting the present state of sexual misconduct cannot be ignored. Women's increased involvement in the workforce and the economy was one of the most significant social transformations during the 20th century.

WOMEN IN THE WORKFORCE

Women's increased participation in the workforce evolved in four distinct phases throughout the 20th century. The first phase occurred from the late-19th century to the 1920s. Women were less educated than men, and many of the jobs available required little to no education or prior experience. Most women were employed as laundresses, in manufacturing, and as domestic workers (housekeeping and caregiving). More professional job opportunities included teaching and clerical work. Nursing, too, began to emerge as an option early in the 20th century.[2]

Significantly, during this era, the women's suffrage movement resulted in the passage of the 19th Amendment to the U.S. Constitution, granting women the right to vote. This gave women a voice in politics, and with a voice in politics, they became instrumental in legislating laws affecting women.

At the same time, more women were pursuing formal education. They were graduating high school and taking advantage of the increasing number of secondary education institutions that gave women the opportunity to pursue a college education.

Many factors contributed to the second phase, from the late 1920s to the early 1950s. One factor was an increasingly educated workforce of women. In 1910, only 9% of women graduated high school; by the late 1920s, 30% of women graduated high school.[2] The rise of many new industrial and corporate jobs led to the need for more clerical workers and factory support staff. However, during this and the prior phase, married women did not account for a majority of the female workforce. There was still an expectation that once married, women would leave the workforce and become homemakers.

World War II radically changed work opportunities for women. The War Manpower Commission, a federal agency established to increase the manufacture of war materials, had the task of recruiting women into employment vital to the war effort. As young men were sent to war, millions of women were employed by factories requiring labor and technical skills not previously offered to women. As a result, Rosie the Riveter emerged as a symbol of this profound shift in the demographics of the industrial workplace. These opportunities shattered long-held beliefs and stereotypes that women were the weaker vessels and simply could not do traditional work dominated by men.

The third phase occurred from the early 1950s through the early 1970s. The number of women in the workforce expanded, and the civil rights movement of the 1960s addressed racism and racial discrimination. There was a rising consciousness that equality was a right.

The last phase, one of the most significant, was revolutionary. In 1950, 25% of married women participated in the workforce; by 1970, 46% of married women were working outside the home. This started a profound shift from women having limited options for careers to an expansion of opportunities.[2]

THE RISE OF SEXUAL HARASSMENT AND MISCONDUCT

With increasing numbers of women participating in the workforce, the prevalence and incidence of sexual harassment and misconduct increased. By the 1970s, the issue gained public attention. Specifically, Catharine MacKinnon, Lin Farley, and other lawyers who represented women in and out of court were able to mount a concerted assault of unprecedented magnitude and force on the practice of sexual harassment. The American legal system began to recognize a woman's right to work free of unwanted sexual advances.

The phrase "sexual harassment" was first coined in 1975 by a group of women at Cornell University. A former employee of the university, Carmita Wood, filed a claim for unemployment benefits after she resigned from her job due to unwanted touching from her supervisor. Cornell had refused Wood's request for a transfer and denied her the benefits on the grounds that she quit for "personal reasons."

Wood, together with activists at the university's human affairs office, formed a group called Working Women United. At a Speak Out event hosted by the group, secretaries, mailroom clerks, filmmakers, factory workers, and waitresses shared their stories, revealing that the problem extended beyond the university setting. The women recounted incidents of men masturbating in front of them, threatening them, and pressuring them to trade sexual favors for promotions. Women had rightfully had enough and wanted strong, corrective action — and justice.[3]

EARLY ATTEMPTS TO ADDRESS THE ISSUE

Title VII of the Civil Rights Act of 1964 made unwanted sexual advances or harassment at work legally actionable, but women faced retribution if they filed complaints. For many women, sexual misconduct and harassment was the price to pay to work. Another attempt to address the issue was the Equal Rights Amendment (ERA), introduced by Representative Martha Griffiths in 1971. Despite wide bipartisan support, Phyllis Schlafly mobilized conservative women to oppose the amendment. It failed to pass the required number of state legislatures by the termination date, June 30, 1982.

By the late 1970s, sexual harassment prevention training programs and videos were produced to educate employees in efforts to prevent the behavior. Rising awareness also led to new and challenging legal cases, establishing new precedents and breaking down the status quo. In 1980, the Equal Employment Opportunity Commission (EEOC) officially established guidelines for sexual harassment in the workplace and provided a formal definition.

In 1986, a landmark case, *Meritor Savings Bank v. Vinson*, determined that if an employer is aware of sexual harassment, the employer is responsible to take action, perform an investigation, and develop a plan to address the situation. The U.S. Supreme Court held that the language of Title VII of the

Civil Rights Act "was not limited to 'economic' or 'tangible' discrimination," finding that Congress intended "to strike at the entire spectrum of men and women in employment...."

The court noted that guidelines issued by the EEOC specified that sexual harassment leading to noneconomic injury was a form of sex discrimination prohibited by Title VII. The court recognized that plaintiffs could establish violations of the Act "by proving that discrimination based on sex has created a hostile or abusive work environment."[4]

Throughout the next three decades, other cases presented new legal challenges and were addressed by the courts and other government agencies. A landmark case before the Supreme Court in 2020, *Bostock v. Clayton County*, determined that Title VII of the Civil Rights Act protects employees against discrimination because of sexuality or gender identity.[5] As slow as it seems, there is progress.

BEYOND LEGAL RULINGS

Sexual harassment and misconduct programs are now ubiquitous in onboarding employees in most industries, yet the behaviors continue. In the past decade, multimillion-dollar settlements and criminal indictments revealed that organizations knowingly failed to address attributed individuals. Most training programs focus on the legal consequences of sexual harassment and do not focus on creating a culture of awareness, prevention, and intolerance.

Cultural change is essential to creating a supportive environment free from harassment. This involves challenging harmful attitudes and behaviors, promoting empathy and respect, and actively working to dismantle systems of oppression and inequality. It requires collective action from individuals, institutions, and society as a whole. It is the responsibility of organizations to foster a good culture and to encourage people to speak when harassment or misconduct occurs. Silence is not an option. In the words of Rev. Dr. Martin Luther King, Jr., "Our lives begin to end the day we become silent about things that matter."

REFERENCES

1. Straus S. Overview and Summary: Sexual Harassment in Healthcare. *Online Journal of Issues in Nursing.* 2019; 24(1).

2. Goldin C. The Quiet Revolution That Transformed Women's Employment, Education, and Family. Richard T. Ely Lecture. American Economic Association Annual Meeting. May 2006.
3. Cohen S. A Brief History of Sexual Harassment Before Anita Hill. *Time*. April 11, 2016.
4. *Meritor Savings Bank v. Vinson.*, 477 U.S. 57 (1986). https://www.oyez.org/cases/1985/84-1979.
5. *Bostock v. Clayton County, Georgia*, 590 U.S. ___ (2020). https://www.supremecourt.gov/opinions/19pdf/17-1618_hfci.pdf.

Scope of the Problem

∞

Chapter 1. Prevalence and Incidence of Sexual Harassment and Misconduct

I T IS DIFFICULT TO ACCURATELY MEASURE the prevalence and incidence of sexual misconduct and harassment due to underreporting or unreported events. However, numerous surveys from research projects, the popular media, and retrospective analyses of reports from the Equal Employment Opportunity Commission (EEOC) indicate the continued high incidence of the behaviors. The April 2022 EEOC Data Highlight reported that between 2018 and 2021, 78% of sexual harassment charges were filed by women. These data are consistent with numerous validated surveys finding that women remain the primary target for sexual harassment and related behaviors.[1]

Since the late 1990s, the number of charges has slowly decreased except for a brief uptick in the number of charges from 2017 to 2020, which corresponds to increased awareness from the #MeToo movement. As shown in Figure 1, the number of charges continues to decline but remains unacceptably high. Thousands of charges are filed annually, and these charges represent a fraction of the total number of charges that could be filed. Fear of retaliation and retribution remains an obstacle and is discussed in greater detail in Chapter 14.

A factor contributing to the decline in the number of reported cases is greater awareness of the problem and, I surmise, the establishment of better processes within organizations to internally manage and respond to allegations and reports promptly — thus negating the need to turn to the EEOC.

In many healthcare organizations, anonymous reporting systems have been created to report not only patient safety concerns but professionalism issues and all other types of harassment, including sexual harassment

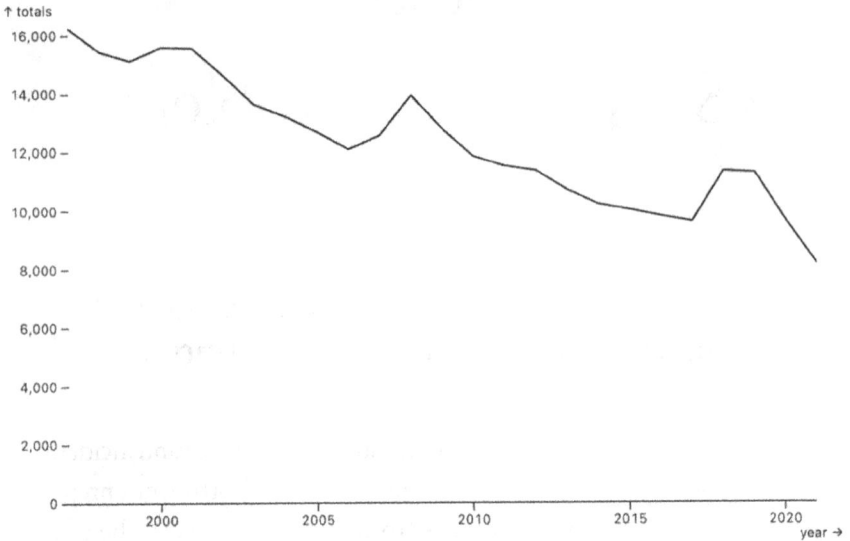

FIGURE 1. EEOC sexual harassment charges, 1997 – 2021.[1]

behaviors. These anonymous reporting systems allow organizations to quickly identify and promptly respond to concerns and take a proactive, not reactive, response.

Nurses provide most of the bedside care around the world, and the frequency and duration of contact with patients and with nurse colleagues on the wards creates an environment for higher rates of sexual harassment and misconduct. In the United Kingdom, where 86% of nurses are female and 14% are male, 60% of nurses say they have experienced sexual harassment at work. Importantly, only 27% of them reported it to their employer.[2]

In addition, 39% of nurses say they have witnessed a colleague being harassed at work, 56% of nurses report verbal harassment, 37% report physical harassment, and 29% experience visual harassment. What's more, 58% of nurses have been harassed by a patient, 26% are harassed by medical colleagues, and 24% are harassed by nursing colleagues.[2] Clearly, the prevalence and incidence of these behaviors in healthcare are unacceptably high.

The number of women in the physician workforce has been rising for decades. In 1980, 25% of medical school graduates were women. As of 2019, 47% of residents and fellows in post-graduate training programs are women and in 2021, 37% of active physicians in the United States were women.[3] An article by Choo, van Dis, and Kass, published in *The New England Journal of Medicine* in 2018, reported that nearly 50% of female medical students will experience sexual harassment by the time they finish medical school.[3] This is unacceptable, and effective interventions to reduce the incidence are necessary.

A 2018 Medscape survey revealed that 28% of physicians experienced sexual harassment by patients.[4] Veterans Affairs outpatient clinics had the highest reported frequency of sexual harassment from patients, followed by outpatient academic clinics.[5]

In 2018, the specialty of dermatology had the dubious distinction of being the specialty with the highest rate of sexual harassment by patients at 46%. Notably, 40% of male providers in a 2020 University of Washington survey of the Department of Dermatology reported sexual harassment.[5] Specific behaviors reported included comments on appearance (85%), questions about marital status (59%), jokes or stories of a sexual nature (35%), and being asked on a date (11%). A contributing factor may be the fact that dermatologists perform full head-to-toe physical exams to screen for skin lesions and abnormalities.

In a 2019 Massachusetts study of resident physicians, 61% of participants reported personal experience with gender-based bias or discrimination during residency, including 93% of women and 24% of men. One-third of women experienced sexual harassment, yet only 5% of women formally reported these events.[6] Barriers to reporting included humiliation, fear of retaliation, and fear of damage to one's career and reputation.[7]

CREATING A SAFE CULTURE

In conclusion, the data and research reveal the continued widespread prevalence and incidence of both discrimination and harassment. Strategies to reduce the behaviors include developing systems and processes that break down the barriers to reporting. Establishing a safe culture takes time and requires employers, schools, and training programs to create an environment where employees, students, and residents feel protected and validated enough to be comfortable reporting an incident or concern.

REFERENCES

1. U.S. Equal Opportunity Employment Commission. Sexual Harassment-Based Charge Data: Total Charge Receipts versus Sexual Harassment-Based Receipts, FY 2016–FY

2020. https://www.eeoc.gov/sites/default/files/2021-12/Sexual%20Harassment%20Charges_FY2020_0.pdf.

2. Mitchell G. Exclusive: Survey Reveals a Majority of Nurses Have Experienced Sexual Harassment. *Nursing Times.* June 3, 2021. https://www.nursingtimes.net/news/workforce/exclusive-survey-reveals-majority-of-nurses-have-experienced-sexual-harassment-03-06-2021/.

3. Choo E, van Dis J, Kass D. Perspective: Time's Up for Medicine? Only Time Will Tell. *N Engl J Med.* 2018;379(17):1592–1593. doi:10.1056/nejmp1809351

4. Kane L. Sexual Harassment of Physicians: Medscape 2018 Report. Medscape. https://www.medscape.com/slideshow/sexual-harassment-of-physicians-6010304?icd=login_success_email_match_norm.

5. Notaro E, Pascoe V, Shinohara MM, DeNiro K. Sexual Harassment from Patient to Provider. *Int J Womens Dermatol.* 2019;6(1):30–31. doi:10.1016/j.ijwd.2019.09.001

6. McKinley S, Wang L, Gartland R, Westfal ML, *et al.* "Yes, I'm the Doctor": One Department's Approach to Assessing and Addressing Gender-Based Discrimination in the Modern Medical Training Era. *Acad Med.*2019;94(11):1691–1698. doi:10.1097/acm.0000000000002845

7. Cortina L, Berdahl J. Sexual Harassment in Organizations: A Decade of Research in Review. In: Barling J, Cooper CL, eds. *The SAGE Handbook of Organizational Behavior: Volume 1 — Micro-Approaches*, SAGE Publications, Ltd; 2008:26, 469-497. doi:10.4135/9781849200448.n26

Chapter 2. The #MeToo Movement

THE #MeToo MOVEMENT is an ongoing awareness campaign against sexual abuse, harassment, and rape culture, in which women publicize their experiences of abuse or harassment. Tarana Burke, a social activist, began using the hashtag #MeToo on her MySpace page in 2006, recalling her experiences of being sexually abused and assaulted as a child and teenager. In 2017, *Time* magazine named Burke Person of the Year.

In October 2017, several Hollywood actresses came forward with claims of sexual abuse against film producer Harvey Weinstein. On October 15, 2017, Alyssa Milano posted on Twitter, "If all the women who have been sexually harassed or assaulted wrote 'Me too' as a status, we might give people a sense of the magnitude of the problem." An avalanche of claims of abuse and assault followed an explosion of the hashtag #MeToo across social media websites as women shared their experiences.[1]

In 2017, an ABC News/*Washington Post* poll found that 54% of American women reported receiving unwanted and inappropriate sexual advances, with 95% of those women saying that the behavior usually goes unpunished. The resulting awareness has led to numerous initiatives, new legislation, and the creation of new programs supporting victims and giving victims a collective voice on the issues. The movement urges men who witness harassment or assault to intervene and stop the behavior; men must be advocates and allies for meaningful change.[1]

Although the movement is no longer in the spotlight, the resulting work and continued awareness of the problem are leading to change and progress. Recently, California passed legislation that bans companies from requiring employees to sign nondisclosure agreements that would prohibit them from speaking about any harassment toward a protected class. A handful of states now require sexual harassment training programs as part of employee onboarding and continuing education. Though slow, these efforts are worthwhile, much needed, and will make a difference. #MeToo lives on.

REFERENCE

1. Gordon S. The #MeToo Movement: History, Sexual Assault Statistics, Impact. Very Well Mind. April 28, 2023. https://www.verywellmind.com/what-is-the-metoo-movement-4774817.

Chapter 3. The High Cost of Sexual Misconduct and Harassment

"Women should not be forced to accept sexual harassment as the price of admission to a life and career in the political world. They should not have to endure unwanted touching, innuendo, and propositioning from men in positions of power." — JB Pritzker, Governor of Illinois

A RECENT EEOC ANALYSIS REVEALED that businesses pay, on average, $37,000–$55,000 on sexual harassment settlements. When harassment lawsuits go to trial, the average payout increases to $217,000.[1] The settlement costs do not include the employer's investigative costs, productivity losses, litigation and legal expenses, potential for reputational harm, and, of course, the individual victim's emotional and/or physical harm.

Regardless of the difficulty in quantifying the indirect costs associated with sexual harassment, the ripple effect of higher turnover and reputational harm can lead to loss of business and difficulty recruiting new employees.

CASE STUDY: COLUMBIA UNIVERSITY PHYSICIAN

In October 2023, Columbia University announced a $100 million fund to compensate victims of Robert Hadden, a former obstetrician-gynecologist at the university convicted of sexual abuse in 2016. Initially, Hadden was not required to serve any jail time, but as the accusations increased, he subsequently was sentenced in 2023 to 20 years in prison.

The Columbia University fund is part of a broader response that includes an external investigation into the failures that allowed the abuse to occur. In addition to the settlement fund, Columbia is establishing a patient safety center to review and improve its health programs and protocols.

More than 6,500 of Hadden's former patients are being informed about his conviction and provided information on available resources as well as their legal rights under the New York State Adult Survivors Act. This act permits survivors of sexual abuse to file lawsuits even after the statute of limitations has expired. Indeed, the downstream consequences affect victims and the organization for years, if not decades.

In a toxic environment, an endless negative loop can exponentially increase the losses as employees leave and are not replaced in a timely manner, and production decreases. Both the quality and quantity of work are affected, and the mental and physical health of the employee is at risk. An environment tolerating sexual harassment and misconduct gives employees a good reason to leave or consider leaving. Figure 1 delineates the types of costs incurred by employees and employers in an environment in which sexual harassment occurs.[2]

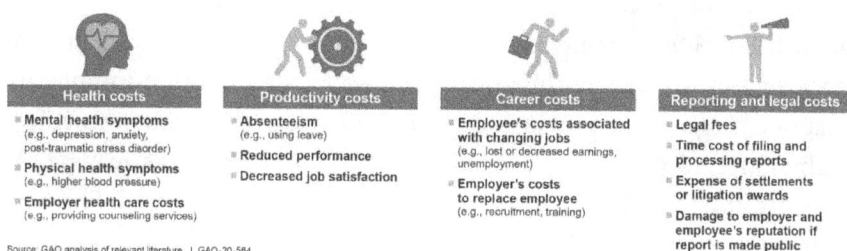

Health costs	Productivity costs	Career costs	Reporting and legal costs
▪ Mental health symptoms (e.g., depression, anxiety, post-traumatic stress disorder) ▪ Physical health symptoms (e.g., higher blood pressure) ▪ Employer health care costs (e.g., providing counseling services)	▪ Absenteeism (e.g., using leave) ▪ Reduced performance ▪ Decreased job satisfaction	▪ Employee's costs associated with changing jobs (e.g., lost or decreased earnings, unemployment) ▪ Employer's costs to replace employee (e.g., recruitment, training)	▪ Legal fees ▪ Time cost of filing and processing reports ▪ Expense of settlements or litigation awards ▪ Damage to employer and employee's reputation if report is made public

Source: GAO analysis of relevant literature. | GAO-20-564

FIGURE 1. Employee and employer costs associated with sexual harassment.[2]

Even in the absence of direct experiences for an organization, learning about a sexual harassment claim gives the public an opportunity to form negative opinions and make assumptions about the organization. Specifically, if the claim involves the sexual harassment of a woman by a man, perceptions and opinions about how the organization treats women are formed — even before an investigation has concluded. Perception can become reality. The initial damage to an organization's reputation can be mitigated, but only if the organization responds quickly and appropriately and takes responsibility.

Organizations can respond to a claim by publicly attacking the accuser or through a formal apology to the victim. Attacking or discounting the claim is a defensive strategy organizations use to distance themselves from the individual and protect themselves from legal liability. Accommodative responses involve active consideration of all parties using an ethical, care-oriented approach considering the emotional needs of all individuals involved. Organizations should consider and act in an ethical manner, respecting all individuals. Denying claims, attacking accusers, and not accepting responsibility can lead to increased harm.[3]

CASE STUDY: ABUSE AND RETALIATION

It is far more common for cases to settle than to go to a jury trial; however, particularly egregious cases in recent years have resulted in significant settlement awards. A recent case involves an employee who sued her employer, a neurological surgery center, alleging repeated sexual harassment by multiple surgeons who were owners/investors.

The employee, Ms. M, a long-tenured physician's assistant, was fired after she repeatedly complained that she observed what she believed were unsafe surgical practices by multiple surgeons — including complaints that one surgeon, Dr. B, who had been sued at least 20 times for medical malpractice, took unnecessarily long breaks during surgeries, leaving his patients under anesthesia for longer than the surgery required. She also stated another surgeon, Dr. R, "is becoming a dangerous surgeon" and that she had been sexually harassed and subjected to misogynistic behavior by numerous surgeons in the group.

She recounted that the surgeons repeatedly made inappropriate, misogynistic, and sexist comments — very often mid-surgery — such as:

"All you women, all you do is complain."
"When was the last time you had sex?"
"[My daughter has] got young perky C-cup breasts."
"If your brains were as big as your breasts, you'd be a genius."
"My wife is my servant."
"Most women who rise to power have done so with their legs open."

Ms. M was retaliated against after "blowing the whistle," which concluded with Dr. B terminating her employment.

When Ms. M was fired, she was offered eight weeks of severance pay. Ms. M accepted this offer in writing. However, incredibly, after Ms. M complained that her termination was unlawful and retaliatory, the surgeons refused to pay her the agreed-upon severance payments, telling her that the severance payments would be made only if she released all claims she had against the organization. The case settled for a substantial, undisclosed amount.[4]

Other cases include a federal judge who awarded a woman $800,000 in damages after a civil jury trial in which the woman said a physician sexually harassed her and managers took no corrective action. In another case, a woman won nearly $168 million in a harassment suit that included a hospital and surgeon. The plaintiff described receiving a needlestick, having someone call her a "stupid chick," and hearing trashy sex talk. She had filed 18 written complaints and was ultimately fired. In 2022, the University of Michigan paid $490 million to more than 1,000 students who said they were abused by Robert Anderson, a sports doctor.

A BURDEN BEYOND MEASURE

For many who have experienced sexual violence, harassment, and discrimination, it is a life-changing event and creates a life-long burden. The financial and reputational damages are substantial. The individuals who suffer from the abuse and misconduct pay a far higher price, as their lives are permanently changed.

Victims often need a supportive, healing journey to move forward, yet there often are economic barriers to receiving continued mental health treatment and support. Additionally, the stigma of being diagnosed with mental health disorders makes some victims reluctant to seek help. The concern or fear of being labeled with mental illness is legitimate and a barrier toward healing. The total economic and emotional toll is beyond measure.

REFERENCES

1. Holman Schiavone, LLC. What Is the Average Settlement for Sexual Harassment in the Workplace? Holman Schiavone, LLC blog. https://www.kdh-law.com/what-is-the-average-settlement-for-sexual-harassment-in-the-workplace/#:~:text=Sexual%20 harassment%20cases%20are%20often,average%20payout%20increases%20to%20 %24217%2C000.

2. U.S. Government Accountability Office. Workplace Sexual Harassment: Experts Suggest Expanding Data Collection to Improve Understanding of Prevalence and Costs. GAO. October 16, 2020. http://www.gao.gov/products/GAO-20-564.

3. Cheng D, Does S, Gündemir S, Shih M. How Organizational Responses to Sexual Harassment Claims Shape Public Perception. *Basic and Applied Social Psychology.* 2024;46(3):169–186. doi: 10.1080/01973533.2024.2313536

4. *Menghini v. Neurological Surgery, P.C.,* CV 15-3534. *Casetext.* 2016. https://casetext.com/case/menghini-v-neurological-surgery-pc.

Chapter 4. Physician Misconduct

"Even what might appear to an outside observer as consensual behavior between a doctor and patient is not truly consensual. The patient is in a vulnerable position." — Brian Zachariah, MD

Larry Nassar, the former physician for the United States women's gymnastics team, was charged with sexually abusing and assaulting 265 young women and girls in what remains one the largest sexual abuse scandals in sports history. He was tried and convicted of multiple crimes, including possession of child pornography, tampering with evidence, and sexual assault. He is now serving a *de facto* life sentence in prison without the possibility of parole. The events and details leading up to his conviction in late 2017 and early 2018 are worthy of exploration and discussion on how institutional failures compound the problems.

In the late 1990s, years prior to the scandal involving the U.S. gymnastics team, complaints about Nassar's behavior were reported to dozens of individuals at Michigan State University. Some athletes stated the abuse started in 1994. USA Gymnastics did not take action against Nassar until 2015, and in September 2016, USA Gymnastics cut ties with him. On September 20, 2016, Nassar was fired by Michigan State University.[1]

MISHANDLING OF MISCONDUCT

Nassar's crimes were particularly heinous in their scope and magnitude, and they cannot be dismissed merely as the deviant behavior of a sociopath. This case should serve as a wake-up call to an industry that has been historically slow to respond to complaints and concerns of sexually inappropriate conduct. The following accounts are from the case after the Michigan State University Police Department (MSUPD) received a complaint in May 2014 involving Nassar and the MSU Sports Medicine Clinic.

The incident was investigated by the MSUPD and referred to the county prosecutor in July 2015; in December 2015, the county prosecutor declined to authorize criminal charges. The police report includes discussions and contact with MSU personnel and states that a Title IX investigation of the complaint was completed in July 2014.

As part of the investigation, William Strampel, dean of MSU's School of Osteopathic Medicine, provided an email exchange with Nassar that explained that the two of them had met to discuss the complaint. As a result of the meeting, Nassar and Strampel agreed to some practices, as follows[1]:

1. Another person would be present (resident, nurse, etc.) whenever a physician was approaching a patient to perform procedures of anything close to a sensitive area.
2. The procedure that caused the patient emotional distress "because of her interpretation of it" would be modified in the future to be sure that there was little to no skin-to-skin contact when in those regions. Should it be necessary, the procedure would be explained in detail with another person in the room for both the explanation and the procedure.
3. New people in the practice would be oriented to make sure they understood the requirements.

When police interviewed Strampel on March 14, 2017, he stated that the Title IX investigation had gone on for three to four months and that he was told that Nassar was "cleared" and could return to work. Strampel also shared that he emailed Nassar to remind him of "common sense medical guidelines," including having a chaperone in the room during sensitive procedures or exams and limiting skin-to-skin contact.[1]

Additionally, Strampel thought he had forwarded the mail to Leif Neitzel, the director of the Sports Medicine Clinic, but was not positive. Ultimately it was discovered that the email was not forwarded to Neitzel, and Strampel did not feel a need to follow up to ensure the agreed-upon guidelines were being followed.

Because Nassar had been "cleared," Strampel did not think it would be appropriate to discuss the investigation with any practitioners at the Sports Medicine Clinic. As a result, a formal chaperone policy was not instituted at the clinic until 2017.

A 2017 MSUPD report recited that 12 assaults at the clinic had been reported since July 2014. Many of the alleged assaults were reported to have occurred in the exam rooms at the Sports Medicine Clinic. Notably, chaperones were not present during sensitive procedures, and the procedures involved un-gloved skin-to-skin contact. Clearly, the abuses never stopped.[1]

In October 2017, Olympic gold medalist McKayla Maroney, using the hashtag #MeToo on Twitter (now X) shared that she had been sexually abused by Nassar from 2008, when she was only 13 years old, until she retired from the sport in 2016. Maroney filed a lawsuit against Nassar, Michigan State University, the United States Olympic Committee, and USA Gymnastics. The lawsuit accused USA Gymnastics of covering up the sexual abuse by requiring her to sign a nondisclosure agreement in her $1.25 million settlement.[2]

On September 15, 2021, McKayla Maroney, Simone Biles, Maggie Nichols, and Aly Raisman testified before the U.S. Senate that FBI agents made false statements regarding their reports about the abuse. Maroney testified that she was met with silence by an FBI agent after telling the agent of Nassar's molestations of her in detail. Raisman testified that the FBI made her feel that the "abuse did not count."

FBI Director Christopher Wray testified and, speaking to the gymnasts, said he was "deeply and profoundly sorry that so many people let you down over and over again." In April 2022, 13 of Nassar's victims filed a lawsuit against the FBI for negligence and other alleged investigatory failures. In 2024, the lawsuit was settled for $138.7 million.[3]

In January 2018, Michigan Attorney General Bill Schuette initiated a full investigation into how Nassar was able to abuse young women for decades while working at MSU. MSU agreed to pay $500 million to 332 of Nassar's alleged victims, settling lawsuits filed by the victims. This was the largest amount of money in history settled by a university for a sexual abuse case.

When leaders are engaged in their own misconduct, it is impossible to create a safe environment. In June 2019, William Strampel, dean of MSU's School of Osteopathic Medicine, was convicted on two counts of willful neglect of duty and one count of felony misconduct in office over sexual comments he made to female students. He was cleared of felony second-degree criminal sexual conduct.

This case, unfortunately, highlights many contemporary and historical concerns, challenges, opportunities, and failures of systems, individuals, policies, and processes. I encourage readers to recall the details of this case while reading the chapters on investigating incidents and concerns, barriers to reporting, individual and institutional responsibilities, the use of chaperones, policies and procedures, creating a culture of psychological safety, and follow-up and disposition. Nothing can "undo" the emotional and physical trauma hundreds of young girls and women endured and continue to endure from Nassar's abuse.

Finally, this case is an example of multiple lapses from multiple individuals from multiple institutions. It remains a searing indictment that more work needs to be done at the system level so individuals receiving reports take them seriously and feel safe conducting a proper investigation. Details of this case emerged as the #MeToo movement gained traction, acting as a catalyst to raise awareness of the issues.

THE STATE OF THE PROBLEM

Despite recent increased awareness, physicians engaged in misconduct remain a problem. Public Citizen, a national nonprofit organization with more than 500,000 members and supporters, represents consumer interests on a broad range of issues, including safe and affordable healthcare. On May 26, 2020, Public Citizen published a 15-year summary of sexual misconduct reported to the National Practitioner Data Bank (NPDB) from 2003 to 2017. Results of the study found a total of 1,354 unique physicians had sexual-misconduct-related reports; 93% of these physicians had only one type of the following reports: 76.6% had only licensing reports, 8.4% had only clinical-privileges reports, and 7.7% had only malpractice-payment reports. The remaining 7.3% had more than one type of these reports.[4]

Collectively, these physicians accounted for only 0.2% of the U.S. general physician population and 1.1% of all physicians with NPDB reports that met their study criteria. Shockingly, these proportions are much lower than the proportion of physicians who have self-reported sexual contact with patients in anonymous surveys. The problem is more extensive than the reports indicate.

The study also found that 90% of the physicians identified were aged 40 years or older, and there were significantly more physicians 50 years or older and fewer younger than 40 years old. The vast majority of physicians, 94%, were men. Physicians from three specialties, family medicine/general practice, psychiatry, and obstetrics-gynecology, accounted for 51% of the reports. In more than 90% of the reports, the victims identified as female. Of the physicians with sexual-misconduct-related malpractice-payment reports, 84.5% committed their misconduct in outpatient settings.[4]

Dubois and colleagues published a study examining 101 cases of sexual violation of patients by physicians and reported a similar profile of the physicians engaged in misconduct. They were older physicians (over the age of 39), not board-certified (70%), practicing in non-academic settings (94%), and routinely examined patients without anyone else in the room (85%).

Interestingly, physicians who were board-certified more frequently engaged in consensual sex with a patient. This rate is unexpectedly high and led investigators to add it as an inductive theory of the case variable in efforts to reduce data to typologies or clusters. Most cases involved more than five victims (57%) who were adults (60%) and women (89%). In 96% of cases, the abuse was repeated; in 58% of cases, the abuse continued for more than two years. In nearly all (88%) cases involved multiple kinds of professional breaches in addition to the misconduct.[5]

Several of these findings are worthy of further research. Why are older males more apt to engage in these behaviors? Why is the sample of men not spread evenly across age groups? What boundary violations occur to account for the higher number of psychiatrists who are reported? Although the number of women who have engaged in sexual misconduct is drastically lower, what are the types of behaviors and characteristics of women and who engage in misconduct?

REFERENCES

1. Locke R. Sexual Harassment By Physicians: Implications for Medical Staff Privileges, Licensure and Physician Practices. Presentation at the American Health Lawyers Association 2018 In-House Counsel Program and Annual Meeting, Chicago, IL.

2. Park A. Who Is Larry Nassar, the Former USA Gymnastics Doctor McKayla Maroney Accused of Sexual Abuse? *Time.* October 18, 2017.

3. Thrush G, Macur J. Justice Department Reaches $138.7 Million Settlement Over FBI's Failures in Nassar Case. *The New York Times.* April 23, 2024.

4. Abudagga A, Carome M, Wolfe S, Oshel R. *15-Year Summary of Sexual Misconduct by U.S. Physicians Reported to the National Practitioner Data Bank, 2003–2017.* Washington, D.C.: Public Citizen's Health Research Group, May 26, 2020. https://www.citizen.org/wp-content/uploads/2523.pdf?eType=EmailBlastContent&eId=cfae6104-8c44-4f07-87b5-f78353346c47.

5. DuBois JM, Walsh HA, Chibnall JT, Anderson EE, Eggers MR, *et al.* Sexual Violation of Patients by Physicians: A Mixed-Methods, Exploratory Analysis of 101 Cases. *Sex Abuse.* 2019;31(5):503–523. doi: 10.1177/1079063217712217

Definitions, Behaviors, Stereotypes, and Consent

∞

Chapter 5. Definitions of Sexual Misconduct, Harassment, and Discrimination

"Sexual harassment is complex, subtle, and highly subjective."
— *Kathie Lee Gifford, TV host, singer-songwriter*

FIGURE 1 GRAPHICALLY REPRESENTS the broad range of sexually harassing behaviors and public awareness and consciousness.[1]

Sexual misconduct and harassment always involve more than one individual and can include more than two individuals. In its guidance, the EEOC defines sexual harassment as[2,3]:

"Unwelcome sexual advances, requests for sexual favors, and other verbal or physical conduct of a sexual nature when: Submission to such conduct is made either explicitly or implicitly a term or condition of an individual's employment. It is a form of aggression and in some cases — violence.

1. *Submission to or rejection of such conduct by an individual is used as a basis for employment decisions affecting such individual.*
2. *Such conduct has the purpose or effect of unreasonably interfering with an individual's work performance or creating an intimidating, hostile, or offensive working environment."*

Unwelcome behavior does not mean "involuntary." A victim may consent or agree to certain conduct and actively participate in it even though it is offensive and objectionable. *Therefore, sexual conduct is unwelcome whenever the person subjected to it considers it unwelcome.* For example, whether the person in fact welcomed a request for a date, sex-oriented comment, or joke

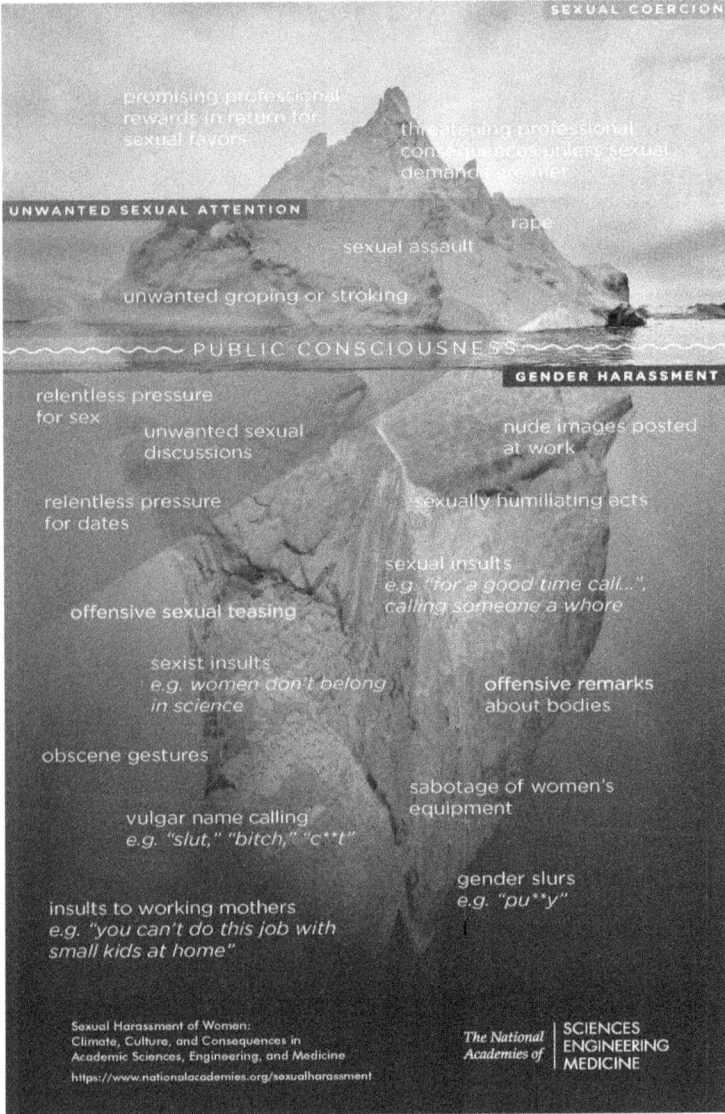

SEXUAL COERCION

promising professional rewards in return for sexual favors

threatening professional consequences unless sexual demands are met

UNWANTED SEXUAL ATTENTION

rape

sexual assault

unwanted groping or stroking

PUBLIC CONSCIOUSNESS

GENDER HARASSMENT

relentless pressure for sex

unwanted sexual discussions

nude images posted at work

relentless pressure for dates

sexually humiliating acts

sexual insults
e.g. "for a good time call...",
calling someone a whore

offensive sexual teasing

sexist insults
e.g. women don't belong
in science

offensive remarks about bodies

obscene gestures

sabotage of women's equipment

vulgar name calling
e.g. "slut," "bitch," "c**t"

gender slurs
e.g. "pu**y"

insults to working mothers
e.g. "you can't do this job with
small kids at home"

Sexual Harassment of Women:
Climate, Culture, and Consequences in
Academic Sciences, Engineering, and Medicine
https://www.nationalacademies.org/sexualharassment

The National
Academies of

SCIENCES
ENGINEERING
MEDICINE

FIGURE 1. Sexual harassment of women:
climate, culture, and consequences.[1]

depends on all the circumstances.[2,3] Coercion can influence decision-making behaviors and responses.

A single, unified definition of terms is not possible. However, sexual harassment can be classified into four categories: verbal/written, nonverbal, physical, and visual. Consider the following examples[4]:

VERBAL/WRITTEN SEXUAL HARASSMENT

- Making remarks of a sexual nature about a person's clothing, personal behavior, or body.
- Making sexually explicit statements, asking inappropriate questions, or sharing jokes or anecdotes that are sexual in nature.
- Requesting sexual favors or dates.
- Spreading rumors about a person's personal or sexual life.
- Using threats to coerce someone into sexual activity.
- Engaging in excessive and unwelcome flirting.

NONVERBAL SEXUAL HARASSMENT

- Looking at a person's body "up and down."
- Making derogatory gestures or facial expressions of a sexual nature.
- Frequently and purposely following or standing too close to a person.
- Whistling or staring in a sexually suggestive or offensive manner.

PHYSICAL SEXUAL HARASSMENT

- Impeding or blocking a person's physical movement.
- Purposefully brushing up against another person.
- Engaging in inappropriate and unwanted touching of a person and/or their clothing, including kissing, hugging, patting, stroking, or rubbing.
- Playing music with offensive or degrading language.

VISUAL SEXUAL HARASSMENT

- Displaying sexually inappropriate pictures, cartoons, posters, calendars, etc.
- Showing pictures, texts, emails, images, or social media posts from others with inappropriate content
- Showing or sharing pornographic images, videos, or audio from media sources.

These behaviors occur in a variety of situations, contexts, and circumstances.

ELEMENTS OF SEXUAL HARASSMENT BEHAVIOR

Several additional elements may be involved in sexual harassment, including coercion, consent, discrimination, hostile environment, quid pro quo, retaliation, hazing, incapacitation, and intimidation.

Coercion. Unreasonable and unwanted pressure to engage in sexual activity. Consent is not provided if coercion is present.

Consent. Permission for something to happen. Consent is not possible in power-dynamic situations, such as physician and patient, resident and medical student, attending physician and resident physician, and supervisor and subordinate employee. Consent is also not possible when any of the parties are under the influence of drugs or alcohol or are otherwise psychologically or medically impaired. Any condition-altering mental status implies the person cannot consent. Consent is discussed in more detail in Chapter 16.

Sex and Gender-Based Discrimination. Any distinction, preference, or other action based solely on an individual's sex and/or gender or gender presentation.

Hostile Environment. An environment where the words and actions of a supervisor, manager, or coworker negatively or severely impact another employee's ability to complete their work.

Quid Pro Quo. With regard to harassment, when employment and/or employment decisions for an employee are based on that employee's acceptance or rejection of unwelcome sexual behavior. For example, a supervisor fires an employee because that employee will not go out with him or her.

The EEOC also states that harassment can occur in a variety of circumstances, including but not limited to the following:

1. The victim and the harasser may be a woman or a man. The victim does not have to be of the opposite sex.
2. The harasser can be the victim's supervisor, an agent of the employer, a supervisor in another area, a co-worker, or a non-employee.
3. The victim does not have to be the person harassed but could be anyone affected by the offensive conduct.
4. Unlawful sexual harassment may occur without economic injury to or discharge of the victim.
5. The harasser's conduct must be unwelcome.

The lack of a unifying, single definition of sexual harassment and misconduct is a challenge for organizations to mitigate and reduce the behaviors. It is important, therefore, for organizations to provide and create comprehensive and explicit codes of conduct.

FILTER TEST: DETERMINING IF CONDUCT IS SEXUAL HARASSMENT

To determine if the conduct is sexual harassment, consider these two questions:

1. *Is the behavior from the complainant by the accused unwanted?*
2. *Is the content or conduct based on the biological sex, gender, gender representation, or sexual orientation of the individual or is the content or conduct sexual in nature?*

If the answer to both questions is yes, it is likely sexual harassment or misconduct, and the best approach is to investigate the concern as a form of sexual harassment or discrimination.

Apply the filter test to the following scenarios.

1. A 24-year-old female bisexual nurse is having lunch with her colleagues. One of the other female nurses is having a side conversation about sexual orientation with another nurse and she states, "I just do not get 'bisexual' people. Are they confused? I mean, people are either gay or straight, and to me, this whole bisexual thing is just a fad, and people who say they are 'bi' just haven't made up their mind."
2. A 32-year-old male medical student is on a rotation with another classmate whom he finds very attractive. She is 29 years old and single, and they get along quite well but have not been dating. One evening during rounds, he makes a series of hand gestures to indicate to her that he finds her attractive, including placing his left hand on his left buttock area and making a hissing noise to convey that he thinks she is "hot."
3. A 60-year-old white male surgeon is having a casual conversation with a 42-year-old gay, white male nurse who recently broke up with his long-time partner of 15 years. In a casual conversation, the surgeon tells the nurse, "I bet finding a new partner is easier for a gay man than a straight man."

All three of these cases depict different types of sexual harassment. In the first case, the nurses invalidating a bisexual sexual orientation is a form of disrespectful microaggression. In the second case, the conduct is clearly meant to imply performing a sexual act in some manner, and he uses inappropriate hand gestures to suggest she is attractive. In the last case, the surgeon is implying that gay men are more open to dating and sex than women.

The most overt act is the case involving the medical student; however, all of these scenarios highlight the fact that if a culture imbued with this conduct is allowed and persists, change is not possible.

REFERENCES

1. Johnson PA, Widnall SE, Benya, FF, eds. *Sexual Harassment of Women: Climate, Culture, and Consequences in Academic Sciences, Engineering, and Medicine.* Washington, DC: National Academies of Science, Engineering, and Medicine; 2018. https://nap.nationalacademies.org/catalog/24994/sexual-harassment-of-women-climate-culture-and-consequences-in-academic.

2. *Preventing Sexual Harassment* BNA Communications, Inc. SDC IP .73 1992 Manual

3. U.S. Equal Opportunity Employment Commission. *Fact Sheet: Sexual Harassment Discrimination.* January 15, 1997. https://www.eeoc.gov/laws/guidance/fact-sheet-sexual-harassment-discrimination.

4. Partners West Africa-Nigeria. Rule of Law and Empowerment Initiative. July 26, 2022. https://www.facebook.com/partnersnigeria/posts/here-are-the-types-of-sexual-harassmentsay-no-to-sexual-harassmentpwan-partnersn/2871440056491753/.

Chapter 6. Gender and Sexual Orientation Differences in Perceptions of Sexual Harassment

"All together now: Women don't cause sexual harassment, harassers do."— *Kirsten Powers, author*

RESEARCH SHOWS THAT PERCEPTIONS of sexually harassing behaviors differ between men and women, and the differences in perception contribute to the ongoing problem of continued sexual harassment in all workplaces. Women are more likely than men to report sociosexual behaviors (comments, looks, gestures (whether complimentary or insulting), touching, and requests for dates) as sexual harassment. In contrast, men may perceive these behaviors as benign or even pleasurable, such as flirting or flirting-type behaviors. However, some men may interpret these behaviors as threatening, degrading, or humiliating, too.[1,2]

Heather Clarke published a unique study in 2022 investigating the perception differences between women and men.[3] Her study included heterosexual men and women and lesbians and gay men. Prior research suggested that gay men have different perceptions of sociosexual behaviors than heterosexual men because gay men, like women, are targets of sexual harassment and violence more frequently than heterosexual men.[4] Clarke's study aimed to determine whether men, particularly heterosexual men, experience sociosexual behaviors differently than women.

The study examined four factors potentially determinative of gender differences. First, the study examined the impact of perspective-taking on perceptions of sexual harassment to explain the inconsistent findings in extant research. Prior studies have suggested there is no difference in the perceptions of sexual harassment between men and women. Vignette studies employ an "imagine-other" perspective-taking or "imagine-self" perspective-taking approach. Clarke's study is the first to incorporate both "imagine-other" and "imagine-self."

Second, the study explored whether gender differences in perceptions of sexual harassment are explained not only by the extent to which the behaviors are experienced as threatening but also by the extent to which they are experienced as discriminatory.

Third, the study rejected the heteronormative assumption underlying much of the research on this subject by incorporating gay and lesbian-identified individuals. Lastly, the study tested a novel psychological process that occurs following exposure to sociosexual behaviors in the workplace.

As mentioned, two types of perspective-taking are found in sexual harassment research. "Imagine-other" perspective-taking, also known as mind reading, involves inferring what the fictional target thinks and feels. Similarity-contingency theory suggests individuals are more likely to project their own beliefs and attitudes on a target if they perceive themselves to be similar to the target. Individuals are more likely to rely on stereotypes and outside information when they perceive themselves to be dissimilar to the target.[5]

When making inferences about a fictional target, female participants are more likely than male participants to perceive similarity to the target because they are more likely to have experienced similar behaviors themselves. Males will more likely rely on stereotypes, as they are less frequently the target and will use objective criteria. Distinct and separate psychological processes occur between males and females to arrive at the same perception.

The second type of perspective-taking, "imagine-self," requires participants to imagine how they would think or feel about the situation if it happened to them. Similar to survey studies of lived experiences, imagine-self vignette studies capture participants' own perceptions and produce gender differences.[6] When imagine-self perspective-taking is employed, females are more likely than males to perceive sociosexual behaviors to be harassment.

Clarke's study had three different hypotheses:

Hypothesis 1: Heterosexual males, but not females or gay males, will report higher perceived discrimination, fear, and perceived sexual harassment when the target is fictional (imagine-other perspective-taking) than when they are the target (imagine-self perspective-taking).

Hypothesis 2: Heterosexual males will report lower perceived discrimination, fear, and perceived sexual harassment than females and gay males when they are the target (imagine-self perspective-taking) but not when the target is fictional (imagine-other perspective-taking).

Further, when subjected to sociosexual behaviors in the workplace, females and gay males will be more likely than heterosexual males to experience fear and perceptions of discrimination, which will in turn predict perceptions of sexual harassment. In addition, these two indirect effects will be moderated by the target of sociosexual behaviors, such that the participant group will predict fear and perceived discrimination ratings when the target of the behaviors is the participant but not when the target is fictional.

Hypothesis 3: Perceptions of sexual harassment will be predicted by a moderated mediation model such that the participant group (heterosexual male, gay male, heterosexual female, or lesbian) will predict perceived sexual harassment through the mediators of fear and perceived discrimination when the target is the participant (imagine-self perspective-taking), but not when the target is fictional (imagine-other perspective-taking) (Figure 1).[3]

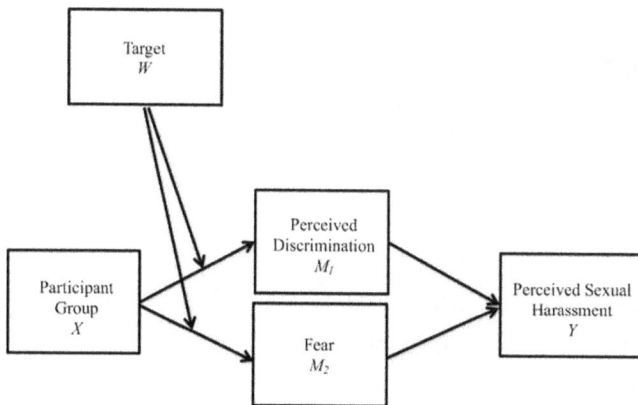

FIGURE 1. Conceptual model predicting moderated parallel mediation.

Approximately equal numbers of heterosexual, gay, and lesbian employed adults were recruited for the study through Amazon Mechanical Turk (MTurk), a crowdsourcing internet marketplace. A total of 876 participants were recruited. The participants were then instructed to read the following fictional scenarios and record responses to four different measures.

The scenario describes an interaction between the target and their manager. With a view to bolstering the realism of the scenario, the gender of the manager was not disclosed so that participants could impute gender based on their own conceptualization or experience of sexual harassment and/ or experience with managers.

In the control conditions, the scenario described a collegial interaction with the manager. In the sociosexual behaviors condition, the scenario described an interaction in which the manager exhibited sociosexual behaviors (touching, leering, and sexual comments) toward the target. The sociosexual behaviors were forms of unwanted sexual attention like those appearing in the sexual experiences questionnaire described in further detail in the section on Validated Instruments to Measure Sexual Harassment and Misconduct.

PERSPECTIVE-TAKING (PARTICIPANT AS TARGET) SCENARIOS

Scenario for Control Condition and Sociosexual Behavior Condition

Imagine that five years ago, you were hired as a sales representative with International Widget Manufacturers Inc. You report directly to the regional sales manager. The job is enjoyable and meaningful to you. To date, you have received positive performance appraisals and feedback from your manager, colleagues, and customers; however, lately, you have felt disenchanted with your job. Recently, a position opened up in the finance department. You decide to apply for the position so you can try something new.

Control Condition: One day, you are eating in the lunchroom at work when your manager enters the room. You say hello, and your manager smiles and says, "I hear that you applied for the finance/HR position." You reply, "Yes, I have." Your manager then asks you some general questions about where you worked before you came to International Widgets and wishes you luck getting the job.

Sociosexual Behavior Condition: One day, you are eating in the lunchroom at work when your manager enters the room. You say hello, and your manager smiles, looking you up and down, seemingly sizing you up. Your manager crosses the room and stands so close to you that your bodies touch. You try to start a conversation, but before long, your manager turns the focus of the conversation from general "small talk" and begins asking personal questions regarding your sex life.

FEMALE TARGET SCENARIOS

Scenario for Control Condition and Sociosexual Condition

Five years ago, Mary was hired as a sales representative for International Widget Manufacturers Inc. She reports directly to the regional sales manager. The job is enjoyable and meaningful to her. To date, she has received good performance appraisals and positive feedback from her manager, colleagues, and customers, but lately she has felt bored with her job. Recently, a position opened up in the finance department. Mary decides to apply for the position so she can try something new.

Control Condition. One day, Mary is eating in the lunchroom at work when her manager enters the room. Mary says hello, and her manager smiles and says, "I hear that you applied for the finance position." Mary replies, "Yes, I have." Her manager then asks her some general questions about her previous work experience before she came to International Widgets and wishes Mary luck in getting the job.

Sociosexual Behavior Condition. One day, Mary is eating in the lunchroom at work when her manager enters the room. Mary says hello, and her manager smiles, looking her up and down, seemingly sizing her up. Her manager crosses the room and stands so close to her that their bodies touch. Mary tries to start a conversation, but before long, her manager turns the focus of the conversation from general "small talk" to asking her personal questions regarding her sex life.

MALE TARGET SCENARIOS

This scenario is identical to the female target scenarios, with "Mark" substituted for "Mary" and feminine pronouns replaced with masculine.

Using a 5-point scale (1=strongly agree, 5=strongly disagree), the four measures included:

1. Perception. The extent to which participants agreed that they/Mark/Mary (depending on condition) were/was sexually harassed in the scenario.
2. Fear. The extent to which a target, they/Mark/Mary, would feel afraid following the incident.
3. Perceived discrimination. The extent to which participants agreed that they/Mark/Mary were/was discriminated against.
4. Experience. Whether or not the participant had personally experienced sexual harassment in the workplace.

Women, gay men, and lesbian women reported very similar percentages of experiences with workplace sexual harassment, ranging from 35.4% to 38.3%. Heterosexual males reported a significantly lower percentage at 15.2%. Notably, the scenarios do not indicate the gender of the manager.

Across conditions and by participants, the manager was likely to be perceived as male.[3]

The study found statistically significant differences between the participants. When the participant was the target of the sociosexual behaviors, females reported higher fear and perceived sexual harassment ratings. Heterosexual male participants reported higher fear, discrimination, and perceived sexual harassment ratings when the fictional target was female than when the target was male.

Sexual stereotyping and sexual prototyping and perceptions of not only what constitutes sexual harassment but also the stereotypical characteristics of a "typical" female victim have the potential to influence how seriously the claim of harassment is taken. Bias, stereotypes, and subjective interpretation continue to influence the outcomes of reports and investigations.

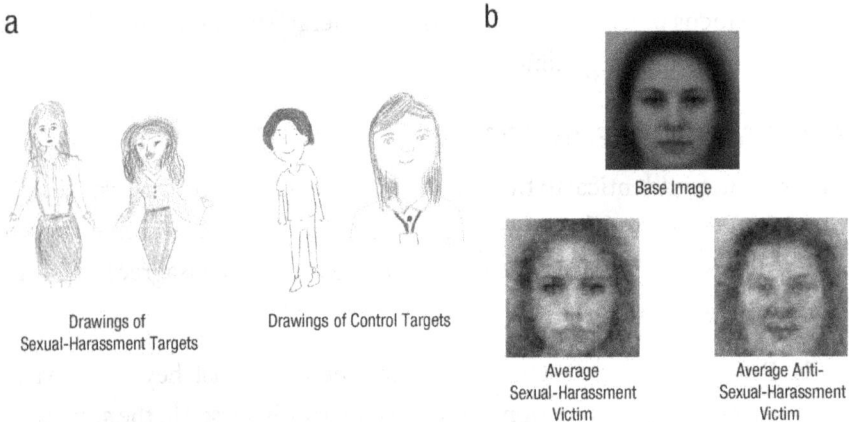

FIGURE 2. The drawings in (a) are examples of participants' renderings of women described as having been sexually harassed and the drawings of the control targets who were knocked over. The images in (b) are examples of the base face and resulting participant-generated reverse-correlation composite images of sexual-harassment targets and anti-sexual harassment targets. The reverse correlation image of the sexual harassment victim was rated as more gender prototypical than the image of the anti-sexual-harassment victim.

Goh and colleagues performed an interesting study that had participants read about a woman whose boss discretely groped her (sexual harassment condition) or accidentally knocked her down (control condition). Participants were then asked to draw the woman under both conditions. Figure

2(a) shows the results, and it is clear that the mental images produced by the participants are prototypically "feminine."

Figure 2(b) shows the results of a more complicated study in which participants were shown a random noise pattern on a base image, and then the inverse noise pattern was separately superimposed on the base image. This resulted in two trial images with opposite noise patterns. Participants then selected which of the two images better represented a sexual harassment victim. Participants chose the more prototypical "feminine" face as the sexual harassment victim.[10]

Responses to sexually harassing behaviors are influenced and interpreted differently depending on the gender of the person reporting the event.[3] Kaiser *et al.*, recently studied how gender prototypes shape perceptions and responses to sexual harassment.[7] Kaiser provides a model describing how the narrow prototype of women having conventionally feminine attributes and identities is a barrier to perceiving sexual harassment and the appropriate claims when victims do not resemble this prototype.

The conventional prototype harms women who diverge from it. Their experiences with sexual harassment are likely not taken as seriously, and they experience increased negative organizational, interpersonal, and legal consequences when they experience and report sexual harassment.[7]

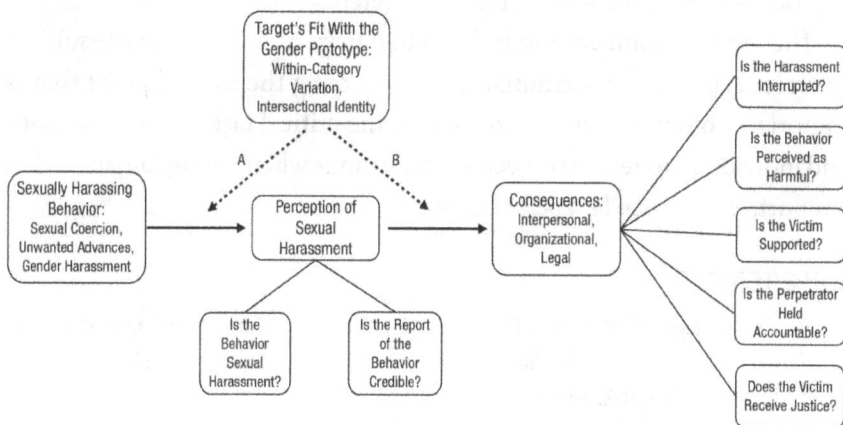

FIGURE 3. The prototype model of sexual-harassment perceptions.

Figure 3 is a graphic model map illustrating two separate paths an investigation with subsequent consequences can take, depending on whether the target fits the prototypical feminine stereotype.

When people think of sexual harassment, they envision prototypical women.[6] Prototypes can moderate whether potentially sexually harassing behaviors are labeled as such and judged as credible (Path A) and can also moderate the consequences of perceived sexual harassment, including interpersonal, organizational, and legal responses (Path B). The gender prototypicality of the harassment victim may shape the extent to which the harassment is interpreted and perceived as harmful, the victim is supported, the perpetrator is held accountable, and the victim has access to justice.

Although a review of research concerning these consequences focuses on their moderation by gender prototypes, they may also be indirectly shaped by gender prototypes via biased perceptions of sexual harassment (e.g., failure to recognize harassment in the first place).[7]

Perceptions of sexual harassment are often subjective and shaped by motivations, life experiences, gender, and cognitive frameworks, as Clarke reported in her study. The result is ambiguity regarding whether the event constitutes sexual harassment.[8] In fact, Tarana Burke, who founded the #MeToo movement, argued that "it's [#MeToo] only for a certain type of person — that it's for white, cisgender, heterosexual, famous women."[9]

The injustices are compounded when targets and victims are subject to stereotypes and discrimination. A recurring theme and point that is important to remember and consider is the critical task for organizations and individuals to remain objective and curious when a complainant makes a report. *Anyone can be a perpetrator, and anyone can be a target.*

REFERENCES

1. Berdahl J, Magley V, Waldo C. The Sexual Harassment of Men? Exploring the Concept with Theory and Data. *Psychology of Women Quarterly.* 1996;20(4):527–547. doi: 10.1111/j.1471-6402.1996.tb00320.x

2. Gutek B, Cohen A, Konrad A. Predicting Socio-sexual Behavior at Work. *Acad Manag J.* 1990;33(3):560–577. doi: 10.2307/256581

3. Clarke HM. #Metoo or #Hertoo? A Moderated Mediation Model of Gender Differences in Perceptions of Sexual Harassment. *Arch Sex Behav.* 2022;51(6):3105–3120. doi: 10.007/s10508-022-02344-1

4. Chen J, Walters, ML, Gilbert LK, Patel N. Sexual Violence, Stalking, and Intimate Partner Violence by Sexual Orientation, United States. *Psychology of Violence.* 10(1): 110–119. doi: 10.1037/vio0000252

5. Ames D, Weber E, Zou X. Mind-reading in Strategic Interaction: The Impact of Perceived Similarity on Projection and Stereotyping. *Organizational Behavior and Human Decision Processes.* 2012;(1): 96–110. doi: 10.1016/J.OBHDP.2011.07.007

6. Dillon H, Adair L, Brase G. A Threatening Exchange: Gender and Life History Strategy Predict Perceptions and Reasoning About Sexual Harassment. *Personality and Individual Differences.* 2015;72, 195–199. doi: 10.1016/j.paid.2014.09.002

7. Kaiser CR, Bandt-Law B, Cheek NN, Schachtman R. Gender Prototypes Shape Perceptions of and Responses to Sexual Harassment. *Current Directions in Psychological Science.* 2022; 31(3):254–261. doi: 10.1177/09637214221078592

8. Kaiser C, Major B. A Social Psychological Perspective on Perceiving and Reporting Discrimination. *Law and Social Inquiry.* 2006;31(4):801–830.

9. Rowley L. The Architect of #MeToo Says the Movement Has Lost Its Way. *The Cut.* October 23, 2018. https://www.thecut.com/2018/10/tarana-burke-me-too-founder-movement-has-lost-its-way.html.

10. Goh JX, Bandt-Law B, Cheek NN, Sinclair S, Kaiser CR. Narrow Prototypes and Neglected Victims: Understanding Perceptions of Sexual Harassment. *J Personality and Social Psychology.* 2022;122(5):873–893. https://psycnet.apa.org/doi/10.1037/pspi0000260.

Chapter 7. Microaggressive Behaviors

"Here I am as a physician, a woman at the table with a room full of other male physicians, and the CEO addressed all of the men as Dr., but when it came time to ask me for my opinion, he always said, "Gloria, what do you think?" This happened all the time, and I got used to it, and I bet he never realized he did it."— Anonymous surgeon

ICROAGGRESSIONS ARE DEFINED AS EVERYDAY, subtle, intentional, and oftentimes unintentional interactions or behaviors that communicate some bias toward historically marginalized groups, including women, underrepresented ethnic or religious groups, the disabled, and the LGBTQ+ community. Chester M. Pierce, a black Harvard University psychiatrist, invented the term *"microaggressions"* in the 1970s to describe slights and insults hurled at black Americans by (usually) their non-black counterparts.

Microaggressions are *"the kinds of remarks, questions, or actions that are painful because they have to do with a person's membership in a group that's discriminated against or subject to stereotypes."*[1] Microaggressions are ubiquitous in society and all work environments. The healthcare environment is certainly not an exception.

Just as there are different types of sexual harassment and discrimination, microaggressions, too, can be broadly categorized. The University of New Hampshire, in its National Science Foundation (NSF)-funded research, breaks down microaggressions into three forms: microassaults, microinsults, and microinvalidations.[2] A fourth form, environmental microaggressions, can be added to the list.

1. **Microassaults:**
   - So-called *"old-fashioned"* discrimination.
   - Name-calling, avoidant behavior, or purposeful discriminatory actions.
   - Likely to be conscious and deliberate.
   - *Example*: Consciously choosing not to promote a manager due to his sexual orientation.
2. **Microinsults:**
   - Subtle snubs that communicate a covert insulting message.

- Convey stereotypes, rudeness, and insensitivity that demean a person's identity.
- Are frequently unknown to the person.
- *Example:* Addressing male physicians in a meeting as "Dr." and addressing the only female physician in the room by her first name. This is also an example of microinvalidation.

3. **Microinvalidations:**
   - Disconfirming messages.
   - Exclude, negate, or dismiss the thoughts, feelings, or experiences of certain groups.
   - May be the most damaging form of the three microaggressions.
   - *Example*: Dismissing a coworker's contribution because of her looks.

4. **Environmental Microaggressions:**
   - Microaggressions accepted as part of the culture in the organization or work environment.
   - *Example:* Using only one demographic group or sex for advertising products.

Additionally, there are numerous types of gender microaggressions, including[2]:

- Sexual objectification.
- Second-class citizenship.
- Use of sexist language.
- Assumption of inferiority.
- Restrictive gender roles.
- Denial of the reality of sexism.
- Denial of individual sexism.
- Invisibility and sexist humor/jokes.

Macrolevel aggressions occur on a systemic and social level, such as unequal pay, the glass ceiling, and media images. Microaggressions can also be based on membership in other marginalized groups related to race, ethnicity, sexuality, age, religion, etc. When we question the validity of microaggression occurrences, that, too, is a microaggression, specifically a microinvalidation. When we repeatedly interrupt a female coworker or speak over her, it is a microinsult. Frequently assigning administrative tasks to female workers is a form of microassault.

When a supervisor calls a meeting to have a *"boys talk"* or invites only male workers out for lunch, or when an organization has an informal *"boys club"* culture that excludes women, it is a microassault. Despite progress, these behaviors continue in the modern workplace and healthcare organizations.

If a male nurse manager, for example, calls a female nurse "babe" when addressing her or attempting to get her attention for any reason, it may or may not be interpreted as open harassment, but there is general agreement that it is not appropriate and creates an unprofessional environment.

In this example, I did not mention the *ages* or *ethnicities* of the individuals involved. Nor did I mention the tenure or duration of the relationship of the individuals. Let's examine a seemingly innocent case scenario to illustrate how our internal biases can affect our emotional response to hearing about a concern.

Scenario:

The house supervisor of a hospital has been working the overnight shift, from 11 p.m. to 7 a.m., for over 20 years. He is in his late 50s and is generally well-liked and respected, but he often refers to his female nurse colleagues as "honey." He does it so frequently and has done it for so long that it is often ignored as part of his normal communication.

A new employee, a 23-year-old female nurse, has just started working the night shift, and the house supervisor calls the nurse to give a brief report. Innocently, he says, "Hey honey, I have a new admit for you. Are you ready for report?" He thinks nothing of the phone call and report. The nurse takes offense at being called "honey" and notifies her charge nurse.

At this point, the charge nurse has an obligation to *acknowledge and take the complainant seriously* that the nurse's interpretation of the house supervisor's use of the word "honey" is demeaning and unwanted. Some might argue, and the charge nurse may even argue or inform the nurse, that this is "just how he is and it's not personal." *This is a mistake.* Allowing non-professional communication maintains the status quo. It becomes tacit complicity, ensuring there is a culture that is microaggressively condescending despite how innocent the word or action may seem.

MICROAGGRESSIONS IN MEDICAL SCHOOL

A recent study by Espaillat and colleagues examined the occurrence and frequency of microaggression experiences of medical students at the University of Florida College of Medicine (UFCOM). In the spring of 2017, a nine-question survey was administered to 545 students, with a response rate of 64%.[3]

A majority of medical students (54%) experienced microaggressions during their medical school years, with most instances occurring during their preclinical years. Notably, before participating in the study, 44% of the students had never heard of the term 'microaggression.' Female medical students were more likely than male medical students, 73% vs 51%, respectively, to experience microaggressions.

A component of the survey included the opportunity to provide a narrative answer to the question: If you have heard of the term "microaggressions," what is your understanding of the term?[3]

Student responses included:

- *"Seemingly small comments or actions made that reflect a larger societal issue of sexism, racism, homophobia, etc. These comments 'seem' harmless (micro) but are harmful to the recipient."*
- *"Male faculty has also shown 'inappropriate dress' pictures, and they only featured women. This made me feel upset that only women could break the dress code."*
- *"In my time on surgery, I was referred to solely in seemingly disparaging terms such as 'sweetheart' in the OR by a young male attending. As a female interested in surgery,*
- *"I felt extremely frustrated that I was not being taken seriously and felt very belittled by the experience."*
- *"I had a Hispanic attending who was joking with a Hispanic medical student about how she would 'never fall for a guy like [me] because [I am] white."*
- *"Our school solely presents gay men in question stems in or to present a question regarding HIV/AIDS. This has made me feel unsafe. We have never been presented with a gay woman, which has made me feel invisible."*

Some students, however, denied the concept of "microaggressions":

- *"Extremely sensitive individuals use this word to describe comments that intentionally or unintentionally offend their fragile egos because they have been accustomed to receiving participation trophies in little league and subsequently have not developed the proper coping mechanisms when encountering someone who does not like them, disagrees with their views, or generally has an opinion different than their own. It's a major development of the so-called 'PC culture.' Using words like microaggression enables the user to declare oneself 'victimized' in an intellectual way."*
- *"To have suffered a microaggression, you must first adopt a 'woe is me' attitude of a perpetual victim who intends to feel threatened by every well-intentioned word, phrase, or action that you may encounter on a daily basis.'*

This paper examined contemporary attitudes and experiences, and the fact that a few students expressed denial of the concept of microaggressions is concerning. These individuals most likely have similar attitudes regarding the presence or prevalence of other forms of discrimination and harassment. It is easy to deny the existence of microaggressions if an individual has not experienced firsthand microaggressions, discrimination, or harassment. This attitude perpetuates the false narrative that these behaviors are not significant enough to address.

Reducing sexual harassment and misconduct requires organizations to raise awareness and address microaggressive behaviors. Awareness leads to understanding, and understanding leads to change, which in turn leads to a better culture that is intolerant of microaggressions. This process does not take place in a vacuum, and the leaders in the organization have a responsibility to model the behavioral expectations they have for everyone else in the organization.

MICROAGGRESSIONS: PART OF A CONTINUUM OF DISCRIMINATION, HARASSMENT, AND ASSAULT

Microaggressions are part of a continuum of behaviors leading to discrimination, harassment, misconduct, and, finally, sexual assault (see Figure 1). Microaggressions are ubiquitous, widely tolerated, and culturally ingrained. Tolerance of microaggressions leads to sex and gender discrimination. Discrimination often leads to harassment, which in turn can lead to misconduct. Effective training requires educating everyone in the organization that microaggressions exist and are antecedent to more serious behaviors and conduct.

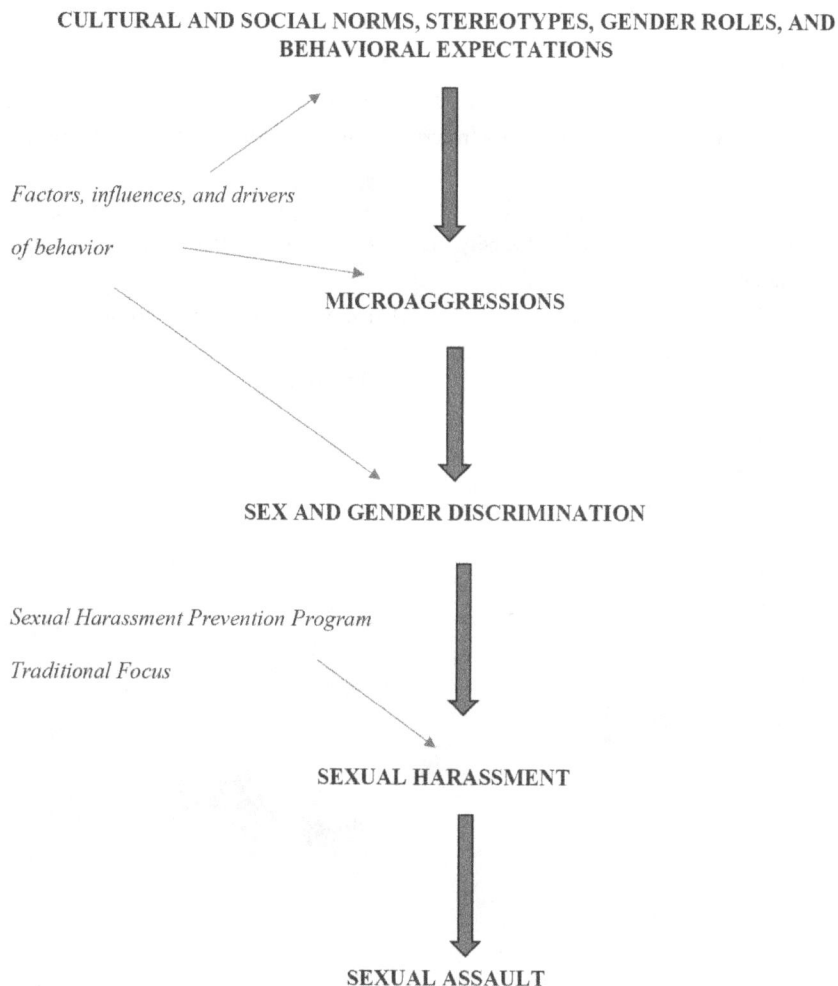

CULTURAL AND SOCIAL NORMS, STEREOTYPES, GENDER ROLES, AND BEHAVIORAL EXPECTATIONS

Factors, influences, and drivers

of behavior

MICROAGGRESSIONS

SEX AND GENDER DISCRIMINATION

Sexual Harassment Prevention Program

Traditional Focus

SEXUAL HARASSMENT

SEXUAL ASSAULT

FIGURE 1. The continuum of microaggressions, discrimination, sexual harassment, and sexual assault.

Most organizations' sexual harassment programs focus on prevention. It is important to consider the impact of societal and social norms and microaggressions as a major contributor to the environment, leading to more serious behaviors: harassment and assault. Ignoring or simply not acknowledging discrimination and microaggressions is a barrier to continued progress. Despite organizations' inability to alter broader cultural and social norms and stereotypes, they can educate staff and employees on these influential drivers of more serious behaviors.

REFERENCES

1. Posh at Work. Microaggressions: Sexual Harassment Subtleties in the Workplace. April 8, 2021. https://poshatwork.com/microaggressions-sexual-harassmentsubtleties-in-the-workplace/.

2. University of New Hampshire. Making the Invisible Visible: Gender Microaggressions. https://www.unh.edu/diversity-inclusion/sites/default/files/media/2021-12/making-the-invisible-visible.pdf.

3. Espaillat A, Panna DK, Goede DL, Gurka MJ, *et al*. An Exploratory Study on Microaggressions in Medical School: What Are They and Why Should We Care? *Perspect Med Educ*. 2019;8(3): 143–151. doi: 10.1007/s40037-019-0516-3

Chapter 8. Beyond Stereotyping: It Can Happen to Anyone

"People forget that stereotypes aren't bad because they are always untrue. Stereotypes are bad because they are not always true. If we allow ourselves to judge another based on a stereotype, we have allowed a gross generalization to replace our own thinking."— George Takei, actor and activist

A MAJORITY OF THE CASES of sexual misconduct, harassment, and discrimination are perpetrated by men to women. To remain objective and fair and engage in an ethically and morally driven investigation into allegations, investigators need to appreciate that harassment and misconduct *can happen to anyone.* Men can be victims, too. Men can harass men, women can harass women, and those who identify as LGBTQ+ can harass other women, men, and LGBTQ+ individuals.

Misconduct and harassment are behaviors that cross all boundaries of sex, gender, race, age, and position, and it is an investigator's and organization's responsibility to remain objective and seek answers without bias or prejudice. Understanding that these are *human-derived behaviors* is the first step in establishing an objective perspective. The individual's status, role or position, race, age, gender, or gender identity are details.

Focus on the behavior. What was done or said? Who engaged in the behavior? Subjective interpretation, bias, or worse, disbelief that an individual does not possess the stereotypical characteristics of someone who would engage in misconduct is not justified. Perpetrators and victims can be anyone.

Kris Hardies recently published a paper examining the prevalence and correlates of sexual harassment in professional service firms in Belgium. The survey included 321 Belgian employees from global accounting and law firms. The results of the study reveal the widespread prevalence of sexual harassment in the work environment: 88.5% of women and 83.3% of men experienced some form of sexual harassment at work at least once or twice during the preceding 24 months. Table 1 presents the survey results.[1]

These data reveal the power of stereotypes and gender roles in perceptions and behaviors. Women, for example, report much higher rates of

TABLE 1. Prevalence of sexual harassment in professional service firms

Sexual Harassment	Item	Total	Men	Women
Traditional	Tried to draw you into a discussion of sexual matters?	27.9%	26.5%	29.0%
Traditional	Told sexual stories or jokes?	65.4%	68.9%	61.8%
Traditional	Displayed, used, or distributed sexual materials (pictures, stories, or pornography)?	16.7%	21.2%	12.2%
Traditional	Made sexist comments or jokes?	72.7%	65.9%	59.5%
Traditional	Gave you sexual attention?	26.2%	24.2%	28.2%
Traditional	Attempted to establish a romantic or sexual relationship despite your efforts to discourage it?	10.3%	9.1%	11.5%
Traditional	Pressured you to "play along" with sexual jokes and behavior?	13.4%	15.2%	12.2%
Traditional	Made you feel you needed to flirt with them to be treated well?	6.5%	4.5%	8.4%
Traditional	Touched your face, butt, thigh, or another "private" part of your body?	11.1%	6.8%	15.3%
Traditional	Exposed a private part of their body to you?	3.4%	6.1%	1.5%
Traditional	Forced themselves on you sexually?	1.5%	2.3%	0.8%
Traditional	Indicated there might be some reward or special treatment if you agreed to engage in sexual behavior?	0.4%	0%	0.8%
Traditional	Made you afraid that you would be penalized if you did not agree to engage in sexual behavior?	0.4%	0%	0.8%
Traditional	Treated you badly for refusing to have sexual relations with them?	1.2%	0.8%	1.5%
Not man enough	Made you feel like you were not tough enough (for example, assertive, strong, or ambitious enough) for the job?	51.3%	42.4%	60.3%
Not man enough	Called you a wimp, sissy, chicken, or some other name implying you are not courageous enough?	16.0%	15.9%	16.0%
Not man enough	Implied they would admire you more if you were stronger or more athletic?	9.2%	12.1%	6.1%
Not man enough	Teased you for being gullible or easily fooled?	32.4%	17.3%	37.4%
Not man enough	Said you were too sensitive?	35.1%	20.5%	49.6%

(N=321).[1]

being told they are too sensitive, gullible, or easily fooled for not being "tough enough" and were touched inappropriately more often. Although this study examines the environment in a professional setting outside of healthcare, there is no reason to suspect that cultural norms and behaviors differ significantly across industries, organizations, or other settings with large numbers of employees.

Social enforcement of rigid gender roles and socially acceptable gender-based behaviors or appearances is a form of microaggressive harassment. Men, for example, are "traditionally" stereotyped as strong, decisive, and courageous, and women have been stereotyped as weaker, more emotional, and timid. When individuals look, behave, or act in ways that are not reflective of these stereotypes, they can be the subject of microaggressions, discrimination, disparaging remarks, and other forms of mistreatment.

Lara Stemple and Ilan Meyer published a study assessing the prevalence and incidence of sexual victimization of men from five federal surveys that the Bureau of Justice Statistics, the Centers for Disease Control and Prevention (CDC), and the FBI conducted independently from 2010 through 2012.

In 2011, the CDC reported results from the National Intimate Partner and Sexual Violence Survey (NISVS) and found that men and women had similar prevalence of nonconsensual sex in the previous 12 months. This remarkable finding challenges stereotypical assumptions about the gender of the victims. Traditional stereotypes reinforce the public's perception and awareness of the problem that men can be victims, too.

Investigators posit several reasons why there is little discussion and research on men as victims. These include the continued belief that:

1. Female-perpetrated abuse is rare or nonexistent.
2. Male victims experience less harm.
3. For men, all sex is welcome.

Male-on-female sexual violence is more common and continues; therefore, it is politically less palatable to raise awareness of female-on-male sexual violence. Males are also less likely to report sexual violence. Traditional stereotypes and the reluctance of males to report incidences "mask" male victimization. A 2012 National Crime Victims Survey (NCVS) of 40,000 households found that 46% of male victims reported a female perpetrator.

These findings suggest further research is necessary to understand the scope of the problem and identify the characteristics of female perpetrators.

Case Study

A 26-year-old black, gay nurse recently accepted a job in the ICU at a local hospital. Staff in the unit are aware of his sexual orientation, as he has mentioned his partner's name a few times while on shift. Approximately two weeks after starting in this position, he is having dinner in the lounge, and two other nurses, a 43-year-old white female, and a 33-year-old white female, sit at the same table as the nurse. After discussing work, the younger female nurse tells him he is very attractive and that he could probably date any woman he wants.

Unknown to her, he has heard this type of remark dozens of times since he came out about six years ago. He knows he is attractive, and he is aware that women find him attractive. He tells her he has heard women say that to him before and that he has a boyfriend. She immediately blurts out, "I bet he's hot, too."

After dinner, everyone returns to the unit and their assignments. He has become exhausted from these types of comments, and the following day, he requests a meeting with the unit manager to discuss the conversation that occurred in the lounge.

Here are some critical questions to ask yourself about this case:

1. Is he "making a mountain out of a molehill" by requesting a meeting?
2. How do you think he feels when a woman tells him he is attractive and that he can have any woman he wants?
3. Do you think the young nurse would make a remark like this to a straight nurse? Why or why not?
4. What is implied when the young nurse says, "I bet he's hot, too?"
5. How would you interpret these events if the 26-year-old gay man were, instead, a lesbian or bisexual woman?
6. How would you interpret these events if, instead, the new nurse were a gay man in his 60s who came out in his late 30s and has been married to his partner for 15 years?
7. How do you interpret this event if the gay nurse is, instead, a young, attractive woman, and the two other nurses are men of similar age?

Would it be okay to tell the young nurse that she could date any man she wanted?

Your answers to these questions reveal your own biases, prejudices, and ideas about gender roles and gender role expectations, cultural norms, social norms, and stereotyping attitudes and behaviors.

Regardless of how open-minded we think we are, everyone has a unique identity shaped by our gender, cultural norms, and other factors that influence how we perceive and interpret what we see and hear. We all inherently possess biases and prejudices. We must consciously recognize our own biases and prejudices when interpreting these events. It is not easy to do.

It is certainly not OK for this young woman to comment on the nurse's attractiveness. The additional comment about his ability to date any woman he wanted to also implies that his sexual orientation matters. What if she said, "I bet you could date any man you wanted to?" A comment like this makes no sense because the fabric of our social norms is grounded firmly in the default stereotype that everyone is cis-gendered and heterosexual until evidence proves otherwise. In summary, it is inappropriate for the nurse to have made those comments. She may have felt her remarks were innocent, but they are not.

Case Study

A 64-year-old female OR director walks up to the OR front desk where a 46-year-old male surgeon is having a conversation with his back to her. With her right hand, she gently taps the surgeon's buttocks for a couple of seconds. The surgeon turns around, surprised, and laughs it off along with two other OR staff members who witnessed the event. Neither the surgeon nor the other staff members file a formal complaint. The OR director and surgeon are not in a romantic relationship.

Here are some questions to ask yourself about this case:

1. Was this sexual misconduct?
2. Why do you think the surgeon did not file a formal complaint?
3. Why didn't the OR staff file a formal complaint?
4. If the OR director and surgeon had a known, romantic relationship, would this conduct at work be acceptable? Why or why not?

Case Study

A 47-year-old recently divorced female nurse is dating a 27-year-old male and is working in the emergency department during a 12-hour day shift. Her shift ends at 7:00 p.m., and she tells everyone she needs to leave quickly, as her boyfriend is picking her up a little after 7 so they can catch a flight to their vacation destination.

Toward the end of the shift, the nurse overhears one of the other female nurses, a 55-year-old female, sarcastically tell a younger nurse, "Yeah, we need to let the 'cougar' get out tonight as fast as possible so she can enjoy a vacation with her cabana boy." The 47-year-old nurse immediately confronts the nurse who made the comment, demanding an apology for the derogatory term that had just been used. Cougar is a slang term for an older woman who dates a younger man, usually at least two decades younger, as in this example. The offending nurse replies, "You do know your new nickname around here is 'cougar,' right?"

Ask yourself these questions:

1. Is this sexual harassment? If so, why? If not, why not?
2. Should the nurse file a formal complaint?
3. You are the unit manager, and the nurse asks to speak to you privately about the event. How will you proceed with investigating this concern?
4. As the unit manager, you discover that many nurses and other staff have been calling the nurse "cougar" behind her back. What will you do to address this behavior?

REFERENCE

1. Hardies K. Prevalence and Correlates in Professional Services Firms. *Front Public Health.* 2022;10. doi: 10.3389/fpubh.2022.1082088

Chapter 9. Impact of Power Differentials in the Healthcare Setting

"Sexual assault and domestic violence are difficult things to talk about. Talk about them anyway." — Mariska Hargitay, actress

PROFESSIONAL AUTHORITY CAN BE SEXUALLY COERCIVE, and there are numerous power differentials in the healthcare setting. First and most obvious is the power differential between a physician and a patient. The nature of the relationship creates an imbalance in power, and this imbalance must be respected and acknowledged by the physician. This is why it is important to establish and maintain professional boundaries with patients at all times. These imbalances produce vulnerabilities, and the power differential and imbalance, already present in the nature of the relationship between physician and patient or nurse and patient, increase or decrease when gender, racial, cultural, and socioeconomic differences are factored into the imbalance.

The "gap" or difference between the physician and patient may be narrow or wide, and the wider the gap, the more vulnerable the patient is, and the greater the opportunity to exploit a wide power imbalance. For example, physicians who practice in affluent regions of a city or suburb often treat patients who belong to the same socioeconomic class as the physician. This reduced power differential increases the likelihood a patient will feel empowered if there is misconduct. Conversely, if a physician works in a rural or impoverished setting, the socioeconomic class difference between the patient and physician is significantly wider.

In addition, it is likely that patients in rural or urban areas with limited resources will not be as well-educated. This increases vulnerability and presents an opportunity for a physician to take advantage of the patient. As well, socioeconomic and even racial differences may influence the "validity" of a patient's claim if there is misconduct. Despite decades of civil rights reforms and increased investment in creating equality, inequalities persist.

In 2010, Devereux presented a model of "idealizing transference," whereby a patient can feel bonded to a professional through the patient's disclosures, which can evolve into dependency.[1] Physicians can also exploit or even create dependency when they encourage more frequent visits than medically necessary. The process of establishing dependence is a form of adult sexual grooming. Sinnamon describes the grooming as a "systematic preparation of a victim"[2]:

> "Establishing trust with the target and their family and social network, normalizing intimate interactions, blurring the lines of what is and is not appropriate behavior, desensitizing their victim to the warning signs of abuse or exploitation, and creating a psychologically, socially, emotionally, and often physically reinforcing experience."

Notably, this process can take *years*. The following story is an example of creating dependence. I have redacted names and altered exact circumstances and details to preserve the anonymity of all parties involved.

Kathy, a white British woman in her 60s, was interviewed about her experiences with the medical system and, in particular, her general practitioner (GP), whom she saw exclusively for years from her teens into her 20s. Of note, in her teens, she was placed into a psychiatric hospital for being "out-of-control" and was the only minor among adult female patients.

Her GP had placed her in the hospital, and after her inpatient course, he scheduled numerous regular appointments with her throughout her teens and 20s. He eventually asked Kathy if she could assist with babysitting his children. Having grown up poor, Kathy felt "special" to be invited to her GP's "beautiful" home.

A few years later, Kathy, now married, felt ill. Her husband was out of town for two weeks on a business trip. She called her GP.

The GP came to Kathy's flat, gave her a tablet to " settle" her down, and then left to attend to another emergency. He returned to Kathy's flat and sexually assaulted her. He returned at the end of the day repeatedly for two weeks and continued to sexually assault her. Distraught, she reported the incidents to the police, and based on her reports, they turned her away, implying she was "troubled." Because she had been in an inpatient psychiatric facility, her credibility was questioned. However, Kathy's husband attempted to confront the physician, and the physician said, "*If you ever do anything with this and try and ruin me, I will ruin you first. Your wife is a psychiatric patient.*"

This case shows how power differentials can create opportunities for inappropriate conduct and, in this particular case, years of repeated sexual assault.

Power differentials and imbalance also include traditional male authority. In a study of anesthesiologists subject to discipline in Canada from 2000 to 2011, 90% of the subjects were male. Age differences can also produce a power dynamic that influences behaviors. Cultural expectations and the power distance between men and women influence the social norms for harassment.[3]

In 1996, Keyton posited that sexual harassment is fundamentally a communicative phenomenon. The relationship through which power is expressed exists within interactions.[4]

Using this concept that harassment is a communication problem is fundamental to understanding the cross-cultural power differences that exist.

In many cultures, for example, women do not have the same status or rights as men. They often must adhere to strict, defined, and rigid gender roles and expectations. There is a large "power distance" between women and men in these cultures, and the greater the power distance, the more likely women are to be victims of misconduct, harassment, and abuse. In some of these cultures, the behaviors are so common and frequent that little attention is given to the issue.[5]

Collectivist cultures value the "group identity" more than individual identity or an individual's personal goals. These cultures are more static and less dynamic, and culture change — including gender roles and expectations — is largely immutable. Western cultures are highly individualistic and recognize the autonomy and sovereignty of an individual. In Western cultures, many women and other marginalized groups have gained rights, social status and position, and the power gap between men and women has been reduced. This transformation is relatively recent, transpiring over the last century.

In summary, power gaps, differentials, and power distance increase the opportunities for misconduct, harassment, and discrimination. Among the many influential factors, the power distance between men and women is the most significant to acknowledge. In many Western cultures, the power distance has been reduced, but it still exists, which is one of the reasons why misconduct and harassment continue.

REFERENCES

1. Devereux D. The Patient's Perspective: Impact and Treatment. In: Subotsky F, Bewley S, Crowe M, eds. *Abuse of the Doctor-Patient Relationship*. London: Royal College of Psychiatrists; 2010:15–27.

2. Sinnamon G. The Psychology of Adult Sexual Grooming: Sinnamom's Seven-Stage Model of Adult Sexual Grooming. In: Petherick W, Sinnamon G, eds. *The Psychology of Criminal and Antisocial Behavior: Victim and Offender Perspectives*. New York: Academic Press;2017:459–487.

3. Alam A, Khan J, Liu J, Klemensberg J, Griesman J, Bell CM. Characteristics and Rates of Disciplinary Findings Amongst Anesthesiologists by Professional Colleges in Canada. *Can J Anesth.* 2013;60(10):1013–1019.

4. Keyton J. Sexual Harassment: A Multidisciplinary Synthesis. In: Burleson BR, ed. *Communication Yearbook 19.* Thousand Oaks, CA: Sage;1996:92–155.

5. Merkin RS. Sexual Harassment Indicators: The Socio-Cultural and Cultural Impact of Marital Status, Age, Education, Race, and Sex in Latin America. *Intercultural Communication Studies.* 2012;XXI:1:154–172.

Chapter 10. Sexual Violence

"That day, I came to a stark realization. I was afraid of men, and the harder I fought, the more intense the fear became. I can't think of an experience that is more harrowing than a woman being sexually harassed or assaulted by a man." — Zahra Hankir, author

SEXUAL VIOLENCE IS ANY SEXUAL ACT, attempt to obtain a sexual act, or other act directed against a person's sexuality using coercion by any person, regardless of their relationship to the victim, in any setting. Nonconsensual sexual touching is one of the most common forms of sexual abuse. It involves any unwanted sexual, physical contact without the explicit consent of the individual involved. Such acts can include, but are not limited to, fondling, groping, or any other form of sexualized touching.

Sexual violence is common among both women and men. Data retrieved from the Global Burden of Disease (GBD) database from 1990 to 2017 determined that nearly 36% of women have experienced sexual violence. Rates of sexual violence against men and boys is lower but is often underreported.[1]

The rates of depression, anxiety disorders, unplanned pregnancies, sexually transmitted infections, and HIV are higher in women who have experienced violence compared to women who have not; other medical conditions can develop long after the violence has ended. Most violence against women is perpetrated by current or former husbands or intimate partners.[2]

The number of reported cases of rape increased dramatically from 2013 to 2022 after the FBI changed the definition of rape (Figure 1). Until 2013, the data gathered used a definition of the term "forcible rape" from 1929: "the carnal knowledge of a female, forcibly and against her will." In 2013, the FBI's Uniform Crime Reporting (UCR) system redefined rape as "penetration, no matter how slight, of the vagina or anus with any body part or object, or oral penetration by a sex organ of another person, without the consent of a victim."[3] The number of reported cases before 2013 would likely be much higher than Figure 1 shows if the new definition was used.

Fewer than 40% of the women who experience violence seek help of any sort. In most countries with available data on this issue, among women

Number of reported forcible rape cases in the United States from 1990 to 2022

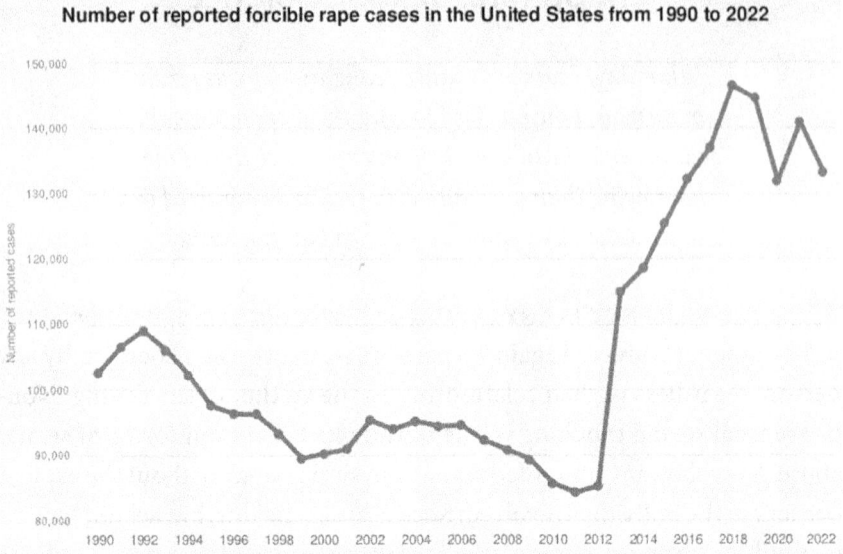

FIGURE 1. Number of reported forcible rape cases
in the United States from 1990 to 2022.

who seek help, most look to family and friends, and very few look to formal
institutions, such as police and health services. Fewer than 10% of those
seeking help reported to the police.[4] The reasons for not reporting events
are explored in more detail in Chapter 14.

REFERENCES

1. Borumandnia N, Khadembashi N, Tabatabaei M, Alavi Majd H. The Prevalence Rate of
Sexual Violence Worldwide: A Trend Analysis. *BMC Public Health.* 2020;20(1):1835.
doi: 10.1186/s12899-020-09926-5

2. UN Women. Facts and Figures: Ending Violence Against Women. https://www.
unwomen.org/en/what-we-do/ending-violence-against-women/facts-and-figures.

3. Federal Bureau of Investigation Criminal Justice Information Services Division. Uniform
Crime Reporting Program Changes Definition of Rape. Crime in the United States
2013. U.S. Department of Justice. https://ucr.fbi.gov/crime-in-the-u.s/2013/crime-
in-the-u.s.-2013/rape-addendum/rape_addendum_final#:~:text=The%20carnal%20
knowledge%20of%20a,permanent%20mental%20or%20physical%20incapacity.

4. United Nations. *The World's Women 2015: Trends and Statistics.* New York: United
Nations Department of Economic and Social Affairs. Statistics Division. 2015; 159.
doi: 10.18356/9789210573719

Chapter 11. The Violence Against Women Act and Its Influence

"The Violence Against Women Act is so important. It provides money to train the cop on the beat, to train the judges that this is a new day, that we won't tolerate this violence and to know how to deal with it." — Patricia Ireland, past executive director, National Organization for Women (NOW)

EXTENSIVE GRASSROOTS EFFORTS in the late 1980s and early 1990s from numerous victim advocacy groups such as The Battered Women's Movement, victim services organizations, law enforcement agencies, prosecutor's offices, the courts, and the private bar urged Congress to adopt legislation to address domestic and sexual violence. The issue was a public health crisis, and with the passage of the Violence Against Women Act (VAWA), which is Title IV of the Violent Crime Control and Law Enforcement ACT, H.R. 3555, originally signed into federal law by President Bill Clinton on September 13, 1994, $1.6 billion was provided toward investigation and the prosecution of violent crimes, including rape, against women. The Act established the Office on Violence Against Women within the Department of Justice.

Until the late 1980s, law enforcement officers were trained to treat domestic violence (DV) as a private matter and ill-suited for public intervention.[1] As an example, the Oakland (California) Police Department's *1975 Training Bulletin on Techniques of Dispute Intervention* explicitly stated[1]:

"[T]he police role in a dispute situation [is] more often that of a mediator and peacemaker than enforcer of the law......[T]he possibility that... arrest will only aggravate the dispute or create a serious danger for the arresting officers due to possible efforts to resist arrest...is most likely when a husband or father is arrested in the home.... Normally, officers should adhere to the policy that arrests shall be avoided....but when one of the parties demands arrest, you should attempt to explain the ramifications of such action (e.g., loss of wages, bail procedures, court appearances) and encourage parties to reason with each other."

Detroit Police Commander James Bannen, in his address to the 1975 American Bar Association convention, described how his police officers respond to domestic violence calls. According to Bannen, the dispatcher would screen calls from battered women and respond only to those women who seemed to be in the most imminent danger. If the woman had only minor injuries when they arrived, the police would become angry and not respond as quickly when she called the next time. Police treated poor women and women of color with less concern than they did middle-class and white women, even when the women were severely injured.[2] In addition to discrimination, racism and racist attitudes influenced law enforcement behavior.

Women were vulnerable, with few options back then. Domestic violence was not perceived as a major problem if law enforcement refused to arrest offenders. Many of the women who were and are victims of domestic violence are also victims of sexual abuse and assault from their partners. The passage of VAWA was a giant leap forward in coordinating efforts from law enforcement, healthcare providers, social workers, and other community programs to support victims.

POSITIVE CHANGES AS A RESULT OF THE VAWA

At the Women of the World Festival in March 2020, HRH The Duchess of Cornwall said, "The campaign to end domestic violence needs the voices of men as well as women, challenging the cultural, economic and political context in which we all experience the world."

The movement toward raising public awareness about domestic violence parallels the movement to create awareness of sexual harassment of women in the workplace. In 1976, Del Martin published *Battered Wives*, a major source of information and validation for the movement. *Battered Wives* legitimized the view that violence against women is caused by sexism and historical attitudes toward women.

Domestic violence and intimate partner sexual violence and assault, now accepted as a public health issue, continue to be addressed through funding of educational and training programs for professionals in law enforcement, healthcare, and other social support services. It required a lot of effort to coordinate and create a support system. It remains complex today; Figure 1 shows the numerous organizations, tasks, and personnel required to support women who are victims of violence.[3]

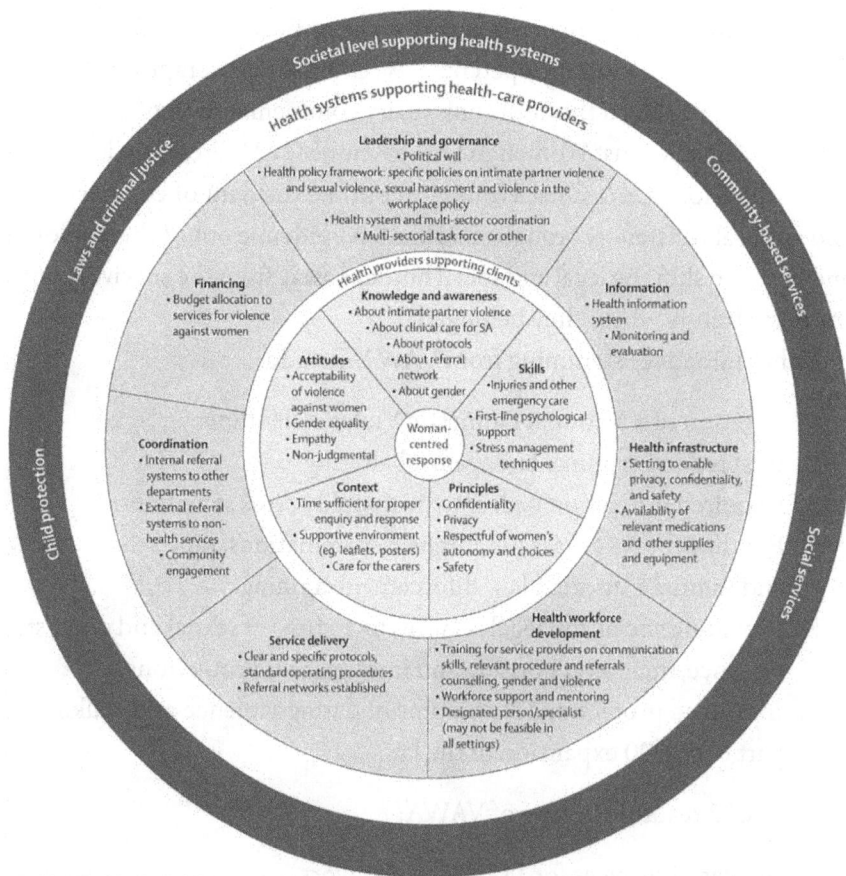

FIGURE 1. Elements of the health system and healthcare response necessary to address violence against women.[3]

Domestic violence and sexual assault and abuse are public health issues and, as such, require appropriately trained and responsive healthcare providers.

Health systems can provide the necessary training and support, and health providers need to appreciate the unique needs of women who are victims of violence and/or sexual assault. Additionally, there are many unique entry points into the healthcare system. A woman who presents to the emergency department will present differently than one who is in an outpatient clinic. Women who present to the emergency department, for example, may require post-rape care and support. Lastly, women will continue to have different needs at different times — with evolving support.

VAWA has been an overwhelming success. Between 1993 and 2022, domestic violence rates dropped by 67%, and the rate of rapes and sexual assaults fell by 56%. At the 30th anniversary commemoration of the passage of the Violence Against Women Act in September 2024, President Joe Biden said, "The Violence Against Women Act broke the dam of congressional and cultural resistance, brought this hidden epidemic out of the shadows, and began to shift the legal and social burdens away from the survivors onto the perpetrators where they belonged."

Other initiatives stemming from VAWA include:

1. Creation of a National Domestic Violence Hotline.
2. First federal criminal law against battering.
3. Required protection orders to be upheld across state lines.
4. Funding for sexual assault forensic examinations, rape crisis centers, and trauma-informed law enforcement training.
5. Providing social and legal services to victims of sexual and domestic violence, including housing and immigration protections.
6. Improved protections for victims of dating violence and stalking as part of a 2000 expansion of the law.

The 2022 reauthorization of VAWA:

1. Increased services for LGBTQ+ survivors.
2. Empowered tribal courts to prosecute non-native perpetrators of domestic and sexual crimes.
3. Added a new National Resource Center on Cybercrimes Against Individuals and prioritized prosecuting of perpetrators of cybercrimes.
4. Led to the Fairness for Rape Kit Backlog Survivors Act, which prevents sexual assault survivors from being unfairly blocked from receiving compensation due to rape kit backlogs.

VAWA is up for federal renewal every five years. An advantage of this renewal process is that it can incorporate new initiatives that reflect new information or needs. The disadvantage is the legislation has been subject to partisan politics, and passing reauthorization funding and provisions has been threatened as recently as 2021. Regardless of partisan politics, VAWA has made a positive difference in women's lives and will continue to evolve.

REFERENCES

1. Zorza J. Criminal Law of Misdemeanor Domestic Violence, 1970-1990. *J Criminal Law and Criminology.* 1992;83(1): 46–72.

2. Schecter S. *Women and Male Violence: The Visions and Struggles of the Battered Women's Movement.* Boston, South End Press;1982.

3. Garcia-Moreno C, Hegarty K, d'Oliveira AFL, Koziol-McLain J, Colombini M, Feder G. The Health-Systems Response to Violence Against Women. *Lancet.* 2015;385(9977):1567–1579. doi: 10.1016/S0140-6736(14)61837-7

Chapter 12. Stalking Behaviors

"Stalking is a crime that deprives victims from basic freedoms and rights. The rights to privacy, free movement, mobility, protection and security are pivotal human rights and victimization should be seen and recognized as a violation of basic human rights." — Jenny Korkodeilou, Victims of Stalking: Case Studies in Invisible Harms

STALKING BEHAVIORS CONSTITUTE A PATTERN of repeated and unwanted attention, contact, harassment, communication, or other conduct directed at an individual that causes a reasonable person to feel fear and intimidation. Similar to crimes of sexual violence, stalking is about power and control. Stalking is one of the four pillars of VAWA, and many sexual assaults follow stalking behaviors; however, estimates suggest fewer than half of stalking victims are assaulted.[1]

The prevalence rate of victimization among females and males in the general population is estimated to be 8%–32% for females and 2%–13% for males. The risk is significantly higher for females, particularly younger individuals (18–29 years).[2] Many victims of stalking had a previous intimate relationship with the perpetrator or have been an acquaintance, friend, or colleague without a history of a romantic relationship with the perpetrator. Stalkers who are not known to the victim are the least common perpetrators. A prior history of any domestic or sexual violence in the relationship increases the chance of becoming a victim of stalking.[3]

Healthcare professionals are particularly vulnerable to stalking behaviors. Several investigations involving psychiatrists, physicians, nurses, and psychologists have shown that this population is at higher risk of victimization than the general population, and estimates range from 12% to 50%. Abrams and Robinson report a prevalence of 14.9% among physicians, with psychiatrists, OB/GYNs, and surgeons showing the greatest risk.[4]

The higher incidence of stalking is likely due to the nature of healthcare work. Patients present with mental and physical disease processes and are vulnerable. A patient might misunderstand the care and compassion of healthcare providers as a desire to form a more intimate relationship with them. Attempts by the healthcare professional to "reset" the nature of the relationship can create a powerful emotional response in the patient, leading to a variety of stalking behaviors.

The various types and prevalence of stalking behaviors reported by victims are shown in Table 1. Four categories of stalking — unwelcome communication, contact, associated behaviors, and violent stalking — and their common behaviors are presented, along with prevalence. Unwelcome communication, not surprisingly, is the most common category. As expected, the least common behaviors were violent, with threats or death threats as the most common in this category. Physical and sexual assault, though not as common as the other behaviors, remain a major concern.

Victims of stalking suffer severe and varied effects that often require assessment and treatment. An analysis of 258 stalking cases reported four categories of impact on victims: psychological and substance abuse, physical health, practical impact on life, and impact on others. Psychological impact is most common and includes anxiety, depression, PTSD, and panic disorders. Duration, relationship, and severity of stalking behaviors increase the risk of severe psychological impact.

The impact on victims of stalkers is well-defined. Less studied and more difficult to research are the reasons *why* individuals engage in stalking behaviors. What motivates stalkers beyond power and control? What are the precipitating events that lead to stalking?

Mullen and colleagues developed a stalking classification system to describe the various stalking typologies. Included in the system is the incorporation of the prior relationship between the stalker and the victim, the stalker's apparent motivation to engage in the behaviors, and finally, the presence and nature of specific types of psychopathology of stalkers. Five stalker "types" emerged from their study[6]:

1. **Rejected:** Stalking behaviors start after the breakup of a close relationship. This includes not only formerly intimate partners but also close friends and family. Rejected stalkers are motivated by a desire for reconciliation, revenge, or both, and are not commonly afflicted with severe mental illness.

2. **Resentful:** These individuals target strangers or acquaintances who they believe have wronged them in some manner. The stalking behaviors seek revenge against their victims as a way to regain power and

TABLE 1. Prevalence of stalking behavior types spontaneously reported by victims.[5]

Category	Stalking Behavior	n	%
Unwelcome communication		**220**	**85.3**
	Texts	130	50.4
	Calls	130	50.4
	Social media	104	40.3
	Emails	85	32.9
	Letters	48	18.6
	Gifts	41	15.9
Contact		**192**	**74.4**
	Visiting home/work	98	38.0
	Following	75	29.1
	Harassing	74	28.7
	Loitering	70	27.1
	Watching	61	23.6
	Hacking	30	11.6
	Spying	24	9.3
	Breaking and entering	19	7.4
	Tracking	8	3.1
	Monitoring	6	2.3
Associated behaviors		**139**	**53.9**
	Third-party contact	104	40.3
	Vexatious complaints	49	19.0
	Criminal damage	46	17.8
Violent stalking behaviors		**127**	**49.2**
	Threats	103	39.9
	Death threat	34	13.2
	Physical assault	24	9.3
	Suicide threat	16	6.2
	Sexual assault	8	3.1
	Revenge porn	5	1.9

control. These individuals may exhibit paranoid traits or may suffer from psychoses that contribute to their sense of injustice.

3. **Intimacy Seekers:** The stalking behaviors of these individuals emerge when the stalker believes they have a loving, intimate relationship,

even when that relationship has not been established. These individuals often suffer from severe mental illness, including borderline personality disorder. The stalker's persistence is accompanied by a delusional conviction the victim either loves them or will love them.

4. **Incompetent Suitors:** Incompetent suitors seek to establish friendships and/or sexual relationships with strangers or acquaintances. They are often motivated by loneliness or lust. These individuals are not suffering from any mental illness but are often socially awkward or have other interpersonal problems.

5. **Predatory:** These individuals target strangers or acquaintances solely for the purpose of sexual gratification, which is often deviant in nature. These individuals often can be diagnosed with paraphilias, substance use disorder, personality disorder, or severe depression.

Obviously, predatory stalkers represent the most concerning type because of the increased potential for sexual assault or violence, but all types of stalkers have that potential. Victims suffering from prolonged and persistent stalking behaviors are at increased risk for developing anxiety, PTSD, depression, and possibly substance use disorders.

CASE STUDIES

Case 1 below is adapted from a paper presented by Douglas Ingram, a clinical professor of psychiatry and behavioral sciences at New York Medical College.

Case 1

A 30-year-old female first-year surgical resident participated in a surgery in which the patient died in the operating room. The patient's brother was an elderly man who was a patient in a locked psychiatric ward at the same hospital. The brother of the patient thought the young intern had killed his sister. Upon completion of the resident's internship, she started her psychiatry residency. Soon after she started, she began receiving letters and postcards from the patient's brother. He had escaped from the psychiatric ward and wrote that she and he would marry after he killed her. He signed each note with a skull and crossbones.

Concerned and worried about her safety, she notified the chair of the department and showed him the letters and cards. Security staff was alerted, and posters of the man were placed throughout the hospital. Eventually, the man did show up at the hospital, and he was quickly arrested and returned to the psychiatric ward at another hospital.

In recounting these events, the young resident said she felt secure and protected because her chair and the administration of the hospital acted on her concerns. The outcome of this case would likely be different if the woman's concerns were not taken seriously.

Case 2

A 38-year-old male urologist who has been in practice for four years began working with a new female certified registered nurse first assistant (CRNFA) in the operating room. The CRNFA had moved recently from another state, and they worked well together — there was nothing unusual in their interactions.

The urologist was a member of a local gym and frequently worked out later in the day. About two months after the new CRNFA started, she purchased a gym membership at the same facility. Late one afternoon, she arrived at the gym about 20 minutes after he arrived and approached him while he was working out on one of the machines. She explained to him that she had just joined the gym and had been a member of a gym at her prior location.

After some small talk, they separated and continued their own workouts; there was no more interaction that day. The next day after work, unbeknown to the urologist, the CRNFA followed him to the gym. She parked next to his car, and after getting out of her car, said hello and walked with him into the gym.

A pattern began to emerge. She showed up at the gym every day after work at the same time he did and began to work out on equipment closer to where he was exercising. For him, it started to feel awkward and intrusive.

One morning, he was at the OR computer preparing for cases and saw a card from the nurse placed on top of the computer. The note described how important he was to her and how much she enjoyed spending time with him.

Concerned, he asked her to stop following him at the gym and said that he was not interested in any further communication. She persisted, and finally, as he was leaving the gym one day, she pulled her car behind his so he could not back out. She confronted him in an aggressive manner and accused him of not caring. She asked repeatedly why she could not work out with him. This incident prompted him to pursue obtaining an order of protection.

The nurse contested the order of protection, and during an investigation, the physician discovered the nurse had engaged in similar conduct in two other states that led to physicians obtaining orders of protection. Clearly, this was a pattern. The judge granted the physician the order of protection, and the hospital administration enforced the terms of the order: She could not work in the same room as the urologist. No further incidents occurred.

Case 3

A 54-year-old female nurse and her 54-year-old male partner, a dentist, worked at the same dental clinic and began dating soon after the dentist's wife passed away. After the dentist ended the relationship, the nurse became fixated on him and launched a relentless campaign of harassment, calling him 965 times in one 24-hour period.

Her obsessive behavior escalated when she broke into his home and waited for him in his bedroom before fleeing through a window. On one occasion, he spotted her following him in her car. He stopped at a local shop and inadvertently left the car unlocked. When he returned to his car and realized it had been left unlocked, he feared for his safety and left his car at the store.

Law enforcement was alerted to this behavior. When the judge said he was prepared to sentence the woman to 12 months in prison, the dentist asked him to show some leniency. Instead, the judge recommended mental health treatment and invoked a restraining order that prohibited the nurse from any further contact with the dentist.

REFERENCES

1. Churcher F, Nesca M. Risk Factors for Violence in Stalking Perpetration: A Meta-Analysis. *FWU Journal of Social Sciences*. 2013;7(2):100–112.
2. Spitzberg B, Cupach W. The State of the Art of Stalking: Taking Stock of the Emerging Literature. *Aggression and Violent Behavior*. 2007;12(10):64–86.
3. Maran D, Varetto A. Psychological Impact of Stalking on Male and Female Health Care Professional Victims of Stalking and Domestic Violence. *Front Psychol*. 2018;9:321.
4. Abrams K, Robinson G. Stalking by Patients: Doctors' Experiences in a Canadian Urban Area. *J Nerv Ment Dis*. 2011;199(10):738–743.
5. Storey J, Pina A, Williams C. The Impact of Stalking and Its Predictors: Characterizing the Needs of Stalking Victims. *J Interpers Violence*. 2023;38(21-22):11569–11594.
6. McEwan T, Shea DE, Daffern M, MacKenzie RD, Ogloff JRP, Mullen PE. The Reliability and Predictive Validity of the Stalking Risk Profile. *Assessment*. 2018; 25(2): 259–276.

Chapter 13. Cross-Cultural Behaviors and Misinterpretation of Actions

*"Cultural differences should not separate us from each other,
but rather cultural diversity brings a collective strength that
can benefit all of humanity."* — *Robert Alan, author*

CULTURAL NORMS, SOCIAL NORMS, GENDER ROLES, gender expectations, power distance between men and women, and the legal rights and status of women vary from nation to nation and within ethnic groups and subgroups. What might be considered rude and inconsiderate behavior may be a welcoming behavior in another culture. Cultural norms for eye contact, personal space and distance, allowable touching behaviors, etc., are culturally distinct enough to produce the unintended consequence and perception of misconduct or harassment when individuals from two cultures interact.

A great deal of research on sexual harassment has focused primarily on gender differences, roles, perceptions, and what behaviors constitute sexual harassing behaviors. There is a dearth of research and literature on the important role of culture.[1] Many organizations and institutions fail to appreciate the impact of culture on behavior, expectations, and interpretations. Developing cultural competence requires understanding these qualitative and quantitative differences in perceptions, behaviors, attitudes, and perspectives. The healthcare workforce is incredibly diverse in many countries, so cultural influence on behaviors cannot be ignored . Ignoring the impact impedes progress.

HOFSTEDE'S CULTURAL DIMENSIONS THEORY

Geert Hofstede was a Dutch social psychologist, former IBM employee, and former professor emeritus of organizational anthropology and international management at Maastricht University in the Netherlands. He is best known for developing one of the earliest and most popular frameworks for measuring *cultural dimensions* in a global perspective.

Hofstede developed a cultural model after using factor analysis to examine the results of a worldwide survey of employee values between 1967 and 1973. *Hofstede's Cultural Dimensions Theory* emerged from this work, and it provides a framework for discussion on the influence of culture on sexual misconduct, harassment, and discrimination (Figure 1). His theory, proposed in 1980, was one of the first quantifiable theories that could be used to explain the observed differences between cultures.[1] The different cultural domains provide a perspective on how individuals relate to each other and within their respective communities.

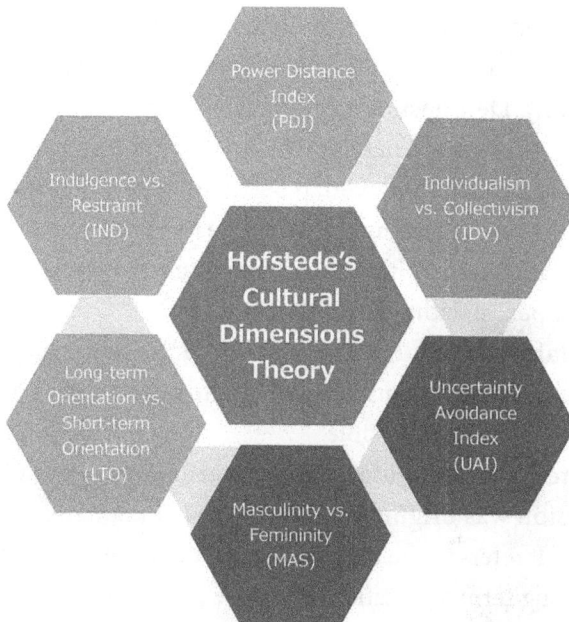

FIGURE 1. Hofstede's Cultural Dimensions Theory.[1]

Hofstede identified and included six unique cultural domains:

1. **Power Distance Index** (PDI): The degree to which authority is accepted or followed. A high PDI score indicates that a society accepts an unequal, hierarchical distribution of power and that people understand "their place" in the system. A low PDI score means that power is shared and widely dispersed and that society members do not accept situations where power is distributed unequally.

2. **Individualism vs. Collectivism** (IDV): This refers to the strength of the ties that people have to others within their community. A high

IDV score indicates weak interpersonal connection among those who are not part of a core "family." Here, people take less responsibility for others' actions and outcomes. In a collectivist society, however, people are supposed to be loyal to the group to which they belong, and, in exchange, the group will defend their interests. The group itself is normally larger, and people take responsibility for one another's well-being.

3. **Masculinity vs. Femininity** (MAS): This refers to the distribution of roles between men and women. In masculine societies, the roles of men and women overlap less, and men are expected to behave assertively. Demonstrating your success and being strong and fast are seen as positive characteristics. In feminine societies, however, there is a great deal of overlap between male and female roles, and modesty is perceived as a virtue. Greater importance is placed on good relationships with direct supervisors and working with people who cooperate with one another.

4. **Uncertainty Avoidance Index** (UAI): In societies that score highly for Uncertainty Avoidance, people attempt to make life as predictable and controllable as possible.

5. **Long-term Orientation vs. Short-term Orientation** (LTO): This dimension was originally described as "Pragmatic vs. Normative (PRA)." It refers to the time horizon of people in a society. Countries with a long-term orientation tend to be pragmatic, modest, and thrifty. In short-term oriented countries, people tend to place more emphasis on principles, consistency, and truth, and are typically religious and nationalistic.

6. **Indulgence vs. Restraint** (IVR): This last dimension is recent. Countries with a high IVR score allow or encourage relatively free gratification of people's own drives and emotions, such as enjoying life and having fun. In a society with a low IVR score, there is more emphasis on suppressing gratification and more regulation of people's conduct and behavior, and there are stricter social norms.

A 1997 study by Pryor and colleagues found that North American, Australian, and German students perceived hostile work environment scenarios more in terms of power abuse and gender discrimination, whereas Brazilian students perceived the same scenarios as innocuous sexual behavior but not harassment. Brazil is considered a high-power index country; the United States and many European nations have a low-power index.[2]

Cultural attitudes toward sex and sexuality also influence individual attitudes. In Brazil, for example, nudity is not socially taboo, and in fact, partial nudity is broadcast on television. In many other countries, this is illegal or considered socially unacceptable. Therefore, the "boundaries" of what is considered acceptable behavior are influenced by social norms, customs, and attitudes.

A 2006 study by Anne Fiedler and R. Ivan Blanco explored the differences in perceptions of various types of sexual harassment among residents of three countries. Using Hofstede's typology for cultural dimensions, the authors found a correlation between a country's ranking on the dimensions and the perception and acceptance of sexually harassing behaviors. Countries that ranked high on the masculinity scale, low on individualism, high on power distance, or high on the uncertainty index have a higher prevalence and acceptance of sexually harassing behaviors. However, we must use caution when broadly applying these findings, as not all individuals in a country will have the same attitude of acceptance or have the same proclivity to engage in harassing behaviors.[3]

Another consideration is the wide variation in training, policies, and legislation between different nations. For example, in Brazil, there are no mandatory anti-harassment policies, and in Australia, sexual harassment training and policies are mandatory. Legislation and cultural expectations and tolerances are intertwined.[4]

The legal system influences the culture, and the culture influences legislation in a loop. In the United States, for example, the suffragist movement gave women a voice and a vote, reducing power distance. Nations and cultures that restrict women's rights negatively affect socially acceptable behaviors. Women are treated as second-class citizens with no agency or authority.

PROVIDING CULTURAL AWARENESS TRAINING TO EMPLOYEES

Cultural differences in perceptions, awareness, and acceptable behaviors must be incorporated into an organization's effort to reduce harassment and misconduct. To reduce the knowledge gap and create cultural competence and awareness, a series of scenario discussions or role-playing exercises demonstrating the differences between cultures in a sensitive manner can show employees how misinterpretations or misunderstandings occur. In this respect, an organization must walk a fine line between showing respect for different cultural attitudes and perceptions while conveying the message that sexual harassment will not be tolerated.

Despite this fine line, in the United States, Title VII, Title IX, and the EEOC's expectations are clear and objective. Therefore, it is important to emphasize to employees that despite cultural differences, actions and behaviors will be interpreted and enforced using legal terms and current legislation.

Doriane Coleman addresses the issue of multicultural sensitivity in applications of the law this way[5]: *"American law has typically attempted to resolve the tension between tolerance and a unified culture by applying the doctrine of ordered liberty."*

This doctrine advocates cultural pluralism, but only within the bounds tolerated by the majority. In other words, cultural liberty is allowed but only within the confines and boundaries of the social order, norms and traditions, and values held by the majority. Critics of this interpretation argue that cultural groups should have the liberty to maintain their uniqueness and have permission to engage in culturally significant practices. This is known as a cultural defense doctrine — the opposite of the doctrine of ordered liberty.

Coleman and Sikora identified six problems with using the cultural defense doctrine. According to them, the cultural defense doctrine[5]:

1. Sets up disparate standards of justice for those of different cultures.
2. Promotes stereotypes of minority cultures.
3. Potentially reinforces cultural norms and practices that depreciate or limit the rights of women and children.
4. Robs victims of justice when a defendant's culture is involved.
5. Limits the deterrent value of punishments through mitigation by cultural agreements.
6. Ignores the fact that the criminal justice system already allows the admission of cultural background evidence to establish mitigating circumstances or argue for a reduced sentence.

Not mentioned but just as important is the practicality of using many different cultural practices and definitions of acceptable behaviors. Applying dozens if not hundreds of different "standards" and "yardsticks" introduces chaos, and without uniform application of definitions and the law, it would be impossible to create a safe, fair, and harassment-free environment. It is impossible to respect and honor every culture's unique perspective.

Another downside to cultural training is the potential for perpetuating stereotypes about cultures. Broad generalizations can have unintended consequences. For example, suppose a training exercise emphasizes that "masculine" cultures tend to tolerate harassing behaviors. A male trainee from Argentina (a highly masculine culture nation) might feel singled out by female trainees as a potential harasser. Female trainees may apply these generalized principles to all men in the organization who are from high-masculine culture-scoring countries.

Offering culturally sensitive training is difficult because of the risk of misinterpretation. People use their own cultural upbringing and social norms as the yardstick for socially acceptable behaviors. We are comfortable with what we are familiar with. Therefore, programs should instruct employees that although cultural values differ *across* nations and cultures, there is considerable variability at the individual level. More importantly, individuals need to be aware of cultural differences and how these differences influence and affect behavior.

As you read the following two case studies, ask yourself these questions:

1. How do you think individuals from other cultures feel when confronted with a different cultural environment?
2. What can you do or say to individuals from other cultures who have different cultural standards and norms to make them feel more comfortable?
3. Should physicians have a right to not treat a patient due to conflicting religious or personal beliefs?
4. How can healthcare professionals reduce their own anxiety when approaching patients with different cultural norms or expectations?

Case 1

A recently hired 32-year-old male scrub tech from a high-power index and high-masculine index country is well-liked by his peers, but he has a habit of putting his arms around the circulating nurses or coming up from behind and placing his hands on their shoulders and whispering to them how great they are to work with.

He is hard-working and a team player, but his behavior has made several of the female circulators uncomfortable. The nurses have spoken about the issue in the locker room after work several times. One of the nurses suggests they draft a brief note of concern they can all sign and submit to the OR manager. The nurses submit the letter, and the OR manager requests a meeting to discuss the issue with all of them present. At the meeting, they all confirm similar behaviors of physical touching and whispering. The OR manager documents the discussion and creates a formal report.

How should the OR manager proceed in this case? Cases involving several individuals need to be addressed and discussed with the chief nursing officer of the hospital. This case, which involves physical touching, can potentially become a legal matter if not handled properly.

What points of discussion are relevant in this case? It might be culturally appropriate behavior in the scrub tech's native country, but physical touch without permission is not permissible behavior in the United States and many other nations. While his intent may not be sexual in nature, the women are uncomfortable and have not given consent to being touched.

Should there be any punishment or disciplinary action in this case? During the interview with the respondent, it is important that he explain why he is touching the women without permission. His answers will provide clarity around intent, and whether or not he recognizes the fact that the women are uncomfortable even if he thinks his behavior is culturally permitted and "normal" in his native country.

The scrub tech shares that he regularly touched women the same way in his native country. He is warm and friendly, and this is the first time it has ever been seen as a problem. He understands the women are not comfortable and agrees to no longer touch the nurses. The nurses are informed of the discussion and his agreement to no longer touch them. The case is resolved, and there are no further incidents.

Case 2

It is late on a Saturday evening, and the OB ward at a Women's Center is busy triaging patients. A new patient arrives in need of an urgent C-section, and the anesthesiologist, a 44-year-old male, is summoned to the triage area to assess the patient prior to going to the OR.

Upon arrival, the anesthesiologist introduces himself, and it is immediately apparent to him there is a concern. The husband of the pregnant woman does not want the male anesthesiologist to touch his wife, and he requests a female anesthesiologist perform the anesthetic. There is no female anesthesiologist available to assist in this case, and the male anesthesiologist informs the husband that he is the only anesthesiologist available.

After some discussion, the husband reluctantly agrees to allow the anesthesiologist to administer the anesthetic if he can be present in the room with his wife throughout the procedure. All parties involved agree, and the case proceeds uneventfully.

Cultural sensitivity includes understanding the unique needs and circumstances of patients. This patient and her husband are Muslim, and male physicians, nurses, or other staff providing bedside care to the patient must consider allowing the husband of the patient to be present. It is also good practice to have a third party of the same gender as the patient present in the room.

REFERENCES

1. Zemojtel-Piotrowska M, Piotrowski J. Hofstede's Cultural Dimensions Theory. In: Shackelford T, ed. *Encyclopedia of Sexual Psychology and Behavior.* Springer Cham; 2025. doi:10.1007/978-3-031-08956-5

2. Mishra V, Davison H. Sexual Harassment Training: A Need to Consider Cultural Differences. *Industrial and Organizational Psychology.* 2020;13(2):163–167. doi: 10.1017/iop.2020.25

3. Pryor J, Desouza E, Erber MW. Gender Differences in the Interpretation of Social-Sexual Behavior: A Cross-Cultural Perspective on Sexual Harassment. *J Cross-Cultural Psychology.* 1997;28(5):509–534.

4. Fiedler A , Blanco R. The Challenge of Varying Perceptions of Sexual Harassment: An International Study. *J Behav and Applied Manage.* 2006;7(3): 274–291.

5. Zimbroff J. Cultural Differences in Perceptions of and Responses to Sexual Harassment. *Duke Journal of Gender Law and Policy.* 2007;14(2):1311–1341.

Chapter 14. Barriers to Reporting

"You're not a victim for sharing your story, you are a
survivor setting the world on fire with your truth. And
you never know who needs your light, your warmth
and raging courage."— Alex Elle, author

DESPITE PROGRESS IN ENCOURAGING the reporting of sexual violence, harassment, and discrimination, barriers for the victim remain. According to the National Intimate Partner and Sexual Violence Survey, one in five women experience attempted or completed rape in their lifetime, and one in 14 men experience an attempted or completed act of being forced to penetrate someone in their lifetime.[1] Few individuals who experience sexual violence report the crime to the authorities. A 2018 National Crime Victimization Survey revealed a sobering statistic; only 24.9% of victims of rape or sexual assault report the events.[2]

A major barrier to reporting the events is fear of retaliation from the perpetrators. Perpetrators are often known to their victims as either family members, friends, acquaintances, romantic partners, or work colleagues. Reporting the event can have a significant impact on the victim's relationships with individuals who know the perpetrator.

Intimate partner violence, especially, places enormous pressure on the victim to keep the crimes secret due to the possible loss of one's family or economic security (if the victim is dependent on the perpetrator). Reporting the events also may lead to physical harm, although this is less common.[3] Individuals are far more likely to report the experience when they do not know their attacker.[4]

Many victims do not report an incident because they believe a lack of physical evidence or witness will cause them to not be believed. In these cases, the perpetrator may deny the allegations. Significant power distances between the victim and perpetrator increase the odds the victim may not be believed, or worse, that the victim will be ignored. In dozens of cases, victims of prominent surgeons and physicians who have engaged in unwitnessed misconduct stay silent out of fear of not being believed. In some cases, when the allegations are found to be true, the disciplinary action against these individuals is kept quiet and sometimes quietly settled. Institutions, especially prominent institutions with elite reputations, are motivated to preserve their reputations.

Speaking out and reporting an event is not entirely risk-free. In some cases, especially when there are no witnesses, the perpetrator can threaten harm to the victim if the victim reports the event. Other reasons for not reporting or delaying reporting events include:

Retraumatization: Recalling the details of a harrowing event is emotionally traumatizing and exhausting. Some victims do not want to have to tell the story numerous times and re-experience the event. Without adequate mental health support, this places another burden on the victim.

Shame or guilt: Some victims may feel as if they are to blame for the abuse, for example, if they are under the influence of drugs or alcohol. Some victims fear others will blame them for the incident.

Harm to reputation: Some victims fear their reputation will be harmed by the event; this is especially true if an investigation is inconclusive. The fear of being labeled as disruptive or a liar can damage an individual's reputation and strain professional and personal relationships.

Won't be believed: Victims may feel their story will not be believed — especially if the accused perpetrator is well-liked in the community, has a good reputation, or has status as a prominent role model or mentor. Additionally, men may not want to report women who engage in inappropriate conduct because of embarrassment or the possibility the story will be minimized due to the respective genders of the perpetrator and victim.

Loss of employment: If the perpetrator is a colleague, reporting the event, especially if the perpetrator is a superior, may lead to retaliation, including termination.

Nothing will be done. Victims often fear nothing will be done to investigate the event. Or, if the perpetrator is found guilty or admits guilt to the misconduct, the consequences may be inadequate.

Embarrassment: Same-sex sexual assaults and harassment are often underreported. If the victim identifies as LGBTQ+ but has not "come out" at work, reporting an event carries the risk the victim will be "outed" at work, not on their own terms.

LGBTQ+ individuals are often the targets of inappropriate comments. Within a predominantly cis-heterosexual social structure, there is a tendency to reduce the LGBTQ+ individual's identity to sex. There is an assumption that the relationships are all about sex, the type of sex, and the frequency of sex. For example, there are LGBTQ+ individuals who identify as lesbian or gay but do not have partners and are not seeking partners. *An individual's identity does not impart anything other than the individual's identity.*

Age: Younger victims have less influence and power than older victims. Consequently, younger victims may feel more vulnerable and afraid of the consequences of reporting an incident.

Doubt: Victims may have doubts about whether the experience was an assault or whether the behaviors qualify as harassment. Doubt is more common when the perpetrator and victim know each other or have a close relationship or the conduct is not violent or forced.[5]

Feeling betrayed: Betrayal produces a powerful emotional response, and reporting an event may exacerbate that feeling. This feeling often occurs within the context of an intimate relationship.

Desire for privacy or normalcy: Victims may not want to recount the events or face their perpetrator. Or they may fear the intrusion into their "normal" lives. One victim stated, *"I was inappropriately touched at work, and I did not want to be at the center of workplace drama."*[6]

Some victims may face multiple barriers to reporting, but the most important take-home message is quite simple: barriers exist, and efforts to reduce barriers and raise awareness that barriers harm victims will create a safer environment for victims to report the events. It is the organization's responsibility, not the victims' responsibility, to create a psychologically safe environment and space to report without fear.

In 2022, Lindsay Orchowski and colleagues published a qualitative analysis of victims who did not report sexual assault and harassment. The victims' statements were tweets that used the hashtag #WhyIDidntReport. Here are a few examples that illustrate the reasons for not reporting assault or harassment. Some of these responses can be powerfully triggering.[6]

- *"I did but no one believed me. It went on for years and was perpetrated by my own stepfather. So that I would have no way of hiding, my mother even took the door off my room."*
- *"I didn't report because men are expected to be tough."* (male victim)
- *"If you miraculously see your perpetrator convicted, the sentences are absolute bullshit."*

- *"I recalled a story of a woman attacked worse than I was, SHE didn't tell authorities. So of course, my assault didn't count."*
- *"I was terrified to say anything. It took me over 15 years to disclose. I was afraid nobody would believe me or that they would judge me."*
- *"He waited until I turned 18 and it was a year before I was able to report it. He threatened—daily—my family, pets, himself. After what he did to me, I thought he'd do it."*
- *"My mom's happiness was more important—I knew if I told the truth it would destroy the family. It did."*
- *"I was 23 when it happened, had just started my career, and I was assaulted by a senior executive in the field. I was alone with him in a living room, thought it was my fault for being there, and quickly realized that if I reported it would end my career."*
- *"If I reported the event, my science career would probably have ended. He was a prominent medical researcher with numerous grants in our lab. It would have ruined my life and other people who worked in the lab if it was shut down. I didn't know what exactly would happen, but I knew it wouldn't be good. I just made sure I was never alone with him again. He had groped me twice late at night in his office."*
- *"I did not want to relive the event again. It was too painful to remember, and I didn't want to tell the story again and again and then possibly face him."*

These statements are heartbreaking and highlight the complex reasons, consequences, and barriers victims face. Tragically, if these crimes and misconduct continue unreported, justice for the victims is denied, and victims pay a tremendous emotional price because of the barriers.

Statistics on prevalence and incidence are drawn from reported events; the *actual* frequency of events is likely higher and difficult to estimate.

REFERENCES

1. Smith SG, Zhang X, Basile KC, Merrick MT, Wang J, Kresnow M, Chen J. *The National Intimate Partner and Sexual Violence Survey: 2015 Data Brief – Updated Release.* Centers for Disease Control and Prevention; 2018.

2. Morgan R, Oudekerk B. *Criminal Victimization, 2018.* U.S. Department of Justice, Office of Justice Programs, Bureau of Justice Statistics. September 2019. (NCJ 253043U). https://bjs.ojp.gov/content/pub/pdf/cv18.pdf.

3. Shepp V, O'Callaghan E, Ullman S. Interactions with Offenders Post-Assault and Their

Impacts on Recovery: A Qualitative Study of Sexual Assault Survivors and Support Providers. *J Aggress Maltreat Trauma.* 2019;29(6):725–747.

4. Zinzow H, Thompson M. Barriers to Reporting Sexual Victimization: Prevalence and Correlates Among Undergraduate Women. *J Aggress Maltreat Trauma.* 2011;20(7):711–725.

5. Russell H. Am I Making More of It Than I Should? *Fam Med.* 2021; 53(6):408–415.

6. Ochowski L. Barriers to Reporting Sexual Violence: A Qualitative Analysis of #WhyIDidntReport. *Violence Against Women.* 2022;28(4):3530–3553.

Chapter 15. Child Sexual Abuse

"When a child reports sexual abuse, it may sound unbelievable — that's what the perpetrator wants. Believe the child. The unbelievable happens all the time." — Paula Goodwin, advocate, founder of Defend Survivors

"A child will never forget sexual abuse; it will never be gone from their memory. They can move forward though, and have healthy emotional and sexual relationships. The brain is fantastic and can heal with treatment." — Celine Hamilton, child and adolescent psychiatrist at Joe DiMaggio Children's Hospital

CHILD SEXUAL ABUSE IS COMMON ENOUGH to be a major public health issue with enormous psychological, social, and economic consequences for the victim. Consider these statistics:

- One in 9 girls and 1 in 20 boys under the age of 18 experience sexual abuse or assault.[1]
- 82% of all victims under 18 are female.[2]
- Females ages 16-19 are 4 times more likely than the general population to be victims of rape, attempted rape, or sexual assault.[3]

What's more, many of the children who are victims know the perpetrator. Out of the sexual abuse cases reported to Child Protective Services in 2013, 47,000 men and 5,000 women were the alleged perpetrators.[4] Women represent approximately 10% of perpetrators; therefore, most children are abused by a male known to the child or adolescent, and a majority of the victims are female.

Reducing the incidence and prevalence of child sexual abuse is a difficult task. Identifying risk factors and developing awareness as a healthcare provider is useful. Researchers have identified several common factors that increase the risk of child sexual abuse risk[5]:

Home Environment. Children who live in two-parent households are less likely to be victimized than those living in single-parent or blended families with a step-parent and/or step-siblings. In addition, if one of the parents has a substance or alcohol use disorder, the risk increases.

Low Self-Esteem. Children with low self-esteem are especially vulnerable due to their need for affection, admiration, and acceptance. Children with low self-esteem are more likely to be drawn to those who offer flattery, gifts, and special attention. This is especially true for children who are targets of bullying or whose parents also display low self-esteem. Without feelings of self-worth, a child may not see the value in the boundaries, respect, and consent they are entitled to.

Loneliness. Loneliness is a powerful emotion that can lead to feelings of neglect, isolation, and alienation. A crucial step in a perpetrator's grooming is isolating the child from their loved ones emotionally and physically. If a child is already feeling isolated, this step will be much easier for a perpetrator to achieve. Also, if a child is frequently left alone or unsupervised, a perpetrator has more opportunities to get close to the child.

Misunderstanding Boundaries. One of the most significant risk-increasers for child sexual abuse is insufficient education or understanding about boundaries. Children who do not have a clear understanding of boundaries are unlikely to distinguish between appropriate and inappropriate behavior. They may not understand when someone has violated their personal boundaries or when they have violated the boundaries of someone else.

With an unclear understanding of what constitutes abuse, they are less likely to disclose any sexually abusive behavior they witness, experience, or hear about. They may also engage in or demonstrate inappropriate behavior that could draw the attention of potential perpetrators.

Domestic Abuse. Sexual abuse is a higher risk in a home where abuse, neglect, and maltreatment occur. This is particularly the case in homes where there is physical abuse. Domestic violence fosters a home environment of instability, insecurity, poor communication, and mishandled aggression. It may also correlate with alcohol or substance abuse among one or more family members.

Each of these factors increases the risk of child sexual abuse. According to researcher Danielle Black, the risk of intra-familial child sexual abuse is six times greater in a family where the mother is a victim of partner aggression.[6]

Prior History of Sexual Abuse. Children who have been victims of prior sexual abuse are at a higher risk of being abused again. This is known as *revictimization.* A child survivor who lacks the support network and tools to cope with their trauma may become more vulnerable to a recurrence of sexual abuse, whether in childhood, adolescence, or adulthood. Also, a child who has been subjected to sexual abuse that has not been dealt with is likely still in an at-risk environment that allows the abuse to continue.

Children Who Identify as LGBTQ+. Children who identify as LGBTQ+ or are in the process of understanding their sexual and/or gender identity can be at risk of feeling socially isolated and alienated from their peers. The fear, anxiety, and uncertainty they may experience could lead them to view themselves as outsiders with no emotional support. A perpetrator may pick up on this vulnerability and need for guidance and might seek to convince the child that they are the only one who understands and accepts them.

When a child is afraid to open up to their parents about their sexuality, a perpetrator can use that secret against them to prevent the abuse from being disclosed.

Unmonitored Use of Social Media and the Internet. Technology provides limitless ways to nurture your child's education, creativity, and communication; it is also a perpetrator's tool to exploit children. The internet provides them with significantly greater access to potential targets, along with added anonymity and secrecy. The phones, tablets, or laptops in the home can be gateways for interaction between a perpetrator and a child. Not only do these devices greatly expand a perpetrator's reach, but they also remove many barriers to contact, such as being able to send inappropriate material.

SIGNS AND SYMPTOMS OF CHILD SEXUAL ABUSE

Children and adolescents exhibit a broad range of signs and symptoms of abuse, and healthcare providers should consider sexual abuse when a child or adolescent exhibits unusual behavior or activities. Some signs and symptoms include[7]:

1. Quieter or more distant than usual.
2. Clingier than usual.
3. New or unusual fears revolving around physical touch, being alone, being with a particular person or in a particular place.
4. Difficulty concentrating or remembering, zoning out, seeming distracted, or not listening.
5. Changes in eating, sleeping, or hygiene.

6. Regressive behaviors such as bed-wetting or soiling after being toilet trained; acting like or wanting to be treated like a baby/younger child.
7. Showing knowledge of sexual behavior beyond their developmental age.
8. Displaying sexual themes in artwork, stories, play, etc.
9. "Acting out" behaviors such as aggression, destructive behaviors, and truancy.
10. Problems with friends and schoolwork/attendance.
11. Vague symptoms of illness such as headache or stomachache.
12. Self-harm, such as cutting; risky behavior.
13. Asking vague questions or making vague statements about topics such as secrets, unusual "games," or adult behaviors.

Case Study

Several years ago, I was performing a history and physical on a six-year-old female patient who was scheduled for dental procedures. As I examined the electronic medical record, I noted the patient had an unusual history of recurrent urinary tract infections and was a patient at a specialty clinic in a large metro area.

I read numerous notes from various physicians about recurrent UTIs, but I could find nothing that would explain the young girl's issues. When I went into the room, the child was sitting in a chair with several relatives and seemed withdrawn. Most children are nervous, but she was exceptionally quiet and made no eye contact. I suspected the child was being sexually abused. By law, my suspicion of sexual abuse required me to file a report.

HEALTH CONSEQUENCES OF CHILD SEXUAL ABUSE

Childhood sexual abuse has a profound impact on the mental, emotional, and physical health of victims; however, awareness of the impact on human development from early experiences of sexual abuse is of relatively recent origin. Many studies have concluded that survivors of childhood sexual abuse are more likely to develop and suffer from a variety of mental health disorders, including depression, anxiety, PTSD, and panic disorder. Eating disorders, personality disorders, substance and alcohol use disorders, suicidal ideation, and other self-injurious behaviors are also common. Survivors are four times more likely than the general population to suffer from substance use disorders, four times more likely to suffer from PTSD, and three times more likely to suffer a major depressive episode.[8]

Case Study

A male 26-year-old first-year medical student presents to the student health clinic with a psychiatrist after going to the emergency room two days prior for chest pain, shortness of breath, and a rapid heart rate. The workup, including an EKG, does not reveal anything wrong physically with the student. The student is discharged home from the emergency department with instructions to follow up in the student health clinic.

During the visit with a psychiatrist at the clinic, the student shares that he grew up in a physically abusive household and was raped at age five and almost raped again at age 13. He shares that he remembers breaking his arm when he was five years old while defending himself from the sexual assault. He shows the psychiatrist his distal radius, which clearly had been fractured without proper healing or treatment. Now, he is not sleeping well, and although he is doing well in his courses, the stress of starting medical school is a bit overwhelming.

The psychiatrist recommends weekly counseling sessions with a psychiatrist and weekly meetings with a local Adult Children of Alcoholics (ACOA) group. He is diagnosed with PTSD and panic disorder. He continues counseling throughout medical school and residency, and the symptoms of PTSD and panic disorder improve. He has been an attending physician for the past 20 years and continues treatment.

This case is about my own journey of healing from my experiences. It certainly has not been easy, but it has given me a profound gift of perspective. There has been suffering, and I live with the physical scar and constant reminder of that night when I look down at my right arm. It has become a symbol of healing but also one of strength that I had enough courage to fight back.

I am finally shattering my own silence. I vividly recall, when I was six years old, sitting in a chair with the sunlight blinding me as it streamed through the window behind Sue, a case counselor from family court services in Fresno County. She asked me a lot of questions about my life from the past year living with my mother. By then, my broken arm had healed, and I never brought it up. And I never brought up the fact I slept in different corners of the house every night to avoid another assault. And I never brought up the fact my brother and I went hungry for weeks on end. I sat, silent.

The last night I spent in that house is seared into my memory. My little brother and I sat in the front seat of a police car, and the slow pulse and glow of red and blue lights drifted across the garage door in front of us. The officer knew we were hungry and offered us his own dinner, a hamburger and fries.

When I was 13, my mother had custody of my brother and me every other weekend through agreed-upon custody arrangements. She rented out all of the rooms in her house to people recovering from alcohol and drug abuse, so when we visited, we never knew who would be at the house or even where my brother and I would sleep. Most times, we slept on the floor in random rooms with a sleeping bag and pillow.

I am sharing this story and more details because some of our patients, colleagues, friends, relatives, and loved ones have had similar experiences. It takes courage to lean in and listen to their stories. Like many survivors of childhood sexual abuse, I don't think there ever is a time when we completely move on from the experiences. We were robbed of our innocence, and for many of us, trusting others is difficult. The perpetrators in my life have been dead for over three decades, and I am telling my story because I think it is important to talk about what happens and what has happened—not only to prevent it but also so we can collectively heal from it through sharing.

Though my life has been profoundly and unalterably impacted by these events, I find solace in the words of Helen Keller: "*Although the world is full of suffering, it is full also of the overcoming of it. My optimism, then, does not rest on the absence of evil, but on a glad belief in the preponderance of good and a willing effort always to cooperate with the good, that it may prevail.*"

REFERENCES

1. Finkelhor D, Shattuck A, Turner H, Hamby S, *The Lifetime Prevalence of Child Sexual Abuse and Sexual Assault Assessed in Late Adolescence. J Adolesc Health.* 2014;55(3):329–333.
2. Department of Justice, Office of Justice Programs, Bureau of Justice Statistics. Sexual Assault of Young Children as Reported to Law Enforcement; 2000.
3. Department of Justice, Office of Justice Programs, Bureau of Justice Statistics. Sex Offenses and Offenders;1997.
4. United States Department of Health and Human Services, Administration for Children and Families, Administration on Children, Youth and Families, Children's Bureau.

Child Maltreatment Survey. Exhibit 5-2 Selected Maltreatment Types by Perpetrator's Sex; 2013:65.

5. Allison B. 11 Factors That Increase the Risk of Child Sexual Abuse. Saprea blog. https://saprea.org/blog/factors-increase-risk-sexual-abuse.

6. Black DA, Heyman RE, Smith Slep AM. Risk Factors for Child Sexual Abuse. *Aggression and Violent Behavior.* 2001;6(2-3):203–229.

7. Bravehearts. What Are the Signs of Child Sexual Abuse ? https://bravehearts.org.au/about-child-sexual-abuse/what-are-the-signs-of-child-sexual-abuse.

8. Mutavi T, Mathai M, Obondo A. Post-Traumatic Stress Disorder (PTSD) in Sexually Abused Children and Educational Status in Kenya: A Longitudinal Study. *J Child Adolesc Behav.* 2017;5(5):357.

Chapter 16. Consent: A Definition with Case Studies

"It's not consent if you make me afraid to say no." — Anonymous

"'No' is a complete sentence." — Anne Lamont, author

B ROADLY DEFINED, CONSENSUAL SEX is sexual activity between two or more individuals when all participants agree to engage in the activity knowingly, voluntarily, and without coercion. *The legal definition of consensual sex is determined individually by each state, country, province, or territory.* Individuals in New York state, for example, can consent to sexual acts at 17 years old. New York clearly defines what constitutes a lack of consent. To constitute a violation of criminal law, a sexual offense based on lack of consent, results from:

- Being forced.
- Being drugged without consent.
- Being physically helpless (unconscious, asleep, otherwise unable to say no).
- Any circumstance under which a victim had clearly expressed, in words or actions, that the victim did not consent and that a reasonable person in that situation would have understood the victim's words or acts as an expression of lack of consent.
- Any circumstance involving the touching of sexual or other intimate parts, directly or through clothing, in which the victim did not expressly or impliedly agree to the sexual contact.

Lack of consent in Arkansas is defined as:

There is a lack of consent if a person engages in a sexual act with another person by forcible compulsion or with a person who is incapable of consent because he or she is physically helpless, mentally defective or mentally incapacitated, or because of a victim's age. (Arkansas Code §§ 5-14-103; 5-14-125)

Lack of consent in Arizona is defined as:

"Without consent" includes any of the following: 1. the victim is coerced by the immediate use or threatened use of force against a person or property;

2. the victim is incapable of consent by reason of mental disorder, mental defect, drugs, alcohol, sleep or any other similar impairment of cognition and such condition is known or should have reasonably been known to the defendant; 3. the victim is intentionally deceived as to the nature of the act; or 4. the victim is intentionally deceived to erroneously believe that the person is the victim's spouse. (Arizona Revised Statute § 13-1401(A)(7))

To meet the state's legal standard, consent is a process that requires adherence to numerous "conditions":

- *Consent is communicated:* Communication for consensual sexual activity must be clearly communicated, and it can be given verbally and/or nonverbally.
- *Consent is mutual:* Consent must be mutually agreed upon by *all* parties involved.
- *Consent can be withdrawn:* Consent can be withdrawn at any time by an individual as long as it is clearly communicated.
- *Consent cannot be assumed:* Consent cannot be assumed if the individual is silent, does not resist, or if there is a prior relationship.
- *Consent is not possible if under the influence of drugs and/or alcohol:* Drugs and alcohol impair judgment and decision-making processes.
- *Consent is not possible for those with physical conditions, mental health issues, or other medical conditions impairing the individual's capacity to consent.*
- *Consent is not possible for those underage:* Each state defines the legal age for consent.
- *Consent is not possible for those who are coerced:* Pressure or threats constitutes coercion.
- *Consent is not possible for individuals in unequal power dynamics:* Physicians, for example, cannot consent patients for consensual sex.
- *Consent does not vary based upon a participant's sex, sexual orientation, gender identity, or gender expression.*

ROMEO AND JULIET LAWS

Romeo and Juliet laws establish and define consent for younger adults and minors. *Statutory rape* is nonforcible sexual activity in which one of the individuals is below the age of consent (the age required to legally consent to the behavior). Although the term usually refers to adults engaging in sexual contact with minors under the age of consent, it is a generic term, and few jurisdictions use the actual term *statutory rape* in the language of statutes. Each state has its own laws and definitions of the term.

Many Romeo and Juliet laws provide that a person can legally have consensual sex with a minor, provided that he or she is not more than a given number of years older, generally four years or less. Other conditions that must be met include: (1) both parties must consent; (2) the younger person must be at least a certain age; (3) the individuals' ages must be within a specified age gap.

To illustrate, consider this question: Can an 18-year-old *date* a 16-year-old in Texas?

While it is not against the law for a legal adult to date a minor in Texas, it is *illegal* to have sexual contact with someone who is 14–17 years old if the older individual is more than three years older than the younger individual, even if the sex is consensual. *Breaking this law is considered statutory rape.* An 18-year-old can engage in sexual activity with a 16-year-old in Texas; however, if the adult is 20 years old, sexual activity with a 16-year-old is illegal because of the age gap.

CONSENT CASE STUDIES

In this case study, the question of consent is relatively clear:

A 48-year-old male attending physician asks a 28-year-old female medical student on her rotation out for a date. He is her attending. She agrees to a date, and they have dinner. She drinks three glasses of wine at dinner, and he invites her over to his house. She agrees to go, and they engage in sexual activity. She wakes up the next morning regretting her decision to sleep with the attending.

Was the sexual contact consensual? No. Her judgment was impaired by alcohol. Additionally, there is a power dynamic between the individuals; she is a student, and he is a teacher on her rotation.

The following case highlights the complexity of what constitutes consent. I am providing direct testimony and verbatim comments from the case to illustrate the difficulty in determining consent in some cases.

In this particular case, consent for continued sexual activity was withdrawn, and the plaintiff alleged that the defendant continued engaging in sexual activity. (*Trigger Warning. This case uses explicit language and depictions of sexual acts some readers may find disturbing, offensive, or triggering*):

Supreme Judicial Court of Massachusetts, COMMONWEALTH v. RICHARD SHERMAN, Jr.[2]

A Superior Court jury convicted the defendant of penile-vaginal and digital-vaginal rape, implicitly rejecting the defendant's testimony that all sexual intercourse between him and the victim had been consensual. On appeal, the defendant claims that the trial judge committed two reversible errors.

First, the defendant contends that, where the deliberating jury asked the judge whether initially consensual sexual intercourse could become rape if the victim withdrew her consent after penetration, the judge erred by failing to instruct the jury that a defendant may not be found guilty of rape under such circumstances unless the penetration continued after the victim communicated the withdrawal of consent to the defendant.

Second, the defendant argues that, where there was no expert testimony regarding the effect of cocaine on perception and memory, the judge erred in admitting evidence of cocaine use for the purpose of allowing the jury to assess the defendant's ability to perceive and recall events. We conclude that the judge erred in failing to provide the jury with an instruction regarding the withdrawal of consent and in admitting cocaine evidence for the purpose of assessing the defendant's memory, but that, in the circumstances of this case, neither error requires reversal of the defendant's convictions. The primary contested issue at trial was whether the victim had consented to sexual intercourse with the defendant. The victim and the defendant offered sharply differing accounts of what happened in the early morning of October 14, 2014. We summarize the evidence at trial.

The victim testified that on the night of October 13, 2014, she drank one beer with a female friend at a pub and then went with her friend to a second pub. The two arrived at the second pub at some time between midnight and 12:15 a.m. Upon arriving, the victim recognized one of her coworkers and the bartender and began speaking with them. The defendant, whom the victim did not know, joined the conversation. The victim and the defendant remained at the pub until approximately 1 a.m., when the pub closed. The victim drank one beer and one shot at the second pub.

The defendant, the victim, and others continued to talk outside the pub after closing. The defendant asked the victim if she wanted to "hang out." The victim agreed but explained to the defendant that it was "just going to be us hanging out" because she was gay. The defendant said that was fine, and the two exchanged telephone numbers before parting.

The victim and her friend then went to a restaurant, where the victim received a text message from the defendant: "I wanna c u 2nite make it happen." The victim texted back, "Thats fine, but you just need to know that i like girls." The defendant asked by text whether the victim wanted him to get condoms. The victim replied by text, "[I]m down to chill but i like girls." After the defendant texted, "K thats cool .," the victim added, "Plus, not to sound gross but im on my period. Lol." The defendant replied by text, "Its all good." The victim then drove her friend home and continued alone to the defendant's apartment, arriving shortly before 2 a.m.

The defendant came downstairs to meet the victim, and the two went up to his apartment. Both the victim and the defendant drank beer in the kitchen while discussing their shared interest in music. The defendant then told the victim that he wanted to show her a record in his bedroom. The victim entered the defendant's bedroom, sat at the foot of the bed, and began looking at the record. The defendant sat down behind the victim and attempted to kiss her on the cheek. The victim responded by putting her hand out and telling the defendant that she was gay and that "it is not going past just hanging out." The defendant apologized multiple times, and then attempted to kiss the victim again. Before she could tell him to stop, the defendant got on top of the victim, put his knees on her thighs, and put his hands on her shoulders. The victim testified that she felt "terrified," that she "froze," and that she was unable to fight back against the defendant.

The defendant then pulled down the victim's pants and pulled her shirt up to her neck. The victim told the defendant to "stop" and to "get the fuck off me," and the defendant asked why. When the victim responded that she was gay, the defendant said "[G]ood" and vaginally raped her with his penis. Intercourse was painful for the victim, who was wearing a tampon, but the defendant "kept going harder and faster."

The defendant then put his penis in the victim's mouth. When the victim turned her head away, he inserted his fingers into her vagina. The defendant then vaginally raped the victim with his penis for a second time. The victim screamed "stop" repeatedly and attempted to push the defendant off her by moving her arms from side to side. The defendant then got off the victim.

The victim dressed rapidly, went into the bathroom, and then collected her things to leave. The defendant told the victim not to "worry about the blood," which the victim observed on the defendant's bed, in the kitchen (located between the bedroom and the bathroom), and on the defendant. The defendant then offered to walk the victim to her vehicle. The victim declined. Nevertheless, the defendant followed the victim downstairs, held her vehicle's door open while she tried to close it, and attempted to kiss her. The victim pushed the defendant and drove away.

Soon after leaving the defendant's apartment, the victim called a friend from her vehicle. After five or six telephone calls, her friend answered and the victim told her, "I've been fucked. It just happened. I just got raped." The friend testified that the victim was so "distraught" and "hysterical" on the telephone that it was initially difficult to understand her.

The victim then drove to her parents' home, and they took her to a hospital where a nurse conducted an evidence collection examination. The nurse testified at trial that the victim — who, the nurse reported, said that she had been assaulted [1] — was "horrified, angry, upset, [and] tearful." The nurse further testified that the victim denied being in pain at that time, and that the nurse observed no trauma to the victim's body.

At around 4:45 a.m., the victim met with Salem police Detective Eric Connolly at the hospital. Connolly testified that the victim was "visibly upset" and crying. After speaking with the victim, Connolly and two uniformed officers went to the defendant's address. They arrived at approximately 6 a.m., and the defendant let them into his apartment. The officers asked the defendant whether he had met anybody that night, and the defendant responded that he had had sexual intercourse with a woman but could not remember her name. Then, while the officers were speaking with him, the defendant lowered his shorts to reveal a "reddish brown stain" resembling blood on his underwear. The defendant also led the officers into his bedroom to show them a bloodstain on his bed sheets. The officers placed the defendant under arrest and transported him to the Salem police department for booking. During booking, Connolly observed that the defendant had "red brownish stains" resembling blood on his left hand.

That same day, officers obtained a warrant to search the defendant's apartment. During their execution of the warrant, officers discovered a paper plate with a spoon on it on the defendant's kitchen counter. The spoon, which appeared burnt, held a white powdery substance believed by Connolly to be cocaine. Connolly observed more white powder next to the plate. Officers also obtained a search warrant for the defendant's cell phone, which led to extraction of the text messages between the defendant and the victim.

On October 20, the victim went to the Salem police department to have photographs taken of bruises that had appeared on her inner arm and inner thigh after the assault.

The defendant testified that he had been at the pub for several hours when the victim, whom he had not met before, arrived. The defendant told the victim that he was recently divorced but "still involved" with his ex-wife. The victim responded that it was not a good idea for the defendant to remain involved with his ex-wife, that he would "probably end up getting hurt," and that he "should move on." The defendant replied, "Move on with you?" The victim told the defendant that she "like[d] girls." When he asked, "[Y]ou don't like men?" she replied, "I didn't say that."

After last call, the defendant asked the victim for her telephone number. The victim provided it, and the defendant texted her soon after to ask whether she wanted to meet later that night. The victim agreed, but repeatedly told the defendant that she liked girls. The defendant understood this to mean that in light of the victim's interest in women, he should not "expect a commitment" from the victim.

When the victim texted the defendant to let him know that she had arrived at his apartment, the defendant went downstairs to greet her, kissed her on the cheek, and brought her upstairs to his home. The two were speaking about music in the kitchen when the defendant kissed the victim on the lips. The victim reciprocated, and the two kissed for several minutes. The victim then walked into the defendant's bedroom, and the defendant followed.

When the defendant entered his bedroom, the victim was sitting on the edge of his bed. The defendant joined her, and the two resumed kissing. They also began touching each other's genitals, although the defendant testified that he never inserted his finger into the victim's vagina. The defendant then lowered his shorts, and the victim got off the bed to perform oral sex on the defendant from the edge of the bed. The defendant did not force the victim to engage in oral sex. After a couple of minutes, the victim removed her jeans and sweatshirt and lay down in the middle of the bed.

The defendant lay down next to her, and the two resumed kissing and touching one another. After several minutes, the victim told the defendant to "just put it in her." The defendant asked the victim about her period, and she responded, "I don't care if you don't care." The two then had consensual vaginal intercourse. The defendant testified that the victim did not ask the defendant to stop, push him away, or twist her body.

Afterward, the victim went into the defendant's bathroom for approximately five to 10 minutes. When she came back into the bedroom, the defendant and the victim spoke for approximately five to 10 minutes about how strange it was that they had never met despite sharing a number of mutual friends. The victim did not seem upset. After this conversation, the defendant walked the victim to her vehicle and kissed her goodbye. The defendant then returned to his apartment. At 3:28 a.m., he texted the victim to say he hoped she got home safely and to ask whether she wanted to get together the next day to "cuddle." The victim did not respond to this message.

Later, police officers arrived at the defendant's door and asked whether he knew the victim. The defendant testified that, at that time, he thought the police might have come to his apartment because the victim had been involved in an accident. The defendant invited the officers into his home and, when asked, told them that he had had sexual intercourse with the victim. The officers also asked the defendant whether he had raped the victim, and the defendant responded that he had not.

The defendant testified that on the night in question, he had a total of three or four beers at the pub and approximately one-half of one beer at his apartment. The defendant also testified that he had not ingested cocaine or any other drug that evening. When asked about the cocaine found on his kitchen counter, the defendant said that he did not recognize the cocaine and had not used it on the night in question. The defendant also confirmed that he lived alone in his apartment.

At the close of the evidence, the judge instructed the jury regarding the law governing the three indictments of rape: digital-vaginal rape, penile-vaginal rape, and penile-oral rape. The judge instructed the jury that "[i]n order to prove the defendant guilty of this offense, the Commonwealth must convince [the jury] beyond a reasonable doubt of two things: First, that the defendant engaged in sexual intercourse with the alleged victim and, second, that the sexual intercourse was accomplished by compelling [the victim] to submit by force or threat of bodily injury and against her will." With regard to the second element, the judge went on to instruct the jury that the Commonwealth "must prove beyond a reasonable doubt that at the time of penetration, [the victim] did not consent."

The judge also instructed the jury that the force requirement would be satisfied if the defendant compelled sexual intercourse by physical force, violence, threat of bodily injury, or constructive force, which "may be by threatening words or gestures" and requires "proof that the victim was afraid or that the victim submitted to the defendant because his conduct intimidated her."

Case Studies

Two traveling nurses, a man and a woman, meet in the ICU, and after a week of working days together, they seem to get along quite well and have mutual interests. She invites him to go out after their shift ends at 7 p.m. They go to a restaurant that's popular with hospital employees, share a light meal, and each has one cocktail. As they part ways, she invites him over to her apartment.

Given the time frame and amount of alcohol consumed, there is no reason to believe either party is impaired, and therefore, if they have sex, it can be considered consensual.

A 17-year-old male presents to the pediatric clinic for treatment of urogenital symptoms, including dysuria. During the history and physical exam, the patient tells the pediatrician he has been having unprotected sex with his boyfriend, age 19, who recently graduated from the high school he attends. They have had a relationship, including sexual contact, for over one year. The 17-year-old states the sexual relationship is consensual.

Is sex between a 19-year-old and a 17-year-old illegal? It depends. If the patient and the patient's partner reside in California, where the age of consent is 18, the pediatrician has the legal authority to use clinical judgment and does not necessarily have to file a report. If, however, the physician suspects non-consensual sex or coerced sex, it is reportable.

Figure 1 shows the age in each state at which an individual can consent to sex.

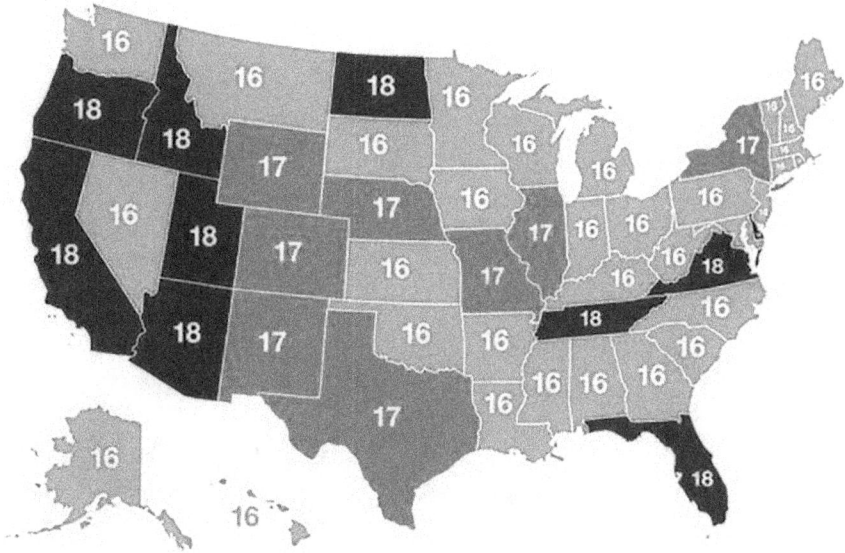

FIGURE 1. Age for consent allowing sexual contact.

In summary, it is important to recognize that consent between individuals is not as straightforward as it may seem. There clearly are conditions and circumstances that meet strict definitions of consent; conversely, there are clear circumstances when it is obvious consent is not possible. The "gray zone" of consent, when consent is not clear, presents a legal, ethical, and moral dilemma.

REFERENCES

1. Consent Laws North Dakota. htpps://.rainn.org/policy/policy-crime-definitions-export.cfm?state=North%20Dakota&group=9.
2. *Commonwealth v. Sherman* (2019). https://caselaw.findlaw.com/court/ma-supreme-judicial-court/1981380.html.

A Universal Problem Affecting All Communities

∞

Chapter 17. Title VII and History of Sexual Harassment Laws in the United States

"When an employer fires a male employee for dating men but does not fire female employees who date men, he violates Title VII. The employer has, in the words of Section 703(a), discriminated against the man because he treats that man worse than women who want to do the same thing. And that discrimination is because of sex, again in the words of Section 703(a), because the adverse employment action is based on the male employee's failure to conform to a particular expectation about how men should behave; namely, that men should be attracted only to women and not to men." — Professor Pamela Karlan in an argument presented to the Supreme Court in 2020

SINCE ITS INCEPTION, TITLE VII has been regarded as a seminal piece of legislation. The law set out to prohibit discrimination based on certain characteristics by mandating that a covered employer would violate Title VII if they:

Fail or refuse to hire or to discharge any individual, or otherwise to discriminate against any individual with respect to his compensation, terms, conditions, or privileges of employment, because of such individual's race, color, religion, sex, or national origin; or to limit, segregate, or classify his employees or applicants for employment opportunities or otherwise adversely affect his status as an employee, because of such individual's race, color, religion, sex, or national origin. (42 U.S.C.A. § 2000e-2)

Title VII has provided a foundation for further legislation as our understanding and awareness of protected individuals and unique cases have evolved. Since the passage of Title VII in 1964, several important landmark cases have transformed the original legislation:

1964: Title VII of the Civil Rights Act of 1964 established the legal foundation for preventing sexual harassment; however, at the time, sexual harassment was not included in the legislation. Although both men and women are covered under Title VII, it was originally intended to protect women from discrimination in the workplace.

1969: The Florida Commission on Human Relations was established to enforce the Florida Civil Rights Act (FCRA), which was modeled after Title VII of the federal Civil Rights Act of 1964.

1972: Title IX of the Education Amendments of 1972 was passed by Congress and signed into law by President Richard M. Nixon. The law prohibits sex discrimination in federally funded schools and broadens the reach of sexual harassment laws.

1974: *Barnes vs. Train,* which is commonly thought to be the first sexual harassment case in the United States (though the term "sexual harassment" was never used), was tried in the U.S. District Court for the District of Columbia. Barnes, who at the time worked for the EPA's Equal Opportunities Division, claimed that her job was eliminated because she rejected her supervisor's sexual advances. The Court ruled that there was no discrimination on the basis that the supervisor found Barnes attractive and felt rejected that she would not have sex with him.

The case was initially dismissed but won on appeal in 1977, *Barnes v. Costle,* when the United States Court of Appeals for the District of Columbia Circuit reversed the original findings and ruled it was sex discrimination for a woman to suffer tangible employment losses for refusing to submit to requests for sexual favors.

1976: In *Williams v. Saxbe,* Williams, a public information specialist at the U.S. Department of Justice, had refused a sexual advance made by her supervisor in 1972 and then was repeatedly harassed and humiliated. She was ultimately terminated later that year. The U.S. District Court for the

District of Columbia ruled in favor of Williams and first recognized *quid pro quo* sexual harassment as a type of gender-based or sexual discrimination.

1977: In *Barnes v. Costle,* the 1974 case was reversed by the U.S. Court of Appeals (DC Circuit). It determined that Barnes was indeed retaliated against by her supervisor and that he sexually harassed her, which violates Title VII of the Civil Rights Act of 1964. Barnes was awarded $18,000 to cover back pay and lost promotions.

1978: The Pregnancy Discrimination Act (PDA) amended Title VII of the Civil Rights Act of 1964 by prohibiting sex discrimination on the "basis of pregnancy, childbirth, or related medical conditions."

1980: The EEOC officially established guidelines for sexual harassment in the workplace and defined it as "unwelcome sexual advances, requests for sexual favors, and other verbal or physical conduct of a sexual nature." It also stated that sexual harassment is a type of sex discrimination that is prohibited by the Civil Rights Act of 1964.

1986: The U.S. Supreme Court addressed sexual harassment for the first time in *Meritor Savings Bank v. Vinson.* This is a landmark case because the Court determined "that severe or pervasive" sexual harassment of an employee by their supervisor violated federal law. In addition, the Court ruled that if the employer knew of the sexual harassment, it was their responsibility to take action against the perpetrator.

1991: In an effort to provide more protection for employees being discriminated against in the workplace, Congress passed the Civil Rights Act of 1991, which was signed into law by President George H.W. Bush. President Bush had threatened to veto the bill prior to Anita Hill's allegations that year against her former boss, Clarence Thomas, who had been nominated for a seat on the U.S. Supreme Court.

Before the Act was passed, employees had limited rights when it came to suing their employers for discrimination and harassment. The Act gave plaintiffs the right to a jury trial in federal court and the right to collect compensatory and punitive damages from their employers.

1992: The Florida Civil Rights Act of 1992 was passed by the Florida Legislature and signed into law by Governor Lawton Chiles. The Act amended the FCRA passed in the 1960s and prohibited discrimination on the basis of race, color, religion, sex, pregnancy, national origin, age, handicap, or marital status. It also changed the procedures for filing employment discrimination complaints and made compensatory and punitive damages available to employees.

1993: In *Harris v. Forklift Systems, Inc.,* the U.S. Supreme Court ruled that victims of sexual harassment don't have to prove that they experienced physical or psychological injury from their harasser for it to be defined as sexual harassment.

1994: The Violence Against Women Act (VAWA) was passed by Congress and signed into law by President Bill Clinton. In relation to sexual harassment in the workplace, it permits evidence of the history of the sexual harasser to be introduced and limits evidence related to the sexual history of the accuser.

1995: The Congressional Accountability Act (CAA) was passed by Congress and signed into law by President William J. Clinton. In essence, the law makes members of Congress subject to the same employment laws as other American workers.

1998: In *Burlington Industries, Inc. v. Ellerth* and *Faragher v. Boca Raton,* the U.S. Supreme Court ruled that employers are liable for sexual harassment by their employees even if threats and favors aren't carried out. However, employers have grounds for defending themselves if they can prove that they took prompt action to prevent harassment by the employee and to respond to complaints of harassment.

2005: The U.S. Supreme Court ruled in *Jackson v. Birmingham Board of Education* that it is illegal to punish someone for reporting sexual harassment and discrimination.

Also that year, Congress passed the Reauthorization of the Violence Against Women Act, which allocates federal funds to aid victims of sexual violence and assault. Among other things, the funds can be used to ensure that victims are able to pay for a fair trial.

2021: President Joe Biden signed the Ending Forced Arbitration of Sexual Assault and Sexual Harassment Act of 2021 into law on March 3, 2022, altering the Federal Arbitration Act. It offers individuals alleging sexual assault or harassment the opportunity to bring these claims to court, regardless of prior agreements to arbitrate such disputes. This option extends to class or collective actions, even if these rights were previously waived.

2022: President Joe Biden signed the Speak Out Act into law on December 7, 2022. Senator Kirsten Gillibrand introduced this act to limit the enforceability of pre-dispute nondisclosure and non-disparagement clauses related to sexual assault and harassment disputes. This legislative action was largely driven by the #MeToo movement's concern over nondisclosure agreements' potential misuse in silencing victims in corporate America.

In conclusion, Title VII is a living piece of legislation that has continued to serve the needs of marginalized members of society.

Chapter 18. LGBTQ+: A History of a Community and Patient Care

"It is absolutely imperative that every human being's freedom and human rights are respected, all over the world." – Jóhanna Sigurðardóttir, former Icelandic Prime Minister and first openly gay head of state

IN THE EARLY HOURS OF JUNE 28, 1969, New York City police raided the Stonewall Inn in Greenwich Village in New York City. The raid ignited a riot and protests lasting nearly six days. The event was a catalyst for the gay rights movement in the United States and around the world.

Three years before Stonewall, the Compton's Cafeteria riot in the Tenderloin District of San Francisco was a response to the violent and constant police harassment of transwomen and drag queens. (*Note: these are the words used to describe individuals during that era, and it is not my intent to disrespect any particular group or group of individuals*). The incident began when a transgender woman resisted arrest by throwing coffee at a police officer. Patrons of the restaurant poured into the street and fought with the police. Both Stonewall and the Compton's Cafeteria riot were a response to the frustration and anger of the LGBTQ+ community after enduring years of continued discrimination, abuse, and marginalization.

A significant number of individuals identify as LGBTQ+, and the number has been increasing over the last decade. In 2012, roughly 3.5% of the population in the United States identified as LGBTQ+. A survey in 2021 reported an increase to roughly 7%. Most surveys indicate that fewer than 1% identify as transgender.[1] In the 2017–2021 Association of American Medical Colleges (AAMC) Graduation Questionnaire, a survey of graduating fourth-year medical students in the United States and Canada, fewer than 5% of responders identified as gay, lesbian, or bisexual, and fewer than 1% identified as transgender.[2]

Legal and social milestones since the Stonewall and Compton's Cafeteria events transformed societal perceptions, yet harassment, abuse, and discrimination continue. An examination of the timeline of significant historical events and milestones affecting the social status, rights, and legal status of members of the LGBTQ+ community is clear evidence that progress, though slow, continues:

June 28, 1970: Christopher St. Liberation Day commemorated the first anniversary of the Stonewall riots. Following the event, thousands of members of the LGBTQ+ community marched through New York into Central Park in what is considered America's first gay pride parade. In the coming decades, the annual gay pride parade spread to dozens of countries around the world.

December 15, 1973: The board of the American Psychiatric Association (APA) voted to remove homosexuality from its list of mental illnesses.

January, 1974: Kathy Kozachenko became the first openly gay American elected to public office when she won a seat on the city council in Ann Arbor, Michigan.

June 7, 1977: Singer and conservative Southern Baptist Anita Bryant led a successful campaign with the "Save Our Children" Crusade to repeal a gay rights ordinance in Dade County, Florida. Bryant faced severe backlash from gay rights supporters across the United States. The gay rights ordinance was not reinstated in Dade County until December 1, 1998, more than 20 years later.

November 8, 1977: Harvey Milk won a seat on the San Francisco Board of Supervisors and is credited with introducing a gay rights ordinance protecting gays and lesbians from being fired from their jobs. Milk also led a successful campaign against Proposition 6, an initiative forbidding homosexual teachers. A year later, on November 27, 1978, former city supervisor Dan White assassinated Milk, motivated by jealousy and depression, not homophobia.

May 21, 1979: Milk's assassin, Dan White was convicted of voluntary manslaughter and sentenced to seven years in prison. Outraged by what they believed to be a lenient sentence, more than 5,000 protesters ransacked San Francisco's City Hall. The following night, approximately 10,000 people gathered on San Francisco's Castro and Market streets for a peaceful demonstration to commemorate what would have been Milk's 49th birthday.

October 14, 1979: An estimated 75,000 people participated in the National March on Washington for Lesbian and Gay Rights. LGBTQ+ people and straight allies demanded equal civil rights and urged the passage of protective civil rights legislation.

July 8, 1980: The Democratic Rules Committee stated that it would not discriminate against homosexuals. At their National Convention on August 11-14, the Democrats became the first major political party to endorse a homosexual rights platform.

July 3, 1981: The *New York Times* was the first to report a rare pneumonia and skin cancer found in 41 gay men in New York and California. The CDC initially referred to the disease as GRID, Gay Related Immune Deficiency Disorder. When the symptoms were found outside the gay community, Bruce Voeller, biologist and founder of the National Gay Task Force, successfully lobbied to change the name of the disease to Acquired Immunodeficiency Syndrome — AIDS.

March 2, 1982: Wisconsin became the first U.S. state to outlaw discrimination on the basis of sexual orientation.

March 10, 1987: AIDS advocacy group ACT UP (The AIDS Coalition to Unleash Power) was formed in response to the devastating effects of the disease on the gay and lesbian community in New York. The group held demonstrations against pharmaceutical companies profiteering from AIDS-related drugs as well as the lack of AIDS policies protecting patients from outrageous prescription prices.

October 11, 1987: Hundreds of thousands of activists took part in the National March on Washington to demand that President Ronald Reagan address the AIDS crisis. Although AIDS had been reported first in 1981, it was not until the end of his presidency that Reagan spoke publicly about the epidemic.

May– June, 1988: The CDC mailed a brochure, Understanding AIDS, to every household in the United States. Approximately 107 million brochures are mailed.

December 1, 1988: The World Health Organization organized the first World AIDS Day to raise awareness of the spreading pandemic.

August 18, 1990: President George Bush signed the Ryan White Care Act, a federally funded program for people living with AIDS. Ryan White, an Indiana teenager, contracted AIDS in 1984 through a tainted hemophilia treatment. After being barred from attending school because of his HIV-positive status, Ryan White became a well-known activist for AIDS research and anti-discrimination.

1991: Created by the New York-based Visual AIDS, the red ribbon was adopted as a symbol of awareness and compassion for those living with HIV/AIDS.

December 21, 1993: The Department of Defense issued a directive prohibiting the U.S. military from barring applicants from service based on their sexual orientation. The policy stated: "Applicants... shall not be asked or required to reveal whether they are homosexual. "This policy is known as "Don't Ask, Don't Tell."

May 20, 1996: In the case of *Romer v. Evans*, the United States Supreme Court decided that Colorado's 2nd Amendment, denying gays and lesbians protections against discrimination, was unconstitutional, calling them "special rights."

September 21, 1996: President Bill Clinton signed the Defense of Marriage Act into law. The law defines marriage as a legal union between one man and one woman and says that no state is required to recognize a same-sex marriage from out of state.

April 1, 1998: Coretta Scott King, widow of civil rights leader Martin Luther King, Jr., called on the civil rights community to join the struggle against homophobia. Members of the black civil rights movement criticized her for comparing civil rights to gay rights.

April 26, 2000: Vermont became the first state in the U.S. to legalize civil unions and registered partnerships between same-sex couples.

June 26, 2003: In *Lawrence v. Texas*, the U.S. Supreme Court ruled that U.S. laws criminalizing consensual sex between two men are unconstitutional.

May 18, 2004: Massachusetts became the first state to legalize gay marriage. The Massachusetts Supreme Judicial Court found the prohibition of gay marriage unconstitutional because it denied dignity and equality to all individuals. In the following six years, New Hampshire, Vermont, Connecticut, Iowa, and Washington D.C. followed suit.

August 9, 2007: Sponsored by the Human Rights Campaign, the Logo cable channel hosted the first American presidential forum focusing specifically on LGBT issues, inviting each presidential candidate to participate. Six Democrats, including Hillary Clinton and Barack Obama, participated in the forum, while all Republican candidates declined.

November 4, 2008: California voters approved Proposition 8, making same-sex marriage in California illegal. The passing of the ballot garnered national attention from gay rights supporters across the United States. Prop 8 inspired the NOH8 campaign, a photo project that used celebrities to promote marriage equality.

June 17, 2009: President Barack Obama signed a Presidential Memorandum allowing same-sex partners of federal employees to receive certain benefits. The memorandum did not cover full health coverage.

October 28, 2009: The Matthew Shepard Act was signed into law by President Obama. The measure expanded the 1969 U.S. Federal Hate Crime Law to include crimes motivated by a victim's actual or perceived gender, sexual orientation, gender identity, or disability. Matthew Shepard was tortured and murdered near Laramie, Wyoming, on October 7, 1998, because of his sexual orientation.

August 4, 2010: A federal judge in San Francisco ruled that gays and lesbians have the constitutional right to marry and that Prop 8 was unconstitutional. Lawyers challenged the finding.

December 18, 2010: The U.S. Senate voted 65-31 to repeal the "Don't Ask, Don't Tell" policy, allowing gays and lesbians to serve openly in the U.S. military.

February 23, 2011: President Obama stated his administration would no longer defend the Defense of Marriage Act, which banned the recognition of same-sex marriage.

June 24, 2011: New York State passed the Marriage Equity Act, becoming the largest state thus far to legalize gay marriage.

June 26, 2015: With a 5-4 decision in *Obergefell v. Hodges,* the U.S. Supreme Court declared same-sex marriage legal in all 50 states.

LGBTQ+ PATIENTS AND DISCRIMINATION

LGBTQ+ individuals have long faced harassment and discrimination within healthcare systems, impacting their access to quality care and overall well-being. Common forms of discrimination and harassment faced by LGBTQ+ individuals in healthcare include:

1. **Refusal of Care:** Some healthcare providers refuse to treat LGBTQ+ individuals or provide essential services, citing personal or religious beliefs. This refusal can delay critical medical attention or prevent individuals from accessing necessary healthcare services altogether.

2. **Disrespect and Mistreatment:** LGBTQ+ individuals may experience disrespectful or insensitive treatment from healthcare providers, including being misgendered, ridiculed, or subjected to derogatory language and attitudes. This can lead to feelings of alienation and reluctance to seek further care.

3. **Lack of Cultural Competency:** Healthcare providers may lack knowledge and understanding of LGBTQ+ health issues, leading to inadequate or inappropriate care. This includes a lack of awareness of specific health needs, such as hormone replacement therapy for transgender individuals or mental health concerns unique to LGBTQ+ populations.

4. **Stigmatization of HIV/AIDS:** Despite advances in HIV/AIDS treatment and prevention, the stigma surrounding the virus persists, particularly within healthcare settings. LGBTQ+ individuals, especially gay and bisexual men, may face judgment, blame, or discrimination when seeking HIV testing, treatment, or support services.

5. **Fear of Disclosure:** LGBTQ+ individuals may fear disclosing their sexual orientation or gender identity to healthcare providers due to concerns about discrimination or negative reactions. This fear can lead to withholding important health information, compromising the quality of care received.

6. **Barriers to Reproductive Healthcare:** LGBTQ+ individuals, particularly transgender and non-binary individuals, may encounter challenges accessing reproductive healthcare services, including fertility treatment, contraception, and pregnancy-related care. Discriminatory practices and a lack of inclusive policies can limit access to these essential services.

In addition to the barriers to access, LGBTQ+ patients are at increased risk of a variety of adverse health outcomes, including sexually transmitted diseases, mental health conditions, substance use disorders, and violent hate crimes. The social stigma, prejudice, and discrimination toward members of the LGBTQ+ community can cause significant, lifelong stress and contribute to maladaptive coping behaviors.[3]

Malik and colleagues performed a qualitative study investigating patient-provider interactions using structured interviews of the experiences of LGBTQ+ patients in healthcare. The individual responses from the patients demonstrate persistent fear, lack of respect, and discrimination from healthcare workers. These comments are disappointing and alarming in a profession that values the importance of being respectful, open, understanding, and compassionate toward *vulnerable people. The following statements are from LGBTQ+ patients*[4]:

- Queer, ciswoman: *"Not just assuming one thing or anything, just asking very open, honest questions… So like instead of saying 'do you sleep with men and do you sleep with women,' 'are you sexually active* [and] *with whom?"*
- Gay, cisman: *"But some people like Dr. B, I think once I told him I was gay, that kind of turned him more, you know, he was kind of standoffish with me."*
- Heterosexual transwoman: *"'What's your pronoun? How would you like to be addressed?' Of if you're looking at someone's file and you see it says 'Ted,' but then you look up, and Ted looks like Tammy. You might want to just say, 'How do you identify?' And if I find that a physician uses words like 'What is your pronoun?' 'How do you identify?' It gives us a sense of comfort. Wow! They're at least on the same page."*

These statements reveal apprehension about disclosure and feelings of disrespect. Addressing these issues requires comprehensive efforts to promote LGBTQ+ inclusivity and cultural competency within healthcare systems. This includes implementing policies that prohibit discrimination based on sexual orientation and gender identity, providing training for healthcare providers on LGBTQ+ health issues, fostering a welcoming and affirming environment for LGBTQ+ patients, and actively engaging with LGBTQ+ communities to understand their unique healthcare needs.

Additionally, promoting the visibility and representation of LGBTQ+ individuals in healthcare leadership and advocacy can advance equality and access. Finding physicians and other health professionals who are culturally sensitive and aware of the unique needs of LGBTQ+ patients can be a significant challenge.

The Providence Oregon Family Medicine Residency Program developed a unique curriculum to address the lack of formal training in providing culturally competent care for LGBTQ+ patients. Titled "Caring for LGBTQ," the curriculum enables participants to:

1. Provide culturally competent care for LGBTQ+ patients.
2. Acquire skills to build empathy.
3. Identify barriers to care for LGBTQ+ patients and methods to decrease or eliminate these barriers.
4. Use communication methods, including population-specific language, to improve the therapeutic patient-physician relationship.
5. Develop the skills necessary to take an inclusive, non-judgmental history.
6. Identify and understand five special healthcare issues for LGBTQ+ patients.

The curriculum includes bias awareness training. Participants are asked to share what comes to mind when they hear the terms lesbian, gay, bisexual, transgender, and queer. Stereotypes are often negative and derogatory, and this exercise builds a foundation for replacing assumptions and stereotypes with facts and knowledge.

The next exercise incorporates learning the various terminology and definitions used in the LGBTQ+ community. For example, The Genderbread Person in Figure 1 is a visually approachable diagram that defines terms. Gender identity is separate from biological sex, attraction, and gender expression. Individuals uniquely fall on a spectrum of identity, expression, and attraction. Case-based small-group discussions with the residents play a significant role in reinforcing these concepts.

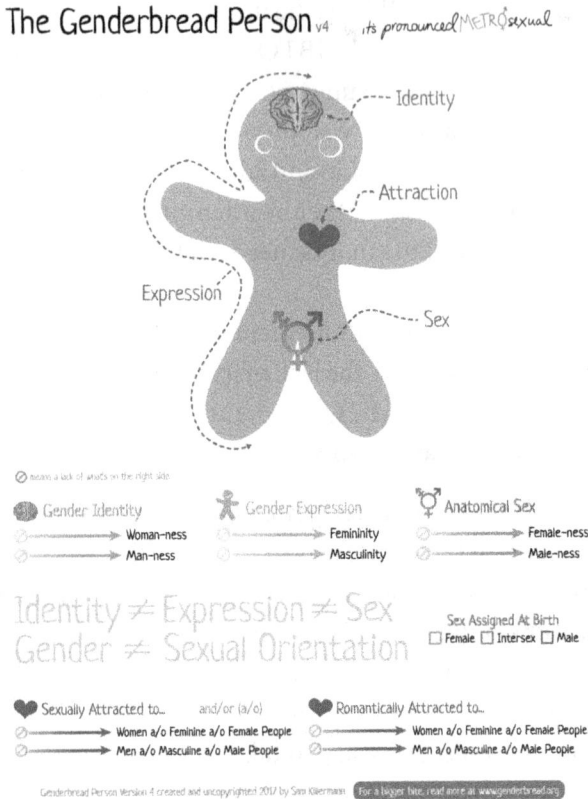

FIGURE 1. The Genderbread Person as a means to understand gender. https://www.itspronouncedmetrosexual.com/about/

Breaking down barriers to care includes learning how to create a safe space for LGBTQ+ patients so they feel comfortable revealing who they are without judgment, discrimination, or bias. The physician can ask open-ended questions and, to avoid making the patient feel singled out, explain that the questions are asked of all patients.

As an example, the physician can state, *"I know these questions might be uncomfortable, but I ask all my patients these questions about their health and sexuality in order to determine any risk factors. Are you comfortable proceeding?"* Using a welcoming tone and body language while asking questions creates trust, and patients are more likely to talk candidly and openly about their health concerns.

LGBTQ+ individuals are at higher risk for mental health disorders, substance use disorders, suicide, and self-harm. The stressors from prejudice, stigmatization, and violence increase rates of anxiety and depression. Open-ended questions in an established, safe relationship provide the foundation for empathic, compassionate care so these issues may be discussed and addressed.

A recent systematic review revealed data related to training medical, nursing, and dental students to reduce LGBTQ+-related bias. Incorporating formal training at the start of professional education in healthcare can, in theory, reduce bias, increase knowledge about the LGBTQ+ community, and increase comfort levels for caring for these patients.[5] Interventions on increasing knowledge included offering relevant material in lectures, readings, videos, interviews, and personal presentations by LGBTQ+ individuals.

Developing a more positive attitude toward the LGBTQ+ community utilized perspective-taking exercises, videos of LGBTQ+ individuals describing discrimination in healthcare settings, and patient panels including LGBTQ+ individuals. Changes in attitudes were measured using the Prejudice Against Sexual and Gender Diversity Scale and the Attitudes Toward Lesbians and Gay Men Scale.[6] Overall, the effects of training programs on LGBTQ+-related attitudes were inconsistent for students in the healthcare professions. There was some indication from the studies that more effective programs involved LGBTQ+ individuals as tutors or in patient panels.

Face-to-face interactions break down assumptions and stereotypes. Of course, some individuals, even in healthcare, have moral or religious beliefs and remain prejudiced regardless of the type of training. *Despite personal attitudes or beliefs, healthcare workers have an ethical and moral duty to treat everyone with dignity, compassion, and respect.*

REFERENCES

1. Jones JM. LGBTQ+ Identification in U.S. now at 7.6%. Gallup. March 13, 2024. https://news.gallup.com/poll/611864/lgbtq-identification.aspx

2. AAMC. Medical School Graduation Questionnaire. 2022. www.aamc.org/data-reports.

3. Meyer IH. Prejudice, Social Stress, and Mental Health in Lesbian, Gay, and Bisexual Populations: Conceptual Issues and Research Evidence. *Psychol Bull.* 2003;129(5):674-697.

4. Malik S, Master Z, Parker W, DeCoster B, Camp-Engelstein L. In Our Own Words: A Qualitative Exploration of Complex Patient-Provider Interactions in an LGBTQ Population. *Canadian Journal of Bioethics.* 2019;2(2): 82–92.

5. Morris M, Cooper RL, Ramesh A, Tabatabai *et al.* Training to Reduce LGBTQ+-related Bias among Medical, Nursing, and Dental Students and Providers: A Systemic Review. *BMC Med Educ.* 2019;19(1):325.

6. Costa AB, de Lara Machado W, Bandeira DR, Nardi HC. Validation Study of the Revised Version of the Scale of Prejudice Against Sexual and Gender Diversity in Brazil. *J Homosex.* 2016;63(11): 1446–1463. https://doi.org/10.1080/00918369.2016.1222829

Chapter 19. LGBTQ+ Health Professionals and Discrimination

"Fears are not facts."— *Chaz Bono, writer, musician, and actor*

"Hope will never be silent." — *Harvey Milk, American politician, and the first openly gay man elected to public office in California*

A N ANALYSIS FROM 2018 FOUND that up to 38% of LGBTQ+ healthcare workers had not disclosed their identity in the workplace — primarily out of fear of job loss and potential harassment or discrimination.[1] And this fear is justified. Stephanie Bizzeth and Brenda Beagan explored the experiences of LGBTQ+ health professionals and students in workplaces in Canada.[2] Although the study sample was small, with only 13 participants, the qualitative statements made by the participants highlight the continuing problem of mistreatment, harassment, bullying, and discrimination.

One participant reported being bullied by a boss, which he perceived was due to his sexual identity. Another participant stated a manager mocked his voice and mannerisms, insinuating gay "flamboyance" was comedic. Some participants in the study felt tokenized and reduced to their sexual orientation or gender identity, with workplace colleagues using nicknames like "Team Rainbow" that focused on their sexual identities. One respondent wrote[2]:

In my medical school, I kind of tried to foster some people being more comfortable talking about these things so we had a little group of us that kind of hung out, like five or six of us, and we kind of got labeled as the "Gay's Anatomy" of the medical school class. Which is in some ways funny but also not funny.

Another medical student wrote[2]:

In orientation week, cause [sic] I lived in a house with two medical students [and] we had offered to host an event where people go from house to house. And they decided to make us the "LGBTQ welcoming house"….It wasn't our idea. We had just signed up to host one of the houses in this welcoming event for the new med students and we kind of got labeled without being asked.

The problem with labels, stereotypes, and assumptions is not only the emotional suffering they create for the individuals but the socially accepted practice of reinforcing the idea that LGBTQ+ people are somehow not human beings. It's a form of aggressive and microaggressive reductionism steeped in cultures infused with heteronormative assumptions made by colleagues and patients and the ways questions and casual conversations convey powerful messages of not fully belonging. The default and assumed identity is universally cisgender and heterosexual. One respondent wrote[2]:

> You're engaged in sort of chat, about whatever. And people would be asking me "Oh, are you married? Do you have kids?" And at the time, I wasn't married. I was single. "No, I don't have children." And the look on their face, like they couldn't believe that. It's always been just the same question: do you have a boyfriend; do you have a husband; do you have kids? Those three basic questions.

Participants in the study also felt pressured to make complex disclosure decisions — whether to be "out" or not and take the risk of being ostracized. Being out with colleagues is a choice between invisibility and potentially unwanted hyper-visibility. Like Odysseus in Homer's *Odyssey*, the choice can be between sailing near Scylla or Charybdis — the origin of the saying, "between a rock and a hard place." There is increased stress in not being authentic at work and not living on one's own terms, or if out to coworkers, there is the stress of navigating a potentially hostile work environment.

In 2022, Hiderscheit and colleagues investigated the national prevalence of mistreatment and poor well-being for LGBTQ+ surgery residents compared to their non-LGBTQ+ peers. A total of 6,956 clinically active residents responded (85.6% response rate). Roughly 4.8% of respondents identified as LGBTQ+. The LGBTQ+ respondents reported discrimination (59%), harassment (47%), and bullying (74.8%). Of note, non-LGBTQ+ identified surgery residents also reported mistreatment — particularly female residents.[3] Attending surgeons were identified as a frequent source of mistreatment and discrimination. Of particular concern, increased suicidality in LGBTQ+ surgery residents is associated with mistreatment.[3]

A 2011 study of the experiences of LGBTQ+ identified physicians found that 10% were denied referrals from heterosexual colleagues, 15% experienced harassment by a colleague, 27% experienced discriminatory treatment of a coworker, and 65% witnessed derogatory comments about LGBTQ+ individuals. Institutions have an obligation to create a respectful, more inclusive environment. LGBTQ+ healthcare workers and professionals should not bear the burden of educating those around them, contributing to the "minority tax," in which further burden is placed on those who are already disadvantaged.[4]

Patients with overt discrimination or hateful and derogatory terms often target LGBTQ+ healthcare workers. A 2008 survey of 502 adults in the United States found that nearly 30% of patients would change practices from a gay or lesbian clinician to a straight clinician.[5] It is clear that LGBTQ+ healthcare workers continue to face discrimination and mistreatment from both colleagues and patients.

REFERENCES

1. Holmberg M, Martin S, Lunn M. Supporting Sexual and Gender Minority Health-Care Workers. *Nat Revi: Nephrol.* 2022;18(6): 339–340.

2. Bizzeth S, Beagan B. "Ah, It's Best Not To Mention Here:" Experiences of LGBTQ+ Health Professionals in (Heteronormative) Workplaces in Canada. *Front Sociol.* 2023;8:1138628. doi: 10.3389/fsco.2023.1138628

3. Heiderscheit E, Schlick C, Ellis R, Cheung E, Irizarry D, *et al.* Experiences of LGBTQ+ Residents in US General Surgery Training Programs. *JAMA Surgery.* 2022;157(1): 23–32.

4. Eliason M, Dibble S, Robertson P. Lesbian, Gay, Bisexual, and Transgender (LGBT) Physicians' Experiences in the Workplace. *J Homosex.* 2011;58(10): 1355–1371.

5. Lee R, Melhado T, Chacko K, White K, *et al.* The Dilemma of Disclosure: Patient Perspectives on Gay and Lesbian Providers. *J Gen Intern Med.* 2008;23(2):142–147.

Chapter 20. Intersexed Patients and Discrimination

"Intersex people exist all around the world. I am certain that everyone on this planet has met somebody else who has been intersex." — Georgiann Davis, associate professor of sociology at the University of New Mexico and author of Contesting Intersex: The Dubious Diagnosis

"INTERSEX" IS AN UMBRELLA TERM for biological markers of sex identity — chromosomes, gonads, hormones, or anatomical structure — such that they do not line up under a rigid male or female classification. For example, people with Klinefelter syndrome often present as male but carry an extra X chromosome and are genetically 47,XXY. Approximately 1.7% of the population has intersex variations. Those who are intersexed continue to be marginalized in both social and medical settings, largely due to the lack of understanding and stigma from not conforming or belonging to the binary views of sex and gender presentation. The "medicalization" of intersex conditions contributes to the stigma.[1]

In 2005, an international conference convened in Chicago on the management of intersex variations. Fifty experts in pediatric endocrinology developed a consensus statement published in January 2006 and updated in 2016. The statement included blueprints for care of intersexed patients in multidisciplinary clinics.

The intent of the conference and the consensus statement were criticized for lacking the involvement of intersexed individuals. In fact, it has been argued that relegating intersex variations to an overly medicalized space has led to the pathologization of what might alternatively be seen as normal human diversity.

A new term for intersex people also emerged from the conference: disorders of sex development (DSD). Intersex advocates have criticized this term because the use of the word "disorder" further pathologizes intersex people.[2]

Teri Merrick wrote an important paper titled "From 'Intersex to 'DSD': A Case of Epistemic Injustice." She challenges our assumptions and provides perspectives to help us understand our own notions of the interplay and definitions of what biological sex, gender identity, gender expression, sexuality, and orientation mean.[3]

In her well-researched account of North American perceptions of intersexuality from the 1950s up to the 2005 conference in Chicago, medical anthropologist Katrina Karkazis notes the tremendous hermeneutical authority accorded to healthcare lexicons[4]:

The power of medicine and science lies in their ability to define what is natural, to name nature and human nature, and in their claim or hope to return individuals to a more natural state of being.

Replacing the word intersex with "disorders of sex development" does nothing to change the perception that these conditions are unnatural and require medical interventions, including surgery.

In fact, the medical approach to normalizing individuals has been a standard approach firmly grounded in the historical notion that gender and anatomy are linked. Children and infants continue to receive early cosmetic genital surgeries as a result.[5,6] This is a bioethical dilemma — a conflict between upholding the bodily autonomy of the child vs. acting on behalf of what is perceived to be the child's best interests. There is little evidence to show surgical intervention is in the best interests of children with DSD.[7]

Many individuals who received procedures as children have suffered physical and psychological harm stemming from complications from the original surgery, continued physical exams, and sexual dysfunction.[6,8] Prominent national and international health organizations and legislative bodies have made recommendations arguing for deferral of elective procedures until the child can participate in the decision-making process.[7] There is anecdotal evidence to support this position. Still, the medical community is divided between deferring interventions vs. intervening early.

The argument for intervention includes the idea it will "normalize" their lives. That is a bold assumption. There is nothing more powerful than hearing from those who are intersex[9]:

Obioma went to an all-girls boarding school in Nigeria but was unsure if she was a girl or a boy. *"Everybody seemed so worried about my body all the time. People kept asking me if I was a girl or a boy and I would answer: 'I don't know. I am just me'."*

Kaisli recalls the secrecy and the silence during adolescence in Finland. *"It was a feeling of not being fully included, of not having a space simply because you didn't fit into a binary worldview."*

Crystal grew up in South Africa thinking she was "a normal girl" until she never got her menstruation like all the girls around her. *"I thought I was the only person in the world like this. I felt alone at school and inadequate as a human. I sometimes don't know how I survived."*

Mauro remembers how a visit to a small pediatric clinic in Argentina at age 13 led to a long series of traumatic medical procedures, psychotherapy, and surgeries throughout the years. *"They couldn't accept that my body was fine the way it was. It was a brutal form of medical violence."*

THE STORY OF DAVID REIMER: IS GENDER A SOCIAL CONSTRUCT?

Of the many cases discussed in this book, this is one of the most tragic. Brian and David Reimer twins were born in Winnipeg, Manitoba, in 1965. At six months of age, the boys were circumcised using the unconventional electrocautery method. Tragically, David's penis was irreparably damaged during the procedure; Brian did not undergo circumcision. Their concerned parents took David to see John Money, a leading gender researcher and sexologist, at Johns Hopkins in early 1967.

Money suggested gender reassignment surgery, and Reimer's parents decided to raise Reimer as a girl. Physicians at the Johns Hopkins Hospital removed Reimer's testes and damaged penis and performed gender reassignment surgery, constructing rudimentary female genitals. Reimer was given the first name Brenda after surgery and raised as a girl. He received estrogen during adolescence to promote the development of female sex characteristics. He was never told he was biologically male.

As part of Money's research, Reimer and his twin brother were directed to inspect one another's genitals and engage in behavior resembling sexual intercourse. Reimer later claimed much of Money's treatment involved the forced reenactment of sexual positions and motions with his brother. In some exercises, the brothers rehearsed missionary positions with thrusting motions, which Money justified as the rehearsal of healthy childhood sexual exploration.

In a *Rolling Stone* interview, Reimer recalled that Money photographed those exercises at least once. He stated that Money observed those exercises both alone and with as many as six colleagues. Reimer recounted anger and verbal abuse from Money if he or his brother resisted orders, in contrast to the calm and scientific demeanor Money presented to their parents.

Ultimately, Money described Reimer's transition as successful and claimed Reimer's girlish behavior stood in stark contrast to his brother's "boyishness." Money referred to Reimer's case as the John/Joan case, leaving out Reimer's real name. For over a decade, Reimer and his brother unknowingly provided data that, according to biographers and the Intersex Society of North America, was used to reinforce Money's theories on gender fluidity and the hypothesis that gender is a social construct. Money's theories and this case justified thousands of sex reassignment surgeries for children with abnormal genitals.

The results of the procedures, treatments, and interventions were tragic. Reimer recalls having severe gender dysphoria. At one point, he told his parents he no longer wanted to visit Money and threatened to commit suicide if they took him back. Reimer claimed that despite receiving female hormones, wearing dresses, and having his interests directed toward typically female norms, he always felt that he was a boy.

In 1980, when Reimer was 15, his father told him the truth about his birth and the subsequent procedures. Reimer assumed a male identity following that revelation, taking the first name David. By age 21, Reimer had received testosterone therapy and surgeries to remove his breasts and reconstruct a penis. He subsequently married a single mother of three in September 1990.

Throughout his adulthood, Reimer suffered psychological trauma due to Money's experiments, which Money had used to justify sexual reassignment surgery for children with intersex or damaged genitals since the 1970s. In the mid-1990s, Reimer met Milton Diamond, a psychologist at the University of Hawaii in Honolulu and an academic rival of Money. Reimer participated in a follow-up study conducted by Diamond, in which Diamond cataloged the failures of Reimer's transition.

In 1997, Reimer began speaking publicly about his experiences, beginning with his participation in Diamond's study. Reimer's first interview appeared in the December 1997 issue of *Rolling Stone* magazine. In interviews and a later book about his experience, Reimer described his interactions with

Money as torturous and abusive. Accordingly, Reimer claimed he developed a lifelong distrust of hospitals and medical professionals.

In his early 20s, Reimer attempted to commit suicide twice. Reimer said marital problems and employment difficulties strained his adult family life. Reimer's brother, who suffered from depression and schizophrenia, died from an antidepressant drug overdose in July 2002. On May 2, 2004, Reimer's wife told him that she wanted a divorce. Two days later, at age 38, Reimer committed suicide by firearm.[10,11]

Gender identity, gender expression, gender roles, and gender role expectations are an amalgam of biological, genetic, anatomical, personal, social, and cultural norms and influences. John Money's narrow perspective on how gender identity is formed and expressed not only led to this tragedy but thousands of others who suffered needlessly. Recent scholars and researchers have since criticized his research. Privately, Money was mortified by the case of David Reimer, colleagues said, and Money did not discuss it. He died in Maryland in 2006.[12]

Regardless of whether or not there are surgical or other medical interventions, people who are intersexed live with their differences, and they pay a social price, too, as they are subject to as much discrimination as members of the LGBTQ+ community.

ANDROGEN INSENSITIVITY SYNDROME CASE STUDY

Androgen insensitivity syndrome (AIS) is a rare genetic condition that prevents the body from responding to male sex hormones or androgens. Consequently, even though they are genetically male, people with AIS develop the physical traits of a female. The following is a narrative from someone with AIS[3]:

"My diagnosis was considered a tragic mistake of nature by both my physicians and my parents. Given that I looked normal, however, my parents undoubtedly took solace in that they did not ever have to reveal the truth about my body to friends or relatives and could keep it a secret even from immediate family members. They were advised by my pediatric endocrinologist to tell me I had a simple hernia when, as a young child, I discovered the abdominal scar just above my pubic region. They were then to say nothing again until the eve of puberty, at which time they should tell me that I had

'twisted ovaries' which had been removed at birth to prevent them from becoming cancerous."

She recounts that the negative silence surrounding her body made it the subject of worrisome half-truths, shocking revelations, and embarrassing ignorance between the time she was 11 and into her mid-30s. She felt isolated and alienated until she found an intersex support group. She shares[3]:

"For the first time I stood side by side with someone who… knew what it was like to have a body that looked and felt like mine, and knew the same secrecy and silence and lies and shame that had been the hallmarks of my existence. My life in earnest had begun."

Recent efforts to reduce access to gender-affirming care for transgender patients will negatively affect the intersex community, too. The medical community must continue to resist efforts to reduce access to sensitive, compassionate care.

REFERENCES

1. Davis G. *Contesting Intersex: The Dubious Diagnosis.* New York: New York University Press;2015.

2. Hughes IA, Houk C, Ahmed SF, Lee, PA, *et al.* Consensus Statement on Management of Intersex Disorders. *Arch Dis Child.* 2006;91(7): 554-563.

3. Merrick T. "Intersex" to "DSD": A Case of Epistemic Injustice. *Synthese.* 2019;196(11): 4429–4447.

4. Karkazis K. *Fixing Sex: Intersex, Medical Authority, and Lived Experience.* Durham, NC: Duke University Press; 2008.

5. Diamond D. Management of Pediatric Patients with DSD and Ambiguous Genitalia: Balancing the Child's Moral Claims to Self-Determination with Parental Values and Preferences. *J Pediatr Urol.* 2018;14(5):416.e1–416.e5.

6. Knight K. *A Changing Paradigm: US Medical Provider Discomfort with Intersex Practices.* New York: Human Rights Watch; 2017. https://www.hrw.org/report/2017/10/26/ changing-paradigm/us-medical-provider-discomfort-intersex-care-practices.

7. Mulkey N, Streed C, Chubak B. A Call to Update Standard of Care for Children with Differences in Sex Development. *AMA J Ethics.* 2021;23(7):E550–556.

8. Daaboul J, Frader J. Ethics and the Management of the Patient with Intersex: A Middle Way. *J Pediatr Endocrinol Metab.* 2001;14(9):1575–1583.

9. United Nations Human Rights, Office of the High Commissioner. A " Big Victory" for Intersex People and Their Rights. April 5, 2024. https://www.ohchr.org/en/ stories/2024/04/big-victory-intersex-people-and-their-rights.

10. Gaetano P. David Reimer and John Money Gender Reassignment Controversy: The John/Joan Case. *Embryo Project Encyclopedia*. Arizona State University. November 15, 2017.

11. Colapinto J. *As Nature Made Him: The Boy Who Was Raised as a Girl*. New York: Harper Collins Publishers; 2000.

12. Carey B. "John William Money, 84, Sexual Identity Researcher, Dies." *The New York Times*. July 11, 2006.

Chapter 21. Transgender and Non-Binary Patients and Providers

"It is revolutionary for any trans person to choose to be seen and visible in a world that tells us we should not exist." — Laverne Cox, actress

"Nature chooses who will be transgender; individuals don't choose this." —Mercedes Ruehl, actress

GENDER-VARIANT PEOPLE HAVE, historically, been a part of the normal fabric of communities, societies, and cultures for thousands of years. In ancient Rome, the Galli priests, who were part of the cult of the goddess Cybele, were born male and castrated. These individuals then dressed in women's clothing and were accepted as a normal part of Roman society. On the North American continent, Native Americans embraced gender variant individuals whom they called "two-spirit" — a third gender. Many of these individuals, born male, performed the gender roles of women and expressed themselves as women. They were often religious leaders and teachers. They were seen as more enlightened and spiritually gifted secondary to their expression as both male (in body) and female (in spirit).

Fluid gender presentations did not "fit" rigid Western European social norms. As Europeans colonized the American continent, two-spirit people, revered in Native American culture, were ostracized and slowly disappeared.

One must use caution, however, when attempting to place labels and definitions on cultures about which we have limited viewpoints and perspectives. The terms used for transgender individuals in the modern era are different as our understanding of transgender individuals has evolved. The only medical procedure for male-born individuals before the 20th century was castration; individuals did not have any options to medically alter their hormonal physiology. Nevertheless, these individuals could function socially as their target gender identity and be accepted as productive members of an accepting society.

In the modern era, there are more options for gender-variant individuals to express themselves through surgery and hormone replacement therapy. However, gender variant and transgender individuals face enormous social pressures and discrimination in many modern societies, including the United States.

"Transgender" is a relatively new term used to refer to gender-variant individuals who exist on an identity spectrum from masculine to feminine. In the previous chapter, the Genderbread Person in Figure 1 shows the complex interplay between gender identity, gender expression, biological sex, sexual attraction, and romantic attraction.

The most recent estimate regarding the prevalence of transgender individuals in the United States is between 1 million and 1.4 million — double the number from 2011. The prevalence has not likely changed, but individuals are now more willing to identify themselves as such, in part due to (until very recently) increased social acceptance and legal protections from discrimination.[1] Regardless, transgender patients, and especially transgender patients from underrepresented ethnic groups, are some of the most marginalized and vulnerable individuals not only in our communities but in healthcare systems, too.

Of particular concern is the exceedingly high rate of completed suicide, suicidal ideation (SI), and suicide attempts (SA). The highest rates of suicide attempt and completed suicide are among transgender youth under age 18. Overall rates of attempted suicide of transgender individuals are estimated to be 30% and above.[2] Additionally, many transgender individuals suffer from disproportionate rates of chronic illness, mental health disorders, substance and alcohol use disorders, trauma and victimization, and housing and employment discrimination.

Exacerbating these issues are significant barriers to compassionate, competent, and nondiscriminatory access to proper healthcare treatment. A 2010 survey of transgender individuals found that nearly one in five transgender patients reported being denied care in both outpatient and inpatient settings.[3] Even if the patients are allowed access to care, 28% of respondents reported verbal harassment, and nearly 50% of respondents had to inform their healthcare provider about transgender healthcare issues.

In the past decade, there has been significant progress in educating healthcare providers about the unique needs of transgender patients. Recently, transgender healthcare, especially for minors, has become a political lightning rod due to the increasing number of transgender minors who want to participate in athletics at school. Transgender minors are also facing decreased access to gender-affirming care as state legislatures pass laws prohibiting or criminalizing treatment. Fueled by fear, ignorance, and misinformation, transgender individuals once again face new challenges and discrimination.

The Williams Institute at UCLA reports that in 2023 and 2024, more than 1,000 separate bills were introduced in state legislatures limiting transgender rights, access to gender-affirming care, and legal recognition.[4] These efforts are negatively impacting many transgender individuals as they fear accessing care or are increasingly at risk of losing access to care.

As access has been restricted, transgender minors have sought treatment in "refuge" states.[4] For example, after Minnesota passed legislation protecting trans rights and access to care, patients began to travel to Minnesota for care from nearby states where transgender care is no longer an option.

Anyone who provides direct bedside care will eventually care for a transgender patient regardless of the setting. Most healthcare workers have not received formal training in taking care of transgender patients, and for those who have not, there may be some discomfort or anxiety. This is understandable. *I cannot emphasize enough the importance of being sensitive and compassionate and treating a transgender patient just like any other patient. We are all human, first and foremost, and our need for respectful, compassionate care is the same.*

Out of respect to the patient, use the *preferred pronouns* the patient desires. Nothing is more disrespectful and demeaning to a patient than to be called a "he" when the patient identifies as a "she" or vice-versa. Not all transgender patients have changed their legal names, and many of these patients will let staff know their chosen name. When staff uses the individual's birth or legal name that the patient no longer uses, this is known as *dead naming*. Dead-naming transgender patients invalidates their existence and is demeaning.

PRONOUNS AND GENDER IDENTITIES

Many individuals who identify along the spectrum of gender identity and expression choose to use and prefer to be called not only by their preferred name but also their preferred pronouns. There are gender-binary, gender-neutral, and non-binary pronouns. For example, Ze, Zie, and Xe are gender-neutral pronouns that communicate a non-binary or gender-neutral identity. These new pronouns reflect a unique identity.

Table 1 lists common pronouns used with examples for use.

SHE/HER/ HERS	She laughs. I called her. Her eyes... That is hers. She likes herself.
HE/HIM/ HIS	He laughs. I called him. His eyes... That is his. He likes himself.
THEY/THEM/ THEIRS	They laugh. I called them. That is theirs. They like themselves.
ZE/HIR/ HIRS	Ze laughs. I called hir. Hir eyes... That is hirs. Ze likes hirself.
ZIE/ZIR/ ZIRS	Zie laughs. I called zir. Zir eyes.. That is zirs. Zie likes zirself.
XE/XEM/ XYRS	Xe laughs. I called xem. Xyr eyes... That is xyrs. He likes xemself.

TABLE 1. Commonly used pronouns in the transgender and non-binary community.

As a healthcare provider, be respectful and ask the patient or colleague which pronouns to use. It's OK to mistakenly use an incorrect or non-preferred pronoun now and then — apologize and move on. It is not OK, however, to consistently and intentionally use non-preferred pronouns. It is disrespectful and falls on the spectrum of harassment, as this is unwanted and unwelcome by the person who has stated preferred pronouns.

NON-BINARY PATIENTS

Some people's gender identities are neither completely male or masculine nor completely female or feminine. Some patients identify as non-binary and use pronouns they or them, for example. These pronouns acknowledge the patient's dual identity as both masculine and feminine. Ask and use the preferred pronouns and name the patient desires.

TRANSGENDER PATIENT EXPERIENCE

Gender transition is a long and difficult journey. Some patients realized as young children that they were different, and most children developed their gender identity by age 3 to 4. Their internal sense of being male or female is a part of their identity. Many transgender patients, as small children, may feel as if there is something different. Some may even exhibit behaviors of the opposite gender or engage in activities typically associated with the opposite gender and desire to dress and present as their gender identity.

Some transgender patients have fully transitioned, some have not started the journey, and still others may be in the transitioning process. *Each transition journey is unique.* Some patients seek only gender-affirming hormone therapy, while others seek a full transition that includes gender-affirming surgeries.

If your institution or organization does not offer training on treating and caring for transgender patients, I encourage you to learn more. This knowledge will give you confidence and comfort. Many patients are anxious and apprehensive about explaining to healthcare providers "who" they are while being treated. Remember, all patients are vulnerable and have a right to receive non-judgmental, respectful care.

TRANSGENDER PHYSICIAN EXPERIENCES

Very few studies investigate the experiences of transgender physicians. In June 2022, Westafer and colleagues published a first-of-its-kind qualitative survey of the professional experiences of transgender physicians using semi-structured interviews.[5] Of 24 physicians interviewed, 33% identified as transgender women, 29% as transgender men, 17% as non-binary, and 8% as genderqueer. Prominent themes throughout the interviews included distress as a result of transphobia, dominance of the rigid gender binary norm, and structural and institutional factors associated with psychological and physical safety. Most also reported feeling isolated as transgender physicians.

Many of the interviewees feared loss of job or license to practice, felt stress from being "stealth" and misgendered, and felt emotionally exhausted. Participants share the following:

Fear of loss of job or license: *"I think, especially for us in healthcare, it's a double-edged sword….we don't get the same privilege of access to mental healthcare because our records can be subpoenaed, because they can withhold medical licenses and things like that. So, for those reasons, for insurance purposes, I didn't come out until I was done with everything… I had my life insurance and disability insurance and everything. I was like, ' You can't take it from me.'"—transgender woman physician.*

Misgendering: *"It's hard at the end of the day to have the bandwidth to like go back and bring this up to folks that you know what? It's actually affecting patient care when you're traumatizing me dozens of times."—non-binary physician.*

Being out because of obligation to the transgender community: *"It's been hard for me to weigh the balance of wanting to be more open for the sake of helping others, and being sort of a beacon and letting other people know that like, yes, this can be done and also not really wanting to deal with that and having fears that my life would be disrupted or people who now very seamlessly are able to navigate my gender identity would you know, suddenly start stumbling where they didn't before when I was presumed to be cisgender."—transgender man.*

Many of the participants in the study described their own difficulty accessing trans-competent healthcare. Caring for transgender individuals is not recent nor is it experimental.

REFERENCES

1. Chipkin S, Kim F. Ten Most Important Things To Know About Caring for Transgender Patients. *Am J Med.* 2017;130(11):1238–1245.

2. Jackson D. Suicide-Related Outcomes Following Gender-Affirming Treatment: A Review. *Cureus.* 223;15(3):e36425. doi: 10.7759/cureus.36425

3. Grant J, Mottet L, Tanis J, *et al.* National Transgender Discrimination Survey Report on Health and Health Care. Washington, D.C.: National Center for Transgender Equality and National Gay and Lesbian Task Force; 2010.

4. Redfield E, Conron KJ, Mallory C. The Impact of 2024 Anti-Transgender Legislation on Youth. Williams Institute, UCLA School of Law. April 2024. https://williamsinstitute.law.ucla.edu/publications/2024-anti-trans-legislation/.

5. Westafer L, Freiermuth C, Lall M, Murder S, Ragone E, Jarman A. Experiences of Transgender and Gender Expansive Physicians. *JAMA Netw Open.* 2022;5 (6):e2219791 doi:10.10001/jamanetworkopen.2022.19791

Chapter 22. Historical and Contemporary Transgender Medical Care

"Gender-affirming health care literally saved my life."— Alexa, transwoman

MAGNUS HIRSCHFELD WAS A GERMAN PHYSICIST and sexologist who started his career advocating for gay rights and treating closeted patients wrestling with their sexuality. His work naturally led him to help the transgender and genderqueer community.

In 1910, Hirschfeld coined the term "transvestite" as a way to medically protect his patients by providing a formal diagnosis yet protecting them from prosecution. Then in 1919, in a more liberal environment under the Weimar Republic, Hirschfeld opened his Institut für Sexualwissenschaft (Institute for Sexual Science) (Figure 1) where he began providing hormone therapy, gender reassignment surgery, and postoperative care for his transgender patients.[1]

FIGURE 1. Institut für Sexualwissenschaft (Institute for Sexual Science)[1]

In comparison to his contemporaries who sought to "cure" transgender people of their supposed mental illness, Hirschfeld supported those seeking their true gender identity and who wanted to live as the gender they felt most aligned with, regardless of sex assigned at birth. His therapeutic care model, called "adaptation theory," was one of the earliest versions of informed consent.[2] His approach to the care of transgender patients was revolutionary, progressive, and emphasized the autonomy of the individual.

One of the most well-known trans women in history is Lile Ebe, whose story is fictionalized in the film *The Danish Girl*, released in 2015. But before Ebe, there was Dora Richter. Dora (Dörchen) left her hometown near the Ore Mountains in 1909 and moved to Berlin to seek a better life. By day, she worked as a "male" waiter in luxury hotels. When off the clock, she lived as a woman. This double life landed her in trouble with the police several times. After one arrest in 1920, she was released to Magnus Hirschfeld at the Institute for Sexual Science. That turning point marked the beginning of the rest of her life. At the institute, Richter received an orchiectomy and worked as a housemaid alongside other trans women. These women volunteered their bodies to refine the institute's techniques. Later, in 1931, Richter received the first full sexual reassignment when she was 40 years old.[3,4]

Unfortunately, Magnus Hirschfeld, who was Jewish, gay, and openly liberal, became a target soon after Adolf Hitler became Chancellor of Germany in early 1933. On May 6, 1933, the Institute for Sexual Science was occupied and looted by young men who were part of the German Student Union. The extensive book collection and other scientific literature at the institute was burned a few days later in Berlin's Bebelplatz Square (Figure 2).[5] A valuable repository of historical information, research, stories, narratives, and scientific contributions to our understanding of LGBTQ+ individuals was lost in an instant.

Hirschfeld, fortunately, was in Paris at the time of these events; he never returned to Germany and died in Paris in 1935. After the attack on the institute, the Nazis continued their persecution of gay men by expanding and enforcing legislation that criminalized homosexuality.

Weeks after Hirschfeld's death, Paragraph 175, a provision of the German Criminal Code, was redrafted to prohibit all forms of male homosexual contact. In total, around 50,000 gay men were detained under these draconian laws. Once confined in jail, they were routinely exposed to inhumane treatment for their sexuality. Around 10,000 to 15,000 were also deported to concentration camps, where many were forced to wear a pink triangle and subjected to castration and medical experimentation. Over half of these prisoners would die from the extreme conditions they were subjected to in the camps. Paragraph 175 was not repealed until March 10, 1994. Many gay men remained in prison for years to come.[5]

FIGURE 2. Nazi Party member burning books in Berlin's Bebelplatz Square, May 10, 1933.[5]

The tragedy and human toll of World War II temporarily slowed research in the field of caring for LGBTQ+ individuals. However, providing treatment for transgender individuals began in earnest soon after World War II, and there are many important milestones:

1940s

Michael Dillon was a transgender man born in London to an Irish family and is the first transgender man to undergo phalloplasty and among the first to access masculinizing hormone therapy. Dillon started on testosterone at the direction of physician George Foss, but according to Dillon's account, he was outed as transgender by his psychiatrist. This made Dillon the subject of public discussion because, as his brother was a Baronet to Lismullen, this would have made Michael Dillon next in line for the inheritance of this position if his legal transition was to be fully recognized.

Dillon moved to Bristol, where he lived as a man and worked in a garage while undergoing testosterone therapy. In 1945, Dillon enrolled in the School of Medicine at Trinity College Dublin to train as a physician. Shortly thereafter, he published *Self: A Study in Ethics and Endocrinology* as a medical, psychological, and philosophical exploration of gender and sexuality. This book affirmed the bodily autonomy of trans people, positing that people should have the right to change their gender and their bodies.

Before being licensed as a physician, Dillon performed an orchiectomy on Roberta Cowell, making her the first British trans woman to receive gender-affirming bottom surgery. This was perhaps one of, if not the first, gender-affirming surgical procedures performed by a trans person for a trans person.[6]

Estrogen and testosterone were manufactured on a larger, less expensive scale and became widely available. Physicians, parents, and ethicists approved the use of hormone therapy for children so they could conform to gender stereotypes, and intersex children were prescribed hormone therapy.

Inspired by Magnus Hirschfeld's 1923 term seelischer Transsexualismus, the term 'transsexual' was introduced in 1949 by David Oliver Cauldwell and popularized by Harry Benjamin in 1966, around the same time "transgender" was coined and began to be popularized.

In 1948, Alfred Kinsey, a pioneer in sexual and gender studies, published *Sexual Behavior in the Human Male*. Soon after publishing this work, he met Louise Lawrence, a transgender artist and activist who advocated for transgender rights and organized the transgender community.

Lawrence lived most of her early adult life as Lew, and after moving to Berkeley and San Francisco in northern California, discovered and joined a cross-dressing and transgender community. Lawrence sought to educate the public about gender non-conformity by acting as a key interface between medical researchers and her network within the transgender community. She wrote, "I am trying to gather as much information... as possible in order that medical men... will be able to help people that come to them."[7] Lawrence had built a community of more than 200 transgender as well as transsexual individuals and incorporated their stories in Kinsey's 1953 follow-up *Sexual Behavior in the Human Female*.

Prior to this, in 1942, she met leading psychiatrist Karl Bowman, the director of the Langley Porter Psychiatric Clinic at the University of California - San Francisco (UCSF). She frequently lectured on transgender topics to Bowman's colleagues at the university. Through Bowman, Lawrence met Harry Benjamin, a researcher in transsexual medicine from Germany, and introduced him to her contacts in the transgender community. [8] According to former colleagues, Benjamin used Lawrence as a "sounding board for many of his ideas," and Lawrence wrote that she appreciated Benjamin as "one of the few medical men in this country who has any understanding of this problem."[8] Lawrence offered talks on the transgender community at UCSF for several years.

1950s

Christine Jorgensen is one of the most famous transgender individuals of the 20th century, as she courageously and boldly sought care to affirm her gender identity in Denmark in the early 1950s. Overnight, she became the face of transgender care in the United States. She influenced the model of transitioning that we know today and helped popularize the term *transgender*, which she came to call herself later in life.

Christine Jorgensen's doctor, Harry Benjamin, began working with transgender patients in 1948 through an affirming model of care. In 1979, he founded the Harry Benjamin International Gender Dysphoria Association, which has since become the World Professional Association for Transgender Health (WPATH). This organization still sets the internationally best-recognized standard of care for transgender people to this day.

In the preface of Benjamin's autobiography, he credits Jorgensen's input into his medical practice for much of his success, demonstrating the effectiveness of a patient-led model of care for transgender people. WPATH has seen many iterations and developments on how best to treat transgender people as Benjamin's ideas were adapted and expanded on. Christine Jorgensen published *Christine Jorgensen: A Personal Autobiography* in 1967, a personal memoir of her experience and her life.[6]

1960s

In 1966, the Johns Hopkins Gender Clinic opened and was the first clinic to offer comprehensive care for transgender individuals, including counseling, gender-affirming hormone therapy, and surgical procedures. Among its innovations was the "Real-Life Test," which required individuals to live for an extended period as their identified gender before being considered for gender-affirming surgery.[6,7] The success of this clinic led to other academic institutions opening gender-identity clinics.[7]

An important figure during this era was John Hoopes, a plastic surgeon. He initially supported gender-affirming surgery (GAS) and was the inaugural director of the clinic.

Milton Edgerton, a pioneer in craniofacial plastic surgery, began to offer a variety of surgical procedures for transgender patients at Johns Hopkins University Hospital and, after leaving Hopkins became the chair of plastic and maxillofacial surgery at the University of Virginia Medical Center.[8]

1970s

The innovative gender clinic at Johns Hopkins faced uncertainty and conflict through the 1970s. Walker Magrath, a medical history student at Johns Hopkins, recently published an excellent article in the October 2022 Annals of Internal Medicine called "The Fall of the Nation's First Gender-Affirming Surgery Clinic." The article explains the many factors leading to the demise of the gender clinic. In 1974, less than a decade after opening the clinic, Dr. John Hoopes, previously a champion for GAS, became disillusioned and expressed disappointment with his operative outcomes.

Hoopes' view of transgender patients also shifted, with him characterizing GAS as "a façade constructed on what once was a male or a female." Furthermore, he described transgender patients as "psychopaths," "masochists," "hysterical," "freakish," and "artificial" in both published and unpublished writings.[9]

A seminal moment occurred when Paul McHugh, notorious for his outspoken pathologization of patients who are LGBTQ, became chief of psychiatry of the clinic in 1975. He arrived with the intent to close the clinic and "concluded" that the clinic was "fundamentally cooperating with a mental illness." His presence accelerated a quorum of hospital leaders already intent on shutting the clinic. The clinic offering GAS closed in 1979.

Progress had hit a wall, and Janice Raymond's transphobic tome, *The Transsexual Empire*, published the same year the Hopkins clinic closed, created a firestorm in the LGBTQ and feminist communities. Psychiatrist

Thomas Szasz commented that "[the book] has rightly seized on transsexualism as an emblem of modern society's unremitting — though increasingly concealed — antifeminism."[10] In a 1980 review, philosopher Sarah Hoagland called it a "fecund discussion of patriarchal deception."

In 1980, lesbian transgender feminist Carol Riddell wrote the first feminist critique of the book, a pamphlet titled *Divided Sisterhood: A Critical Review of Janice Raymond's The Transsexual Empire*, which became heavily cited in transgender studies. Riddell builds on the earlier work of transgender feminists and argues the book ran counter to the emphasis placed on subjectivity in feminist consciousness-raising, criticized its portrayal of gender identity clinics as an "empire" rather than institutions marginalized by the medical patriarchy which forces transsexuals to conform to gender roles and suffer, and stated the book is "dangerous to transsexuals because it does not treat us as human beings at all, merely as the tools of a theory." Riddell argued in 1996 that *The Transsexual Empire* "did not invent anti-transsexual prejudice, but it did more to justify and perpetuate it than perhaps any other book ever written."[11]

The closure of the Hopkins gender clinic accelerated the demise of all but two of the 20 other gender clinics in other academic departments.

1980s

In June 1981, the Centers for Disease Control and Prevention's *Morbidity and Mortality Weekly Report* about five gay men with a syndrome that came to be called AIDS cast a long dark shadow on the provision of equitable healthcare in the LGBTQ+ community. Gay and bisexual men and transgender women, in particular, were ostracized in their communities and subject to discrimination and mistreatment in most healthcare systems. As a result, government action was slow and muted partly because of the broad stigma against who was most affected.

In the 1980s, 20 states, many in the South, still had sodomy laws that criminalized sex between members of the same sex or all nonprocreative sex. In 1986, in *Bowers v. Hardwick*, the Supreme Court reinforced stigma when it upheld the right of Georgia to enforce a sodomy law prohibiting homosexual conduct, even when it occurred in a private home. The progressive era in efforts to improve our understanding of transgender care from the 1960s through the late 1970s ground to a halt.

Despite increased attention to transgender people, the first two editions of *The Diagnostic and Statistical Manual of Mental Disorders* included no mention of gender identity. It was not until 1980, with the publication of *DSM–III*, that the diagnosis of "transsexualism" first appeared.

1990s

Transgender individuals continued to struggle to find access to gender-affirming care and treatments. The diagnosis of Gender Identity Disorder (GID) carried significant weight, and healthcare providers were hesitant to provide care. Most physicians were not provided culturally or medically appropriate training in medical schools and graduate training programs. Even for healthcare providers who wanted to treat transgender patients, the diagnosis of GID entailed extensive psychological testing before a patient was offered the option for medical transition.

"Gatekeeping, "the power of the healthcare provider to deny transgender patients access to hormones or other medical and surgical treatments, remained a problem for the community.

One of the most groundbreaking technological developments in the 1990s was the introduction of the internet. In 1994, from her home computer in San Francisco, computer programmer Gwendolyn Ann Smith (also known as *Gwenners*) started the Gazebo AOL chat room, the first specially hosted for transgender people.

When she initially signed up for the free AOL account, Smith noticed that there was an embargo on organizing a chat room using the words "transgender," "transsexual," and "transvestite," which led her to press the issue with the company, which reversed the policy by the end of 1992. By then, the coded "Gazebo" chat room had provided a gathering place and resource center with a bulletin board that within a few years attracted tens of thousands of unique visitors every month. Users were rapidly exchanging information about their lives, including the actress and already famous gender activist Kate Bornstein.[12,13]

Just five years later, in 1999, in response to the murder of trans woman Rita Hester, Smith began the "Remembering our Dead" archiving web project to inventory and memorialize all murdered trans persons the world over. The Transgender Day of Remembrance is held every year on November 20.[13]

The LGBT rights group Parents and Friends of Lesbians and Gays (PFLAG), founded in 1972, also became more supportive of transgender people at this time. In 1998, gender identity was added to their mission after a vote at their annual meeting in San Francisco.

PFLAG was the first national LGBT organization to officially adopt a transgender inclusion policy for its work. PFLAG established its Transgender Network, also known as TNET, in 2002 as its first official "Special Affiliate," recognized with the same privileges and responsibilities as its regular chapters.

Transgender history also began to be recognized around this time. In 1996, Leslie Feinberg published *Transgender Warriors,* a history of transgender people.

With the release of *DSM–IV* in 1994, "transsexualism" was replaced with "gender identity disorder in adults and adolescents" in an effort to reduce stigma. However, controversy continued with advocates and some psychiatrists pointing to ways in which this diagnostic category pathologized identity rather than a true disorder.

2000s

In 2002, Pete Chvany, Luigi Ferrer, James Green, Loraine Hutchins, and Monica McLemore presented at the Gay, Lesbian, Bisexual, Transgender, Queer and Intersex Health Summit, held in Boulder, Colorado, marking the first time transgender people, bisexual people, and intersex people were recognized as co-equal partners on the national level rather than gay and lesbian "allies" or tokens. In 2004, the first San Francisco Trans March was held; it has been held annually since and is one of the largest trans events in the world.

In February 2007, Norman Spack co-founded Boston Children's Hospital's Gender Management Service clinic — America's first clinic to treat transgender children. In 2009, America's professional association of endocrinologists established best practices for transgender children that included prescribing puberty-suppressing drugs to preteens, followed by hormone therapy beginning at about age 16. The American Academy of Child and Adolescent Psychiatry echoed these recommendations in 2012.

2010s

With the publication of *DSM–5* in 2013, "gender identity disorder" was eliminated and replaced with "gender dysphoria." This change further focused the diagnosis on the gender identity-related distress that some transgender people experience (and for which they may seek psychiatric, medical, and surgical treatments) rather than on transgender individuals or identities themselves.

The *DSM–5* articulates explicitly that "gender non-conformity is not in itself a mental disorder." The fifth edition also includes a separate "gender dysphoria in children" diagnosis and for the first time allows the diagnosis to be given to individuals with disorders of sex development (DSD). *DSM–5* also includes the optional "post-transition" specifier to indicate when a particular individual's gender transition is complete.

In this "post-transition" case, the diagnosis of gender dysphoria would no longer apply, but the individual may still need ongoing medical care (e.g., hormonal treatment). Nevertheless, discussions continue among advocates and medical professionals about how best to preserve access to gender transition-related healthcare while also minimizing the degree to which such diagnostic categories stigmatize the very people that physicians are attempting to help.[14]

In 2011, the Center of Excellence for Transgender Health published the first protocols for transgender primary care, and the Veterans Health Administration issued a directive stipulating that all transgender and intersex veterans are entitled to the same level of care "without discrimination" as other veterans, consistent across all Veterans Administration healthcare facilities.

Despite progress in mainstream media, entertainment, and politics, transgender individuals began to face significant backlash, and providing gender-affirming care for transgender children and adolescents is challenged by political opponents. In 2017, the Trump administration made efforts to reverse many protections afforded to transgender individuals, including banning transgender individuals from the military and eliminating transgender employees from Title VII protection. This set off a long legal battle.

Although several judges issued injunctions to delay Trump's proposal, the Supreme Court ultimately allowed the Trump administration to proceed with its plan. From April 2019, existing transgender personnel could continue to serve, but new transgender personnel could not join. In 2017, the Trump administration, through the Department of Justice, reversed the Obama-era policy which used Title VII of the Civil Rights Act to protect transgender employees from discrimination. President Joe Biden reversed the policy in January 2021.

2020s

As of December 2024, about half the states have banned transgender minors' access to puberty blockers and hormone therapy. On December 4, 2024, the Supreme Court agreed to hear a case listed as *U.S. v. Skrmetti*. The question in this case is whether Tennessee's law banning gender-affirming hormone therapies for transgender minors violates the Equal Protection Clause of the U.S. Constitution.

The American Medical Association, the American Psychiatric Association, and the American Academy of Pediatrics oppose these restrictions, which have already forced thousands of families across the country to travel to maintain access to medical care or watch their children suffer without it. In July 2023, the Sixth Circuit Court of Appeals rejected requests from families and medical providers to block laws in Tennessee and Kentucky banning gender-affirming medical care for transgender youth. The Supreme Court's decision is expected by June 2025.

In 2024, more than 500 additional anti-LGBTQ+ bills were introduced, and over 40 passed into law across 14 states. The vast majority of the bills introduced since 2023 have specifically targeted transgender people in an attempt to take away the transgender community's basic freedoms. While many transgender people are choosing to flee hostile states in what has become known as the "trans exodus," Joelle Bayaa-Uzuri Espeut, a black trans activist, says lower-income black and brown trans people do not always have that option[15]:

> *"The trans exodus is a direct response to the anti-trans bills being proposed and passed, as well as the increased violence towards the trans community. Trans-identifying persons are feeling less and less safe. The real harm is being done to Black and brown trans people who do not have the financial means or resources to move."*

Gender-affirming care for adults is also threatened. In 2023, Florida passed a law requiring that adults seeking transition care sign an informed consent form, undergo psychological evaluations to continue hormone therapy, and receive all related care from a physician in person. In June 2024, a federal judge overturned the law. Also that year, Missouri Attorney General Andrew Bailey put forward emergency rules that placed barriers to gender-affirming care for minors and adults. These efforts are an unprecedented onslaught against human rights. In the words of Dr. Martin Luther King, Jr, "Nothing in all the world is more dangerous than sincere ignorance and conscientious stupidity." Most of these efforts to restrict and ban care are politically motivated. The narrative continues.

CASE STUDIES

Case 1

A 23-year-old patient, presenting as female, presents to a family practice clinic. The patient recently moved from another state and is seeking a new primary care physician. The patient has long known his gender identity is male and is seeking care to start his transition journey. (Note that even though the patient is presenting as female, I am acknowledging the patient's gender identity in telling this story.)

The physician has no experience providing transgender care. The physician communicates this to the patient and says she is willing to provide primary care for the patient but must defer offering gender-affirming hormone therapy, as she is unfamiliar with prescribing hormone therapy for transgender patients. Proactively, she suggests making an appointment with another physician top whom she will refer him.

This is a common scenario for many transgender individuals as they start their journey. First, they must often awkwardly explain to the providers (MD, NP, or PA) who they are and then nervously wait for any negative reaction. In this case, the family practice physician is being courteous and respectful and not dismissive. It is a great approach.

Case 2

A 45-year-old transgender woman presents to the emergency department with an acute abdomen. She is in the middle of her transition, and her voice is still deep enough that when she speaks, she sounds "male" despite her appearance as a woman. When she was admitted, she told the admitting nurse she had not legally changed her name from David and informed her that she preferred to be called Diane.

The emergency room physician ordered a CT scan of her abdomen, and when she arrived at the scanner, the technician looked at her identifying bracelet and saw that it stated, "David J." The electronic medical record also identified Diane as biologically male but preferred the pronouns she/her/hers.

The tech, confused, asked her if she was David, and she said that was her legal name, she preferred to be called Diane. Just prior to the start of the CT scan, the tech performed a "timeout" to ensure he was doing the right procedure on the right patient. He then asked the patient to identify herself and provide a date of birth. When she said "Diane," the technician said she had to use her legal name for the "time out," and she said, "David. "As the CT scan proceeded, she was in tears over what had just happened.

When the CT scan was complete, the technician called patient transport and told them "he," the patient, was ready to go back to the emergency department.

- How do you think the patient feels about how she was treated?
- What could the technician have done differently?
- Do you think the technician intentionally used the wrong pronoun, or was it a mistake?
- What can organizations and institutions do to ensure staff acknowledges transgender names and pronouns?
- If the patient files a complaint with a patient advocate about the experience , how should the patient advocate proceed?
- Is the patient being "too sensitive"?

The patient deserves to be treated with respect and addressed by her preferred pronouns. Staff should have received training on the appropriate way to address and treat transgender patients. If a staff member does not feel comfortable taking care of a transgender patient and using preferred pronouns, he or she should defer providing care for the patient.

Case 3

Louie Bullock, a transgender teen who uses they/them pronouns, didn't always feel so welcome in the community where they lived. They moved with their family to Rochester, Minnesota, from their home state of Texas in June 2022 due to safety concerns and an influx of anti-transgender legislation in the Lone Star State.

In the Midwest, both Iowa and South Dakota passed bans this year that prevent trans youths from seeking this care. North Dakota is on track to follow their lead. Furthermore, Iowa has passed a bill that prohibits individuals from using restrooms that align with their gender identity if that differs from their gender assigned at birth.

"These bills are incredibly harmful to trans people ... it's just so very scary," Bullock says. "It has you wondering at what point is this about protecting anybody, you know?"[16]

Bullock is not the only trans person to move to Minnesota in response to safety concerns. Minnesota is seen as a haven by many due to local legislation pushes, such as Gov. Tim Walz's executive order that protects the right to receive gender-affirming care and efforts by the state legislature to establish Minnesota as a "trans refuge" state. It's 2025. We can do better.

REFERENCES

1. Brennan T, Hegarty P. Magnus Hirschfeld, His Biographies and the Possibilities and Boundaries of "Biography" as "Doing History." *Hist Human Sci.* 2009;22(5):24-46. doi: 10.1177/0952695109346642

2. Bullough V. Magnus Hirschfeld, an Often Overlooked Pioneer. *Sexuality and Culture.* 2003;7:62–72. doi: 10.1007/s12119-003-1008-4

3. Serena K. The Real Danish Girl: Lili Elbe's Tragic Life as a Transgender Pioneer. AllThatsInteresting.com. May 14, 2023. https://allthatsinteresting.com/lili-elbe.

4. Rivera J. La première chirurgie de reassignation sexuelle réussie : Magnus, Dora et l'institut de sexologie de Berlin en 1931 [The first successful sex reassignment surgery: Magnus, Dora and the Institute of Sexology, Berlin in 1931]. *Ann Chir Plast Esthet.* 2024;69(5):338-342. French. doi: 10.1016/j.anplas.2024.06.003

5. Holocaust Memorial Day Trust. 6 May 1933: Looting of the Institute of Sexology. https://hmd.org.uk/resource/6-may-1933-looting-of-the-institute-of-sexology/ #:~:text=Jewish%2C%20gay%20and%20outspokenly%20liberal,Hirschfeld%20 was%20working%20in%20Paris.

6. Trans Healthcare Action. Celebrating the History of Trans Healthcare for LGBT History Month. February 25, 2024. https://www.transhealthcare.ie/post/celebrating-the-history-of-trans-healthcare-for-lgbt-history-month#:~:text=1940s%3A%20 Michael%20Dillon%20becomes%20one,to%20access%20masculinising%20 hormone%20therapy.

7. Meyerowitz J. *How Sex Changed: A History of Transsexuality in the United States.* Boston: Harvard University Press;2002.

8. Stryker S. *Transgender History.* New York: Seal Press;2017.

9. Magrath W. The Fall of the Nation's First Gender-affirming Surgery Clinic. *Ann Intern Med.* 2022;175:1462–1467.

10. Szasz T. Male and Female Created He Them. *The New York Times.* June 10, 1979:3.

11. Caslin S. "Trans Feminism and the Women's Liberation Movement in Britain, c. 1970–1980. Gender and History. January 15, 2024. doi: 10.1111/1468-0424.12767

12. Bromberger B. Bio Highlights Trans Columnist's Activism. *Bay Area Reporter.* November 8, 2017. https://www.ebar.com/news/news//251702/bio_highlights_trans_columnists_activism.

13. Steinbock E. The Early 1990s and Its Afterlives: Transgender Nation Sociality in Digital Activism. *Social Media + Society.* 2019;5(4). doi: 10.1177/2056305119881693

14. American Psychiatric Association. Gender Dysphoria Diagnosis. https://www.psychiatry.org/psychiatrists/diversity/education/transgender-and-gender-nonconforming-patients/gender-dysphoria-diagnosis.

15. Jamerson N. 2024 Is Shaping Up To Be a Bad Year for Anti-Trans Laws. *Word in Black.* February 28, 2024. https://wordinblack.com/2024/02/2024-is-shaping-up-to-be-a-bad-year-for-anti-trans-laws/.

16. Castle Work M. Transgender Teen Moved Cross Country Due To Safety Concerns. *Inforum.* April 18, 2023. https://www.inforum.com/news/minnesota/transgender-teen-moved-cross-country-due-to-safety-concerns.

Discrimination in the Healthcare Setting

"Privilege is invisible to those who have it." — Peggy McIntosh,
author of White Privilege: Unpacking the Invisible Knapsack

∞

Chapter 23. Gender Bias

"Gender bias is so steeped in the culture, their results implied,
that women were themselves discriminating against other
women." — Angela Saini, British science journalist

L AKSHMI PURI, WHO SERVED as the UN Assistant Secretary-General and Deputy Executive Director of UN Women, stated in a 2013 speech, "Gender inequalities affect health outcomes and must be addressed accordingly." If gender equality saves lives, then the converse is also true: gender inequality costs lives.[1]

Gender bias in healthcare, treating women differently than men, contributes to increased morbidity and mortality, missed or incorrect diagnoses, and decreased access to care, and it remains endemic in healthcare. Despite some progress, many physicians, nurses, and other healthcare personnel rarely receive training and education addressing gender bias and how to consciously reduce it by acknowledging its impact.

There is a long history of treating women differently than men. For example, the diagnosis of "hysteria," which is no longer a formal diagnosis, can be traced back to the Ancient Greeks. Sabine Arnaud writes in *On Hysteria: The Invention of a Medical Category between 1670 and 1820* that doctors from the 17th to 19th centuries used this term to give it more credibility as a diagnosis.

The term originally applied to both men and women, but it soon became a term for many health complaints made exclusively by women, including premenstrual syndrome, anxiety, depression, and PTSD. Of course, these diagnoses did not exist at the time, but historical accounts of symptoms of these conditions accurately describe some of these diagnoses.

By the end of the 1800s, treatment of hysterics in Paris's Salpêtrière Hospital was sold as entertainment for the public.[1] Sigmund Freud refined the diagnosis through faulty and biased research. In 1980, "hysterical neurosis" was finally removed from the *Diagnostic and Statistical Manual of Mental Disorders*. The legacy of using "hysteria" to describe women with a variety of ailments, unfortunately, lives on through gender bias.

Diane Hoffman and Anita Tarzian showed in their 2001 study, "The Girl Who Cried Pain: A Bias Against Women in the Treatment of Pain," that women are treated differently than men in healthcare. Hoffman and Tarzian state, "In general, women report more severe levels of pain, more frequent incidences of pain, and pain of longer duration than men, but are nonetheless treated for pain less aggressively." They attribute this to gender bias and the long history of society treating women's reasoning capacity as "limited."[1] Gender bias and inequality have far-reaching consequences that affect the health and well-being of communities worldwide.

Women's legal rights in many countries conflict with their human rights and requirements for quality reproductive healthcare. The United Nations Population Fund (UNFPA) estimates that 6.5% of women around the world want to avoid pregnancy but lack access, endure social stigma, or are subject to harmful gender norms. The UNFPA also estimates that nearly 25% of all women feel unable to say no to sex with their partner.[1] With the reversal of *Roe vs. Wade* in the United States, American women now lack access to evidence-based emergency medical treatments in states limiting abortion.

Another issue underpinning gender biases in healthcare includes a lack of equity in research. Symptoms for the same condition, for example, may manifest differently in women than in men, and medications may have different side effects in women than in men. Janine Clayton, director of the Office of Research on Women's Health at the National Institutes of Health (NIH), explains that "much of medical science is based on the belief that male and female physiology differ only in terms of sex and reproductive organs. Because of this, most research has been conducted on male animals and male cells." She states, "Because we have studied women less, we know less about them. The result is that women may not have always received the most optimal care."[2]

OVERCOMING BIAS IN HEALTHCARE

Two forms of bias affect women in healthcare: (1) *implicit bias,* an unconscious attitude or belief about a group or individual that can lead to discriminatory healthcare practices, and (2) *explicit bias,* a more overt and *conscious* effort to treat someone differently through actions or words. Implicit bias is more common than explicit bias, but both forms of bias negatively affect healthcare access and outcomes for women. Women from underrepresented or marginalized groups are often subject to multiple forms of bias.

Denise Davis, a professor of medicine at UCSF, offers practical solutions to reduce the impact of gender bias. She states, "Biases are not moral failings; they are habits of mind." She suggests using effective bedside communication strategies and quantifiable and objective data collection.[2] Consider the following strategies:

Diverse healthcare teams. Explicitly encouraging discussion of gender or other biases during team huddles can help team members feel comfortable speaking up about any concerns. Diverse healthcare teams also provide a variety of perspectives and increase the opportunity for gender-sensitive and culturally sensitive care for patients.

Open-ended questions. Questions that elicit a limited range of responses from patients are more easily contaminated by bias. Open-ended questions pave the way to optimal patient care. For example, clinicians can ask, "What are your concerns today? What am I missing that is important for us to talk about?" The opportunity for the patient to engage in a free narrative approach is an opportunity for a patient to feel respected and listened to.

Substitution and stereotype. If a physician thinks bias may be slipping into the patient interaction, the physician can consciously "substitute" the patient's gender to eliminate the potential for bias. For example, a physician might be more likely to ask a young male patient about substance use or risky behavior, such as having guns at home. A young female patient may not be asked the same question.

Conversely, some physicians might assume a female patient has an ample social support system when there may be no evidence to suggest this is the case. Any of these assumptions can lead to missed opportunities for more comprehensive patient care. Many of these biases are rooted in stereotypes. The "stereotypical" young male takes more risks, and young females are assumed to have an extensive social network.

Data collection and analysis. Collecting and analyzing data can illuminate differences in care that would otherwise go undetected. If disparities in screening questions or other routine care practices have been detected, for example, measuring the results highlights the extent of the problem.

Checklists and guidelines. Computerized checklists that prompt providers to ask patients about risk factors, for example, can help ensure that all patients undergo the same evaluation. Similarly, clinical guidelines for patient care can ensure that clinicians follow evidence-based methods for all patients.

Training opportunities. Bringing in practice coaches or attending training opportunities on patient experience or patient communication can help clinicians become aware of their own biases.

REFERENCES

1. ConcernUSA. The Deadly Inequities of Gender Bias in Healthcare. September 26, 2022. concernusa.org.
2. Paulsen E. Recognizing, Addressing Unintended Gender Bias in Patient Care. Duke Health. January 14, 2020. https://physicians.dukehealth.org/articles/recognizing-addressing-unintended-gender-bias-patient-care

Chapter 24. Gender and Racial Discrimination

"Of all the forms of inequality, injustice in healthcare is the most shocking and inhuman." — Dr. Martin Luther King, Jr.

B LACK MATERNAL MORTALITY is a public health crisis and cannot be explained by socioeconomic factors alone. According to the CDC, black women have the highest maternal mortality rate in the United States: 69.9 deaths per 100,000 live births for 2021, almost three times the rate for white women.[1]

In May 2021, U.S. Representative Cori Bush from Missouri recounted her own experience as a black OB patient at a House Oversight and Reform Committee.[2] She said she saw a sign in her doctor's office encouraging patients to speak up about anything unusual. She did, telling her physician she was having severe pains. Her concerns were swiftly dismissed, and she was sent home. One week later, she went into early labor. She told committee members, "At 23 weeks, my son was born, one pound, three ounces. His ears were still in his head. His eyes were still fused shut. His fingers were smaller than rice, and his skin was translucent, a Black baby, translucent."

Bush recalled that the doctor who delivered her son apologized for not listening to her. But when she was pregnant with her second child, she faced the same situation. She again went into early labor, and a different doctor refused to help her, telling Bush in a clear reference to her race: "You can get pregnant again because that's what you people do." Her story is far from unusual.

Twenty-nine black women who completed focus questionnaires described differential treatment by staff based on their insurance status (public vs. private) and described a lower quality of prenatal care based on providers' racism. They describe their interactions with their doctors or supporting staff as prejudiced.[3]

While there may not be evidence that differential treatment of black pregnant patients leads to maternal death, literature does support that black patients do receive differential treatment. Black cancer patients needing chemotherapy, for example, were less likely to be counseled about fertility preservation.[1,4] For many black women, the perception of racial bias is their reality. This impacts their willingness to engage with their obstetricians.

Self-reflection about racial bias can be the first step in addressing this systemic and pervasive problem. Some physicians and other caregivers may challenge the notion they treat patients differently solely based on their race or socioeconomic class. Implicit bias remains a problem.

Black maternal deaths also impact families and local communities in a "starburst effect," as illustrated in Figure 1.[3] The crisis of black maternal mortality and disparities in care threatens to widen the perception of racism within the medical community, and the relatively high rate in the United States challenges the dogma that the U.S. can be a champion for human rights. As Rolanda Lister and others state in their paper addressing black maternal mortality, it truly is the elephant in the room. Ignoring or denying it exists exacerbates the injustice and perpetuates the problem.[3]

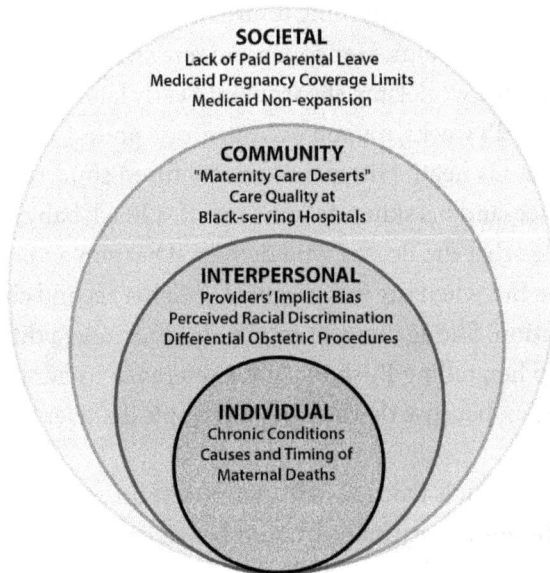

FIGURE 1. Starburst effect of maternal mortality.[3]

REFERENCES

1. Stafford K. Why Do So Many Black Women Die in Pregnancy? One Reason: Doctors Don't Take Them Seriously. *AP News.* May 23, 2023. https://projects.apnews.com/features/2023/from-birth-to-death/black-women-maternal-mortality-rate.html

2. Olson L. Cori Bush Testified Before Congress About Black Maternal Deaths, Pregnancy Complications. *Missouri Independent.* May 7, 2021. https://missouriindependent.

com/2021/05/07/cori-bush-testifies-before-congress-about-black-maternal-deaths
-pregnancy-complications/

3. Noursi S, Saluga B, Richey L. Using the Ecological Systems Theory to Understand Black/
   White Disparities in Maternal Morbidity and Mortality in the United States. J Racial and
   Ethnic Disparities. 2021;8:661-669. https://doi.org/10.1007/s40615-020-00825-4

4. Lister R, Drake W, Scott B, Graves C. Black Maternal Mortality—The Elephant in the
   Room. *World J f Gynecol Womens Health.* 2019;3(1):10.33552/wjgwh.2019.03.000555.
   doi: 10.33552/wjgwh.2019.03.000555.

Chapter 25. Gender and Sex Discrimination of Professional Women in Healthcare

"After almost over 40 years [in the health care industry],
it still is a disappointment to me that [women]
disappear as we get to the top." — Cathy Jacobson,
CEO of Froedtert ThedaCare Health, Inc.

A RECENT REPORT ON WOMEN'S LEADERSHIP stated, "…when women thrive, organizations thrive — and nations thrive too."[1] Women in healthcare, however, are beset by an almost intransigent obstacle to their leadership aspirations. The so-called *glass ceiling* is real as women face this invisible obstacle on their career ladders. Despite the social progress and legislation addressing discrimination, various factors contribute to and, in some cases, strengthen the glass ceiling, which has led to the underrepresentation of women in leadership roles.[2]

Women compose more than 80% of healthcare occupations, yet only 25% of leaders in the healthcare sector are women.[3,4] And only 18% of hospital CEOs were women in 2017.[2]

A 2012 survey of healthcare executives by the American College of Healthcare Executives (ACHE) noted a disparity in the proportions of women and men who advanced to the CEO position. Between 2006 and 2012, women obtained CEO positions at nearly half the rate of their male counterparts. This was a decline from the 63% rate from the 2006 survey.[5]

The ACHE study revealed two findings that offer insight into the reasons women lag behind men in leadership roles. First, there is a greater proportion of men than women in general leadership roles (62% vs. 50%), and second, a greater percentage of men achieved their first leadership position at the rank of vice president or higher. In the survey, women tended to have more highly specialized and niche management roles. Men who occupy more general management roles may be perceived as having the necessary skillset to succeed and are therefore chosen for greater leadership roles.[5]

What are the barriers facing women as they advance to greater leadership roles? Considerable research has been devoted to identifying common barriers. According to the National Academy of Sciences, "It is not talent, but unintentional biases and outmoded institutional structures that are hindering the access and advancement of women."[6] Both conscious and unconscious biases and gender stereotypes play a role in hindering women's access to higher levels of leadership, including senior and executive leadership roles. Typical "male" characteristics are used to measure how women are expected to perform. Typical "female" characteristics are devalued.

Women also face higher levels of scrutiny for reasons other than ability (appearance, for example), and are frequently evaluated more severely — this is especially true for women in executive positions.[7] Women face "damned if they do and damned if they don't dilemmas." If they are not assertive enough, they are perceived as not tough enough to be competent, and if they are too assertive, they are penalized for being too tough. This double bind results from entrenched stereotypes and perceived gender roles and expectations for behaviors. Women are penalized for this double bind more often than men.[7]

With fewer women in senior leadership positions, there are fewer role models, mentors, and sponsors for up-and-coming potential leaders. The importance of mentorship and sponsorship to the success of women pursuing executive roles cannot be overstated.[7] Sponsors take on the role of promoter and market, advocate, and advance the causes of others.

Another factor is the lack of support for maintaining a work-life balance that includes family responsibilities. Women frequently must take time away from work for maternity leave or to care for family members. Men are, for the most part, less willing to participate in household tasks or caring for other family members.[5] Men do not pay a social price for investing more time in their careers. In fact, it is expected that men focus on career success even at the expense of time with family or other obligations. It's a nefarious double standard.

The salary gap between men and women is real. In the ACHE survey, women healthcare executives earned 20% less than male executives.[5] The numerous barriers to women's leadership are expansive and entrenched in both the societal and organizational psyche. Reducing the impact of these barriers will take time and a concerted effort.

CASE STUDY

Gina Bilotti, a senior executive who worked for Johnson & Johnson (J&J), filed a lawsuit against J&J, alleging she was fired for complaining about the "old boys club" culture. She was fired after a 25-year career at the company, winning numerous awards and recognition as she climbed the ladder to executive positions. In 2017, a new CFO was hired and, according to the suit, immediately treated Bilotti in a harassing manner. In the lawsuit, he allegedly told her to "shut up," asking, " Did I tell you you could talk?" and saying "Fuck you, Gina," and " Obviously, I need to explain this to you in words you be able to understand."[8]

In addition to his discriminatory and harassing behavior, the CFO acted unethically when he misled Matthai Mammen, the global head of R&D, regarding the past performance and efficiency of Bilotti's group by reporting a number that had been inflated to more than three times what the data confirmed.

When Bilotti complained about the misrepresentation, the CFO threatened her, saying " Sure, go and tell someone, see if I care, but just remember, even if they change your reporting line, I control your headcount and your budget, and there are 350 lives that depend on you, so think about that before you go to bed at night."[8]

J&J's HR department took more than a year to investigate the initial complaints about the CFO's behaviors despite other complaints about him.

The CFO was not the only individual allegedly involved in inappropriate behaviors. In early February 2018, Bilotti began formally reporting to Mammen, with whom she already had a working relationship. On December 17, 2017, Mammen wrote to Bilotti in an email stating, "Did I tell you recently how thrilled I am to be working closely with you?" On January 25, 2018, Bilotti expressed hesitancy about taking on an additional role as Mammen's senior strategic advisor. Mammen responded by email, "I'd really like to speak live again … I must say I have become addicted to you and need you badly to re-create our amazing R&D org….I need you."

The next day, during a call, Mammen said, "I don't typically believe in fate, but I do have this strong feeling that we were brought together for a reason, our paths crossed for a reason. We were somehow meant to meet at this exact point in time. You to help me here in JRD and me, because I understand all too well about the grief you're going through. I know we're going to do great things together!" Mammen, who was in the United States during these conversations, may have been grooming Bilotti, who was in Belgium, for a sexual relationship.

Mammen subsequently asked for access to her Facebook page. When Bilotti asked Mammen why, Mammen responded, "Just wanted to connect that way too. Normally reserved for family and close friends" and "deep trust."

Bilotti told Mammen that she was a private person and tried to draw a line between her work and her private life. However, she felt she had no choice but to allow Mammen access to her private Facebook page. After Mammen had access to her Facebook page, he became aware that she is gay. Thereafter, Mammen began to treat her dramatically differently, significantly reducing his contact with her and interacting with her in an abrupt and demeaning manner

She met with CEO Alex Gorsky, telling him about the discrimination she had been subject to. Gorsky said it was "a big, big problem" but never followed up despite a promise to do so. The same day, Bilotti was stripped of the responsibility for two departments, and the next day, her membership on four committees was revoked. Two days later, she was subject to a "bogus and merciless" audit investigating her financial practices spanning five years.[8]

Bilotti took disability leave in 2019, falling ill due to stress at the prospect of losing her pension and medical benefits ten months before her planned retirement. In 2020, her physician released her to work, and she was terminated. The case was dismissed with prejudice on August 8, 2022, after the dispute had been "amicably resolved."

According to a 2019 Korn Ferry survey of CEOs and other C-suite healthcare executives, 63% of respondents said that compared to 2014, there was more opportunity for women to advance to senior leadership positions; however, 55% believe women in their organization were passed over for promotion based on their gender; 59% stated the organization would be more profitable with greater gender parity; and 64% said greater parity would lead to less employee turnover. Two-thirds rank their organization's development programs for women as fair, poor, or non-existent. Finally, 76% said their organizations do not have sponsorship programs to help women advance.

Institutions and organizations must investigate strategies and implement initiatives and programs to reduce the impact of gender bias and discrimination. There are individual responsibilities, but without an institutional framework focused on change, individual efforts fail. Chisholm *et al.*, suggest the following efforts[2]:

1. Acknowledge the existence of gender bias and barriers.
2. Create a committee focused on diversity, equity, and inclusion with a specific charter to reduce the impact of gender bias and discrimination.
3. Conduct workforce assessments to identify the current state and address current gaps in efforts.
4. Cultivate leadership aspirations of early and mid-careerists.
5. Create a mentorship, sponsorship, and focused leadership development program.
6. Identify specific challenges and barriers and design strategies to overcome these challenges.
7. Actively recruit women for senior leadership and executive positions.
8. Create networking opportunities.
9. Develop, assess, and share inclusivity policies and practices.
10. Offer and support educational and training programs and personal development opportunities.
11. Encourage membership in nationally recognized healthcare leadership and executive organizations such as the American College of Healthcare Executives and the American Association for Physician Leadership.
12. Encourage completing formal educational programs and degrees, including MBA, MHA, or MPH degrees.

Additionally, setting targets for advancing women in leadership creates an objective goal. Tracking leadership metrics (e.g., the number of women versus men in leadership roles relative to organizational size) is a strategy to set benchmarks and create an urgency for change. Organizations should also identify potential leaders and encourage them early in their careers. There is strength in diversity. Homogeneity stifles creative thinking and creates a "group think" mentality. Per Boatman and colleagues, "Having a better balance of women in top leadership positions can mean a more diverse team of leaders with different perspectives and a greater ability to contribute to new ideas."[9]

"To move the needle in having more women in leadership positions in healthcare, there must be a shared responsibility between professional

women and their organization. Key to this is engaging organizational leaders to become more agile and adaptive in how they recognize, support and develop female leaders at all levels of the organization."— Katie Bell, Korn Ferry global lead for the healthcare sector.

REFERENCES

1. Warner J. The Women's Leadership Gap. The Center for American Progress. November 20, 2018. https://www.americanprogress.org/article/womens-leadership-gap-2/.

2. Chisholm-Burnes M, Spivey C, Hagemann T, Josephson M. Women in Leadership and the Bewildering Glass Ceiling. *Am J Health Syst Pharm.* 2017;744:312–324. doi: 10.2146/ajhp160930

3. Bureau of Health Workforce, Health Resources and Services Administration. Sex, Race, and Ethnic Diversity of U.S. Health Occupations (2010-2012): Technical Documentation. U.S. Department of Health and Human Services. January 2015. https://bhw.hrsa.gov/sites/default/files/bureau-health-workforce/data-research/diversity-us-health-occupations-technical-2012.pdf.

4. Lennon T. Benchmarking Women's Leadership in the United States. University of Denver Colorado Women's College. 2012. https://www.issuelab.org/resources/26706/26706.pdf.

5. American College of Healthcare Executives. A Comparison of the Career Attainments of Men and Women Healthcare Executives. December 2012. https://www.ache.org/-/media/ache/learning-center/research/2012genderreportfinal.pdf.

6. Bernstein L. At NIH, One Woman Says Gender Bias Has Blocked Promotions. *The Washington Post.* August 28, 2016. https://www.washingtonpost.com/national/health-science/at-nih-one-woman-says-gender-bias-has-blocked-promotions/2016/08/28/e529171e-63cf-11e6-96c0-37533479f3f5_story.html.

7. Johns M. Breaking the Glass Ceiling: Structural, Cultural, and Organizational Barriers Preventing Women from Achieving Senior and Executive Level Positions. *Perspect Health Inf Manag.* 2013:10(Winter):1e. www.ncbi.nlm.nih.gov/pmc/articles/PMC3544145.

8. *Gina Bilotti vs. Johnson & Johnson.* (December 17, 2020). https://www.smithmullin.com/wp-content/uploads/JJ-Complaint.pdf.

9. Boatman J, Wellins R, Neal S. Women Work: The Business Benefits of Closing the Gender Gap. DDI Global Leadership Forecast. 2001. https://www.yumpu.com/en/document/read/38861808/women-work-the-business-benefits-of-closing-the-gender-gap.

Chapter 26. Intersectionality

"Intersectionality is a lens through which you can see where power comes and collides, where it interlocks and intersects. It's not simply that there's a race problem here, a gender problem here, and a class or LBGTQ problem there....If we aren't intersectional, some of us, the most vulnerable, are going to fall through the cracks." — Kimberlé Crenshaw, researcher

NTERSECTIONALITY HAS ROOTS in the black feminist movement of the late 20th century, particularly articulated by scholars like Kimberlé Crenshaw, who first used the term in 1989. Intersectionality is used to describe how race, class, gender, and other individual characteristics "intersect" with one another and overlap to form an individual's unique identity. It emerged as a response to the limitations of single-axis frameworks in understanding the experiences of marginalized groups.

Crenshaw's work highlighted how systems of oppression, such as racism and sexism, intersect to create unique forms of discrimination that are often overlooked in traditional analyses.[1,2] Using an intersectional approach to understand an individual's perspective and experience is more complete, accurate, and comprehensive.

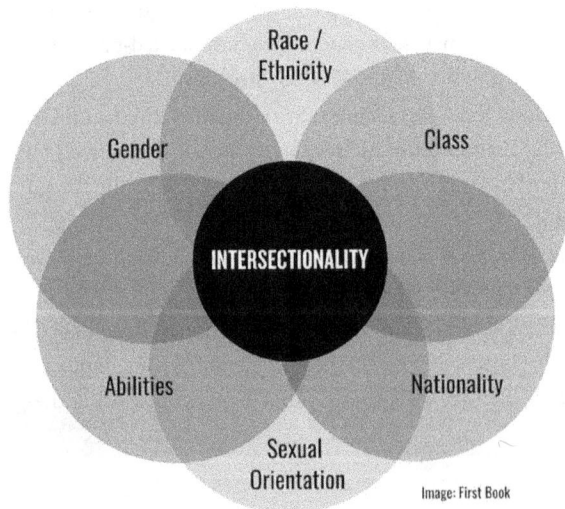

Image: First Book

FIGURE 1. Contributors to intersectionality.

Intersectionality compounds legacy systems of oppression at multiple levels of society to perpetuate inequalities. A key domain in reducing inequality is access to healthcare, and access to healthcare depends on numerous sociodemographic factors. Figure 2 represents how intersectionality impacts individual health.

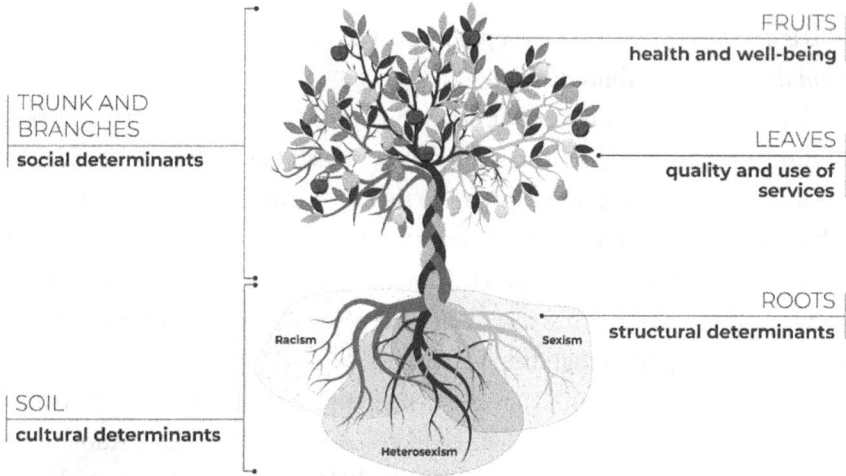

FRUITS
health and well-being

TRUNK AND BRANCHES
social determinants

LEAVES
quality and use of services

ROOTS
structural determinants

Racism

Sexism

SOIL
cultural determinants

Heterosexism

FIGURE 2. Intersectional impact on healthcare access and outcomes.[3]

Figure 2 uses a growing tree to symbolize distinct levels of the determinants of health equity, starting with ideological "soil" and ending with health and well-being, or the "fruits." Culturally oppressive ideologies such as racism, sexism, and heterosexism overlap in the soil in which the tree grows and intersect in all other parts of the tree. In turn, they affect structural determinants of health, social determinants of health, quality, and use of services, and finally, health and well-being experienced by individuals.

We focus on racism, sexism, and heterosexism to provide a clear illustration, recognizing that this is an oversimplification of intersectionality and how it operates. Systems of oppression not pictured in the figure include, but are not limited to, classism, ageism, ableism, fatphobia, ethnocentrism, colorism, and cisgenderism.

Interventions to reduce intersectional impacts include structural and institutional efforts and interventions at the personal level. Dismantling structural racism, sexism, and classism requires a conscious effort at the organizational level. This is partially accomplished through diversity, equity, and inclusion (DEI) efforts. Health policy efforts and public health initiatives specifically acknowledging and incorporating intersectional identities are necessary to reduce the negative impact.

CASE STUDY

This is a condensed interview synopsis by Davina Hayes, as told to Amy Leipziger from the Free to Be Youth Project.

A young, black transgender woman recounts facing numerous forms of discrimination and trauma. She states, "I also fall under some of many other statistics: I'm among the up to 40% of homeless youth in the U.S. who identify as LGBTQ+. I'm one of approximately 8,400 queer youth in New York City who are homeless ....I was sexually assaulted at 18 and again at 22. And the other times it may not have been called sexual assault, but something happened that didn't feel right."[4]

Young black and LatinX transgender females are among the most vulnerable population groups in the United States. A Survey of Today's Adolescent Relationships and Transitions Project in 2018 clearly demonstrated how intersectionality impacts healthcare access. The average predicted probability of experiencing problems accessing healthcare due to gender ranged from 10% for white non-binary identified youth compared to 42% and 40% for Hispanic and black transgender females.

Transgender females were least likely to be insured, least likely to have a current medical provider, least likely to be out to a provider, and most likely to experience gender-based problems with healthcare. Qualitative interviews with transgender women suggest they frequently encounter dehumanization and suspicion from providers as reactions to their gender identity and expression.[5] Individuals experiencing "double discrimination" or even "triple discrimination" through intersectional influences are at a distinct disadvantage and are uniquely positioned and vulnerable to, as stated, fall through the cracks.

REFERENCES

1. Crenshaw K. Demarginalizing the Intersection of Race and Sex: A Black Feminist Critique of Antidiscrimination Doctrine, Feminist Theory and Antiracist Politics.

University of Chicago Legal Forum. 1989;1(8). https://chicagounbound.uchicago.edu/cgi/viewcontent.cgi?article=1052&context=uclf.

2. Vohra-Gupta S, Petruzzi L, Jones C, Cubbin C. An Intersectional Approach to Understanding Barriers to Healthcare for Women. *J Community Health.* 2022;48(1):89–98.

3. Michaels E, Wesley D, O'Neill S. Intersectionality: Amplifying Impacts on Health Equity. *Mathematica.* January 26, 2023. https://vaccineresourcehub.org/resource/report-intersectionality-amplifying-impacts-health-equity.

4. Hayes D, Leipziger A. Homeless Trans Youth Are More Than Just Statistics — We're Fully Realized People. *Teen Vogue.* June 21, 2023. https://www.teenvogue.com/story/homeless-trans-youth-pride.

5. Hudson K. (Un)doing Transmisogynist Stigma in Health Care Settings: Experiences of Ten Transgender Women of Color. *J Progressive Human Services.* 2018; 30(1):1–19. doi:10.1080/10428232.2017.1412768

Chapter 27. Diversity, Equity, and Inclusion

"If we cannot now end our differences, at least we can help make the world safe for diversity." — President John F. Kennedy

"Diversity is having a seat at the table, inclusion is having a voice, and belonging is having that voice be heard." — Liz Fosslien, author and keynote speaker

STEVEN COVEY, AUTHOR of *The 7 Habits of Highly Effective People*, wrote, "Strength lies in difference, not in similarities." Over the last 50-plus years, efforts have been made to initiate changes in policy, practice, and programs that address persistent gender, racial, and socio-economic disparities and other related issues within the sociocultural context of the practice of medicine.

Investment in diversity programs and training has increased exponentially in the past two decades. In 2003, corporations spent nearly $8 billion on diversity programs, and a 2019 survey found that spending on DEI efforts had increased 27% over the five preceding academic years.[1] Future and continued investment in DEI efforts are now unclear.

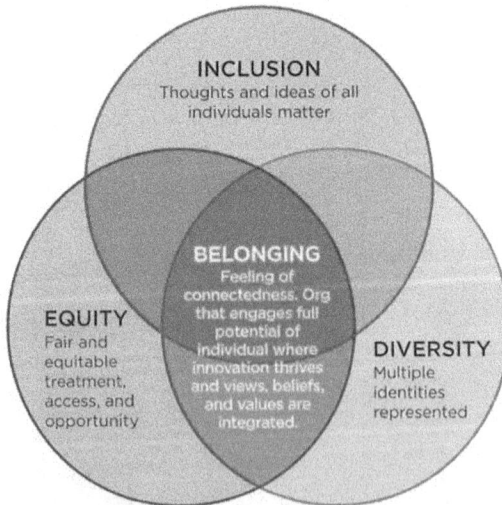

FIGURE 1. Overlap of diversity, equity, inclusion, and belonging.

Figure 1 shows the overlap between diversity, equity, and inclusion, and in the middle of the graphic, belonging. Belonging is the idea that knits the concepts and practices of DEI together into a cohesive whole. *Diversity* is how many different identities are represented, including race, gender, ethnicity, religion, sexual orientation, gender identity, and age. *Equity* ensures equal access, opportunity, and influence. It is the fair and just treatment of all members of a community. *Inclusion* refers to an intentional effort to ensure people from different identities are able to fully participate in all aspects of an organization, including leadership.

In summary, DEI is representation, equal access to opportunities, and a voice in the decision-making processes in organizations. Verna Myers stated that "diversity is being asked to the party. Inclusion is being asked to dance."[3] A fully inclusive, diverse workforce with equity allows individuals to feel a sense of belonging and being valued. These efforts have a powerful history worth examining.

In 1960, approximately 1,000 women applied to U.S. medical schools; only 600 were accepted. Women comprised 7.3% of matriculants and only 7% of accepted students.[1] Black students were not accepted into all U.S. medical schools until 1966. The American Medical Association (AMA), created in 1847, did not allow most black physicians to join until the late 1960s. Black physicians were excluded from professional and career advancement opportunities without acceptance into the AMA. Without equal access to medical schools, black students were forced to attend separate medical schools.

By the end of the 19th century, there were 14 medical schools for black students. After the Flexner report in 1910, only two remained.[2] Today, black physicians make up only 3.6% of full-time faculty at U.S. medical schools.

CASE STUDY

Fatima Cody Stanford, an obesity medicine physician-scientist, educator, and policy maker at Massachusetts General Hospital and Harvard Medical School, recalls an event she experienced as a medical student at the Medical College of Georgia School of Medicine. As a new medical student starting in 2003, she and the rest of her classmates were shown numerous pictures from the medical school archives. She noticed one black man appeared in many of them. Curious, she discovered his name was Grandison Harris, a slave whose ownership was shared among the school's seven faculty members in the 1800s.

Harris stole bodies from graveyards — mostly poor and black community members — for the medical school for over 50 years. These bodies were used as cadavers for medical student education.

Stanford, the newly elected freshman class president, said she wanted to acknowledge Harris's contributions to medical education during the school's cadaver memorial services.

In response, Stanford faced severe backlash from other students. When she arrived at class the next day, students threw items at her, and a newsletter was emailed to faculty and fellow students in which Stanford's face and body were mocked in detail. This was 2003.

According to Stanford, the harassment was one of her most horrific experiences as a black medical student. Racism is not just in the past — it is something black medical students are still facing today. Stanford reminds us that the problem is, as she says, "We aren't always welcome."[3-5]

This story illustrates that the recent backlash against diversity, equity, and inclusion (DEI) efforts is in fact a reactionary defense to preserve the status quo. Efforts to reduce or eliminate DEI programs are also an attempt to protect political and economic power. A lot of work still needs to be done to erase the unjust legacy of racism and sexism that continues to act as a barrier to much-needed progress.

Many individuals opposed to DEI efforts have not experienced discrimination or harassment firsthand and cannot relate to the lived experiences of marginalized individuals on a day-to-day basis. DEI programs recognize all historically marginalized groups, including women, LGBTQ+ individuals, underrepresented racial and ethnic groups, and the disabled. Continued support and creation of robust, effective DEI programs is essential and must continue.

REFERENCES

1. INSIGHT Staff. An INSIGHT Investigation: Accounting for Just 0.5% of Higher Education's Budgets, Even Minimal Diversity Funding Supports Their Bottom Line. Insight into Diversity. October 16, 2019. https://www.insightintodiversity.com/an-insight-investigation-accounting-for-just-0-5-of-higher-educations-budgets-even-minimal-diversity-funding-supports-their-bottom-line/.

2. Global Industry Analysts. Global Diversity and Inclusion (D&I) Industry. October 2022.

3. The Verna Mayers Company. https://learning.vernamyers.com.

4. Tan T. Principles of Inclusion, Diversity, Access, and Equity. *J Infect Dis.* 2019;220 (S2):S30–S32.

5. Tenet M. Racial Inequality in Medicine: How Did We Get Here? *Georgetown Medical Review.* 2021;5(1). doi: 10.52504/001c.25142

The Psychology, Impact, and Consequences of Sexual Misconduct

∞

Chapter 28. Perspectives on the Causes of Sexual Misconduct and Harassment

"In a world where women are systemically subjected to men's violence — it is the responsibility of men, not women, to prove that it's 'not all men.' And you don't prove it by convincing women to trust men; you prove it by convincing men not to violate women." — Farida D., Arab gender researcher and poet

THE LACK OF A UNIFYING and concise definition of sexual misconduct and harassment is a persistent problem. No single theory explains why sexual harassment, in particular, occurs. Pina and colleagues identify three widely recognized theories: sociocultural, organizational, and natural-biological theories.

Broadly, sociocultural theories incorporate the view that continued gender inequality and sexism are part of a root problem. Organizational theories focus on status inequities in organizations. Most executives and middle managers are men, and this power differential in the organization foments an environment that tolerates the behaviors. Lastly, the natural-biological theories posit that biological attraction between individuals is natural, and men are predisposed to sexually harass women due to a higher sex drive.[1]

These theories have been criticized for being too simplistic. The four-factor model, which incorporates many of the elements from these theories, proposes that sexual harassment depends on four factors[2]:

1. Motivation to harass (power, control, sexual attraction).
2. Overcoming internal inhibitions (moral restraints).
3. Overcoming external inhibitions (specific organizational workplace barriers).
4. Target resistance (assertiveness of the targets' relative status within the workplace).

Examining these theories reveals that these behaviors are a consequence of many environmental and individual influences and circumstances. An individual with few internal inhibitions placed in a tolerant environment with no barriers and vulnerable individuals sets up the behavior to occur. Conversely, an environment intolerant of these behaviors with significant barriers and empowered individuals reduces the opportunities for individuals who overcome internal inhibitions or have a proclivity to harass others.

Another motive for engaging in harassing behaviors is the preservation or exertion of social and psychological power and status. Some behaviors, especially demeaning or degrading comments or gestures, microassaults, and other microaggressions, are consciously used to create an openly hostile environment with the preservation of the extant power dynamic.

I suggest that a major reason for the recent resistance to continued funding and efforts to create an environment focused on diversity, equity, and inclusion is the fact progress is being made, and this threatens the traditional power structures in many organizations.

We get the behaviors we tolerate.

REFERENCES

1. Pina A, Gannon T, Saunder B. An Overview of the Literature on Sexual Harassment: Perpetrator, Theory, and Treatment Issues. *Aggression and Violent Behavior.* 2009;14(2):126–138.
2. O'Hare E, O'Donohue W. Sexual Harassment: Identifying Risk Factors. *Arch Sexual Behav.* 1998;27:561–580.

Chapter 29. Psychological Profiles of Offenders and Perpetrators

R ESEARCH HAS CLEARLY SHOWN the short- and long-term negative impact and psychological consequences to victims of sexual misconduct and discrimination. Only recently have studies begun to examine the personality profiles and traits of those who engage in the behavior — from less extreme forms of the behavior to sexual assault and violence. Who is more likely to engage in the behavior, and why are they engaging in the behavior?

One explanation for the dearth in the literature on this subject is the difficulty in finding study participants. Prospective studies are difficult to perform, and retrospective studies are observational and often incomplete. Despite these challenges, efforts to understand what drives the behaviors are necessary to construct more effective prevention strategies and programs.

Lee and colleagues examined the personality characteristics associated with men's sexual harassment proclivities using the Likelihood to Sexually Harass (LSH) scale developed by Pryor in 1987.[1] Pryor, a professor at Illinois State University, developed the scale in an effort to measure the likelihood that people would engage in rape if they thought they might get away with it. The more current LSH focuses only on one type of sexual harassment: coercion — a quid pro quo, bribe, or threatening punishment if there is a refusal to participate in sexual activity.

Evidence has shown that men who perform acts in one situation are likely to do the same in another situation.[2] A male's tendency to behave in a sexually exploitative manner toward women may be predicted by the LSH in combination with certain social normative factors that permit or condone such behavior.[3,4]

Lee and colleagues designed the study to examine and measure *nonoffenders'* proclivity toward sexual harassment and correlated the results with major personality traits from the Big Five and Five Factor Model developed by Costa and McCrae in 1992, in addition to incorporating the emerging sixth dimension of personality: honesty–humility.[3,4] This new personality dimension represents a willingness or reluctance to engage in behaviors that exploit others. This dimension, therefore, is useful in predicting future behaviors.

The LSH is a 10-item test administered using a variety of scenarios between men and women. In it, the individual chooses a course of action based on the situation or opportunity presented. The LSH grades responses on the spectrum of Likely (1) and Very Likely (5). Higher LSH scores correlate with a higher probability or inclination to engage in sexual harassment.

The study revealed a strong negative relationship between LSH and honesty-humility. This result is not surprising, as low honesty-humility scores represent a tendency to take advantage of others.

Although it is not legal to administer this evaluation tool to potential or current employees, it is important to understand that individuals within every organization and business have these traits and can and do take advantage of individuals if the circumstances allow it. Because training programs cannot change an individual's inclinations, organizations need to implement a zero-tolerance approach toward the behavior.[5,6]

ANTI-SOCIAL AND NARCISSISTIC PERSONALITY DISORDER CHARACTERISTICS

A recent study by Arbanas explored the prevalence of personality disorders (PDs) of sex offenders using a retrospective analysis of more than 500 individuals referred for psychiatric evaluation. Not surprisingly, 67% of sexual offenders were diagnosed with a PD. Of these offenders, 38% had antisocial PD and 32% had narcissistic PD. These two PDs are characterized by the following[6]:

Anti-Social Personality Disorder (ASPD) Characteristics:
- Repeatedly breaking the law.
- Repeatedly being deceitful.
- Being impulsive.
- Being irritable and aggressive.
- Having reckless disregard for safety for self and others.
- Being consistently irresponsible.
- Lacking remorse.

Narcissistic Personality Disorder (NPD) Characteristics:
- Having a sense of self-importance.
- Being preoccupied with power, beauty, and success.
- Feeling entitled.

- Surrounding themselves with only important or special people.
- Being interpersonally exploitive for their own gain.
- Being arrogant.
- Lacking empathy.
- Needing to be admired.

A common characteristic for both PDs is the lack of remorse or empathy. These individuals do not care about their behaviors' impact on others. It is important to note that the term *sociopath* is outdated and inaccurate. Individuals with ASPD possess sociopath tendencies and exhibit ASPD behaviors.[6]

Glen Gabbard, a contributor to *Physician Sexual Misconduct*, evaluated and treated physicians who engaged in sexual misconduct.[7] Using a psychodynamic approach, Gabbard proposed physicians fall into four distinct psychodynamic categories. It is important to keep in mind, however, that within these categories, there is considerable variation based on the unique psychodynamic features of the physician involved. This classification system is still useful, as it helps in terms of understanding motives and assists in guiding rehabilitation efforts discussed in Chapter 37[7]:

1. **Lovesickness:** These physicians cross professional boundaries after falling in love or developing strong feelings for a patient and then engaging in unethical behaviors. From Gabbard's experiences, these physicians are usually middle-aged, may be male or female, and are much older than their patients. Some of these physicians suffer from obsessive-compulsive or borderline personality disorders.

2. **Masochistic Surrender:** These physicians are devoted to their patients and "give in" to the demands and special treatment patients seek. In a typical scenario, the physician submits to a patient's tormenting demands by violating one nonsexual boundary after another. This slippery slope of boundary violations can lead to a sexualized relationship.

3. **Predatory Psychopathy and Paraphilias:** These physicians often have anti-social personality and narcissistic traits and engage in some of the most egregious sexually abusing behaviors. These physicians frequently engage in unprofessional conduct and other criminal behaviors. Before the National Practitioner Data Bank (NPDB) was

established, these physicians could easily move from state to state to continue practicing if there were behavioral or professionalism issues.

4. **Psychotic Disorders:** Physicians with psychosis or developing psychotic features are exceptionally uncommon. These physicians frequently suffer from untreated mental disorders, substance abuse, or other medical reasons that lead to the behaviors.

Tom Ealey and Cynthia Krause, in their book *Sexual Harassment: Health Care Edition: Management, Policy, and Training*, group harassers into six basic types[8]:

1. **Mr. Macho:** These individuals claim, "I am so sexy I cannot control myself."
2. **Great Gallant:** Chivalrous and charming, these individuals use charisma to persuade others.
3. **Opportunist:** If the situation allows harassment or misconduct, these individuals take advantage of the opportunity.
4. **Power Player:** These individuals use their positions of authority to intimidate and coerce others.
5. **Serial Harasser:** These individuals pursue multiple targets at any opportunity.
6. **Situational Harasser:** This is someone who usually has no past history of engaging in harassment but takes advantage of conditions that create opportunity.

Case Study: A Physician with Psychosis

A female resident physician became manic with psychotic features, thinking the television was telling her she could cure schizophrenia through love. She helped a male patient with schizophrenia escape from the hospital and had sex with him to cure him. She went on a chaotic cross-country trip and repeatedly had sex with the patient. Subsequently, she was hospitalized and obtained appropriate treatment for her mania.

REFERENCES

1. Lee K, Gizzarone M, Ashton M. Personality and the Likelihood to Sexually Harass. *Sex Roles: A Journal of Research.* 2003;90(2):59–69.
2. Pryor JB. Sexual Harassment Proclivities in Men. *Sex Roles: A Journal of Research.* 1987;17:269–290.

3. Martin M. How Likely Is Someone to Sexually Harass Others? This Scale Determines. *NPR Heard on All Things Considered.* January 14, 2018.

4. Pryor J B, Giedd J L, Williams K B. A Social Psychological Model for Predicting Sexual Harassment. *J Social Issues.* 1995:51(1): 69–84.

5. Pryor J B, LaVite C, Stoller L. A Social Psychological Analysis of Sexual Harassment: The Person/Situation Interaction. *J Vocational Behavior.* 1993;42(1):68–83.

6. Arbanas G. Personality Disorders in Sex Offenders, Compared to Offenders of Other Crimes. *J Sexual Medicine.* 2022;19(Suppl. 4):S39.

7. Gabbard G. Psychodynamic Approaches to Physician Sexual Misconduct. In: Bloom J, Nadelson C, Notman Meds. *Physician Sexual Misconduct.* Washington, DC: American Psychiatric Press;1999.

8. Ealey T, Krause C. *Sexual Harassment: Health Care Edition: Management, Policy, and Training.* Ealey Publishing; 2019.

Chapter 30. Female Perpetrators of Sexual Misconduct

"Although I wish I had recognized the abuse earlier, talking to someone openly and honestly about what I have experienced helps me understand that I am not to blame." — Anonymous

"I was sexually abused by my mom for several years. I felt ashamed about being forced and asked to do things she asked. I hated it, and when I was a young teen, I started cutting myself and thought about suicide. Who was I supposed to tell? I lived alone with her, and she drank constantly. I knew once she started drinking, it would happen. I left the house at 17 to live at a friend's house. I still feel shame as an adult, and I still cannot believe it happened. It is a secret only a few people know about." — Anonymous male survivor

OTHER THAN A FEW CASE REPORTS, not much is known about the characteristics of females who engage in sexual abuse and misconduct. A recent study found that 882 nurses were reported to the NPDB for sexual misconduct. Most were aged 35–54; 63.2% were male and 36.8% were female. The study did not analyze the types of behaviors or misconduct involved in the reports, and nothing was reported on other characteristics besides age and gender.[1]

Female-perpetrated sexual misconduct and abuse, though not as common as male-perpetrated abuse, does occur, and it is less well studied due to the stereotype that women are largely seen as incapable of engaging in misconduct and predatory behaviors.

There is no reason to suspect major differences in motivation or personal characteristics between females working in the healthcare professions and other service professions who engage in sexual misconduct. A handful of studies have examined female teachers who have sexually abused their students, and a recent qualitative study explored the characteristics of 35 female teachers who sexually abused their students.[2]

Most of the abuse, approximately 63%, occurred after numerous professional boundary violations, including inappropriate contact and text messages and provocative comments in the classroom. Of the sample cohort, 19% described their relationship with the student as a friendship before the abuse; 17% indicated they sought emotional support from the student following a traumatic event.

When asked if she used her profession to gain access to victims, one of the perpetrators stated, "I am a great teacher and went into the profession to help children and make a positive difference." Many of the offenders used leverage to begin sexual relations with their students, such as alcohol, drugs, gifts, threats of lowering grades, and tutoring. Many of these women slowly violated professional boundaries for a variety of reasons using a variety of means.[1]

Many of the offenders had past histories of being sexually or physically abused as children or adolescents. There is evidence linking being a victim and being a perpetrator. Still, a limitation of extending these findings to women is that most studies have only investigated male perpetrators and offenders.[3] Although the qualitative and quantitative evidence supports the assertion that perpetrators are more likely to have a history of abuse, this does not necessarily mean those who have been sexually abused will become perpetrators.

Another critical difference when comparing female teachers and health-care professionals is the amount of time teachers spend with victims in a learning environment vs. the amount of time female healthcare professionals spend with patients in the healthcare environment. Very few female teachers engage in inappropriate contact without establishing some form of emotional bond or other relationship. Daily and frequent contact with students allows these bonds to form. Contact with the same individual in a healthcare environment is temporal and brief in comparison; there is less opportunity to bond with patients.

In the healthcare setting, psychologists and psychiatrists spend many hours with patients. In these settings, creating an emotional connection that can break down barriers and lead to crossing boundaries is far easier. In a study published in the mid-1990s, four out of 40 women who a therapist sexually abused said a female therapist abused them. The study was not large enough to draw any conclusions about the motives or characteristics of the female providers.[4]

The goal for organizations is to create a culture that is consciously aware of the problem and has communicated that any conduct concerns will be taken seriously regardless of who is engaged in the behaviors. Psychological safety and objective and unbiased investigations thwart individuals more apt to take advantage of others. It's an institutional and organizational responsibility to accept accountability and have the courage to make changes for improvement.

REFERENCES

1. AbuDagga A, Wolfe SM, Carome M, Oshel RE. Crossing the Line: Sexual Misconduct by Nurses Reported to the National Practitioner Data Bank. *Public Health Nurs.* 2019;36(2):109–117. doi: 10.1111/phn.12567

2. Steely M, Ten Bensel T. Child Sexual Abuse within Educational Settings: A Qualitative Study on Female Teachers Who Sexually Abuse Their Students. *Deviant Behavior.* 2019;41(11): 1440–1453. doi: 10.1080/01639625.2019.1624288

3. Glasser M, Kolvin I, Campbell D, Glasser A, Leitch I, Farrelly S. Cycle of Child Sexual Abuse: Links Between Being a Victim and Becoming a Perpetrator. *Br J Psychiatry.* 2001;179: 482–494. doi: 10.1192/bjp.179.6.482

4. Quadrio C. Sexual Abuse in Therapy: Gender Issues. *Aust N Z Psychiatry.* 1996;30(1):124-131.

Chapter 31. Mental and Physical Health Impact on Victims

"You took away my worth, my privacy, my energy,
my time, my safety, my intimacy, my confidence,
my own voice... until now." — Anonymous

"There is no timestamp on trauma. There isn't a formula
that you can insert yourself into to get from horror to healed.
Be patient. Take up space. Let your journey be the balm."
— Dawn Serra, clinical counselor and relationship coach

As discussed in Chapter 14, victims of sexual misconduct or harassment may not come forward for a variety of reasons. However, it can be difficult for victims to hide the consequences of the misconduct or harassment.

If a colleague suddenly becomes withdrawn or does not seem to be "himself or herself" at work, that individual may be a victim of misconduct or harassment. A decline in productivity, increased absenteeism, changes in appearance, changes in attitude, and avoidant behaviors can be signs of abuse but may also be the result of other conditions, including illness, substance use disorders, or mental health disorders. Physical signs include bruising or unusual physical injuries.

It is often difficult to determine the causes of many of the behaviors of victims, and employees do not have a legal obligation to report their own abuse. Although it may seem uncomfortable, work colleagues should ask colleagues open-ended questions about any alarming changes in appearance or behavior. *Something* is not going well in that person's life — whether at home or at work. Sexual misconduct or harassment might be a reason.

Victims of sexual assault, misconduct, and harassment often develop an array of serious mental and physical health problems. Victims can develop depression, anxiety, sleep disorders, eating disorders, lower self-esteem, and weight loss or gain. Increased absenteeism or job loss can exacerbate these conditions and cause additional stress that can begin to take a toll on the victim's physical health.

PTSD is common for victims of sexual assault, and feelings of fear, shame, anger, and guilt can affect personal and social relationships. Negative coping mechanisms include using drugs or alcohol, which can have an immediate and long-lasting impact on the physical well-being of victims.[1,2] Figure 1 shows the results of a 2019 study finding an association between a history of sexual assault and sexual harassment and the development of a higher incidence of hypertension, sleep disorders, depression, and anxiety.[3]

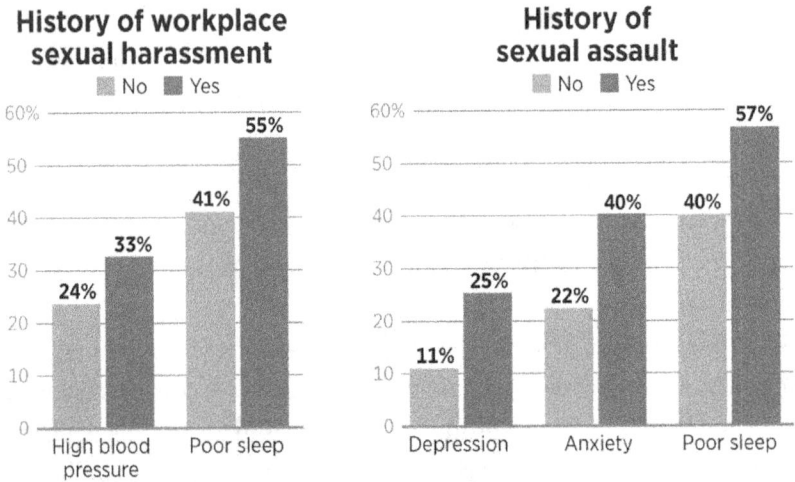

FIGURE 1. Association of history of sexual harassment and sexual assault with prevalence of hypertension and poor sleep.[3]

Almost one-third of rape victims develop PTSD, and nearly 10% continue to suffer from PTSD years after the event. Additionally, one-third of victims of rape experience at least one major episode of depression. Victims are 13 times more likely than non-victims to develop alcohol use disorders and 26 times more likely to develop substance use disorders than non-victims. Suicidal ideation is four times more likely, and attempted suicide is 13 times more likely in victims than non-victims.[1]

Given the high incidence and prevalence of sexual violence and assault, it remains a significant public health issue. Analysis of the 1995-1996 National Violence Against Women Survey (NVAWS) revealed that 41.5% of intimate partner assaults resulted in physical injury, 28.1% of which led to medical treatment; approximately 28% of those who experienced physical assaults, rape, and stalking by an intimate partner received some type of mental health counseling.[4]

REFERENCES

1. Kilpatrick D. The Mental Health Impact of Rape. National Violence Against Women Prevention Research Center. Medical University of South Carolina, 2000. https://mainweb-v.musc.edu/vawprevention/research/mentalimpact.shtml.

2. Dworkin E, Menon S, Bystrynski J, Allen N. Sexual Assault Victimization and Psychopathology: A Review and Meta-Analysis. *Clin Psychol Rev.* 2017;56:65–81.

3. Thurston RC, Chang Y, Matthews KA, von Kanel R, Koenen K. Association of Sexual Harassment and Sexual Assault with Midlife Women's Mental and Physical Health. *JAMA Intern Med.* 2019;179(1):48–53. doi:10.1001/jamainternmed.2018.4886

4. McLean G, Gonzalez-Bocinski S. The Economic Cost of Intimate Partner Violence, Sexual Assault, and Stalking. Fact Sheet Institute for Women's Policy Research. August 2017. https://iwpr.org/wp-content/uploads/2020/10/B367_Economic-Impacts-of-IPV-08.14.17.pdf.

Chapter 32. The Second-Victim Effect

"Behind every brave face is a heart that has carried
the weight of countless stories." —*Unknown*

THE DIRECT PSYCHOLOGICAL IMPACT on victims and targets of sexual assault and discrimination is well investigated and studied; there is less research on "second victims" — those who witness events, listen to stories of events (therapists and investigators), and those who know the victims personally.

For example, close family members of a sexually abused individual can feel the impact of the trauma. When this trauma impact is unacknowledged, it can become disenfranchised grief — grief that is not or cannot be, openly acknowledged, socially validated, or supported. In many households where sexual abuse occurs, a "code of silence" may be enforced by the perpetrator and then reinforced indirectly by the victim because of a fear of retaliation or harm.[1,2]

A study from the late 1980s investigating the effects on children who witnessed the sexual assaults of their mothers found that all of the children who witnessed the event developed moderate to severe PTSD symptoms.[3]

CASE STUDY

This case study is an account by a woman who describes the events following the discovery of her father sexually abusing her sister as a small child.[4]

I was eight years old when I found out my father had been sexually abusing my sister. It was later that I began to learn the details, which included the number of years and what sexual abuse meant. My frame of reference at that time was a TV movie in which a coach was abusing a 5-year-old member of his team. At that time, I did not fully understand that it involved more than inappropriate touching.

When my mother found out, she reported it to the police and took my sister through the beginning of the legal and medical processes. I, on the other hand, went to one of my favorite places in the world, my aunt's house, to visit with my cousins. I played all day without a care in the world. That evening, my mother, who I knew was distraught about something, told me that my father had left us. My response was to reassure her that he would come back. I do remember being sad because I was "daddy's girl." Up to that point, we had never been apart. During the next few days, we relocated temporarily out of state.

Two months later, we moved back to our home so I could return to school. During this time, my father was arrested, released on bail, and was awaiting trial. The false narrative that I created in my 8-year-old mind was that he was off somewhere thinking that he had made a mistake to leave our family and would return soon.

With the encouragement of a therapist, my mother told me what my father had done. I remember staring at the ground when my mom told me why my father was no longer in our lives. I understood that my father had touched my sister in a sexual way and that it was wrong. According to my mother, my reaction was to call her a liar and to tell her that my father would never do that. There was an understanding that outside of the counselor's office, I was not supposed to talk about what happened. I began to know that our family was "different" and damaged.

I struggled with reconciling the father that I knew with the perpetrator that my sister knew. There was guilt, because he hurt her, and he didn't hurt me. I was confused about how I should feel about him and how I should feel about my sister. I was sad that I had lost him. I didn't feel special anymore. I became the "hidden child" in the household. I physically and emotionally lost my dad. I couldn't talk about him; I couldn't mourn him. It was like he didn't exist. But he was still very much at the center of our world because we had to deal with what he did. His actions dictated everything in our lives at that time.[4]

EXTENDED TRAUMA

In addition to caring for the victims of primary abuse, physicians, psychologists, and social workers should appreciate the impact of witnesses and the second victims. Therapy, support, and the opportunity to address mental health issues and disorders should be offered if necessary. Rather than keeping family members out of the immediate circle of support, including them with transparency, honesty, and openness can help second victims process the events.[4]

Another phenomenon is the secondary trauma therapists experience when counseling and treating victims of sexual abuse and assault. Therapists working with clients who have been traumatized can develop long-lasting, detrimental effects, including PTSD.[5] Preventing secondary trauma and mitigating the negative psychological effects on counselors is a worthy goal. Judith Herman sums up the issue well when she states, "Just as no survivor can recover alone, no therapist can work with trauma alone."[6]

Several organizational approaches prevent secondary trauma and create a supportive environment. Catherall developed a five-step plan for institutions[7]:

1. Identify staff level of exposure to secondary trauma.
2. Develop a plan with staff on handling the stress of secondary trauma and creating avenues for discussion.
3. Provide psychoeducation for staff on secondary trauma.
4. Create a "preparedness structure" to highlight the organization's philosophy and plan on mitigating and handling secondary trauma.
5. Evaluate the plan for effectiveness.

Munroe and colleagues posit that there are three basic tenets in dealing with secondary trauma in a team setting: (1) accepting the reality of secondary trauma, (2) understanding that secondary trauma is not a personal defect but a natural response, and (3) finally, accurately responding to secondary trauma.[8]

Munroe further states, "A community absorbs the traumatic experience of an individual by diffusing its effects among many people and demonstrating that the survivor's feelings are understood." Using a team approach and fostering open discussion normalizes the therapist's responses and creates a safe environment for discussion and diffusion of personal impact.[8]

As much as individuals have a responsibility for self-care, institutions have a responsibility to create, maintain, and monitor supportive, safe environments, recognizing the impact of secondary trauma not only on therapists but for all caregivers in the healthcare setting. Nurses and physicians in emergency departments also develop secondary trauma care for victims of assault and sexual assault.

Emergency room care is vastly different from an outpatient, structured, and scheduled setting with less time pressure and immediate stress. The effects are the same, and there is less time for healthcare workers in acute settings to make time for decompression and discussion in a high-pressure, time-pressured environment. As a result, healthcare workers in these settings receive less organizational support, and creating a "team" environment is logistically difficult. A different approach is necessary; end-of-shift huddles or briefings can help. It is important to emphasize that no one is alone.

Families, close friends, and co-workers can also suffer from the second-victim effect. The issues are difficult to discuss, and most people do not know how to provide emotional support for victims of sexual assault.

For victims, intimacy and navigating sex and sexuality after a sexual assault is challenging. Changes in sexuality include a loss of interest in sex, an increase or change in sexual partners, or an increase in sexual behaviors. Some survivors of sexual trauma also experience being triggered by sexual intimacy as a result of PTSD. Dissolution of relationships and difficulty forming new relationships is also difficult.

REFERENCES

1. Doka K, ed. *Disenfranchised Grief: New Directions, Challenges, and Strategies for Practice.* Research Press;2002.

2. Corr C. Enhancing Concept of Disenfranchised Grief. *Omega.* 1998;38(1):1–20.

3. Pynoos R, Nader K. Children Who Witness the Sexual Assaults of Their Mothers. *J Am Acad Child Adolesc Psychiatry.* 1988;27(5):567–572. doi: 10.1097/00004583 -198809000-00009

4. Zoll L, Davila L. Disenfranchised Trauma: The Impact on Indirect Victims. *The New Social Worker.* Winter 2021. https://www.socialworker.com/feature-articles/practice/ disenfranchised-trauma-impact-indirect-victims/.

5. Hesse A. Secondary Trauma: How Working with Trauma Survivors Affects Therapists. *Clinical Social Work Journal.* 2002;30(3): 293–309.

6. Herman J. *Trauma and Recovery.* Basic Books;1992.

7. Catherall D. Preventing Institutional Secondary Traumatic Stress Disorder. In C.R. Figley, ed. *Compassion Fatigue: Coping with Secondary Traumatic Stress Disorder in Those Who Treat the Traumatized.* New York: Taylor & Francis;1995:232–248.

8. Munroe J, Shay J, Fisher L, Makary C, Rapperport K, Zimering R. Preventing Compassion Fatigue: A Team Treatment Model. In C.R. Figley, ed. *Compassion Fatigue: Secondary Traumatic Stress Disorder from Treating the Traumatized.* New York: Taylor & Francis;1995:209–231.

Chapter 33. Trauma-Informed Care

"Being trauma-informed can help us change the message from 'what is wrong with you' to 'what happened to you?'" — Marci Gordeyko, clinical director and clinical psychologist, University of Toronto

TRAUMA-INFORMED CARE (TIC) or trauma and violence-informed care (TVIC) is a framework for helping patients who have experienced negative consequences as a result of exposure to or as a victim of violence, severe accidents, sexual abuse, sexual violence, or trauma.

Mental health practitioners Maxine Harris and Roger Fallot published a research paper in 2001 introducing a structured approach to treating children who've lived through a traumatic experience resulting in spiritual, emotional, and psychological damage.[1] Government agencies and researchers immediately began exploring the concept, including the Substance Abuse and Mental Health Services Administration (SAMHSA), which began measuring the effectiveness of TIC programs. In 2000, the U.S. Congress created the National Child Traumatic Stress Network (NCTSN), which the SAMHSA administers.

The Australian National Trauma-Informed Care & Practice Advisory Group states that trauma-informed care "... acknowledges and clearly articulates that no one understands the challenges of the recovery journey from trauma better than the person living it. This requires that practitioners are attuned to a person's experience and the dynamics of trauma and acknowledge, respect, and validate that experience."[2]

A cornerstone in caring for patients who have experienced trauma is interacting with the patients in a manner that does not further traumatize them. This approach uses new questions: Instead of asking patients "What's wrong with you?" ask, "What happened to you?"[2] This helps patients begin to understand they are not to be blamed for the event. This reframing of the event is the first step in addressing patients' and survivors' needs.

RESPONDING TO A DISCLOSURE OF SEXUAL ASSAULT OR INTIMATE PARTNER VIOLENCE

Using a patient-centered approach is at the center of providing care. The most important skill is communicating empathically and compassionately when a patient discloses a traumatic event. Julia Palmieri and Julie Valentine suggest using acknowledging and affirming statements and questions. They stress the importance of believing the patient and accepting without judgment[3]:

1. *Use acknowledging statements.*
   - "Thank you for sharing."
   - "I'm so sorry this happened to you."
2. *Avoid blaming the survivor.*
   - Avoid questions that can be perceived as placing blame on the survivor.
   - Never ignore or distract from a disclosure.
3. *Ask how you can help.*
   - "How can I help?"
   - "What can I do during your visit to help you feel comfortable?"
   - "I see that you marked 'yes' on the screening survey. Would you like to talk about it?"
   - "Sharing these events can sometimes bring back negative feelings. I want this to be a place where you can feel safe and healing. What can I do to help you feel more comfortable during your visit?"
   - "Many of my patients who have shared similar experiences have benefited from seeing a team member who does behavioral health. They are good at supporting you while working through those experiences. Can I give you a referral?"
4. *Ask questions that promote resiliency.*
   - "What has given you strength in the past during a hard time?"[6]
   - "Who in your life do you have a strong connection with?"
   - "What are you doing when you have moments of happiness?"
   - "What thoughts or actions give you hope?"
   - "What do you do to take care of yourself or others?"

Raja and colleagues created specific suggestions in five domains for implementing a trauma-informed approach to caring for patients[4]:

1. **Patient-Centered Communication and Care**
   Ask every patient what can be done to make them feel more comfortable. Explain physical exams and present a brief summary of what

needs to be done. Give the patient an opportunity to shift an item of clothing out of the way rather than putting on a gown. If the patient appears anxious, offer them a way to signal distress verbally or with a hand gesture .

2. **Understanding the Health Effects of Trauma**

   Maladaptive coping behaviors, including substance abuse, alcohol use, overeating, and high-risk sexual behaviors may indicate a past history of trauma. Engage the patient in a non-judgmental way and explain the adverse health effects of continued maladaptive coping behaviors.

3. **Interprofessional Collaboration**

   Patients with a history of trauma often require care from healthcare professionals across multiple disciplines. Creating and maintaining relationships and connections with specialists and counselors provides the patient with access to necessary care. Using an engaging team-centered approach also ensures some degree of continuity of care.

4. **Understanding Your Own History and Reactions**

   Healthcare providers with their own history of trauma experiences are influenced by those experiences, and this may affect patient care. Healthcare providers who lack insight into how their experiences influence patient care may or may not provide objective care. Healthcare providers must be keenly aware of their own burnout and learn good self-care.

5. **Screening**

   Screening tools for past and present trauma are often specialty-specific. Additionally, choosing a face-to-face or self-reporting form for disclosure is an important consideration. Staff should be trained on how to communicate with a patient with a past or current history of trauma. This is best accomplished with role-playing and practice.

Equity-centered trauma-informed care anchors the core principles of trauma-informed care with an appreciation of the intersectionality of the patient (Figure 1). SAMHSA identifies a sixth principle, the "hub" in the equity-centered wheel that identifies the ways in which[5]:

"... The organization actively moves past cultural stereotypes and biases (e.g. based on race, ethnicity, sexual orientation, age, religion, gender-identity, geography, etc.); offers access to gender-responsive services; leverages the

healing value of traditional cultural connections; incorporates policies, protocols, and processes that are responsive to the racial, ethnic and cultural needs of individuals served; and recognizes and addresses historical trauma."

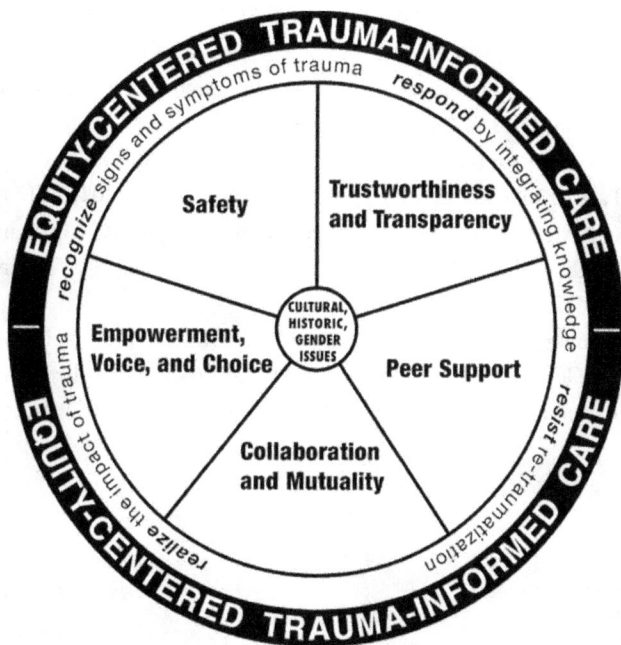

FIGURE 1. Equity-centered trauma-informed care.

SAMHSA describes trauma-informed care through the 4 Rs: *realizing* the widespread impact of trauma, *recognizing* signs of trauma, *responding* to trauma with efficacy and compassion, and *resisting* retraumatization.[6] Effective trauma-informed care requires organizations to appreciate cultural differences, legacy racism, and historical inequities.

The wheel in Figure 1 forces one to examine trauma-informed care as a dynamic interplay; importantly, however, once cultural, historical, and gender issues become the lens through which we view, analyze, and practice the principles of trauma-informed care, we effectively shift "margin to center" and begin the work needed to create an equity framework for trauma-informed care.

REFERENCES

1. Harris M , Fallot R. Envisioning a Trauma-Informed Service System: A Vital Paradigm Shift. *New Directions for Mental Health Services.* 2001;89:3–22. doi:10.1002/yd.23320018903. PMID 11291260

2. Bateman J, Henderson C. *Trauma-Informed Care and Practice, Consultation on the Development of a National Approach To Trauma-Informed Care and Practice (TICP).* Mental Health Coordinating Council, Sydney, Australia; 2011.

3. Raja S, Hasnain M, Hoersch M, Gove-Yin S, Rajagopalan C. Trauma-Informed Care in Medicine: Current Knowledge and Future Research Directions. *Fam Community Health.* 2015;38(3):216–226. doi: 10.1097/FCH.0000000000000071

4. Palmieri J, Valentine J. Using-Trauma-Informed Care To Address Sexual Assault and Intimate Partner Violence in Primary Care. *J Nurse Practition.* 2021;17(1):44–48.

5. Thompson P, Marsh H. Centering Equity: Trauma-Informed Principles and Feminist Practice. In: Thompson P, Carello J, eds. *Trauma-Informed Pedagogies.* Palgrave Macmillan, Cham;2022. doi: 10.1007/978-3-030-92705-9_2

6. Substance Abuse and Mental Health Services Administration. SAMHSA's Concept of Trauma and Guidance for a Trauma-Informed Approach. Rockville, MD: Substance Abuse and Mental Health Services Administration; 2014.

Chapter 34. Burnout Implications

"Although I wish I had have recognised the abuse earlier
talking to someone openly and honestly about what I
have experienced helps me understand that I am not to
blame." — *Anonymous domestic abuse survivor*

BURNOUT IS UBIQUITOUS IN MEDICINE, and nearly half of all health-care professionals exhibit at least one sign or symptom of burnout.[1,2] First described and reported in 1974 by Herbert Freudenberger, burnout is best described as a state of mental, physical, and emotional exhaustion caused by prolonged and excessive stress. Among the many contributing factors and conditions affecting the prevalence and incidence of burnout in healthcare is sexual harassment.

In 1981, Christina Maslach introduced the Maslach Burnout Inventory (MBI) to assess levels of burnout in three separate domains: emotional exhaustion, personal accomplishment, and depersonalization.[2] Participants answer 22 questions in the three domains, and an aggregate score is used to quantify and qualify the level of burnout. It remains the standard measurement instrument in research on burnout.

Multiple studies have shown associations between sexual harassment and burnout.[3,4,5] In a survey of female surgeons, rates of burnout were higher when they experienced sexual harassment.[3] Women physicians experiencing sexual harassment also report lower job satisfaction, reduction in professional effort, and a desire to reduce work hours.[4]

Female medical students who experience sexual harassment report higher rates of burnout, particularly when the behaviors are recurrent.[5] Indirect harassment increases burnout in women faculty, and a 2019 study of radiation oncology residents reported a 27% incidence rate of sexual harassment and an overall 95% burnout rate.[6]

Even more concerning is a finding that work stresses, including sexual harassment, may increase the risk for suicide in women physicians.[7]

Sexual harassment creates conditions that act as a catalyst for burnout. Cynthia Stonnington and Julia Files, editors of *Burnout in Women Physicians: Prevention, Treatment, and Management,* include powerful accounts of female physicians who are subjected to racism, sexism, and discrimination in rural areas.[8] Unwelcome environments increase burnout and importantly, these physicians often choose to leave and establish practices elsewhere.

Burnout is also common in nursing and other allied healthcare professionals, including physical therapists, occupational therapists, pharmacists, and respiratory therapists. Not surprisingly, women allied healthcare professionals and nurses are at increased risk for burnout if they experience sexual harassment.[9] Lack of support, fear of retaliation, and facing barriers to safely reporting the behaviors exacerbate the negative work environment and circumstances.

Glomb *et al.*, published a study examining the consequences of both direct and indirect exposure to sexual harassment as a workplace stressor.[10] Although this study did not investigate burnout directly, it did propose that both direct and indirect exposure to sexual harassment would negatively impact job satisfaction, health conditions, and psychological conditions.

Figure 1 presents the antecedents and consequences of two groups in their study: those who directly experienced sexual harassment and another group who experienced indirect *or ambient sexual harassment* of other group members.[10]

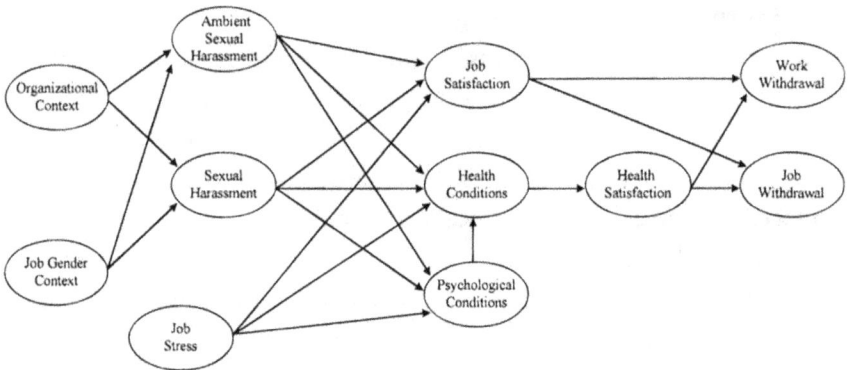

FIGURE 1. Integrated model of antecedents and consequences of ambient sexual harassment and sexual harassment.

The impact on job satisfaction, health conditions, and psychological conditions is pervasive for *both* groups. The results of their study suggest that work environments tolerant of sexual harassment negatively impact all members of the work environment. The results of this study led me to believe burnout rates are higher for women in organizations tolerant of sexually harassing behaviors. A relatively recent study found that sexually harassing behaviors from patients lead to higher rates of emotional exhaustion.[9]

REFERENCES

1. Stodolska A, Wojcik G, Baranska I, Kujowska V, Szczerbinska K. Prevalence of Burnout Among Healthcare Professionals During the COVID-19 Pandemic and Associated Factors — A Scoping Review. *Int J Occup Med Environ Health*. 2023;36(10; 21–58. doi:10.13075/ijomeh.1896.02007

2. Iwanicki E, Schwab, R. A Cross-validation Study of the Maslach Burnout Inventory. *Educational and Psychological Measurement*. 1981;41(4): 1167–1174.

3. Ceppa D, Dolejs S, Boden N, Phelan S, *et al.* Sexual Harassment and Cardiothoracic Surgery--#UsToo? *Ann Thorac Surg*. 2020:109(4):1283–1288.

4. West C, Dyrbye LN, Shanafelt TD. Physician Burnout: Contributors, Consequences and Solutions. *J Intern Med*. 2018;283(6):516–529.

5. Cook A, Arora V, Rasinski K, Curlin F, Yoon J. The Prevalence of Medical Student Mistreatment and Its Association with Burnout. *Acad Med*. 2014;89(5):749–754.

6. Osborn V, Koke K, Griffith K, Jones R, Lee A, Maquilan G, Masters A, *et al.* A Survey Study of Female Radiation Oncology Residents' Experiences to Inform Change. *Int J Radiat Oncol Biol Physics*. 2019;104(5):999–1088. doi:10.1016/j.ijrobp.2019.05.013

7. Fridner A, Belkic K, Marini M, Minucci D, Paven L, Gustafsson K. Survey on Recent Suicidal Ideation Among Female University Hospital Physicians in Sweden and Italy (The HOUPE Study): Cross-Sectional Associations with Work Stressors. Gend Med. 2009;6(1):314–328. doi:10.1016/j.genm.2009.04.006

8. Stonnington C, Files, J. *Burnout in Women Physicians: Prevention, Treatment, and Management*. Springer Nature;2020.

9. Linos E, Lansky-Fink J, Halley M, Sarkar U, Mangurian C. Impact of Sexual Harassment and Social Support on Burnout in Physician Mothers. *J Women's Health*. 2022;31(7):932–940.

10. Glomb T, Richman W, Hulin C, Drasgow F, Schneider K, Fitzgerald L. Ambient Sexual Harassment: An Integrated Model of Antecedents and Consequences. *Organizational Behavior and Human Decision Processes*. 1997;71(3):309–328. doi: 10.1006/obhd.1997.2728

Chapter 35. Psychological Safety

"Psychological safety at work takes effort. It's not the norm, but it's worth the effort."— Amy Edmundson, organizational leadership expert

WILLIAM KAHN FIRST INTRODUCED psychological safety in 1990.[1] Psychologically safe environments allow and encourage individuals to challenge the status quo in order to innovate and evolve their operations or practices without fear of negative consequences. Organizations and institutions that promote and create a safe environment are more productive, and employees are more engaged.

Medicine is a profession in which the achievement of a psychologically safe environment would seem essential to provide safe, effective, high-quality patient care; unfortunately, the medical profession has a problem with overt psychological toxicity.[2,3] All forms of harassment (including sexual harassment), bullying, and other unprofessional behaviors continue to occur. A recent survey of German physicians reported that 70% had experienced workplace harassment, and a report from the National Academy of Sciences in the United States revealed that more than 50% of women experienced sexual harassment in academic medicine environments.[4] In Canada, 75% of resident physicians report experiences of harassment — up 30% from that of a comparable survey of Canadian trainees conducted over a decade ago. This rate of harassment is simply unacceptable.[5]

How can a healthcare organization that promotes patient safety be indifferent (or oblivious) to the harm caused by harassment? How is it that despite knowing the benefits of cultivating psychological safety, organizations fail and seem unable to achieve it? A major barrier to improving culture is our collective acceptance of harassment as part of our professional experience. We have normalized the behaviors.

Promoting professionalism and respectful communication and behaviors is part of the process for improvement. Creating and maintaining a psychologically safe environment to reduce sexual harassment and misconduct requires addressing all forms of harassment and bullying behaviors, as well as racism and discrimination. I posit that an organization tolerant of unprofessional conduct will have issues with *all* forms of harassment — including sexual harassment.

Historically, professional behavior and professionalism have often been promoted through self-regulation, meaning holding each other accountable for our behaviors. However, if self-regulation worked, codes of conduct and training programs would not be necessary.[3]

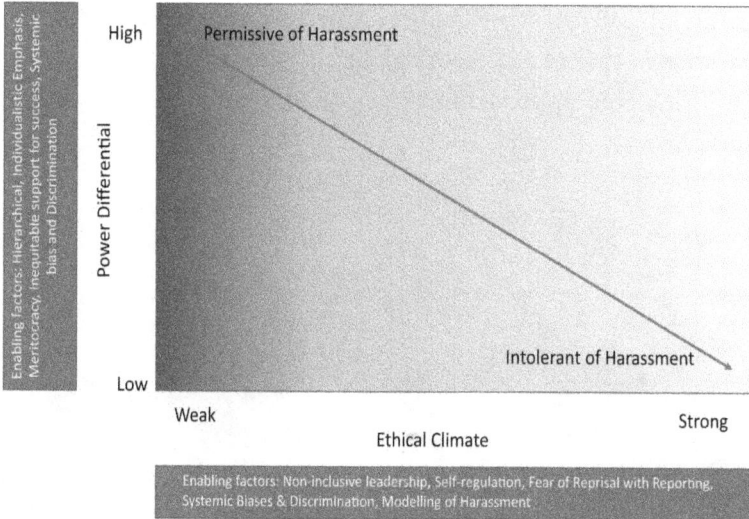

FIGURE 1. Determinants of psychological safety.[3]

Fartoon Siad and Doreen Rabi created the graphic in Figure 1 to demonstrate the relationship between power differentials and ethical climate. The ethical climate of an organization is the shared perception of its members toward its own practices. In strongly ethical work and learning environments, there is an intolerance of harassment; conversely, in environments that are ethically weak with large power differentials, there is increased tolerance.[3] Several cultural practices and beliefs in medicine contribute to a weak ethical climate.

First, there is a belief that medical training is inherently dehumanizing. Medical trainees endure long hours of training, lack of sleep, and no time for self-care in a high-pressure environment. Second, intolerance of these behaviors is often perceived as a sign of weakness or lack of professional fit. Compounding this problem is the collective cultural perspective that a career in medicine requires self-sacrifice. Acceptance of the behaviors is just part of the journey.

Institutions offering programs emphasizing personal resilience are tacitly validating the perspective that medicine is a rough business. While providing and promoting resilience training is important, completely offloading institutional responsibility onto individuals to learn how to navigate a toxic and harassing environment is a moral and ethical failure. Shifting the culture toward an ethically strong climate requires institutions to be responsible for investing in change and creating a safe environment.

A multifaceted approach is required to create a safe environment (Figure 2).

Power & Knowledge Sharing	Evaluation & Accountability
1) Inclusive leadership (compassionate, courageous, collaborative, culturally intelligent, cognizant curious)	Track and report on admission, hiring, wellness, harassment, promotion and pay
2) Incentivize and reward collaborative success	Potential Key Performance Indicators:
3) Value and seek diverse experience & expertise	- Representation at every level
4) Intentionally inclusive admission, hiring & promotion practices	- Closure of gaps in opportunity
5) Commitment to competency in equitable & inclusive medicine & education	- Closure of gaps in wellness
	- Elimination of workplace harassment
Creating a Strong Ethical Environment	
1) Culture of humility (normalize apologies)	
2) Clearly stated standards of practice re: equitable & inclusive professional behavior	
3) Clearly articulated accountability for breaches in standards	
4) Emphasis on collective wellbeing	
5) Responsiveness when harm occurs (emphasis on restorative Justice)	

FIGURE 2. Creating psychologically safe environments.[3]

In addition to the initiatives and actions outlined in Figure 2, there must be an effort to recruit equity-deserving individuals who have historically faced discrimination, provide training in implicit and explicit bias, provide training in bystander intervention, develop competency in health equity, and adopt restorative justice models of accountability. There must be acknowledgment of and a willingness to reflect with honesty and humility on how the field of medicine has created a culture that permits ongoing harm to colleagues and, by extension, patients.

Establishing and maintaining psychological safety is the responsibility of the organization's executive leadership. Little progress will be made if the organization lacks strong leaders who create and endorse initiatives that advocate for change and support change efforts. I posit that a reason these behaviors continue to occur is due to the fact many C-suite executives are not comfortable addressing the issues of misconduct and harassment directly and clearly. It is a difficult topic to discuss publicly, but remaining silent and relying solely on human resources departments to "carry the torch" is not enough. Speaking about it publicly is the first step in creating a psychologically safe environment. This creates a collective consciousness about the issue. The following case study highlights the need for organizations to recognize all forms of harassment — not just sexual harassment.

CASE STUDY

In 2016, Wynand Wessels, a white, South African-born surgeon in Alberta, Canada, hung a noose on an operating room door where both black and indigenous physicians worked.[6] This incident was immediately reported to leaders in administration and to the provincial regulatory body, the College of Physicians and Surgeons of Alberta (CPSA).

In 2020, a tribunal determined that although the noose might be seen as a symbol that could intimidate and threaten OR staff, the tribunal did not recognize it as race-based harassment or intimidation, citing insufficient evidence to determine the perpetrator was motivated by racism. The tribunal did find the perpetrator guilty of unprofessional behavior. Further details make it abundantly clear this was racist behavior meant to intimidate one individual and indirectly threaten lynching.

It took four years for this case to resolve, and the events that unfolded reveal how institutional failure can perpetuate and create a psychologically unsafe environment.

First, the alleged target for the noose was Oduche Onwuanyi, a Nigerian-born surgical assistant. During the investigation into the matter, Scott Weins, a colleague of Wessels, confirmed that Wessels told him the noose was for Onwuanyi.

The incident was reported to the hospital administration minutes after it happened. Over the next four years, at least three doctors reported it to the hospital's administration, Alberta Health Services, the college, and then-health minister Tyler Shandro. Wessels was never suspended and faced no discipline.

The college subsequently admitted it had failed to investigate the incident in a timely manner. Alberta Health Services (AHS), which manages the province's healthcare system, said it believed the matter had been dealt with. The college announced a hearing for Wessels shortly after CBC News revealed the noose incident. Indeed, the matter went unresolved until the incident was made public in a news story.

Nearly five years after the incident, in January 2021, a CPSA hearing panel found Wessels guilty of misconduct. Remarkably, the all-white panel called no witnesses, including Onwuanyi. Wessels told the panel he was unaware of the violent symbolism behind a noose. He claimed the noose does not carry the same racist and violent connotations in South Africa, where he is from, as it does in North America. The panel ruled there was insufficient evidence to conclude Wessels was motivated by racism or intended to create a racist symbol. An independent consultant hired by Alberta Health agreed it was not racism.

An all-white disciplinary tribunal of the College of Physicians and Surgeons of Alberta issued Wessels a four-month suspension and ordered him to pay 75% of the costs of the investigation and two hearings. An attorney for the college pushed for a one-year suspension, calling the noose a "deadly threat" and an attempt to intimidate.

The president of the Black Physicians' Association of Alberta, Kannin Osei-Tutu, called the tribunal's sanction "......an affront to the Black community; I think it is an affront to all racialized people. I think that tribunal needs to look at itself and say, 'What have we done here?'" He also stated, "Because it is not just the message they are sending to people in Alberta. The entire country is looking at this and will pass judgment on this decision."

If the noose was not "racist," then what was it? Labeling it as "unprofessional behavior" minimizes what the noose represents and the aim of taping it to the door of the OR: a way to instill fear, threaten violence, and intimidate. It is also difficult to believe Wessels is ignorant of the crime of lynching blacks in the South in the United States. Even highly educated individuals from other cultures are aware of the symbol of racism the noose represents.

CULTURE OF TRUST AND SAFETY

Organizations need to create a culture of trust to establish a psychologically safe environment. Trust is gained through consistent, objective, and clear messaging and actions. This means everyone is held accountable for their actions regardless of the position or title of the individual involved. Disciplinary actions against individuals must not utilize a "double-standard" approach.

For example, a prominent, high-earning physician must be treated in the same manner and with the same objective approach as a floor nurse who is accused of the same category or type of conduct. Using different yardsticks for individuals based on titles, authority, or other reasons will erode or destroy trust that the organization is just, fair, unbiased, and objective.[7]

The fundamental value system needs to be dismantled and replaced with one that values inclusion and safety. To dismantle the current system, there must be a willingness to reflect with honesty and humility on how legacy racism, sexism, and marginalization of other minority groups continue to negatively impact individuals and their work environments. Organizations in the healthcare industry can and should be leading by example in creating a psychologically safe environment for everyone.

REFERENCES

1. Kahn W. Psychological Conditions of Personal Engagement and Disengagement at Work. *Academic Management Journal.* 2017;33(4):33.
2. Clark T. *The 4 Stages of Psychological Safety: Defining the Path to Inclusion and Innovation.* San Francisco: Berrett-Koehler;]2020.
3. Siad F, Rabi D. Harassment in the Field of Medicine: Cultural Barriers to Psychological Safety. *Canadian J Cardiology Open.* 2021;12:S174–S179.
4. Jenner S, Djermester P, Prugl J, Kurmeyer C, Oertelt-Prigione S. Prevalence of Sexual Harassment in Academic Medicine. *JAMA Intern Med.* 2018;179(1):108–111.
5. Phillips S, Webber J, Imbeau S, Quaife T, Hagan D, *et al.* Sexual Harassment of Canadian Medical Students: A National Survey. *EClinical Medicine.* 2019;7:15–20.
6. Rusnell C , Russell J. Surgeon Handed 4-Month Suspension for Noose Incident at Alberta Hospital. CBC. December 6, 2021. https://www.cbc.ca/news/canada/edmonton/alberta-surgeon-noose-hospital-1.6274942.
7. Gardiner E. Alberta Surgeon Found Guilty of Professional Misconduct for Hanging a Noose in the Hospital. Blog. RosenSunshine blog. February 11, 2021. https://www.rosensunshine.com/blog/sxr5w9gy1bnjc5o1y314uwrne3c8ln.

Chapter 36. Support Groups

"We are all healers of each other. Look at David Spiegel's fascinating study of putting people together in a support group and seeing that some people in it live twice as long as other people who are not in a support group. I asked David what went on in those groups and he said that people just cared about each other. Nothing big, no deep psychological stuff-people just cared about each other. The reality is that healing happens between people."— Rachel Naomi Remen, pediatrician

"We don't heal in isolation, but in community."— S. Kelley Harrell, author

SHARING MY STORY WITH OTHERS has been invaluable on my journey. There is value in not feeling isolated, sharing similarities and differences, and finding common ground to heal. Listening is powerful, healing, and empathic. It validates our feelings and experiences, and when another person or groups of people feel safe enough to ask vulnerable questions, trust is created. New bonds between people are created. New friendships and relationships can be forged out of tragic experiences.

My first experience with support groups was Alcoholics Anonymous (AA) meetings my mother frequently attended while I was a teen. I did not fully comprehend the process, but I did listen to the stories, the heartfelt sorrow, and the gratitude expressed by those attending. What struck me most was the atmosphere of caring and listening. It was a powerful experience.

Support groups are available in formal and informal settings and on online platforms. Resources are available for victims to participate through in-person, online video interaction via multimedia platforms such as Zoom and through group forum chats, both live and static.

Recent research on the efficacy of group work on reducing symptoms of depression, PTSD, anxiety, or increased well-being suggests formal, semi-structured survivor groups are effective in college-aged women who have experienced sexual trauma.[1] Other studies have confirmed that group therapy has potential as a valuable support service for survivors, but more rigorous research and evaluations are required to better capture outcomes and understand how to design and implement effective interventions.[2,3]

Online applications (apps) are also available for victims of sexual assault. Research on the usefulness of these online apps is not encouraging. A content analysis of 700 random narrative-style posts on an online app for survivors of sexual assault found that the narratives were mostly being shared in conjunction with a negative-laden effect and a hopeless tone; 86% of the disclosures were considered hopeless or depressing. In addition, 28% of disclosures included negative self-talk. This is particularly concerning given that negative self-appraisals maintain PTSD symptoms and are related to emotion regulation difficulties and low self-compassion.[4,5]

I surmise the lack of a mental health professional who can respond to the posts or redirect conversations or offer alternative perspectives is one of the reasons an online app may only be effective in sharing the narrative about the event; they likely do little else to help victims process the events.

Virtual platforms and face-to-face virtual meetings provide the opportunity for more thorough and meaningful discussions. For victims who live in rural areas, for example, an online resource group may be the only option available. Virtual support communities may positively affect the emotional well-being of survivors by providing spaces for a sense of justice through "being heard." More vulnerable survivors are more likely to communicate online, and they do so to tell their stories and have their experiences validated by a listening audience.

Survivors of sexual assault consider being heard as an essential part of seeking justice. Considering the insufficient systems for victims to be heard and acknowledged in the mainstream justice system, online communities offer an alternative.[6]

Another advantage of online support groups is the option to remain anonymous or create a fictitious name. This affords the individual the opportunity to feel safe in disclosing events, especially if publicly discussing an event without anonymity may be discovered by the assailant or other attributed individuals. Given the increased use of online platforms and virtual forums for support groups, I predict their continued use. It is an area ripe for research into which platform methods are effective.

Researchers from the University of Nebraska and Brown University recently published a paper to critically examine "what we know" and "what we don't know" about sexual assault disclosure and social reactions to disclosure that occur in an online forum (i.e., blog post, Twitter, Facebook, or other social media site). Drawing upon "what we don't know" about how sexual assault disclosure occurs in online contexts, they generated suggestions for research, as well as strategies for understanding how best to create safer and more supportive experiences for survivors of sexual victimization who choose to disclose their experiences online.[7]

Zielinski and colleagues examined incarcerated women's perspectives on the impact and acceptability of group psychotherapy involving imaginal exposure to sexual assault memories. Most women who are incarcerated — 56%–82% according to best estimates — have experienced sexual violence and assault. The cohort in their study included 80 incarcerated women divided into 15 separate groups. Each group had 4-8 participants.[8]

Women were asked to share their memory of a sexual assault or abuse experience in narrative form, using as much detail as possible, including the five senses and what they were thinking and feeling. The participants then imagined the scene. This process is known as imaginal exposure. After the narrative was complete, group participants were asked to provide feedback to the sharer. The impact of listening to other group members' sexual assault and abuse memories was positive.

Included in the study are direct quotes from participants who responded. The researchers categorized the responses into three themes: *Realized I am not alone, Positive interpersonal impact, and Miscellaneous.* Here are direct quotes from participants in the three categories:[8]

REALIZED I AM NOT ALONE

"Realizing I'm not alone and that there are others out there who has [sic] been through similar traumatic events and that people are willing to help."
"It helped me see that I'm not alone and I have a right to my feelings."
"That it's okay to feel the way I do. I'm not alone, my story matters."

POSITIVE INTERPERSONAL IMPACT

"Taught me to trust."
"A sense of closeness, understanding."
"Strong impact. Helped in making me more comfortable in sharing my story."

MISCELLANEOUS

"It helped me identify some of the things I was blocking out from my own experiences."

"I was emotional, it was hard listening to their stories. I know I found myself counting or trying to focus on something when it became overwhelming."

"I wished I would have been able to do this as a kid. It would have saved me a lifetime of problems."

"I don't feel so alone and being able to talk and deal with my feelings and feeling accepted by other women."

Not mentioned in the study is the power of validation for their experiences. The participants' *feelings* are validated as well. Additionally, sharing an intimate personal experience such as sexual trauma with strangers or those who are only acquaintances is not easy. The participants become vulnerable once more, and recounting a traumatic event produces a wellspring of negative feelings. Despite these challenges, the participants of the study felt the group work was acceptable and beneficial.[8]

MALE SURVIVORS AND SUPPORT GROUPS

Males are less willing than females to seek individual counseling or group support for several reasons. For males, the masculine stereotype of strength and stoicism is challenged when revealing sexual assault or forced engagement in nonconsensual sex. As discussed in Chapter 14, some men feel they will not be believed, and sharing in a support group is not worth the risk of feeling invalidated. Men are socially expected to want sex and may feel conflicted, embarrassed, and ashamed for having been a victim of an unwanted experience.

A recent study found that men hesitate to disclose past histories of childhood sexual abuse. The cohort included 253 participants aged 18–59 who were recruited through websites for males with childhood sexual abuse histories. On average, the participants waited roughly 15 years before disclosing the abuse.[9]

Boys who have been sexually abused by women are unlikely to report or disclose the abuse that they have experienced, perhaps because social structures surrounding the sexual abuse of boys by women are designed to minimize, excuse, or even encourage such sexual contact.[10] The constellation of psychological, social, and emotional barriers for males to disclose abuse and participate in a support group hinders healing and negatively impacts the survivor's health and well-being.

The conflicting nature of the traditional views of masculinity and the culture of therapy contribute to male victims' exclusion from the survivor community.[11] Without a connection to a healing community, men are left to live in their misconceptions, distortions, and false beliefs. Group therapy provides an avenue for men to have those internal experiences identified and normalized. Group counseling allows for catharsis, which holds long-lasting benefits for male sexual survivors, including reducing feelings of shame.[12]

Moreover, group therapy offers the opportunity to use role-play and psychodrama. Both experiential methods can empower clients to act assertively, an often-counter narrative to the actual assault. Male victims can also act out existing or latent feelings within a non-judgmental and supportive environment.[13]

I did not disclose my past history of sexual abuse until I was 26 years old, and I did not share my experiences as a participant in the local Adult Children of Alcoholics (ACoA) meetings. I openly discussed other concerns and issues, but I had not personally processed what I experienced as a child until I started individual counseling sessions with a psychiatrist in medical school. I was unwilling to make myself vulnerable in front of strangers.

Finding healing through group therapy does not have to be part of the journey for all survivors, but for some, it is the only option due to cost or geographical constraints — especially in rural areas. With cost constraints facing healthcare systems and providers, and with the ongoing shortage of mental health providers and increased costs for access, I anticipate increased demand for virtual and online support.

REFERENCES

1. Murn LT , Schultz LC. "Knowing I'm Not Alone": The Development of a Support Group for College Victims and Survivors of Sexual Assault. *J College Student Mental Health*. 2023;38(3):391–414.

2. Heard E, Walsh D. Group Therapy for Survivors of Adult Sexual Assault: A Scoping Review. *Trauma, Violence, Abuse*. 2023; 24(2):886–898. doi: 10.1177/15248380211043828

3. Hébert M, Bergeron M. Efficacy of a Group Intervention for Adult Women Survivors of Sexual Abuse. *J Child Sex Abus*. 2007;16(4): 37–61. doi: 10.1300/J070v16n04_03.4

4. Collaton J, Barata P, Lewis SP. Understanding Discussions of Sexual Assault in Young Women on a Peer Support Mental Health App: A Content Analysis. *J Interpers Violence*. 2022 ;37(23-24):NP22811-NP22833. doi: 10.1177/08862605211073112

5. Barlow M R, Goldsmith Turow R E, Gerhart J. Trauma Appraisals, Emotion Regulation Difficulties, and Self-Compassion Predict Posttraumatic Stress Symptoms Following Childhood Abuse. *Child Abuse Negl.* 2017;65:37–47. doi: 10.1016/j.chiabu.2017.01.006

6. O'Neill T. "Today I Speak": Exploring How Victim-Survivors Use Reddit. *International Journal for Crime, Justice and Social Democracy.* 2018;7(1): 44–59.

7. Bogen K W, Orchowski LM, Ullman S. Online Disclosure of Sexual Victimization and Social Reactions: What Do We Know? *Women & Therapy.* 2021;44(3/4):358. doi:10.1080/02703149.2021.1961448.

8. Zielinski MJ, Karlsson ME, Bridges AJ. "I'm Not Alone, My Story Matters": Incarcerated Women's Perspectives on the Impact and Acceptability of Group Psychotherapy Involving Imaginal Exposure to Sexual Assault Memories. *Health Justice.* 2021; 9(1): 25 . doi:10.1186/s40352-021-00148-4

9. Romano E, Moorman J, Ressel M, Lyons J. Men With Childhood Sexual Abuse Histories: Disclosure Experiences and Links with Mental Health. *Child Abuse Negl.* 2019 ;89:212–224. doi: 10.1016/j.chiabu.2018.12.010.

10. Fraser J, Bradford J, Pritchard C, Moulden H. Childhood Sexual Abuse by Women of Boys Who Go On to Sexually Offend: Review and Critical Analysis. *Curr Psychiatry Rep.* 2024 ;26(3):45–52. doi: 10.1007/s11920-024-01486-4

11. Rochlen AB. Men in (and Out of) Therapy: Central Concepts, Emerging Directions, and Remaining Challenges. *J. Clin. Psychol.* 2005;61:627–631. doi: 10.1002/jclp.20098

12. Yam WH. Review of *The Theory and Practice of Group Psychotherapy* by Irvin D. Yalom and Molyn Leszcz. Group. 2022;46(1):105–107. doi: 10.1353/grp.2022.0006

13. Mulkey M. Recreating Masculinity: Drama Therapy with Male Survivors of Sexual Assault. *Arts Psychother.* 2004;31(1):19–28. doi: 10.1016/j.aip.2003.11.003

Chapter 37. Offender Treatment and Rehabilitation

"It can be argued that rapists deserve to be raped, that mutilators deserve to be mutilated. Most societies, however, refrain from responding in this way because the punishment is not only degrading to those on whom it is imposed, but it is also degrading to the society that engages in the same behavior as the criminals." — Stephen Bright, attorney and professor

SEX OFFENSES ARE A SERIOUS SOCIAL ISSUE due to their lasting impact on their victims and as a concern of public safety for those in the community at large. While sexual offenders are stigmatized by many groups, including law enforcement, the media, and the community, they are also degraded through general discussion, research focus, and paper titles.[1] As a result, the concept of offering treatment to these individuals is regarded as controversial.

The first documented efforts to treat sex offenders occurred at the end of the 19th century. Two approaches were utilized: psychological and medical. Psychological approaches included helping offenders change how they thought and acted and teaching them how to avoid committing sex crimes. Medical treatments included surgical castration and, beginning in the 1940s, chemical castration using diethylstilbestrol to reduce testosterone and libido.[1–3]

Modern treatments emerged in the 1970s, including the development of phallometric evaluations, the broadening of behavioral interventions, and more comprehensive treatment programs.

Phallometry (also known as penile plethysmography or penile tumescence testing) is an objective method of assessing male sexual arousal. Psychiatrist Kurt Freund developed the penile plethysmograph in Czechoslovakia in the 1950s. At the time, homosexuality was illegal in many jurisdictions and regarded as a mental disorder, and the technology was first directed at identifying homosexual or "androphilic" desires. Although early applications included aversion therapy to "cure" homosexuality, phallometric evidence of the immutability of sexual orientation supported the biological basis of homosexuality, and Freund came to lobby successfully for the decriminalization of homosexuality in Czechoslovakia.

Academic interest in phallometry and offending has remained remarkably consistent over the past 30 years, with 87 publications on the topic in the 1990s, 86 in the 2000s, and 88 in the 2010s.[4] In forensic psychiatry, phallometry is primarily deployed in the management of people who have committed sexual offenses, especially those who have offended against children.

Some clinics utilize phallometric testing in the management of men with suspected paraphilias not known to have acted upon their problematic sexual interests (PSIs) to commit offenses. Occasionally, phallometry has been used in other settings, such as family court proceedings and occupational health.[4]

Phallometry may be important to the management of people who have committed sex offenses (PCSOs) because specific sexual response profiles predict recidivism, and phallometric tests are valid indicators of paedophilic interests, both for PCSOs against children and controls.[4] Thus, it is incorporated into the evaluation of PSIs, into risk assessment, and into measuring response to sex offender treatment.

One of the most significant contributions to emerge in the 1980s was the adaptation and use of the relapse prevention model from the field of addiction medicine. Researchers identified commonalities between addictive behaviors and sexual aggression, especially in terms of their association with signs of relapse.[5] Relapse prevention helps the offenders identify problematic situations that may place them at risk for offending, teaches strategies for coping, and helps them control their sexual behavior.

MODERN TREATMENT

More treatment programs and an explosion in research in the 1990s led to a completely new approach to treatment using integrative models. There was recognition that previously formulated theories regarding the cause of sexually offensive behaviors, including biological, environmental, social learning, and behavioral, were too simplistic to conceptualize sexual offending as the result of actions in only one domain.[1] A more comprehensive approach to treatment combined physiological, psychological, social, and environmental influences on the development and maintenance of sexual offending behaviors.

The current treatment approach incorporates the complex nature of the behavior. The treatments are much more extensive and target many areas, including deviant sexual arousal, distorted cognition, pro-offending attitudes, problems with impulse control, social skills deficits, poor emotion regulation, and environmental triggers. Multi-component cognitive-behavioral therapy (CBT) incorporating relapse prevention has been the preferred treatment for decades and remains dominant today.

CBT is based on several core principles, including that psychological problems are based, in part, on faulty or unhelpful ways of thinking and on learned patterns of unhelpful behavior.

CBT treatment involves efforts to alter thinking patterns:

- Learning to recognize one's distortions in thinking that are creating problems and then to reevaluate them in light of reality.
- Gaining a better understanding of the behavior and motivation of others.
- Using problem-solving skills to cope with difficult situations.
- Learning to develop a greater sense of confidence.

CBT treatment also usually involves efforts to change behavioral patterns. These strategies might include:

- Facing one's fears instead of avoiding them.
- Using role-playing to prepare for potentially problematic interactions with others.
- Learning to calm one's mind and relax one's body.

Utilizing and offering effective treatment approaches is an essential public health and safety concern, as the majority of convicted sex offenders are eventually released back into the community.[6] Over the last decade, there has been extensive research on the effectiveness of modern treatments, and there is substantial evidence the current approaches are working.[1,7] As our understanding of this important topic continues, new treatment modalities will be incorporated.

Most of the research on rehabilitation has focused on males as perpetrators. The effectiveness of treating female perpetrators is not well-researched. Gender has historically been downplayed or overlooked within treatment considerations for females, and using the same interventional approach and strategies in the treatment of males may not be as effective in the treatment of females.[8]

Priebe *et al.*, examined consideration of the treatment of females sentenced for child sexual abuse (FCSA). There is a high prevalence of past and ongoing trauma in women incarcerated for FCSA. Untreated substance use disorders and mental health conditions are common, as are problems with illicit drug use and alcohol abuse as well. In a sample of 85 female child sex offenders, 64 reported problems with mental health, drug use, violence, and past sexual, physical, and psychological abuse.[8] A significant proportion of female child sex offenders have histories of being sexually abused — one study found an incidence of up to 80%.[9,10]

Over time, important distinctions between male and female offenders have emerged, including significant variations in motivations, pathways, and offensive characteristics. The motives for females who engage in CSA differ significantly from those of males. Although some engage in the behavior as a form of seeking intimacy, others engage in the behavior out of sexual attraction toward children. Some female offenders report idealizing children and having a desire to nurture them, viewing sexual behavior with children as less harmful or abusive compared to male sexual offenders.

Unfortunately, there are female offenders who believe men should be entitled to behave as they wish toward women and children and, as a result, participate as co-offenders with male offenders.[11] Still, there still appears to be no "typical" pattern concerning the motives of female offenders in their behaviors.

Given the fact many female offenders have past histories of childhood trauma, the starting point for treatment is addressing past trauma and treating the psychological sequelae and other mental health disorders, including substance use disorders. Thoroughly understanding the needs of female offenders is still in its infancy, and specific treatments have not yet been developed.

Some researchers have suggested that the Good Lives Model (GLM), currently used in treating male offenders, may benefit females. The GLM, developed by Professor Tony Ward and colleagues in 2002, is a novel approach to instilling behavioral change and reducing recidivism. Rather than focus on risk reduction, the GLM aims to equip individuals with internal and external resources to live a "good" or "better" life — a life that is socially acceptable and meaningful. There is some evidence the GLM is effective in reducing recidivism, but further research is needed to investigate its efficacy over other treatment models.

The Risk-Need-Responsivity (RNR) model, developed in the late 1980s and early 1990s, assesses risk, analyzes needs, and identifies effective strategies and barriers to reduce recidivism.[12] Each component represents separate but interlocking principles (Figure 1). The Risk-Need-Responsivity (RNR) model provides a sound theoretical foundation for the effective treatment of people who have become delinquent. Such treatment aims to reduce the risk of reoffending and to enhance the chance of a pro-social lifestyle. Treatment effectiveness increases when treatment addresses all three core principles of the RNR model.[13-15]

What Questions Does the Risk-Need-Responsivity Model Ask?

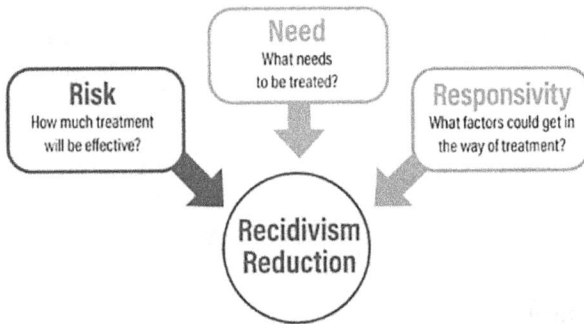

Need
What needs to be treated?

Risk
How much treatment will be effective?

Responsivity
What factors could get in the way of treatment?

Recidivism Reduction

FIGURE 1. Principles of the RNR Model.[12]

While the *Risk Principle* (treatment intensity depends on the level of recidivism risk) and the *Need Principle* (treatment is based on individual criminogenic needs associated with delinquency) are well investigated, the *Responsivity Principle* is still insufficiently examined.[13,16,17] The RNR model implies that the, *General Responsivity* principle is met by treatment offers based on cognitive-behavioral and social learning approaches., *Specific Responsivity* is, however, defined rather vaguely: the better the treatment fits a client's personality, cognitive style, skills, and attributes, the more effective it is.[13,18]

ASSESSING RECIDIVISM RISK

Formal surveys and questionnaires are used to assess recidivism risk, which is obviously important. Individuals with a higher risk of recidivism pose a greater threat than those of lower risk.

Criminogenic needs are dynamic risk factors directly linked to criminal behavior and recidivism, meaning they are factors that can be changed and addressed to reduce the likelihood of reoffending. Assessment of criminogenic needs is common; the STABLE-2007 is the most frequently used instrument. Evaluators are also increasingly likely to consider protective factors, which are social, environmental, or psychological features that help with desistance from crime. While a majority of evaluators use actuarial instruments,

Most evaluators have now adopted modern actuarial instruments, with the Static-99R and Static-2002R being the most commonly used. A substantial minority employ Structured Professional Judgment (SPJ) instruments.[19] Static-99R is a 10-item actuarial assessment instrument created by R. Karl Hanson, PhD, and David Thornton, PhD, for use with adult males with a history of sexual offending who are at least 18 years of age at the time of release to the community.

In 2012, the age item for the original scale (Static-99) was updated, creating Static-99R. Static-99R is the most widely used sexual recidivism risk assessment instrument in the world and is used extensively in the United States, Canada, the United Kingdom, Australia, and many European nations.[20]

These tools predict risk but are by no means complete. The tools are actuarial; the output measures are objective, not subjective, and there have been significant challenges regarding the legal admissibility of the scores. Static-99R provides an important baseline risk assessment based on static risk factors. It may be particularly useful in triaging large numbers of individuals for resource allocation. It should not be mistaken for a comprehensive risk assessment.[21]

These tools are far from perfect, but there are no other alternatives to obtain objective data. Rehabilitation efforts and continued research investigating effective interventions and predicting risk is especially important as economic constraints are reducing resources for interventions and corrections.

REFERENCES

1. Harrison JL, O'Toole SK, Ammen S, Ahlmeyer S, Harrell SN, Hernandez JL Sexual Offender Treatment Effectiveness Within Cognitive-Behavioral Programs: A Meta-Analytic Investigation of General, Sexual, and Violent Recidivism. *Psychiatr Psychol*

Law. 2020;27(1):1–25. doi: 10.1080/13218719.2018.1485526. Erratum in: *Psychiatr Psychol Law.* 2020 Feb 03;27(1):168. doi: 10.1080/13218719.2020.1722388

2. Laws D, Marshall W. A Brief History of Behavioral and Cognitive Behavioral Approaches to Sexual Offenders: Part 1. Early Developments. *Sexual Abuse.* 2003;15(2): 75–92.

3. Scott C, Holmberg T. Castration of Sex Offenders: Prisoners' Rights Versus Public Safety. J *Am Acad Psychiatry Law.* 2003;31(4):502–509.

4. Bickle A, Cameron C, Haswsan T, Safdar H, Khalifa N. International Overview of Phallometric Testing for Sexual Offending Behaviour and Sexual Risk. *BJPsych Int.* 2021 ;18(4):E11. doi: 10.1192/bji.2021.17

5. Marlatt G, Gordon J, eds. *Relapse Prevention: Maintenance Strategies in the Treatment of Addictive Behaviors.* New York: Guilford; 1985.

6. Moster A, Wnuk D. Cognitive Behavioral Therapy Interventions With Sex Offenders. J *Correctional Health Care.* 2008;14(2): 109–121. doi:10.1177/1078345807313874

7. Rocha ICO, Valença AM. The Efficacy of CBT Interventions to Sexual Offenders: A Systematic Review of the Last Decade of Literature. *Int J Law Psychiatry.* 2023; 87:101856. doi:10.1016/j.ijlp.2022.101856

8. Priebe B, Rayment-McHugh S, McKillop N, Christensen LS. What Women Want: Program Design for Females Sentenced for Child Sexual Abuse. *Victims and Offenders.* 2024;20(2):255–257. doi: 10.1080/15564886.2024.2400994

9. Johansson-Love J, Fremouw W. Female Sex Offenders: A Controlled Comparison of Offender and Victim/Crime Characteristics. J *Family Violence.* 2009;24(6): 367–376.

10. Bickart W, McLearen AM, Grady MD, Stoler K. A Descriptive Study of Psychosocial Characteristics and Offense Patterns in Females with Online Child Pornography Offenses. *Psychiatr Psychol Law.* 2019;26(2): 295–311. doi:10.1080/13218719.20 18.1506714

11. Elliott I, Eldridge HJ, Ashfield S, Beech A. Exploring Risk: Potential Static, Dynamic, Protective and Treatment Factors in the Clinical Histories of Female Sex Offenders. J *Family Violence.* 2010;25(6): 595–602.

12. Batastini A, Morales I, Dillon M. The Psychology of People Who Commit Crimes. What the TV Shows Don't Tell You. *Eye on Psi Chi.* 2024; 28(3). doi:10.24839/2164-9812.Eye28.3.30

13. Bonta J, Andrews DA. *The Psychology of Criminal Conduct.* New York: Routledge; 2017. doi.org/10.1111/bjop.12254

14. Gannon TA, Oliver ME, Mallion JS, James M. Does Specialized Psychological Treatment for Offending Reduce Recidivism? A Meta-Analysis Examining Staff and Program Variables as Predictors of Treatment Effectiveness. *Clin Psychol Rev.* 2019;73: 101752. doi:10.1016/j.cpr.2019.101752

15. Hanson R K, Bourgon G, Helmus L M, Hodgson S. Meta-Analysis *of the Effectiveness of Treatment for Sexual Offenders: Risk, Need, and Responsivity* 2009-01. Ottawa, ON: Public Safety Canada; 2009.

16. Cohen TH, Whetzel J. The Neglected "R" — Responsivity and the Federal Offender. *Federal Probation.* 2014;78(2):11–18.

17. Jung S, Dowker BA. Responsivity Factors Among Offenders. *J Offender Rehabilit.* 2016;55(3):148–167. doi:10.1080/10509674.2016.1148090

18. Schmucker M, Lösel F. The Effects of Sexual Offender Treatment on Recidivism: An International Meta-Analysis of Sound Quality Evaluations. *J Experiment Criminol.* 2015;11: 597–630. doi: 10.1007/s11292-015-9241-z

19. Kelley SM, Ambroziak G, Thornton D, Barahal RM. How Do Professionals Assess Sexual Recidivism Risk? An Updated Survey of Practices. *Sex Abuse.* 2020;32(1):3–29. doi:10.1177/1079063218800474

20. Stück E, Briken P, Brunner F. Changes in the Risk of Sexual Reoffending: The Role and Relevance of Perceived Self-Efficacy and Adult Attachment Styles in Correctional Treatment. *Sex Abuse.* 2022 ;34(8):891–922. doi: 10.1177/10790632211054048

21. Helmus LM, Kelley SM, Frazier A, Fernandez YM, Lee SC, *et al.* Static-99R: Strengths, Limitations, Predictive Accuracy Meta-Analysis, and Legal Admissibility Review. *Psychology, Public Policy, and Law.* 2022;28(3):307–331. doi:10.1037/law0000351

Investigating Concerns and Allegations

∞

Chapter 38. Legal Obligations and Reporting Requirements

"Think of the consequences if you do nothing." — Unknown

THERE ARE EFFECTIVE AND INEFFECTIVE methods and procedures to investigate reported events and concerns; incorrect, omissive, or illegal processes can expose the organization and individuals to legal action and avoidable consequences.

It is a moral and ethical duty to investigate all claims or concerns regardless of personal interpretation of the event. Organizations have a duty to protect patients, employees, complainants, and other staff from further incidents. Failing to investigate and intervene harms individuals and maintains a status quo, tolerant, and psychologically unsafe environment and culture. Numerous cases presented in this book are examples of organizational failures.

A thorough and complete investigation requires accurate and complete documentation of evidence, interview discussions, lists of witnesses, time stamps, date stamps, copies of texts, emails, pictures, social media posts, etc. Every phone call, conversation, and any objective information ***must be documented.*** If it is not documented, it becomes hearsay unless a cooperative individual confirms or agrees to any findings, conversations, or content of any conversations. This task may be tedious, but it is necessary. It ensures transparency, and transparency creates faith and confidence in the process for everyone involved.

Every organization has unique structures and chains of command for reporting events, and in the case of criminal behaviors, the authorities must also be notified. In these cases, the authorities, human resources departments, risk managers, and legal counsel are necessary to ensure processes follow regulatory and legal requirements. Details on specific processes are beyond the scope of this book, but physician leaders, managers, directors, and nurse and pharmacy managers and directors should be trained and educated on the processes in the organization.

Chapter 39. Reporting Child and Elder Abuse

REPORTING SUSPECTED CHILD or elder abuse is a legal obligation for healthcare workers, teachers, and social workers. Each state has its own requirements for notification of authorities within a specific timeframe. In Connecticut, for example, unless the child or adult is in immediate danger, in which case the authorities must be contacted immediately, the reporting requirement is within 12 hours.

The Department of Health and Human Services has a hotline, Eldercare Locator, for reporting suspected or known cases of abuse during normal business hours, Monday through Friday. Trained operators direct individuals to report to their respective local agencies and organizations within their state. The requirements and other legal obligations for each state vary.

Chapter 40. Middle Management's Role

"Middle managers are the muscle and bone of every sizable organization, no matter how loose or "flattened" the hierarchy, but they are largely ignored despite their immense importance to our society and economy." —
Andrew S. Grove, former CEO of Intel Corp.

ORGANIZATIONAL SUCCESS requires effective C-suite leadership and scores of well-trained and supported middle managers, including supervisors, floor managers, assistant directors, etc. The importance of their role cannot be emphasized enough, as middle managers have the responsibility and authority to implement and enforce an organization's policies, rules, regulations, and duties with frontline staff.

Without question, it is a difficult task for middle managers due to the concurrent pressure to lead and assist bedside nurses and caregivers while being held accountable for the overall operations and culture of the unit or floor. Senior leaders and those in the C-suite expect managers to not only monitor the professional behaviors of the staff but also ensure policies are enforced. The pressure from above and below is an inherent, immutable part of the role. Conduct concerns involving patients and nurses are often first reported to or discussed with either a unit charge nurse, manager, supervisor, or director. Managers and directors have the unique position of often being the first person with responsibility and authority to listen to an incident or concern. In organizations with anonymous reporting systems, managers receive daily reports of patient safety and professional behavior concerns, including sexual misconduct or discrimination. Therefore, it is critical for middle managers to feel confident and competent to initiate any formal policy or reporting process.

Failure to adhere to a process or failure to formally acknowledge an incident or concern exposes the organization to potential legal consequences but, more importantly, foments a culture of silence. Managers set the initial tone for how an organization investigates and handles the complainant's issues and concerns. An off-the-cuff insensitive comment or body language and tone that is dismissive will undoubtedly become known by other employees at some point, as the complainant may talk about the negative incident. Not taking a complaint seriously adds insult to injury.

Sexual harassment can knock on a manager's door softly or with the force of a sledgehammer. A "direct hit" is when the employee asks to meet and lays out clearly what has occurred. And it can literally be any type of event. These events are easier to investigate because the employee is usually able to fill in all of the details. As a manager, documenting the points of the discussion is critical; it protects all parties and the organization.

Some issues or concerns brought to a manager's attention include the gray zone of what may or may not constitute sexual harassment. As an example, is it sexual harassment when a female colleague tells a male colleague his haircut is "feminine looking"? Is it harassment when a male colleague tells another male colleague he has poor taste in choosing women? Is it sexual harassment if colleagues at work continually ask an employee about an extramarital affair?

In these cases, it is better to document the concern and treat the event as sexual harassment. The reason is twofold. First, the events are *unwanted*, and the employee is bringing it to a manager's attention. Second, from a legal perspective, it is better to take the complaint seriously and follow a formal process—at a minimum documenting the concern.

Some organizations and managers may not necessarily document the concern and, instead, have a "coffee cup" conversation with the accused. The main problem with a coffee cup conversation is strikingly simple: What events warrant a coffee cup conversation versus those that should be formally investigated? The coffee cup is not a good practice because of the subjective interpretation of the event.

If an employee arrives with a complaint about conduct that mentions *anything* about appearance that seems gendered, intimate relationships, or out of line with other professionalism issues, document it and treat it formally. Not only is that the safe approach, but it also demonstrates that the concerns will be handled formally and taken seriously.

Some managers may know about sexual misconduct or harassment and do nothing about it. If you recall, in *Meritor Savings Bank v. Vinson*, having a complaint procedure that an employee ignored may not absolve the organization from responsibility for the conduct if the employer had reason to know about the sexual harassment concerns.

Similarly, employers or supervisors may become aware of a sexual misconduct or harassment concern through back channels, small talk, observation, or gossip. It is the manager's responsibility to follow up and determine if harassment has occurred. Failing to follow up and claiming ignorance is not good enough.

Managers need to use what I call the "Four C" approach when handling sexual harassment or misconduct concerns:

1. Caring. Managers must show, through speech and body language, that the concern is serious and that the manager cares. *Caring sets the tone.*
2. Competence. Managers must be competent to handle the situation. Managers should know the process and be *trained* on the process. (For a more extensive discussion, see Chapter 54.)
3. Confidence. Managers need to confidently move through the process, knowing they will have support from superiors and the employees will be supported.
4. Consistency. Managers must be *objective and fair.* Playing favorites, "protecting" an employee, or engaging in any behavior perceived as special treatment is a risk. Consistency also applies to the investigation process. Always use a standardized approach.

Chapter 41. Human Resources

"The job of human resources is to make sure that resources come to work with their hearts and go back to their homes with happiness." — Amit Kalantri, author of Wealth of Words

EMPLOYEE RETENTION STARTS before an employee's first day. The delicate balance and equilibrium between management, executive leadership, and employees is maintained through a well-run human resources (HR) department. HR departments engage in all aspects of the organization, vertically and horizontally, including onboarding, offboarding, and training and guiding employees. How HR functions during the onboarding process sets the initial tone and culture of the organization for a new employee.

HR departments are also responsible for providing employee training, including training and education on sexual misconduct, harassment, and discrimination.

HR departments are often in the unique position of being made aware of formal complaints by employees; therefore, an organization's reputation depends on how HR staff interact with employees. Bad news travels fast, and if the HR department is perceived as uncaring or nonchalant, recruitment and retention of employees are more difficult.

HR department activities that influence an institutional approach to sexual harassment include:

Managing workplace dynamics: HR has a responsibility to communicate and enforce policy and to recognize the delicate nature of relationships between managers, supervisors, and employees. HR departments should foster an environment of open communication and offer guidance during conflicts.

Encouraging collaboration: Many organizations, especially healthcare organizations, are comprised of individuals from various cultures and backgrounds. Diverse workforces present challenges when developing teams, and as discussed previously, understanding cultural influences on behavior is critical.

Cross-functional collaboration can help HR build a more united front and framework for reducing sexual harassment. Team-building exercises and workshops on cultural differences are important. Most organizations do not provide cultural competence training.

Communicating with sensitivity: Effective, sensitive, compassionate communication is paramount when dealing with sexual harassment concerns.

Providing counseling and support: Many organizations have employee assistance programs (EAPs), which HR departments are responsible for overseeing and for ensuring the programs are available for employees who need assistance. During an investigation, for example, both the accuser and accused may need support. A good employee assistance program can help reduce anxiety and other negative conditions brought on by an event.

Navigating legal and organizational realities: HR departments must operate within the legal and regulatory environment and framework while understanding the unique dynamics of their organization. Legal pitfalls are costly, and mishandling concerns is a liability that can negatively affect the organization's reputation.

Balancing management and employee interests: Employees are often distrustful of HR departments because they perceive HR as a "mouthpiece" for management. An "us vs. them" culture is toxic. Protecting the organization is the responsibility of HR departments, but their responsibility to support the employees cannot and should not be discounted or discouraged. The employer/employee relationship is fundamentally transactional, and the nature of the power dynamic inherently complicates perceptions.

Fostering a cultural shift: While the C-suite and other executives are responsible for helping craft the vision and shape an organization's culture, HR does the heavy lifting. HR departments are the "torch bearers" for company culture and, as such, should drive toward the goal that sexual misconduct or harassment is unthinkable in the organization's culture. It's not an easy task and takes concentrated effort.

BARRIERS TO PROGRESS

Employees' negative perception of HR departments is a significant barrier to reducing sexual misconduct and harassment. Employees want and need to be treated with respect. Without an atmosphere of trust and support, employees may hesitate to report conduct.

Some employees anthropomorphize their organization, personalizing and humanizing an inanimate entity.[1] As in the *Wizard of Oz*, there is no "person" behind the curtain of an organization. This tendency to instill human characteristics in an organization can create a great deal of tension when the organization responds in what's perceived as an uncaring manner. A well-run HR department treats employees with dignity and respect.

REFERENCE

1. Wang Y, Kim S, Rafferty A, Sanders K. Employee Perceptions of HR Practices: A Critical Review and Future Directions. *Inrl J Human Resource Manag.* 2020;31(1): 128–173. doi:10.1080/09585192.2019.1674360

Chapter 42. State Boards, Formal Reporting Requirements, and the National Practitioner Data Bank

STATE MEDICAL BOARDS ARE THE AGENCIES that license medical doctors, investigate complaints, discipline physicians who violate the Medical Practice Act, and refer physicians for evaluation and rehabilitation when appropriate. The overriding mission of medical boards is to serve the public by protecting them from incompetent, unprofessional, and improperly trained physicians. Medical boards accomplish this by ensuring that only qualified physicians are licensed to practice medicine and that those physicians provide their patients with a high standard of care.

After physicians are licensed in a given state, they must reregister periodically to maintain their active status. During this reregistration process, physicians must demonstrate that they have maintained acceptable standards of ethics and medical practice and have not engaged in improper conduct.

The duty of the medical board, however, goes beyond the licensing and reregistration of physicians. The board evaluates whether a physician's professional conduct or ability to practice medicine warrants modification, suspension, or revocation of the license to practice. Board members devote much time and attention to overseeing physicians' practice by reviewing patient complaints, malpractice data, information from hospitals and other healthcare institutions, and reports from government agencies.

When a board receives a complaint about a physician, and there is reason to believe the physician has violated the Medical Practice Act, the board has the power to investigate the claim, hold hearings, and if necessary, impose discipline.[1] The state statute commonly known as the Medical Practice Act defines unprofessional conduct in each state. Although laws vary by jurisdiction, some examples of unprofessional conduct include:

- Physical abuse of a patient.
- Inappropriate relationships and sexual misconduct.
- Inadequate record keeping.
- Not recognizing or acting on common symptoms.
- Prescribing drugs in excessive amounts without legitimate reason.

- Impaired ability to practice due to addiction.
- Failure to meet continuing medical education requirements.
- Performing duties beyond the scope of a license.
- Dishonesty.
- Conviction of a felony.
- Inappropriately delegating the practice of medicine to an unlicensed individual.

CASE STUDY

(Based on an actual case. Names and places redacted.)

The state medical board has revoked the license of Dr. K, an OB/GYN, saying he entered into a sexual relationship with one of his patients at the River Rock medical group, according to the regulatory agency.

According to that complaint, Dr. K began treating "Patient A" in January 2003, serving as an obstetrician for three of her pregnancies and delivering two of her babies. The patient's last in-person visit was in September 2012, the complaint stated. The medical board's executive director stated, "The inappropriate relationship between Dr. K and his patient is an egregious violation of the law and especially concerning to the Board."

Dr. K is accused of sexual misconduct, sexual exploitation, unprofessional conduct, gross negligence, and repeated negligent acts and incompetence.

Dr. K was placed on leave in January 2016 and has been prohibited from seeing patients since then. The affair between Dr. K and the woman, who started working as a nurse for River Rock Medical Group in 2008, began in October 2013 and lasted until June 2014.

Their first sexual encounter occurred on the second night of an out-of-town conference. Both were married to others at the time. "Within the next two to three weeks, they drove out to an undisclosed location and had sexual intercourse in a car...... Patient A would go to his office when she got off of work around 3:30 p.m., while he was still working, and they would have sex in his office," according to the complaint.

The complaint said the two would meet for sex in the clinic when it was closed during his night call shifts and in his office while he was on duty and was supposed to report for patient care. In February 2014, the nurse learned she was pregnant, and Dr. K prescribed Misoprostol, a drug that can induce miscarriages, to abort the baby in an attempt to conceal the relationship from his then-wife, the medical board said in a statement.

The relationship deteriorated after that, and the nurse reported the relationship to her employers and to the medical board. State investigators would later learn that Dr. K had backdated the Misoprostol prescription to conceal the affair, the medical board said.

THE CHALLENGE OF INVESTIGATIONS

The course of events, timeline, and complexity of the investigation leading to the revocation of the physician's medical license highlights the difficult task medical boards face when receiving formal complaints. Every state medical board's requirements, processes, and procedures are unique. Some states, for example, will reinstate a medical license for physicians who have had a history of sexually abusing their patients after a specified length of time, for example, two or three years.

This was the case in California until a new law was passed in 2022 prohibiting the state's medical board from granting a license to clinicians whose credentials were previously surrendered or revoked on grounds of sexual misconduct with patients, with no chance of winning an appeal. Before the new law — which appears to be the only of its kind in the nation — a clinician whose license was revoked or surrendered because of earlier sexual misconduct violations could reapply after two or three years and return to practice if approved.[2]

Consumer groups' reactions to the passage of this new law were mixed. Eric Andrist of the Patient Safety League, a frequent critic of the Medical Board of California, said the new law only applies to physicians in the context of their relationships with their patients. He said it "turns a blind eye" to doctors who get in trouble for sexual misconduct with non-patients, including fellow staff members. "I mean, what difference does it make who the misconduct was with?" he said. "Yes, it's an even worse breach of the doctor-patient relationship when it's a patient, but sexual misconduct is wrong across the board."[2] He is correct — sexual misconduct is wrong across the board.

Other states have drafted and passed or attempted to pass similar legislation, including Michigan, Florida, and Georgia. In June 2021, Florida passed a bill that was narrower in focus than the California bill. It specifically addresses a physician's sexual acts involving children or those with mental illness or intellectual disability, as well as actions related to sex trafficking and deriving profits from prostitution. In Georgia, a new bill appears to "provide for the refusal, suspension or revocation of the license of a physician who has committed a sexual assault on a patient" but doesn't require it as California's new law will. Two recent bills introduced in Michigan failed to pass.[2]

The continuing problem of physician sexual misconduct prompted the Federation of State Medical Boards (FSMB) to convene a focused workgroup led by the then-chair of the FSMB, Patricia King, in May 2017. King charged the workgroup with addressing these concerns[3]:

1. Collecting and reviewing available disciplinary data, including incidence and spectrum of severity of behaviors and sanctions related to sexual misconduct.
2. Identifying and evaluating barriers to reporting sexual misconduct to state medical boards, including, but not limited to, the impact of state confidentiality laws, state administrative codes and procedures, investigative procedures, and cooperation with law enforcement on the reporting and prosecution/adjudication of sexual misconduct.
3. Evaluating the impact of state medical board public outreach on reporting.
4. Reviewing the FSMB's 2006 policy statement, *Addressing Sexual Boundaries: Guidelines for State Medical Boards*, and revising, amending, or replacing it, as appropriate.
5. Assessing the prevalence of sexual boundary/harassment training in undergraduate and graduate medical education and developing recommendations and/or resources to address gaps.

The workgroup adopted a broad approach to scrutinizing the current practices of individual state medical boards and other regulatory bodies in the United States and abroad. The workgroup identified an important element contributing to the problem: *culture*. The workgroup "... acknowledged the existence of several highly problematic aspects of sexual misconduct in medical education and practice, many of which permeate the *prevailing culture* of medicine and self-regulation."[3]

The National Academies of Sciences, Engineering and Medicine 2018 report, *Sexual Harassment of Women: Climate, Culture, and Consequences in Academic Sciences, Engineering, and Medicine,* states that organizational culture plays a primary role in enabling sexual harassment and that sexually harassing behaviors perceived license to engage these behaviors, and patients are ultimately at risk of dire consequences in an environment in which sexual misconduct exists.[4]

There remains wide variability in the investigative and adjudicatory processes designed to address sexual misconduct, including state medical board procedures and policies, state laws, and transparency of each state's medical board processes. Another factor is a lack of formal education and training among board investigators, attorneys, law enforcement personnel, and medical regulators.

Without standardization, it is nearly impossible to determine whether or not a given process or policy is effective. The FSMB workgroup offers solutions to these issues.

DUTY TO REPORT

Many instances of misconduct are never reported despite the legal requirement and ethical responsibility for any healthcare worker to report a physician to a medical board if they have witnessed misconduct. Evidence suggests that less egregious violations often lead to more egregious behaviors. Although several factors contribute to less reporting, the increasingly corporatized care environment, including corporate-owned practices and institutions, has led to the false belief that internal processes alone are sufficient to address the issue. An institution failing to report sexual misconduct to a medical board is neglectful and lacks transparency. The public has a right to know.[3]

Physicians fail to report other physicians for many of the same reasons victims of sexual misconduct fail to disclose, including fear of retaliation, retribution, and lack of faith in the process. Physicians may also feel moral distress and apprehension. Numerous studies have found that only 40–50% of physicians report impaired colleagues or those who engage in unprofessional behaviors, including sexual misconduct.[5]

Physicians fear they may damage their own reputations by being labeled as "whistleblowers," become more involved in the process, which is professionally and personally disruptive, and finally, increase the group's workload, especially if the physician is in a small group, and the group might suffer reputational harm. The stakes are quite high.

Furthermore, power dynamics may affect a physician's willingness to report. For example, can new employees or those on a partnership track feel confident reporting a director, chair, or senior partner? I doubt it.

Case Study

Dr. M, a recent graduate from a prestigious program, is a new employee on the partnership track in a small neurology group comprised of four other partners. She has been with the practice for six months and is doing quite well. She enjoys her patients and the group.

The group has an exclusive contract with the hospital and recently became an accredited and certified primary stroke center with The Joint Commission. The hospital has been advertising the new certification on local billboards and television commercials. Dr. M is a featured physician in one of the commercials.

Dr. L is one of the original founders of the group and plans to retire in three years. He was instrumental in the hospital's efforts to become stroke-certified and is a frequent donor to the hospital. He has been providing patient care at the hospital for 33 years.

One afternoon, while rounding in the hospital, Dr. M overhears a couple of nurses in the medication room discussing a recent event involving Dr. L. She is surprised to hear Dr. L had been accused of groping one of the charge nurses late one evening after evaluating a patient. One of the nurses states, "The only reason they aren't doing anything about what he did to Jackie is because he is too important and untouchable. The hospital won't dare make a big deal of this after all of his efforts. It's unfair, and those of us who know him are not surprised he did it in the first place. He has always been a little creepy."

A couple of weeks later, Dr. M is in the clinic, and Dr. L asks her if she can see his last patient, as he is late to a meeting. She agrees to see the patient. During the appointment, the patient discloses that Dr. L had touched her breasts in a way that surprised her during an appointment one month ago. Further discussion revealed Dr. L had fully touched her breasts with a cupped hand while telling her there was a new requirement for all physicians to do a manual exam for breast cancer screening. The patient was very uncomfortable, as Dr. L had not explained this to her until after the exam.

The patient was relieved to see Dr. M, and because no one else is present in the office but the secretary at the front desk, she feels comfortable disclosing the events of the last appointment to Dr. M.

The patient then states that she is considering reporting the incident to the state medical board but is afraid she won't be believed. The patient is also aware of Dr. L's reputation in the community and at the hospital, and she believes this will make it even more difficult for others to believe her story. She asks Dr. M if she is willing to contact the state medical board on her behalf.

At this point, Dr. M should reassure her patient the medical board will take her complaint seriously, and though she is willing to make a report on her behalf, it is in her best interest to report the incident directly. Dr. M takes this approach, and the patient still refuses. Dr. M is now legally and ethically obligated to make a report on the patient's behalf.

Dr. M makes a report, and the medical board notifies Dr. L there has been a complaint filed against him alleging inappropriate touching of a patient. Dr. L is allowed to continue to practice during the investigation.

The hospital is notified of the complaint by the state medical board, and the medical staff leadership holds an emergency meeting to discuss the case. The medical executive committee votes to temporarily suspend the physician's privileges until the investigation is completed and the state medical board is notified of these actions.

NATIONAL PRACTITIONER DATA BANK

Congress established the National Practitioner Data Bank (NPDB) in 1986 as part of the Health Care Quality Improvement Act (HCQIA). The NPDB collects and maintains reports on medical malpractice payments, federal and state licensure and certification actions, and adverse clinical privilege actions. Before the creation of the NPDB, physicians could move from one state to another and practice after adverse actions against their licenses or malpractice claims.

All licensed healthcare practitioners are reportable in the NPDB, including nurses, techs, physician assistants, dentists, chiropractors, pharmacists, podiatrists, and psychologists.

Entities that are required to submit information to the NPDB include:

- **Hospitals:** Required by federal law to query.
- **Other healthcare entities:** Required to report or query, depending on the type of organization and its ownership.
- **State agencies:** Required to report, including state licensing and certification authorities, state Medicaid fraud control units, and state agencies administering or supervising state healthcare programs.
- **Federal agencies:** Required to report, including federal licensing and certification agencies, and agencies administering federal healthcare programs.
- **Professional societies:** Required to report, including those with formal peer review.
- **Peer review organizations:** Required to report.
- **Private accreditation organizations:** Required to report.
- **Medical malpractice payers:** Required to report.
- **State law enforcement agencies:** Required to report.
- **Drug Enforcement Administration (DEA):** Required to report.
- **HHS Office of Inspector General:** Required to report.

Comprehensive and current guidance related to the NPDB is available online at npdb.hrsa.gov.

Case Study

The following case is a summary of *Jason C. Chang MD v. The Rehabilitation Hospital of the Pacific*, 2019 WL 3430767 (US District Court, Hawaii July 30, 2019)

In early 2019, two employees brought claims of sexual harassment against Dr. Jason Chang, CMO of the Rehabilitation Hospital of the Pacific. The hospital hired an outside attorney to investigate, and Chang was placed on "restrictions and directives" pursuant to medical staff bylaws. The hospital's attorney determined that Chang had engaged in unwelcome sexual activity, including sexual intercourse, toward the employees using coercion and intimidation. After the required process, Chang's medical privileges were summarily suspended.

In response, Chang filed a complaint for declaratory and injunctive relief, citing violations of federal and state constitutional due process rights, federal and state law, and hospital bylaws. Chang requested the court to enjoin the hospital from reporting his suspension to the NPDB.

The court found that the hospital did not violate hospital bylaws by issuing a summary suspension on a non-patient care case because it followed HCQIA due process requirements of a formal hearing and that sexual harassment of an employee is on the same level of wrong-doing as impairing patient safety.[6] As reference, in 2008, The Joint Commission released *Sentinel Event Alert 40*: Behaviors That Undermine A Culture of Safety.[5] The Joint Commission asserted that disruptive and unprofessional behaviors impacted patient care. Although not specifically addressed in the Alert, sexual misconduct and harassment certainly is disruptive and does harm patients.[7]

REFERENCES

1. *Carlson D, Thompson JN. The Role of State Medical Boards. Virtual Mentor. 2005; 7(4):311-314. doi: 10.1001/virtualmentor.2005.7.4.pfor1-0504*

2. Clark C. New California Law: Docs Who Sexually Abuse Patients Can't Get Their Licenses Back. *Med Page Today*. September 27, 2022. https://www.medpagetoday.com/special-reports/exclusives/100935.

3. Federation of State Medical Boards. Physician Sexual Misconduct Report and Recommendations of the FSMB Workgroup on Physician Sexual Misconduct. May 2020. https://www.fsmb.org/siteassets/advocacy/policies/report-of-workgroup-on-sexual-misconduct-adopted-version.pdf.

4. Johnson PA, Widnall SE, Benya FF, eds. *Sexual Harassment of Women: Climate, Culture, and Consequences in Academic Sciences, Engineering, and Medicine*. Washington, DC: National Academies Press; 2018. doi:10.17226/24994.

5. DesRoches C, Rao S, Fromson J, Birnbaum J, Iezzoni L, Vogeli C, Campbell E. Physician's Perceptions, Preparedness for Reporting, and Experiences Related to Impaired and Incompetent Colleagues. *JAMA*. 2010;304(2):187-193.

6. Paterick Z, Paterick T, Paterick B. The National Practitioner Data Bank: Requisite Medical and Legal Issues for Physicians. *J Med Pract Manage*. December 8, 2020. https://www.physicianleaders.org/articles/national-practitioner-data-bank-requisite-medical-legal-issues-physicians.

7. The Joint Commission. Behaviors that Undermine a Culture of Safety. The Joint Commission Sentinel Event Alert. Issue 40, July 9, 2008; updated June 18, 2021. https://www.jointcommission.org/-/media/tjc/documents/resources/patient-safety-topics/sentinel-event/sea-40-intimidating-disruptive-behaviors-final2.pdf.

Chapter 43. Standardizing the Processes

"Trust is built with consistency." – Lincoln
Chafee, former governor of Rhode Island

INVESTIGATIVE TEAMS TRAINED to conduct interviews, write and present reports, and suggest interventions ensure the investigation processes are standardized, complete as possible, and satisfy the legal and compliance requirements to protect the individuals and organization. A haphazard, incomplete approach or process can set up the organization for failure, and individuals involved may not be treated fairly or objectively. The emotional toll on all involved, too, can have devastating consequences.

To standardize the approach for investigating allegations of sexual misconduct or harassment, a small workgroup composed of experts in law, leadership, human resources, medicine, and healthcare operations recently convened and identified the necessary steps and processes to help organizations create a methodical approach to investigating allegations of sexual boundary violations in healthcare. Their work, published in *The Joint Commission Journal on Quality and Patient Safety* in 2023, is a must-read for all healthcare leaders, managers, and directors in any setting. The strategies and approaches suggested in their paper are timely and relevant.[1]

The group proposed creating a classification scheme to identify and triage the types of behaviors. They analyzed and used cases derived from two national professional accountability programs coordinated by the Vanderbilt University Center for Patient and Professional Advocacy (CPPA) for their proposal.

CPPA oversees a nearly 200-hospital network that sends electronic reports of unsolicited patient complaints and safety event reports alleging unprofessional behavior directed toward coworkers as a part of the Patient Advocacy Reporting System (PARS) and the Coworker Observation Reporting System (CORS).[1-3] Using a novel coding system, the behaviors reported are identified and classified, including sexual boundary violations.

From 2017 to 2022, PARS and CORS processed approximately 358,000 patient complaints and coworker concerns. Among the reports, approximately 0.1% contained information suggesting possible sexual boundary violations (SBVs). The group reviewed a sample of 50 de-identified reports that had been flagged as potential SBVs. During the review, the group identified themes that described both severity and acuity, the role of complainant and respondent, and the possible context of the behavior (Figure 1).[1]

Final Classification Scheme

Severity/Acuity	Roles/Relationships (consider all that apply)	Context

• **Severity**
  ○ Inappropriate/unexpected speech, communication, or gesture
  ○ Flirtatious behavior or touching in front of others (who observe but are not involved in the activity)
  ○ Invasions of sexual privacy for a sexual purpose:
    ▪ watching or enabling others to watch the complainant's nudity/sexual acts; or
    ▪ making or attempting to make photographs (including videos) or audio recordings, or posting, transmitting, or distributing such recorded material, depicting the complainant's nudity/sexual acts
  ○ Inappropriate, unexpected, or unwanted physical contact
  ○ Inappropriate, unexpected contact with sensitive areas, face, neck, breasts, legs, genitals
  ○ Forced sexual activity
 	
• **Acuity**
  ○ Recent event
  ○ Remote event
  ○ Chronic history of event(s)—including a range of unprofessional behaviors
	• **Employment context**
	  ○ Supervisory relationship between complainant and respondent, or respondent has a leadership role
	  ○ Bullying or assertions of physically being stronger
	
	• **Patient care context**
	  ○ Patient or patient caregiver, or occurs in care environment
	  ○ Patients who may misinterpret a standard examination procedure
	  ○ Patient as respondent
	  ○ May require consideration of medical necessity and/or appropriateness of clinician actions
	
	• **Educational context**
	  ○ Educational supervisor
	  ○ Trainee in any role
	  ○ Active teaching/evaluating role
	
	• **Other role and relationships issues**
	  ○ Interactions that occur in a nonprofessional setting (for example, social setting or another context)
	  ○ Events invoking multiple regulatory requirements that may require prioritization and collaboration (for example, criminal law, Title IX, medical staff processes)
		• **Relationship Elements**
		  ○ Hierarchy implied or invoked or affects reporting or response
		  ○ Quid pro quo assertions
		  ○ Hostile environment
		
		• **Prior History**
		  ○ Respondent: Repeated events (consider all reporting sources). Consider how to address prior reports that may have been vague or unfounded after investigation but still may represent concerning prior behaviors. Evidence that the behavior was specifically driven by intended sexual gratification.
		  ○ Complainant: Ensure that reports from patients with language or other information suggesting the patient has a behavioral health condition are addressed consistently and adequately.

FIGURE 1. PARS and CORS final classification scheme for investigations.[1]

The authors of the scheme suggest that organizations investigate and report *all* complaints. For example, some organizations dismiss complaints from delirious or demented patients. *This is a mistake.* Consistently using the same approach to an investigation reduces the possibility of personal bias.

Out of this classification scheme, the group suggested organizations utilize a triage process immediately after a report (Figure 2).[1]

The group also suggests organizations use these guiding principles:

1. Balance and consider the safety of all individuals.
2. Consider the potential and risk for recurrence during the triage and investigatory period.
3. Respect the rights of the complainant, respondent, and any other relevant witnesses or other personnel directly involved in the case.

In addition to a centralized, systematic approach, the authors highlight the importance of a strong workplace culture as a preventative strategy. A

Severity / Acuity (Type of Reported Behavior and Timing)

Need for law enforcement engagement?

Contact Law Enforcement
Coordinate internal response

Recent vs. Remote Event or Suggestive of Multiple Complainants

Recent
Consider need to remove respondent from practice
Explore need for additional information from complainant and best path to connect

Remote or Multiple Complainants
Consider resources needed for investigation
Consider whether wider investigation to identify potential additional complainants is needed

Roles / Relationships (Consider all that apply)*

Employment Role

Engage Human Resources support

Patient Care Role

Engage risk management, medical leadership, and follow appropriate pathways based on the respondent's relationship(s) to the organization (employed, credentialed, contracted, faculty, etc.)

Educational or Training Role

Consider statutory requirements. Refer to appropriate investigatory path according to law, regulation, or policy

*Complex cases may involve multiple roles for respondent, complainant, and others who may be affected. Collaboration among key stakeholders is essential to identify relevant policies and the optimal way to coordinate investigations and responses.

Contextual Issues (Elements of relationship and prior history)

Review all available data to identify if any previous issues or findings

Consider prior events for respondent and special circumstances for complainant (i.e., patient with behavioral health condition). If so, these should inform the response to ensure equity and consistent process

Review whether aggravating factors are present (e.g., quid pro quo)

If so, may necessitate consideration of additional review and/or action

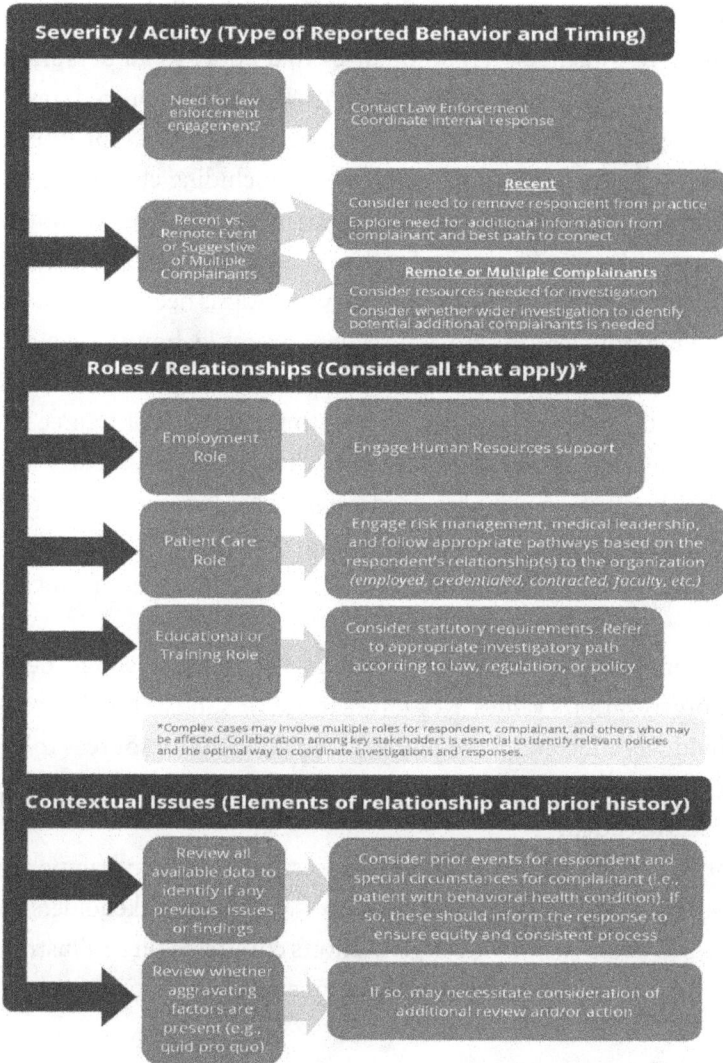

FIGURE 2. Triage process for initial review and management of reports of sexual boundary violations in the healthcare setting.[1]

few cases reported to PARS and CORS involved high-profile individuals who were given preferential treatment. *I cannot emphasize enough that granting preferential treatment or minimizing the behavior of high-profile individuals will derail any efforts an organization makes to reduce the behaviors.* Double standards destroy good work cultures and prevent improvement.

The organization should review and align the policies and procedures pertaining to interpersonal boundaries that apply to all persons in the healthcare environment, including patients. Policies and procedures should specifically address and include performance expectations for appropriate interpersonal sexual boundary interactions, including chaperone policies for sensitive history and physical examinations, as well as standards to guide the timing and procedural rules for the investigation of complaints.

Different subtypes of sexual boundary violations need to be considered in following policies and procedures. For example, boundary violations involving a student or trainee and faculty as respondent or complainant necessitate considering policies relevant to the student or trainee and the relevant policies for the faculty member (for example, faculty manual, academic institution policies, medical staff bylaws). Review processes should include appropriate key stakeholders to guide which policies and procedures need to be considered and the potential order in which issues need to be resolved.

The steps to report and the implications of the findings should be guided by the organization's values. Resources to address the well-being concerns of individuals affected by the reported violation and resources to investigate and adjudicate potential cases should be identified and made readily available as needed.[1]

Once an organization establishes a process, sustaining and supporting the members of committees, employees, leaders, and other stakeholders ensures the process "lives" within the organization's culture. Figure 3 illustrates the support structure necessary to provide an effective approach.

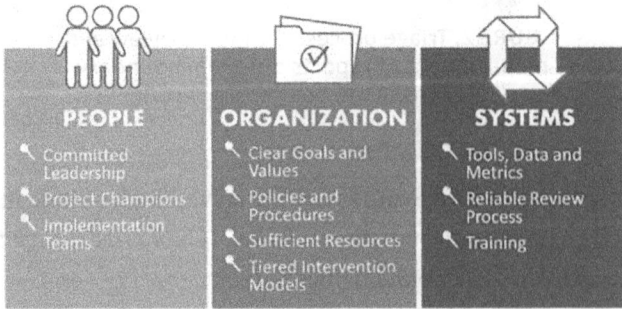

PEOPLE
- Committed Leadership
- Project Champions
- Implementation Teams

ORGANIZATION
- Clear Goals and Values
- Policies and Procedures
- Sufficient Resources
- Tiered Intervention Models

SYSTEMS
- Tools, Data and Metrics
- Reliable Review Process
- Training

FIGURE 3. Supporting practices needed for sustainable processes.[1]

Using a standardized approach to the process, with trained individuals having clearly defined roles and responsibilities, reduces the stress of the individuals involved in the investigation. Sharing responsibilities forces accountability, and forcing accountability forces organizations to address the issues. This reduces liability and creates a just culture.

REFERENCES

1. Cooper WO, Foster JJ, Hickson GB, Finlayson AJR, Rice K, *et al.* A Proposed Approach to Allegations of Sexual Boundary Violations in Health Care. *Jt Comm J Qual Patient Saf.* 2023; 49(12):671–679. doi: 10.1016/j.jcjq.2023.08.006.
2. Vesentini L, Dewilde K, Matthys F, De Wachter D, Van Puyenbroeck H, Bilsen J. Dealing with Sexual Boundary Violation in Mental Health Healthcare Institutions by Government Policies: The Case of Flanders, Belgium. *BMC Med Ethics.* 2022;23(1):40. doi: 10.1186/s12910-022-00778-9
3. Freischlag J, Files K. Sexual Misconduct in Academic Medicine. *JAMA.* 2020; 323(15):1453-1454. doi: 10.1001/jama.2020.3344

Chapter 44. Interviewing Complainants, Respondents, Witnesses, and Victims

"A lot of times the interview relies not so much on the interviewee, but on the interviewer." — Ernie Johnson Jr., American sports commentator

INTERVIEWING INDIVIDUALS INVOLVED in sexual misconduct and harassment cases is one of the most challenging, emotionally charged tasks one can undertake in management and leadership. The questions and responses can produce incredibly painful and awkward moments for those interviewed, and the interview can sometimes be triggering for the interviewer. Unfortunately, few people receive formal training on how to interview individuals involved in these events; however, these skills can be learned and, once learned, make the process far less anxiety-provoking.

Depending on the organization, the initial report of misconduct may be made directly to a manager or supervisor, or it may be a formal, written concern documented in anonymous reporting systems. Of note, many healthcare organizations now use anonymous reporting systems to document safety and conduct concerns.

Of course, some employees may feel uncomfortable revealing their identity for fear of retaliation or, worse, that the concern will simply go unaddressed, but an anonymous report of misconduct does not resolve the situation. This is why it is important for organizations to create a culture that fosters a safe, positive, supportive environment. Organizations are responsible for informing all employees and associates about the process for reporting behavior concerns, including sexual misconduct, harassment, and discrimination.

A manager, director, chair, or supervisor may be the individual who initiates the investigative process. The manner in which a manager conducts him or herself at the outset of the investigation can affect the course of events. Despite the informality of an initial meeting or report, it is important to document points of discussion from the complainant, even if no one else is present.

INTERVIEWING THE COMPLAINANT, RESPONDENT, AND WITNESSES

A formal interview is a legal process, so there are pitfalls to avoid. First, conducting interviews with at least one other person present is in your best interest. Interviewing an individual alone can lead to an individual (especially the attributed individual) challenging what was asked or stated during the interview process. Witnesses in interviews protect you, the interviewee, and the organization.

Dos and Don'ts for Interviews

Before we discuss the interview process in detail, consider the following list of dos and don'ts during the interview process.

Do:

- Treat all complaints seriously regardless of how innocuous they may seem.
- Believe the complainant is telling the truth.
- Listen carefully.
- Ask the complainant to be as thorough as possible.
- Ask follow-up and probing questions to get as many facts as possible.

Don't:

- Promise absolute confidentiality (safety concerns may be involved).
- Disclose your own personal feelings or impressions.
- Ask about the complainant's sex life, history, or sexual proclivities.
- Suggest the complainant is being too sensitive.
- Defend the attributed individual.
- Delay the interview process.
- Criticize or debate with the complainant.
- Take any action on your own outside of the organization's processes.

INTERVIEWING THE COMPLAINANT

Interviewing the individual who filed the concern requires sensitivity, objectivity, and thoroughness (SOT). This SOT approach creates a safe, fair, and complete process for information gathering. Interviewing the complainant professionally, respectfully, and sensitively sets the tone for the entire process, so it is important to do it correctly.

First, explain the investigative process and steps involved, giving some assurances about confidentiality and against retaliatory actions. Second, create a safe space for the individual to tell their story. To set the tone, tell the interviewee that some of the questions may be difficult to answer and that details are important. ***Tell the individual they can take their time answering the questions, as the questions can illicit unsettling memories and emotions.*** This level of sensitivity is empathic and validating. Finally, ask if they are comfortable proceeding. On occasion, the time might not be right for an interview. In that case, reschedule as soon as possible.

After this brief introduction to the process and explanation of how the interview will be conducted, proceed by asking the following questions:

1. Ask the complainant to describe the incident or occurrence in as much detail as possible, including who, what, when, where, and how. Inform the individual of the importance of accurate days, times, and who else might have witnessed the event. While asking this question, inform the complainant he or she may be interrupted to clarify any details. This part of the interview process is open-ended, and it gives the complainant an opportunity to tell their story.
2. Ask about the reporting relationship. Is the attributed individual in a position of authority, a manager, supervisor, or coworker? The nature of the relationship in healthcare is often quite clear. A charge nurse, attending physician, or department chair is clearly a position with managerial responsibility and authority.
3. Determine the nature of the relationship between the complainant and the attributed individual. Inform the interviewee that they are not required to answer this question if they are not comfortable. Ask if they were friends, socialized outside of work, or were romantically involved at some point. It may seem awkward to ask this question, but if there is a concern for unwelcome physical contact or communication, it is important to establish whether or not there was an intimate relationship. It also helps establish the credibility of the complainant's story.

Again, it is critical to remain objective and fair. On occasion, there may be an ulterior motive. For example, if the individuals were romantically involved, one of the individuals may want to seek revenge for a non-amicable break-up . This possibility is explained in greater detail in Chapter 46, which discusses how to investigate false accusations.

Ask the complainant if they communicated to the attributed individual that the conduct was unwelcome. If so, how did the attributed individual respond? Details about the incident help substantiate the claims. A general answer stating the conduct was harassment without any further details is not helpful.

1. Ask how the incident has affected the complainant in terms of any adverse consequences or harm.
2. Ask if the complainant feels safe or needs to be reassigned. Organizations cannot reassign complainants unless the complainants agree; otherwise, reassigning an individual can be interpreted as a retaliatory action.
3. Be prepared to answer questions about how the investigation will proceed. Inform the complainant that the investigation includes interviewing the respondent and, if there are witnesses, the witnesses, too. At this point, it is important to reassure the individual that confidentiality will be maintained as much as possible.
4. Be prepared for inquiries about your impression, opinion, or judgment. Some complainants may ask you to validate their claims. Do not be tempted to make any statements or answer the complainant's questions. Simply state that the investigation includes examining evidence and interviewing all parties and that any conclusions prior to the end of the investigation are premature. The manner in which this is stated to the complainant must incorporate an appreciation for the emotional impact of the complainant's experience.

It is helpful for you to validate how the individual feels. For example, you can say, *"I know this has been a difficult interview, and we care about you and your willingness to discuss this incident. At this time, we have not completed the investigation, but rest assured we will complete it in a timely manner and keep you informed."* Saying it in this manner is empathic and respectful.

INTERVIEWING THE RESPONDENT

Interviewing the respondent (attributed) individual is the most challenging task during an investigation. The stakes are extremely high for the individual;

in some cases, the individual will not cooperate without a lawyer present. If this is the case, the organization should have counsel present. This protects you and the organization.

Interviewing the respondent should always start with disclosure statements, including confidentiality, cooperation, and fairness, and, similar to interviewing the complainant, an explanation of the process. Additionally, stress the seriousness of the report of the event and that part of investigating an incident includes interviewing all parties. Most organizations have signed or time-stamped records of completion that employees understand the code of conduct policy regarding professional conduct and sexual harassment.

Remain respectful and professional, and do not broadcast judgment through your tone of voice or body language. Never engage in small talk prior to the start of the interview.

Additionally, be aware of your own biases or preconceived perceptions of the nature of the complaint. It is easy, for example, to pass quick judgment on a respondent if the individual has an extensive history of such behaviors and is now being held accountable. Unless those past transgressions resulted in formal correction, action, or discipline, consider the interview as a separate part of the process. Your own biases can derail the interview.

At the start of the interview, explain all of the complainant's allegations. This includes all details, regardless of how graphic or embarrassing they may be. The attributed individual must be given an opportunity to respond. Missing critical details places the organization at risk.

At this point, ask the respondent to explain what happened in his or her own words. Allow time and space and only interrupt the individual to ask for clarity.

If the attributed individual denies the behaviors or allegations, ask if there is any reason to believe the complainant is not telling the truth or is concealing any facts. Refer to the notes from the interview with the complainant to identify any inconsistencies.

Respondents often conceal or downplay details; if the event was not witnessed, it is difficult to validate the complainant's concern. If the respondent seems to not want to share any details, respectfully inform the respondent of the importance of sharing as much information as possible. If the respondent does not wish to provide any further details, do not continue to ask. They are either telling the truth or concealing information.

At the end of the interview, thank the respondent for the time and opportunity and discourage any further contact with the complainant as the investigation continues.

INTERVIEWING WITNESSES

Witnesses are important for corroborating and confirming the allegations the complainants state in reports or interviews. However, interviewing witnesses can also undermine the investigation if not done properly.

Just as it is important when interviewing complainants and respondents, introduce yourself, briefly describe the alleged incident, and clearly state that the individual is being questioned because they witnessed the event or you were told the individual saw the event, either by the complainant or respondent.

Again, ensure you remain objective. Witnesses might tell a different story or state conflicting details, contradicting the complainant or respondent's narrative.

Your task is to let the witnesses provide their own version of events. Standardizing the questions ensures you, as the interviewer, ask the same questions of all witnesses. After the introduction and brief explanation of the complaint, proceed as follows.

1. Ask the person if they witnessed the complainant's account of events firsthand. Ensuring the witness did not "hear" about the complainant's allegations is important.
2. Ask the witness to describe the events from the complaint in as much detail as possible. Let the witness tell their story without interruption. If any points need clarification, take notes and ask these questions after the witness has finished.
3. Ask the witness about the nature of the relationship between the complainant and the respondent.
4. Ask the witness if they have observed anything unusual between the complainant and respondent since the incident.
5. Finish the interview by asking any additional questions for clarification and conclude with the final question about any further details or concerns.

Witnesses can often be a source of gossip and rumors when staff, hungry and eager for any details, badger them with inappropriate questions. In my practice interviewing witnesses, I have instructed them not to tell anyone who asks for details. A simple response is, "I know you would like information or my opinion, but I cannot share any details out of respect for all involved." Stress the importance of confidentiality.

After the interviews are complete, your own observations about tone of voice, cadence, body language, etc., can help discern whether or not an interviewee was forthright and honest. To help gauge credibility, use the following:

1. Uneasy demeanor during the interview. Was the interviewee nervous? Was the interviewee using irregular speech, fidgeting, etc.? Did something not quite seem right?
2. Failure to make eye contact (may be nervousness, too).
3. Blanket denials or terse denials. Quick responses.
4. Motives to lie (revenge, seeking to damage someone's reputation).
5. Changing or inconsistent story.
6. Contradicting story.
7. History of lying.
8. Stating erroneous facts.

A witness may have motivations to lie, including protecting the respondent or seeking revenge against a complainant or respondent. Consistent accounts of events are reassuring, but a false witness can be convincing.

INTERVIEWING VICTIMS OF SEXUAL ASSAULT

I include this section to highlight the need to understand how the authorities have changed their approach when interviewing victims of sexual assault. In the past 20–30 years, the process has evolved to recognize the impact of a trauma victim's emotional and mental response. Consider these guidelines, focusing on three dimensions: thoughts, feelings, and sensory information:

1. Allow one or two sleep cycles after the incident before conducting interviews.
2. Use a victim-centered approach.
3. Ask the victim to talk about their experience as they remember it.

4. Ask about the five senses experienced during the assault.
5. Avoid "why" questions.
6. Go at a slow pace and be patient.

Some victims of sexual assault do not report the event immediately, especially if it involves a non-stranger assault. This can be due to denial, shock, self-blame, and embarrassment. It is important to respect someone's decision if they choose not to participate in an investigation and to note that an investigation can be re-activated when or if the victim is ready — as long as it is within the statute of limitations.

Trauma affects emotions and behavior. Some decisions the victims make during traumatic events do not make sense, and it is critical to understand there is no "normal" victim response to trauma.[1] Giving time and space prevents further victimization through an insensitive or disrespectful interview process. Some victims of sexual assault may not be willing to participate in an interview to avoid reliving the event in great detail to prevent secondary revictimization, lack of clarity about the process, fear of not being believed, and fear of the criminal justice system. Victims may also fear retaliation unless safety can be assured.

INTERVIEWING CHILDREN

There is nothing more heartbreaking than interviewing children who are victims of sexual abuse. The child may experience fear, anxiety, and sadness. The interviewer, too, might feel sad and angry, powerless, and frustrated.

First and foremost, it is important to remember that the child's responses to your questions depend on the child's stage of mental development. Charles Darwin introduced the idea of childhood development in the late 1800s, and in the early 20th century, Jean Piaget proposed four operational stages of childhood development. Appreciating these developmental differences is essential when conducting interviews with children:

1. **Sensorimotor stage.** This occurs from birth to around age 2. This stage is characterized by the development of basic motor skills and ability to interact with people and objects.
2. **Preoperational stage.** Children from ages 2 to 7 begin to develop language and symbolic thinking. This stage is characterized by egocentrism. Children cannot separate themselves from their environment and often

blame themselves for the abuse. The internalized idea the child has done something "wrong" shapes the child's interpretation of cause, effect, and consequences. The result produces shame, anxiety, fear, and guilt.

3. **Concrete operational stage.** As children mature, around ages 7–11, they enter the concrete operational stage and become aware that their feelings and thoughts are unique. They can separate themselves from the environment and learn cause and effect. During this phase, children realize that abuse is not about themselves.

4. **Formal operational stage.** Starting at around age 11, adolescents are able to think abstractly, hypothetically; they are fully cognitively developed by their late teens.

Monit Cheung developed a Child Sexual Abuse Interview Protocol (CSAIP) to standardize the process for use in forensic videotaping interviews.[2] Using a checklist of specific items to address, in four distinct stages, ensures an account of the alleged abuse that satisfies ethical and legal obligations. The four stages of the protocol are rapport, free narrative account, questioning, and closing the interview.

Rapport is established by telling the child the purpose of the interview and setting ground rules. The child's competency can be determined by asking about a non-abusive event for narrative practice. Can the child, for example, answer who, when, where, what, and how?

To understand the child's competency level, the interviewer can tell the child their friend went to the park yesterday and played with a ball. The child is then asked the specific details of this brief narrative event. If the child struggles to explain the event, the child may not be competent enough to provide an interview.

Stage two, the free narrative account, is an opportunity to ask critical open-ended questions. Ask the child *what* happened and explain they can tell what happened in their own words. Use dolls or drawings only after the child has disclosed the content of sexual abuse.

Once the free narrative is complete, stage three begins with more formal questioning. Finally, closing the interview is an opportunity to affirm the events, allow the child to ask questions, and reassure the child.

There are several pitfalls to avoid when interviewing children, including using leading questions, asking "why," and behaving in a tense or awkward manner. Additionally, avoid being judgmental and be aware of potential confirmation bias. Confirmation bias is selectively seeking, focusing on, and attaching greater weight to evidence that supports rather than refutes one's own beliefs.[3] Although rare, there is always a possibility the child could be lying or misinterpreting events.

LEARNING HOW TO INTERVIEW

Interviewing complainants, respondents, and witnesses is a skill one can learn, and practicing how to interview through simulation and role play with constructive feedback provides a safe space to make mistakes and gain confidence without consequences. I strongly encourage healthcare organizations to provide the time to train managers, supervisors, committees, and appointed investigators charged with the responsibility and authority to interview everyone involved. With practice comes confidence, and this new skill set makes navigating the process less emotionally charged. That comfort and confidence are usually perceived by the interviewees.

Case Study

A 44-year-old female nurse claims a 47-year-old male nurse pinned her against the wall in the break room and attempted to kiss her. She filed a formal report a week after the alleged event. According to the report, the event occurred at approximately 3 a.m. and was unwitnessed. She states she verbally told him to back off, and he complied with no further incidents.

She was able to avoid further contact with the attributed individual for the rest of the shift but did inform the charge nurse the following day. Initially reluctant to file a formal report, she changed her mind and made a request to no longer work any shifts with this nurse.

You are the primary investigator for this case and are responsible for interviewing both the complainant and the respondent. Relevant facts for the case include video evidence from a hallway camera of the complainant and respondent entering the breakroom together at 2:46 a.m. and leaving the break room at 3:10 a.m.

The following is a transcript of the interview.

Complainant Interview

Interviewer: Good morning. My name is Judy Johnson, and this is my colleague, Steven Page. We are part of a team of individuals who investigate claims of sexual harassment and misconduct here at St. Elsewhere. We understand this interview may be difficult, and we want to assure you this interview will remain confidential.

Part of the process of investigating the report includes interviewing all parties involved. We will keep you informed in as much detail as possible, and if you have any questions or concerns after this interview, please contact us.

As we ask the questions, if you need time to gather your thoughts or need a moment for any reason, take your time. Before we proceed, do you have any questions and are you comfortable continuing?

Complainant: I don't have any questions, and I am OK to have the interview.

Interviewer: Can you please tell us in as much detail as possible what occurred in the breakroom during the night shift?

Complainant: It was about 3 a.m. when Mike and I both went to the breakroom for a quick bite to eat. I sat down along the wall, and there was not much room between the back of the chairs and the wall. As I was finishing eating, I got up out of the chair, and Mike got out of his chair, too. As I was standing at the sink rinsing my plate, he quickly walked over to me, pressed me against the wall and tried to kiss my cheek. I was not expecting any of this to happen, and I quickly told him to stop and back off and not try that again. He quickly stepped back, and I left the room.

The breakroom is in a corner around the hall away from the nurse's station and charge. No one was around when this happened, and my tone of voice was enough to send him the message it better not happen again. I simply avoided any contact with him for the rest of the shift and told the day charge nurse the following day. Mike is a traveling nurse who has only been working on the floors for about three weeks.

Interviewer: You have known or worked with him only since his arrival about three weeks ago. Is this correct?

Complainant: Yes. That is right.

Interviewer: Thank you. This may seem awkward, but have you had any contact with Mike before or after this event?

Complainant: Yes. When Mike first arrived, he asked me if we could have some coffee after completing our overnight shift. We went to this restaurant a couple of blocks from the hospital and had some breakfast. This was about two weeks ago. Other than some small talk about the hospital, we both went home separately. He seems like a nice guy, and we got along fine at work. The next week he asked me if he could take me out to dinner. I told him thank you but politely declined the offer.

Interviewer: Just to clarify, other than having breakfast after your shift, you have had no other contact outside of work?

Complainant: Yes. That is correct.

Interviewer: Has he made any attempts to contact you since this event?

Complainant: Yes. He has texted me several times. He asked me to go out again, and I responded saying I do not wish to go to dinner.

Interviewer: Do you have anything else you would like to share with us at this time?

Complainant: Not at this time. I would like him to stop asking me out and texting me. I made it pretty clear I was not interested in dating him.

Interviewer: Thank you for sharing this with us. Again, I wish to reiterate this interview is confidential. Do you feel safe working with this individual? We can reassign you to another floor but only if you agree. You do not have to change assignments if you do not want to.

Complainant: I feel safe. I am avoiding him during our shifts, and he is a traveler. I doubt he will be getting another assignment here after this. But temporarily working on a different unit will make me more comfortable at work.

Interviewer: We will make the arrangements.

Respondent Interview

Interviewer: Good morning. My name is Judy Johnson, and this is my colleague, Steven Page. We are part of a team of individuals who investigate claims of sexual harassment and misconduct here at St. Elsewhere. We understand this interview may be difficult, and we want to assure you this interview will remain confidential.

Part of the process of investigating the report includes interviewing all parties involved. We will keep you informed in as much detail as possible, and if you have any questions or concerns after this interview, please contact us. As we ask the questions, if you need time to gather your thoughts or need a moment for any reason, take your time.

A formal complaint was filed about an incident that took place at approximately 3 a.m. while you were on shift with a fellow female nurse. She states you pinned her against the wall and attempted to kiss her cheek. In your own words, can you tell us about the event?

Respondent: Certainly. I am not sure why this is being reported, but here is what happened. We went to the break room to have a bite to eat, and she was washing a plate when I tried to squeeze by her. I tripped and briefly, I pushed her to the wall as I was falling forward. It's a pretty tiny room, and I had no choice but to put my hand up to brace my fall, and I guess my head came too close to hers.

I was not trying to kiss her as she claims. She told me to back off, and of course, I did. I am not sure if she realized I tripped. She then quickly left the room and did not say anything to me the rest of the night. I am not quite sure why I am here. I am a bit confused.

Interviewer: Before this event, did you have any contact with her?

Respondent: A few days after I arrived, we finished a shift and went to a place down the street for breakfast. I found out she was single and asked her if she would like to maybe go out for dinner sometime. She said she would let me know.

Interviewer: She states you offered to take her out on a dinner date via text. Did you ask her out for dinner the following week?

Respondent: Yes. I did text her. I had mentioned it at breakfast and did not really hear from her, so I decided to text her. She said she was not interested.

Interviewer: After the event during that morning, she says you have sent several texts asking her out. Is this true?

Respondent: Yes.

Interviewer: She stated she was not interested. Is this correct?

Respondent: Yes.

Interviewer: As this investigation is ongoing, we are politely asking you to avoid any further contact with her. Do you agree to comply with this?

Respondent: Yes.

Interviewer: This interview is confidential, and we will keep you informed as the investigation continues. If you have any other questions or concerns, please contact us.

ANALYSIS OF THE INFORMATION

Based on the information from the interviews alone, even if the respondent had tripped, the complainant's interpretation of the event was that it was intentional and not accidental. Since it was unwitnessed, it is impossible to verify the complainant's account.

However, another form of harassment developed around this single event. The respondent repeatedly asked her for a date she did not want, and she feels uncomfortable at this point. Even if she has not filed a formal complaint about the unwanted offers, the investigators are obligated to inform the respondent that continuing to ask her on dates is harassment, and the behavior must stop.

Notably, he did not deny attempting to ask her out, and he seemed forthright in telling his version of the event. Had he not answered the questions honestly, the veracity of his account of the event is questionable. The resolution of this case should involve a formal letter requesting the respondent no longer make any contact with the complainant. Assigning the complainant to a new work location will likely be temporary, as the respondent will move on to a new assignment.

It is a useful exercise to hypothetically consider how alternative responses to the interview questions influence the course of the investigation. For example, what if the respondent denied the account of the events? What if, during the investigation, the complainant lied about making contact and had a dinner date a few days prior to the event? There are dozens of scenarios to consider, and the outcome and course of the investigation is influenced by the narratives and responses revealed during the interviews.

The take-home points while conducting interviews are to remain objective, sensitive, consistent, respectful, and, as much as possible, without bias. Everyone's emotional responses during the interviews are a natural part of the process. People cannot change how they feel about a situation, but they can regulate *how* they respond.

Approaching the interview process with a high degree of emotional intelligence, confidence, and competence makes the process less intimidating. The sample interview form that follows can be a useful guide. Feeling comfortable interviewing grows over time.

REFERENCES

1. Rock A. How to Conduct Trauma-informed Sexual Assault Investigations. *Campus Safety*. October 18, 2023. https://www.campussafetymagazine.com/clery/how-to-conduct-trauma-informed-sexual-assault-investigations/.

2. Cheung M. Child Sexual Abuse Interview Protocol (CSAIP). Graduate College of Social Work. University of Houston, Texas; 2012.

3. O'Dononue W, Cirlugea O. Controlling for Confirmation Bias in Child Sexual Abuse Interview. *J Am Acad Psychiatry Law*. 2021; 49 (3): 371–380.

INTERVIEW FORM

Date: _____

Time: _____

Location of Interview: _____

Interviewer: _____

Interviewee: _____

    (circle one) Complainant Respondent or Witness

Co-interviewer/Witness: _____

Who was involved? _____

Names of witnesses: _____

When did it occur? _____

Where did it occur? _____

What happened? _____

Nature of relationship: _____

Contact before or after event: _____

Does the interviewee feel safe? _____

If necessary, does the complainant agree to a work reassignment? _____

_____

Summary: _____

_____

_____

_____

_____

_____

Chapter 45. False Allegations and Consequences

F ALSE ALLEGATIONS OF SEXUAL ASSAULT or misconduct are not common, and an analysis of 10 years of reported cases of sexual assault found that approximately 6% of reported cases of rape were false.[1] False accusations of sexual assault or misconduct can have devastating consequences for the accused, their families, and even survivors of assault whose voices may be doubted as a result.

Determining the validity of false claims of harassment can be difficult, but consistently using the same investigative approach can help confirm or refute claims. Consistency in investigating incidents is critical.

Inconsistent narratives in the victim's story are a red flag, and spinning a web of lies requires remembering details that did not occur. More probing questions followed by long pauses or *changes in details* from complainants with different interviewers or the authorities can indicate the allegations are false. However, due to barriers in reporting, some victims may not come forward until months or even years after the events. Details about what occurred can be forgotten.[2] Traumatized victims may not recall the assault in a "linear" fashion — the memories are often fragmented. As a result, determining whether or not the allegation is true is challenging for investigators.

CASE STUDIES

Case 1

In 2017, Dr. M, a highly respected pediatrician with over 20 years of experience, faced a wrongful accusation of sexual misconduct that shook his career and reputation. Dr. M had been practicing at a well-known children's hospital for over a decade when a teenage patient, who we'll call Emma, accused him of inappropriate behavior during a routine examination. Emma alleged that Dr. M had touched her inappropriately and made suggestive comments during the examination.

The accusation shocked Dr. M and his colleagues, as he had always been known for his professionalism and compassionate care. Dr. M denied the allegations, stating that his interactions with Emma had been entirely appropriate and focused solely on her medical care. The hospital, obligated to take all allegations of misconduct seriously, launched an investigation into the matter. Dr. M cooperated fully with the investigation, providing his account of the examination and presenting evidence to support his innocence.

As news of the accusation spread, Dr. M faced public scrutiny and condemnation. He was suspended from his duties pending the outcome of the investigation, which further fueled speculation and damaged his reputation. Throughout the investigation, Dr. M maintained his innocence and received overwhelming support from his patients, their families, and fellow medical professionals. Many attested to his integrity and dedication to patient care, casting doubt on the credibility of the accusation.

The investigation ultimately concluded with a finding of insufficient evidence to support Emma's allegations. The hospital reinstated Dr. M to his position, but the damage had been done. His reputation had been tarnished, and he faced challenges in rebuilding trust with patients and colleagues.

Dr. M's experience underscores the devastating impact of wrongful accusations of sexual misconduct on healthcare professionals. It highlights the importance of due process, thorough investigations, and preserving the presumption of innocence until proven guilty. While Dr. M was ultimately vindicated, the ordeal took a toll on his mental and emotional well-being. It served as a stark reminder of the need for fairness, transparency, and accountability in addressing allegations of misconduct in healthcare settings.

Case 2

A 34-year-old male-to-female transgender patient presented with acute psychosis, depression, and PTSD with suicidal ideation. The patient had been reluctant to participate in treatment because, she says, "No one treats me well in the hospital." She requests a private room because, she says, other patients have called her a "freak." The patient regularly met with a therapist during her initial course, and a plan was created for her to be discharged. The patient refused and demanded to be transferred to another state for "original pain" work.

The therapist refused to respond to this request, and the patient alleged the therapist demanded sexual favors from her. The patient, in fact, threatened to contact the district attorney's office. The patient was then interviewed by the program director and the local police. The patient indicated there may have been a misunderstanding and withdrew the allegation.

Case 3

A 23-year-old female with a history of sexual abuse from ages 8 to 11 and major depression was admitted to the hospital for a suicide attempt. She had recently taken legal action against her family members for the abuse. Nine days after admission, the patient experienced confusion, difficulty organizing her thoughts, and dissociation. An EEG was ordered to rule out a potential lesion. The EEG was performed without issues, but seven hours after returning to the floor, the patient reported that a male staff member had sexually penetrated her during the EEG.

She demanded to be taken to a rape crisis center and was transported to another hospital. An examination was performed, and there was no evidence of any trauma or sexual activity. A review of the study showed no abnormalities and no tracing artifact that would appear with any significant motion. It was physically impossible for the events she described to occur with this evidence.

Case 4

A 45-year-old female nurse alleged that a 53-year-old male nurse who worked on the same floor grabbed her breasts and attempted to put his hand down her pants in the medication room. She told her supervisor at the end of the shift. An investigation into the matter revealed several important details.

The female nurse reported that the incident took place at about 9:30 p.m. The male nurse denied being in the room at the same time as the female nurse. Time-stamped computer entries confirmed that the male nurse was in a patient's room performing an admission, which takes at least 20 minutes. His timed entries in the electronic medical record confirmed that he was logged in and entering data from 9:25 to 9:50 p.m. The female nurse left the medication room at 9:36 p.m.

When the female nurse was confronted with this evidence, she retracted her claim. She stated that she and the male nurse had been having an affair (both are married) for about six months, and about one week prior to her reporting the incident, he decided to break it off. Angry, she said this was a way to "get back at him" for dumping her. After the retraction, the male nurse asked to be reassigned to another unit.

MOTIVES FOR MAKING FALSE CLAIMS

The motives for making false claims are varied:

Exploitation. False claims are often made to obtain financial rewards or other clinical treatment support. In the case of the transgender patient mentioned, the patient desired special treatment by refusing to accept the treatment plan.[2]

Retaliation. After a sexual or emotional relationship, if the decision to separate is not mutual, one party may feel upset and angry. The motive may be to inflict emotional pain or other suffering.[3]

Psychopathology. A patient's past experiences and emotional trauma may be so severe they have a distorted sense of reality. The patient who was sexually abused as a child, for example, may have been reliving past trauma during the EEG exam. In a dissociated or psychotic state, the patient can hallucinate. The intent is not malicious, as the experience from the patient's perspective is that these events are real.

Personality disorders are difficult to diagnose and treat, but patients and employees with Cluster B type personality disorders (narcissistic, borderline, and anti-social) exhibit certain traits and behaviors that can lead to false allegations. Collectively, individuals with these disorders experience volatile, unpredictable, and dramatic emotions.

Individuals with borderline personality disorder have a variety of symptoms; the most common include[4]:

1. Fear of abandonment.
2. Unstable relationships.
3. Unstable self-image.
4. Impulsive behaviors.
5. Self-harm.
6. Emotional instability.
7. Feelings of emptiness.
8. Inappropriate anger.
9. Stress-related paranoia.

Individuals with borderline personality disorder may have chaotic and unstable personal relationships. This may or may not impact the individual's capacity to perform at a high level professionally.

Individuals with histrionic personality disorder crave being the center of attention, can engage in inappropriate or provocative behaviors, are easily influenced, and can sometimes feel the relationship is more intimate than it is.

Patients who are delirious, demented, psychotic, or under the influence of drugs or alcohol can also make false claims.

Fabrication to Feel Special. Some patients fabricate an intimate liaison or encounter to feel special or unique. Work colleagues, too, may engage in similar behaviors.

Hide an Affair or Inappropriate Relationship. Some people falsely claim consensual sex as an assault to absolve the victim of responsibility for his or her decisions.

RESPONSES TO FALSE CLAIMS

Knowing whether an allegation is true is often difficult at the start of any investigation. It is an ethical and moral imperative to take every claim seriously. *The response to every claim must be thoughtful, respectful, prompt, and confidential.* When a claim is filed, the process and substance of the investigation and inquiry should be carefully documented. Because of the potential destructive impact of a false claim, if the inquiry can proceed confidentially, it is in the best interest of all parties. The professional reputation and career of an individual who is falsely accused can have devastating personal and professional consequences.

REFERENCES

1. Lisak D, Gardinier L, Nicksa SC, Cote AM. False Allegations of Sexual Assault: An Analysis of Ten Years of Reported Cases. *Violence Against Women.* 2010;16(12):1318–1334.
2. De Zutter AWEA, Horselenberg R, van Koppen PJ. Motives for Filing a False Allegation of Rape. *Arch Sex Behav.* 2018;47(20):457–464. doi:10.1007/s10508-017-0951-3
3. Sederer L, Libby M. False Allegations of Sexual Misconduct: Clinical and Institutional Considerations. *Psychiatr Serv.* 1995;46(2):160–163.
4. Engle J, O'Donohue W. Pathways to False Allegations of Sexual Assault. *J Forensic Psychol Pract.* 2012;12(2): 97–123. doi:10.1080/15228932.2012.650071

Chapter 46. After an Investigation, Disposition, Follow Up, and Management

ONCE AN INVESTIGATION AND DISPOSITION are complete, many important tasks remain. First, a time limit is essential if an attributed individual is required to complete any remedial training or coursework. Any delays in completing required work or a refusal to complete required work need to be addressed.

Some employees might feel they can "test" the system. This is rare, but it has occurred. In this case, medical staff affairs, human resources, and possibly legal counsel must be made aware of the lapse, and a clear course of action and plan must be created.

Organizations should have clearly outlined procedures, processes, and policies delineating the organization's responsibilities and the individual or individuals involved. As an example, in the Larry Nassar case, there were email exchanges between Nassar and William Strampel discussing the conduct concerns at the clinic. A formal and, if necessary, certified letter detailing expectations or disposition is the best approach. It is a legal document. Haphazardly treating the communication process via email, while convenient, does not protect the confidentiality of the individuals or the organization. It is unprofessional and fails to communicate the seriousness of the concerns.

When I was chair of professional behavior, the committee met with attributed individuals and sent a follow-up letter to the physician after discussing the meeting and disposition. The process was transparent, professional, and respectful. Each institution has its own set of bylaws, rules, and regulations. If you are personally or professionally involved in a case or its investigation and/or disposition, do not discuss the case with anyone not directly involved. Maintain confidentiality at all times.

Prevention in the Workplace

*"Trying to rely on the sheer good luck of avoiding bad outcomes
indefinitely would simply guarantee that we would eventually fail
without the means of recovering." — David Deutsch, British physicist*

PREVENTING SEXUAL MISCONDUCT, harassment, and discrimination in the workplace is a moral and ethical responsibility of individuals and the organization. *Everyone* in the organization is responsible for conducting themselves in a manner conducive to eliminating the problem. Employees, staff, and leaders — people — are the organization. However, creating and offering programs, prevention efforts, policies, and training are the responsibility of organizational leadership and owners. Effective prevention should entail much more than a checkbox approach so often offered during the onboarding process.

Nearly 75% of companies offer formal harassment training, and a third of these firms spend as much as $100,000 on training programs. Many organizations purchase video modules, offer webinars to employees, or use handouts and electronic policy statements to educate employees and staff. These approaches are, in my opinion, less effective because they are informative rather than instructive, and the learning modules are passive in nature.

A radical new approach uses the principles of andragogy adult learning theory — and incorporates experiential learning, hands-on learning, self-directed learning, role-playing, and live discussions.

∞

Chapter 47. Ethics and Moral Obligations

*"The United States had a system for muting sexual harassment claims,
which often enabled the harassers instead of stopping them. Women
routinely signed away the right to talk about their own experiences.*

Harassers often continued onward, finding fresh ground on which to commit the same offenses. The settlements and confidentiality agreements were almost never examined in law school classrooms or open court. This was why the public had never really understood that this was happening. Even those in the room with long histories of covering gender issues had never fully registered what was going on." — Jodi Kantor, author of She Said: Breaking the Sexual Harassment Story That Helped Ignite a Movement

ONE OF THE MODERN MYTHS in medicine is the belief that the phrase *"First, do no harm"* is part of the Hippocratic Oath. It is not, and the closest approximation can be found in Hippocrates work, *Of the Epidemics,* which states, "The physician must be able to tell the antecedents, know the present, and foretell the future — must mediate these things, and have two special objects in view with regard to disease, namely, to do good or to do no harm."

The phrase "First, do no harm" is believed to have originated with Thomas Sydenham, an English surgeon in the 19th century.[1] Hippocrates did, however, describe the importance of four ethical principles for physicians to consider when caring for patients:

- **Autonomy** – respect for the patient's right to self-determination.
- **Beneficence** – the duty to "do good"
- **Non-Maleficence** – the duty to "not do bad."
- **Justice** – to treat all people equally and equitably.

The ethics of sexual misconduct and harassment prevention encompass a broad spectrum of considerations aimed at fostering a safe, respectful, and equitable environment for all individuals. The ethical principles that guide sexual harassment prevention include respect for individual dignity, fairness, accountability, and the promotion of a culture of respect and inclusion.

As healthcare providers, we have an obligation to not serve our own interests at the expense of caring for patients, and organizations share that obligation and responsibility to act in an ethical manner.

KEY ETHICAL PRINCIPLES FOR INVESTIGATORS AND ORGANIZATIONS

Respect for Individual Dignity: Every person deserves to be treated with respect and dignity, free from any form of harassment or discrimination.

This principle underpins the ethical imperative to prevent sexual harassment and to protect the rights and well-being of all individuals.

Fairness and Justice: Ethical sexual harassment prevention policies and practices must ensure fairness and justice for all parties involved. This includes providing due process for those accused of harassment and ensuring that allegations are thoroughly and impartially investigated.

Accountability: Organizations and individuals must be held accountable for preventing and addressing sexual harassment. This includes implementing clear policies, providing training and education, and taking appropriate action when harassment occurs.

Confidentiality and Privacy: Respecting the confidentiality and privacy of all parties involved in sexual harassment allegations is crucial. This helps protect the identities and reputations of both the accuser and the accused while ensuring a fair investigation process.

Support and Protection: Providing support and protection for victims of sexual harassment is essential. This includes offering resources such as counseling, legal assistance, and ensuring that victims do not face retaliation for reporting harassment.

Transparency: Maintaining transparency in how sexual harassment allegations are handled is important for building trust within an organization. This involves clear communication about policies, procedures, and outcomes of investigations while balancing the need for confidentiality.

IMPLEMENTATION OF ETHICAL
SEXUAL HARASSMENT PREVENTION

Policy Development: Organizations should develop comprehensive sexual harassment policies that clearly define what constitutes harassment, outline reporting procedures, and specify the consequences of such behavior. These policies should be regularly reviewed and updated to reflect best practices and legal requirements.

Education and Training: Regular training and education on sexual harassment prevention should be provided to all members of an organization. This creates awareness, fosters a culture of respect, and equips individuals with the knowledge to recognize and prevent harassment.

Prompt and Impartial Investigations: Allegations of sexual harassment must be investigated promptly and impartially. This ensures that all parties are treated fairly and that appropriate actions are taken based on the findings of the investigation.

A Culture of Respect: Fostering a culture of respect and inclusion is essential for preventing sexual harassment. This involves promoting values such as empathy, integrity, and mutual respect within the organization.

Leadership Commitment: Ethical prevention of sexual harassment requires strong commitment from organizational leadership. Leaders must model appropriate behavior, support policy enforcement, and allocate resources for prevention efforts.

CHALLENGES AND OTHER CONSIDERATIONS

Balancing Rights and Interests: Ensuring the rights of both the accuser and the accused can be challenging. Ethical policies must balance these interests to provide justice while preventing harm to any party involved.

Cultural Sensitivity: Organizations must consider cultural differences and sensitivities in their approach to sexual harassment prevention. This includes being aware of how cultural norms and values may influence perceptions and experiences of harassment.

Continuous Improvement: Sexual harassment prevention is an ongoing process that requires continuous improvement. Organizations should regularly assess the effectiveness of their policies and practices and be willing to make necessary adjustments or alter program offerings and training.

KEY MORAL PRINCIPLES

The moral obligation to prevent sexual harassment in healthcare is particularly significant due to the unique and sensitive nature of the environment. Healthcare professionals are entrusted with the care and well-being of patients, often in vulnerable situations. This trust necessitates a higher standard of conduct and a robust commitment to ethical principles. Here are key aspects of this moral obligation:

Duty of Care

Patient Trust and Safety: Healthcare professionals have a moral duty to ensure the safety and trust of their patients. Sexual harassment undermines this trust and can cause significant emotional and psychological harm, which is contrary to the fundamental principles of healthcare.

Vulnerability of Patients: Patients often find themselves in vulnerable positions due to illness, injury, or dependency on medical professionals. This vulnerability heightens the moral obligation to protect them from any form of exploitation, including sexual harassment.

Professional Integrity

Ethical Standards: The healthcare profession is governed by stringent ethical standards that emphasize respect, compassion, and integrity. Preventing sexual harassment is integral to upholding these standards and ensuring that care is delivered in a respectful and dignified manner.

Role Modeling: Healthcare professionals serve as role models in society. Their behavior sets a standard for others in the community. By actively preventing sexual harassment, they reinforce the importance of respect and ethical behavior in all professional behaviors, communication, and interactions with others.

Legal Obligations

Compliance with Laws: There are legal frameworks in place that mandate the prevention of sexual harassment in the workplace. Healthcare institutions have a moral obligation to comply with these laws to protect their employees and patients.

Institutional Responsibility: Healthcare institutions have a moral duty to create and enforce policies that prevent sexual harassment. This includes training staff, providing clear reporting mechanisms, and taking prompt action when incidents occur.

CREATING A CULTURE OF RESPECT

Education and Training: Continuous education and training about sexual harassment and respectful behavior are crucial in creating a culture of respect. Healthcare institutions have a moral obligation to provide this education to all staff members.

Zero Tolerance Policy: Implementing and enforcing a zero-tolerance policy for sexual harassment sends a clear message that such behavior will not be tolerated. This is essential in fostering a safe and respectful environment.

Support Systems: Providing support systems for victims of sexual harassment, including counseling and legal assistance, is part of the moral obligation of healthcare institutions. Ensuring that victims feel supported and safe to report incidents is crucial.

THE COMPLEXITY OF THE ISSUE

There are a number of ethical implications around sexual harassment in organizations and workplaces that make it complex:

1. **The reasonable person test.**

   A challenge in dealing with sexual harassment is the fact that many have markedly different views on what constitutes harassment. The complexity here is that applying subjective values to sexual harassment can make a mockery of the law. In order to deal with this in harassment cases, courts can apply the reasonable person test. In this test, an ideal model of what constitutes a reasonable man or woman with reasonable values is used to determine the threshold at which a specific behavior is considered sexual harassment.

2. **The responsibility of the employer.**

   An employer has a responsibility to prevent sexual harassment in the workplace. This means enforcing a strict code of conduct, modeling good behavior, and possibly implementing a whistleblower hotline for anonymous reporting of unethical behavior. However, what companies are required to do in this regard varies by state. For example, California law requires that employers are liable for harassment by their managers.

3. **The hostile work environment.**

   The broader implication of sexual harassment in the workplace is that it can create a hostile work environment for some employees. This may lead to loss of productivity, high staff turnover, legal and financial ramifications, and brand damage.

The moral obligation to prevent sexual harassment in healthcare is driven by the duty to protect patients, uphold professional integrity, comply with legal and ethical standards, and ensure high-quality care. By fostering a culture of respect, providing continuous education, and implementing strict policies, healthcare institutions can fulfill their moral obligation and create a safe and supportive environment for both patients and staff.

Case Study

A 15-year-old adolescent male is scheduled for a visit with his local pediatrician for a routine physical exam and screening to participate as a high school football team player. The patient is accompanied by his father, who picked him up after school for the appointment.

The patient is brought into a private exam area while the father waits in the waiting room. The physician introduces herself to the young patient. As the history and physical exam proceed, she asks him if he is sexually active, and he begins to get tearful and silent. Concerned, she asks what is wrong, and he says, "My parents do not know this, but I am gay, and I do not know what to do. I am afraid they will disown me if I tell them or if they find out. I am having sex with a classmate, and his parents don't know about him or us. It is a big secret, and I am scared if anyone finds out."

Does the physician have an ethical and/or legal duty to include the patient's sexual orientation and activity in the patient's chart?

What if the patient shared with the physician that he was feeling suicidal because of his sexual orientation and the intolerance he feels at home and with other friends?

The patient's mother finds out about her son's sexual orientation when she looks at his electronic medical record a few days later. Upset, she calls the physician's office and demands to speak with the physician. During the conversation, the mother of the patient demands to know why she was not informed about her son's sexual orientation and activity. She is angry the physician offered her son advice and education on safe sex practices.

How should the physician respond?

REFERENCE

1. Shmerling R. *The Myth of the Hippocratic Oath*. Harvard Health Blog, November 25, 2015. https://www.health.harvard.edu/blog/the-myth-of-the-hippocratic-oath-201511258447.

Chapter 48. Organizational Responsibilities to Respond to Claims

"Vulnerability sounds like truth and feels like courage. Truth and courage aren't always comfortable, but they're never weakness." — Brené Brown, author, professor, and podcaster

A PROMINENT ORTHOPEDIC SURGEON at a teaching hospital in Los Angeles was fired after a two-year investigation. Investigators found that Louis Kwong sometimes looked under the surgical covers of black males who were under anesthesia and discussed the "genitals of the day," according to his discharge notice. Kwong also discussed his favorite sex positions and his preference for "auto-erotic asphyxiation," his colleagues told investigators.[1,2]

In 2013, Maria Garibay, then a medical secretary, told the county's human resources department that Kwong would have discussions with his staff about the women he operated on and "the variations in which they groom their pubic areas." According to Garibay, rather than investigate the claims, her supervisors transferred her to another office away from Kwong. Kwong was also reported to have carried a gun into the operating room and failed to disclose financial relationships with medical device companies that provided products for his surgical procedures.[1]

In 2019, a medical student accused Kwong of entering an operating room to peek "under the hood" and look at a patient's genitalia. The comments, posted on a site used to rate orthopedic programs, were flagged for the hospital's director of risk management, who responded that they had "started working on this."[1] These allegations about the orthopedics department burst into public view in 2023.

Two female orthopedic surgeons and one female emergency room physician, a former director of the emergency medicine residency program, sued the county. In their lawsuits, the plaintiffs say they were demoted or retaliated against when they reported or complained about Kwong's behavior. Before they sued, all three physicians tried other remedies over many years, according to their suits, including filing grievances with the county and complaining to superiors.[2]

The hospital did not launch an investigation until the fall of 2021, and it wasn't until the spring of 2022 that Kwong was put on paid leave during the investigation.[1] This case illustrates how an organization can fail to listen and respond to allegations of sexual harassment and unprofessional behavior. As a result, the misconduct continued to the point of creating a toxic atmosphere and unsafe patient care environment.

As much as individuals are responsible for their own behaviors, institutions, too, are responsible to take claims seriously and immediately begin an objective investigation. In my opinion, these actions were delayed for numerous reasons in Kwong's case.

First, orthopedic surgeons generate millions of dollars in revenue for hospitals. Second, taking any negative action would become public and harm the reputation of the facility. Third, hospital administrators might not have felt comfortable proceeding with an investigation involving a prominent surgeon.

Preventing these events and mitigating this conduct is not an option. The next chapters in this section provide insight into policies, behaviors, training, and programs to formally address and understand this complex topic. Organizations can successfully navigate through these incidents, but it is not possible if there is indifference, fear, or lack of strong policy and expectations.

REFERENCES

1. Ellis R. Harbor-UCLA Doctor Is Fired After County Finds He Regularly Gawked at Patients' Genitalia. *Los Angeles Times.* April 20, 2024. https://www.latimes.com/california/story/2024-04-20/doctor-paid-leave-fired.
2. Morgensen G. Three Female Doctors Sue L.A. County, Alleging It Ignored Complaints About an Abusive Boss at Harbor-UCLA Hospital. *NBC News.* October 11, 2023. https://www.nbcnews.com/health/health-news/female-doctors-sue-la-county-ignored-complaints-abusive-surgeon-rcna119562.

Chapter 49. Conduct Policies and Setting Expectations

"For employers to effectively prevent sexual harassment, assault, or rape from occurring, they must not only have strong policies, but they must also enforce those policies." — Rebecca Lucero, commissioner, Minnesota Department of Human Rights

CONDUCT POLICIES SPECIFICALLY ADDRESSING sexual discrimination, harassment, and misconduct are nearly universal in all industries and organizations. To the best of my knowledge, all healthcare organizations have formal policies. However, there is no universal written policy or standard policy in use. Each organization has created unique documents compliant with local, state, and federal laws, regulations, and requirements.

KEY COMPONENTS OF A SEXUAL HARASSMENT POLICY

An effective sexual harassment policy should encompass several key elements:

- **Purpose and Scope** — Describes the policy's goals and the range of behaviors it covers, reinforcing its applicability to all employees, regardless of position or status.
- **Definitions of Harassment** — Provides specific, legal definitions of sexual harassment, including examples to guide understanding.
- **Guidelines for Conduct** — Provides a detailed description of acceptable and unacceptable behaviors to prevent ambiguity and encourage compliance.
- **Reporting Procedures** — Clearly outlines the process for reporting incidents, ensuring confidentiality and protection from retaliation.
- **Investigation and Enforcement** — Details the procedures for investigating reports of harassment and the subsequent actions that will follow a confirmed violation.
- **Penalties for Violations** — Enumerates possible sanctions for policy breaches, emphasizing the seriousness of infractions.
- **Acknowledgment of Understanding** — Requires employees to affirm their comprehension and agreement to abide by the policy's stipulations.

Retaliation for reporting is unlawful. Equal Employment Opportunity Commission laws prohibit punishing job applicants or employees for asserting their rights to be free from employment discrimination, including harassment.[1] Asserting these Equal Employment Opportunity (EEO) rights is called "protected activity," and it can take many forms. For example, it is unlawful to retaliate against applicants or employees for:

- Filing or being a witness in an EEO charge, complaint, investigation, or lawsuit.
- Communicating with a supervisor or manager about employment discrimination, including harassment.
- Answering questions during an employer investigation of alleged harassment.
- Refusing to follow orders that would result in discrimination.
- Resisting sexual advances, or intervening to protect others.
- Requesting accommodation for a disability or religious practice.
- Asking managers or co-workers about salary information to uncover potentially discriminatory wages.

Participating in a complaint process is protected from retaliation under all circumstances. Other acts to oppose discrimination are protected as long as the employee was acting on a reasonable belief that something in the workplace may violate EEO laws, even if he or she did not use legal terminology to describe it.

Engaging in EEO activity, however, does not shield an employee from all discipline or discharge. Employers can discipline or terminate workers if motivated by *non-retaliatory and non-discriminatory* reasons that would otherwise result in such consequences. However, an employer is not allowed to take action in response to EEO activity that would discourage someone from resisting or complaining about future discrimination.

For example, depending on the facts, it could be considered retaliation if an employer takes the following types of actions in response to an employee's EEO activity:

- Reprimand the employee or give a performance evaluation that is lower than it should be.
- Transfer the employee to a less desirable position.

- Verbally or physically abuse the employee.
- Threaten to make or make reports to authorities against the employee, such as reporting immigration status.
- Increase scrutiny of the employee.
- Spread false rumors about the employee and/or their family.
- Make the person's work more difficult, such as purposefully changing the employee's work schedule to conflict with family responsibilities.

The EEOC has a public portal to report retaliation.

How organizations approach sexual harassment conduct expectations sets the tone for organizational tolerance. Setting expectations begins during the onboarding process. I advocate telling new employees the organization has a zero-tolerance stance on sexual abuse, misconduct, and harassment. This messaging makes it abundantly clear that the issue is a serious matter that will be strictly enforced. Anything less than a strong, concise, clear, and consistent message can lead to failure.

PATIENT AND VISITOR CODES OF CONDUCT

In the same spirit as a professional conduct and sexual harassment policy for staff and employees, many healthcare systems have created a separate and comprehensive code of conduct for patients and visitors. The following is an example:

Patient and Visitor Code of Conduct: Blue Ridge River Valley Medical Center

Blue Ridge River Valley Medical Center (BRRVMC) is committed to providing high-quality care to our patients and communities in a safe and respectful environment that supports health and healing. To ensure our hospitals and care locations are safe, caring, and inclusive, we ask that patients and visitors follow the example of BRRVMC providers and associates by adhering to our Patient and Visitor Code of Conduct, which includes the following:

- Everyone will be treated with kindness, dignity, and respect. Offensive comments about race, religion, gender, sexual orientation, or personal traits are not acceptable, and neither is the refusal to see a clinician or associate based on these traits.

- All patients and visitors will use respectful, appropriate language and behavior. Physical or verbal threats or assaults, suggestive or explicit words, phrases, gestures, or actions will not be tolerated.
- All patients and visitors will respect patient privacy and avoid disrupting other patients' care or experiences.
- All patients and visitors must obtain the consent of everyone involved for any photographing or video/audio recording within all hospitals and patient care locations.

If these guidelines are not followed:

- Patients may be asked to leave and make other plans for their non-emergent immediate care, and for severe violations, future non-emergency care at BRRVMC may require review. In cases of non-compliance, patients will have an opportunity to explain their perspective, which will be considered prior to any decisions regarding future care at BRRVMC.
- Visitors may be asked to leave and could be restricted from future visitation.

Every day, our providers, nurses, and associates are committed to providing the highest levels of care to our patients. Please show them the respect they deserve and that you expect as a patient or visitor.

The document must be thorough, simple, and accessible to all patients and visitors. Some healthcare institutions require patients and visitors to acknowledge reading a code of conduct and attesting that he or she understands and is willing to comply with the expectations.

REFERENCE

1. EEOC. Retaliation. https://www.eeoc.gov/retaliation.

Chapter 50. Credentialing, Privileging, and Background Checks

HOSPITALS, PHYSICIAN GROUPS, and hospital systems have a duty to protect the public from harm from physicians, and the credentialing process is part of that duty.

Red flags on an application include unexplained time gaps in work history, references that raise issues, negative or no response from a reference, disciplinary actions, any claims or investigations of fraud, unusually high number of malpractice claims, and discrepancies between information provided by the applicant and what is received from references or other sources. Organizations have been blindsided by physicians when past incidents or other claims were not disclosed during the credentialing process.

A major flaw in our current healthcare system is the lack of a consistent and standardized process for credentialing and giving physicians privileges. Every state medical board has a separate licensing authority, and institutions and hospital systems also have different methods and procedures. With variations in processes, errors and other important information can be missed.

CASE STUDY

A middle-aged male anesthesiologist applies for privileges at a local community hospital as a locum tenens physician. In the application for privileges, the physician discloses that he had been arrested for assaulting his wife during a sexual encounter. Specifically, the physician was accused of biting his wife on the lip during sex.

The charges were subsequently dropped, and the physician reported that the issue was resolved. There was a significant time gap in the physician's career, including a one-year gap two years ago and a six-month gap three years ago. The physician disclosed the reasons for the gaps as a personal matter that has been resolved.

The three references were contacted and stated he was an excellent clinician, and they have no reservations in recommending him. Other than the resolved arrest and the time gap, the rest of the application is clean. Should the credentials committee approve this physician's application?

As chair of the credentialing committee, I presented and discussed this physician's application. It was one of the most uncomfortable and awkward cases I have ever discussed with a committee. Something seemed "off" about the applicant, but we had no choice but to offer him privileges. There were no legal grounds for our committee to deny his application, and we consulted an attorney to discuss this case, as I had reservations about approving his application.

My suspicion that there were deeper issues and concerns with this physician was proven true when, at another hospital in the state, he performed a wrong-site nerve block on a patient and attempted to hide it. He was reported to the medical board, and his license was temporarily suspended. He also filed several lawsuits against two groups who had used his services as a locum physician. Upon learning about the suspended medical license, we immediately suspended his privileges at our hospital as well.

Chapter 51. Effectiveness of Formal Prevention Programs

I N MAY 2020, THE *HARVARD BUSINESS REVIEW* (HBR) published an article titled *Why Sexual Harassment Programs Backfire* based on a paper by Frank Dobbin and Alexandra Kalev published in 2019.[1] The authors conclude that "neither the training programs that most companies put all workers through nor the grievance procedures that they have implemented are helping to solve the problem of sexual harassment in the workplace."

In 1998, the Supreme Court reviewed and established legal precedent regarding the two most common sexual harassment programs in workplaces: sexual harassment grievance procedures and training programs through two landmark cases: *Faragher vs. City of Boca Raton* and *Burlington Industries, Inc. vs. Ellerth*. In these cases, the court established that employers can be held vicariously liable for sexual harassment by supervisors unless they demonstrate that they took reasonable action to prevent or correct such harassment. By 1998, 95% of companies had grievance procedures and 74% had training.

According to Dobbin and Kalev, raising awareness of misconduct and harassment may seem to "backfire" because recognition of harassment can be an antecedent to an increase in reports and complaints. Victims also fear retaliation if they complain.[1] It is notoriously difficult to measure the prevalence and incidence of harassment in workplaces where employees do not feel comfortable reporting events. Therefore, measuring the overall effectiveness of training programs is challenging but not impossible.

BARRIERS TO EFFECTIVE TRAINING

In 1980, training and grievance protocol education was virtually non-existent. By 1987, 75% of federal workers had completed training, and by 1994, 80% knew how to file a grievance.[2]

Did harassment decline from 1980 to 1994? When federal workers were asked questions about specific forms of harassment in 1980, 42% of women reported harassment over the prior two-year period. In 1994, there was a very slight *increase* to 44%.[2] The programs implemented were failing to address the problem of harassment. Dobbin and Kalev posit the training programs amount to managerial "snake oil" and organizations are using the wrong approach.

An atmosphere and environment tolerant of sexual harassment or having ineffective grievance procedures causes women to leave managerial positions.[2] Managers are liaisons between subordinate employees and executive management in business organizations and are often the first individuals to receive a report of harassment. Dobbins and Kalev suggest that a reduced rate of sexual harassment would be reflected by women staying in management and that the number of women in management should increase.

In Chapter 14, which discusses barriers to reporting, I point out that many victims choose not to report harassment or misconduct due to distrust in the process, fear of retaliation, and failure to remove or discipline the harasser. Indeed, research has shown that filing a grievance is perilous. A 2003 study found that 66% of women who filed complaints faced retaliation.[3]

A high rate of retaliation is reflective of an unsafe environment for filing a grievance and is a sign of organizational failure. As Marcellus in Shakespeare's *Hamlet* states in Act 1, "*Something is rotten in the state of Denmark.*" A non-supportive, toxic culture is a fertile breeding ground for continued misconduct and harassment.

Another concern is evidence that suggests that women who file a report show worse career, mental health, and health outcomes compared to those who do not file.[4] Everyone suffers in these environments. There is a paucity of research on the effectiveness of sexual harassment training for managers. Most programs educating middle managers focus on reviewing methods to prevent harassment, recognizing the signs, methods for intervention, and how subordinates can use the grievance process. The education of middle managers resembles bystander intervention training (see Chapter 54).

Lastly, employee training often treats employees as potential perpetrators, not victims' allies. Many training programs explicitly outline forbidden actions and review sexual harassment law. Improving knowledge about sexual harassment and grievance procedures *does not necessarily change behaviors*. In fact, men who score high on "likely harasser" and "gender role conflict scales" — the men many training programs seek to reform — have strongly negative reactions to this type of "forbidden behavior" training, scoring higher on these scales after training.[5]

These findings were based on a one-hour video training program presented to 90 undergraduate male students with an average age of 20.[6] I posit that the maturity level of these individuals is not reflective of older, more mature males who participate in a more extensive training program.

Most organizations use the programs for legal protection to avoid legal actions. This approach is reactive, not proactive. Rulings in the *Burlington Industries, Inc. v. Ellerth* and *Faragher v. City of Boca Raton* court cases stipulated that if organizations engaged in activities to prevent sexual harassment (training, awareness, and reporting mechanisms) *and* the target of harassment *did not utilize those mechanisms for reporting*, the employer would have significantly less liability.[7]

In *Hanley v. Doctors Hospital of Shreveport,* the organization was held liable to pay punitive damages to the plaintiff in a sexual harassment and retaliation case partially due to its lack of a sexual harassment and prevention training program. Many organizations offer short, EEOC-focused training programs solely to prevent legal action. This approach is short-sighted and ineffective.

From a victim's standpoint, the training seems perfunctory. If an employee sues the organization for sexual harassment, the employee will face an uphill battle because the organization offers training. Training is then nothing more than "file cabinet compliance" and another in the long list of checkbox items. Also, the indirect message is that the employees' work environment is unimportant to the organization.

Another contributor is the belief that change will happen overnight once training is completed. This expectation of immediate results is a setup for organizational failure and does not appreciate the time and process required to change the *organization's culture*. In Chapter 58, I outline the barriers and challenges organizations must overcome to create a new environment and lasting, positive change. It is a notoriously difficult task with no "finish line."[7]

There is often a disconnect between the characteristics of the training and the expected outcomes. A brief, one-shot training program lasting only one or two hours is not comprehensive enough to address the topic, provide adequate scenario-based training, and demonstrate effective bystander intervention training. This training is important, but one empirical study found that a three- or four-hour highly interactive employee training program and a two-day intensive workshop for managers were not as effective as expected in reducing harassment three and six months after training.[8] I posit these findings reflect the lack of sufficient time to create meaningful cultural change.

Individual-level factors influence the effectiveness of training. An individual's sense of cynicism toward training directly impacts their motivation to learn. Without motivation to learn, there is no motivation to change. Organizations contribute to this negative pretraining attitude if there is a perception the organization is not offering the training to create meaningful change. For example, a short, one-hour course online or at staff meetings is not adequate training. Notably, researchers have found, anecdotally, that cynicism of training is widespread and prevalent.

Contributing to this negative bias is the absence of senior leaders and management during in-person training and prominent employees who blatantly disregard the sessions by reading during the session, looking at their phones, etc. Evaluations and quizzes can often be "gamed" by participants who take the opportunity to retake the exams until they pass. If organizations treat training as a checkbox item, employees can also rush through the training as another checkbox item. When senior leaders and executives exempt themselves from the training, the message is clear to the employees: employees are the source and cause of the behavior.

REFERENCES

1. Dobbin F, Kalev A. Why Sexual Harassment Programs Backfire. *Harvard Business Review.* May-June 2020. https://hbr.org/2020/05/why-sexual-harassment-programs-backfire.
2. Dobbin F , Kalev A. The Promise and Peril of Sexual Harassment Programs. *Proc Natl Acad Sci USA.* 2019;116)(25):12255–12260.
3. Cortina L, Magley V. Raising Voice, Risking Retaliation: Events Following Interpersonal Mistreatment in the Workplace. *J Occup Health Psychol.* 2003;8(4): 247–265.
4. McLaughlin C, Uggen C, Blackstone A. The Economic and Career Effects of Sexual Harassment on Working Women. *Gend Soc.* 2017;31(3):333–358.
5. Kearney LK, Rochlen, AB, King EB. Male Gender Role Conflict, Sexual Harassment Tolerance, and the Efficacy of a Psychoeducative Training Program. *Psychology of Men and Masculinities.* 2004;5(1):72–82. https://awspntest.apa.org/doi/10.1037/1524-9220.5.1.72
6. Robb LA , Doverspike D. Self-Reported Proclivity to Harass as a Moderator of the Effectiveness of Sexual Harassment- Prevention Training. *Psychol Rep.* 2001;88(1): 85–88.
7. Zelin A, Magley V. Sexual Harassment Training: Why It (Currently) Doesn't Work and What Can Be Done. In: Geffner R, White JW, Hamberger LK, Rosenbaum A,

et al, eds. *Handbook of Interpersonal Violence and Abuse Across the Lifespan.* Springer Nature;2022: 3941–3961.

8. Magley VJ, Fitzgerald LF, Salisbury J, Draasgow F, Zickar MJ. Changing Sexual Harassment within Organizations via Training Interventions: Suggestions and Empirical Data. In: Burke R, Cooper C, eds. *The Fulfilling Workplace: The Organization's Role in Achieving Individual and Organizational Health.* Surrey, UK: Glower; 2013:225–246.

Chapter 52. Training Programs: A New Approach

"You can't get different results by doing things the same way." — Richard Moran, philosopher, Harvard professor

A T THE TIME CATHARINE MACKINNON's book *Sexual Harassment of Working Women* was published in 1979, some organizations, including healthcare organizations, offered sexual harassment training to employees. The first programs consisted of video vignettes, often of senior executives or "handsy" bosses who made sexually charged comments or touched a female employee in an inappropriate way. The videos showed only the most overt acts of misconduct and harassment and were largely informative rather than instructional.

These programs focused on interpersonal responsibility and dynamics while ignoring the contributions of social structures, environment, and company culture. Fundamentally, the videos and training focused on sex and civility rather than power and civil rights. As a result, these programs were not effective.

In the past three decades, however, sexual harassment training has become ubiquitous and a part of onboarding new employees not only in healthcare but nearly every industry. Although the prevalence and incidence of misconduct and harassment have decreased over the last few decades, it continues to be a problem. Part of the reason for the failure is that organizations present sexual harassment training as an equal part of the variety of content they provide in onboarding presentations and materials. An employee or physician watches videos on infection control, compliance, corporate conflicts of interest, and sexual harassment training without emphasizing the importance or relevance of one over the others.

Education and training around sexual harassment should be separate from the rest of the onboarding program. Effectiveness requires a holistic approach that offers employees an immersion course with more interactive lessons and demonstrations. The program should use case-based, small-group learning using effective techniques gleaned from adult learning theory and methods. Programs should offer, at minimum, the following content:

- History of sexual harassment and Title VII of the Civil Rights Act of 1964.

- Definition and examples of misconduct, harassment, and discrimination.
- Cultural and social factors that have normalized and influenced sexual harassment.
- Myths, stereotypes, and gender-based assumptions.
- Role-playing exercises to demonstrate the effect and foster empathy.
- The branching consequences of misconduct and harassment, including second-victim effect and cultural erosion.
- LGBTQ+ awareness and sensitivity training.
- Cultural influences.
- Reporting processes and procedures.
- Investigative and interview training for managers, directors, etc.

Organizations should keep a separate repository of records of events and should use validated surveys and instruments to measure the effectiveness of the programs. To ensure new employees receive timely education and training, monthly or quarterly workshops addressing professionalism and sexual misconduct can be offered. This approach is expensive, time-consuming, and difficult to implement; however, consistent, frequent effort will create a cultural change over time.

CASE STUDY

Just before the #MeToo movement in 2017, the Mayo Clinic began to track and separate sexual harassment and misconduct claims from other types of harassment. More importantly, leadership recognized the failures of traditional training programs. Their approach incorporates many of the suggestions discussed above[1]:

- Facilitated dialogue with top leadership teams and the board of governors, using case examples.
- Email messages from the president and CEO to all staff.
- Scenario training for new supervisors.
- Online training of all supervisors addressing their role in handling complainants, the accused, and any bystanders.
- Case-based education with the staff.

This approach led to a decrease in allegations of misconduct in 2018. It was a bold and important step in the right direction — made possible only because leadership had the courage to be open, transparent, and accountable.

REFERENCE

1. Rihal CS, Baker NA, Bunkers BE, Buskirk SJ, Caviness NJ, *et al*. Addressing Sexual Harassment in the #MeToo Era: An Institutional Approach. *Mayo Clin Proc*. 2020;95(4): 749–757.

Chapter 53. Professional Communication and Boundary-Setting

*"Compassionate people have boundaries
of steel." — Brene Brown, author*

SETTING BOUNDARIES AS A MEDICAL PROFESSIONAL can prevent misconduct. Most physicians and nurses choose a career in medicine to help people, and helping people requires empathy, compassion, and listening. Patients share personal information and details about their lives they would otherwise not share with others besides close family and friends. To be effective, healthcare providers must connect with their patients as individuals.

The environment and type of work healthcare providers perform is a setup for boundary violations leading to sexual misconduct or inappropriate relationships. Setting boundaries, therefore, is essential.

The family and social environment we are raised in influences our boundary structures. Our family background, upbringing, and other social experiences influence our relationships with others. Most of us are unaware of the influence our childhood and family environments have on our own perceptions of what is or is not a boundary violation. Some individuals who have been sexually abused as children, for example, may struggle with creating healthy boundaries, but not all struggle.[1]

As the one who possesses the power in the physician-patient relationship, physicians have the responsibility to establish and maintain boundaries. Kent Garman, former president of the medical staff at Sequoia Hospital in San Mateo County, California, wrote several articles advising physicians on maintaining professionalism and boundaries. The Medical Board of California published a synopsis of these guidelines and refers to them as the Garman Guidelines.[2] These guidelines are especially useful for solo practitioners.

THE GARMAN GUIDELINES

1. Allow patients to disrobe and dress in private and offer cover gowns and appropriate drapes. Some physicians do not practice these simple steps.

2. Have one of your office staff in the room whenever possible, especially during breast and pelvic exams. I have talked to many physicians who feel this is silly and an added burden on their office staff. However, many women are very offended if these exams are done without another person in attendance. It would be reasonable to have your office nurse ask your patient if she would prefer to have an attendant in the room.

3. Improve your communication with the patient about the reasons for and methods of examinations. If you feel a breast examination for axillary lymphadenopathy is necessary for a hand infection, tell the patient why you are doing it.

4. Avoid any flirtatious behavior toward patients. Since you are perceived as a "power" figure, the patient may be hesitant to complain directly to you about jokes or other "innocent" behavior that they find troubling or offensive.

5. Ask someone else to review your office procedures regarding physical exams with a view to avoiding any risky procedures and make necessary changes. One series of complaints was dealt with by asking the physician's female office staff to review and change standard examination procedures to avoid future problems.

Sexual misconduct, inappropriate relationships, and other misdeeds often begin with so-called "minor" boundary violations. Giving more time to a patient for no clinical purpose, taking small gifts or giving small gifts, checking your appearance before seeing a patient, communicating about nonclinical subjects outside of the professional environment, or meeting for a cup of coffee are slippery slope behaviors that can lead to far more serious behaviors. Emotional affairs are common, and it is easy for an emotional affair to become physical over time.

PROMOTING PROFESSIONALISM

The Vanderbilt University School of Medicine (VUSM) has been teaching professionalism for two decades.[3] Although the approach used by VUSM is employed broadly, the principles, processes, and concepts from the VUSM approach are applicable to professionalism around sexual harassment.

An effective approach is a standardized process for guiding interventions using a pyramid for identifying, assessing, and dealing with unprofessional behavior.[3] The pyramid developed by the Vanderbilt Center for Patient and Professional Advocacy (CPPA) escalates interventions through different levels. Individuals with persistent patterns of behaviors continue the behaviors if there are no escalating consequences. The result is an increasingly toxic environment. CPPA's escalation and tiered approach:

Informal Intervention: Cup of coffee. Utilized if there is a single concern or first-time offense.

Level 1: Awareness intervention. A pattern becomes apparent.

Level 2: Guided intervention by authority. A persistent pattern of behaviors despite prior interventions.

Level 3: Intervention through formal process. No change is noted despite interventions. At this point, the organization must take a more formal approach, including the possibility of termination or loss of privileges.

Note: Reports are screened to identify potentially egregious or mandated reports that may require immediate investigation/intervention.

Six key drivers contribute to continued unprofessional behavior[3]:

1. Substance abuse disorders or untreated psychological issues.
2. Narcissism, perfectionism, or selfishness.
3. Spillover of chronic or acute family/home problems.
4. Poorly controlled anger.
5. Bad behavior gets the desired results.
6. Clinical, administrative, and institutional inertia. The behavior is frequent enough to be normalized and accepted.

Mitigating sexual misconduct, harassment, and discrimination requires an organization to make a parallel effort to reduce *all* unprofessional conduct. Lumping sexual harassment into the same bucket as "unprofessional" behaviors is a mistake. In my opinion, the influence and consequences of administrative and institutional inertia are major reasons organizations fail to make progress. Whereas some drivers are individual issues and concerns, those behaviors occur in the context of and within an organization.

The financial pressures in many healthcare organizations are increasing, and funding new projects and initiatives is challenging. Promoting professionalism within an organization and addressing unprofessional behaviors is an ethical imperative. It is the right thing to do, and it can have a cascading and indirect benefit on an organization's finances through increased staff retention and satisfaction, improved patient safety, and reduced liability exposure and risk-management activity. A professional, safe environment increases productivity and cooperation and creates a more desirable work environment.

REFERENCES

1. White RD, Montgomery JC. *The Ethical Risks of Professional Boundaries: When to Say WHOA, When to Say NO*. St. Petersburg, FL: Book Locker;2021.
2. Garman JK. Accusations of Harassment Against Physicians. Medical Board of California. www.mbc.ca.gov/Licensing/Physicians-and-Surgeons/Practice-Information/Sexual-Misconduct.aspx.
3. Hickson GB, Wichert JW, Webb LE, Gabbe SG. A Complementary Approach to Promoting Professionalism: Identifying, Measuring, and Addressing Unprofessional Behaviors. *Acad Med.* 2007;82(11):1040–1048.

Chapter 54. The Bystander Effect

"Whenever one person stands up and says, 'Wait a minute, this is wrong,' it helps other people do the same."
— Gloria Steinem, journalist, feminist, and activist

IN 1964, KITTY GENOVESE, a 28-year-old bar manager living in Queens, New York, finished her late-night shift and headed home. Just outside her apartment building, she was robbed, raped, and stabbed to death while 38 people watched or listened to her screams and did nothing to stop the attack.

The *New York Times* published the story on the front page two weeks after the murder, and it began: "For more than half an hour, 38 respectable, law-abiding citizens in Queens watched a killer stalk and stab a woman in three separate attacks in Kew Gardens." The story and the number of people who apparently witnessed the event originated with a conversation between New York City's police commissioner and Abe Rosenthal, then the *New York Times* city editor. The number of people was exaggerated and inadequately checked before publication. The story shocked the local community and nation, especially the reports that no one intervened.

In the following years, a new term emerged, the "Kitty Genovese effect," which evolved into the " bystander effect," which postulates that the greater the number of bystanders, the less likely someone will intervene.

The haunting story of Kitty Genovese led to several positive social and legal changes; for example, Good Samaritan laws were passed in New York City and other areas of the United States to encourage people to step in, act, and prevent violence or assault. The murder also helped create the 911 system. In her detailed book *Kitty Genovese, A True Account of a Public Murder and Its Private Consequences*, Catherine Pelonero says the case of Kitty Genovese's murder was the most cited incident in social psychology literature until the September 11 terrorist attacks in 2001.

After the story took root, closer inspection revealed a different story. Several books and documentaries questioned and challenged the reported facts. The number of eyewitnesses was indeed exaggerated; no one saw the attack completely, those who heard it thought it was a drunken brawl or lovers' quarrel, and some people did call the police.

In fact, Sophia Farrar, who lived across the hall from Kitty, rushed to her aid and told a neighbor to call the police and an ambulance.[1] People did intervene. And the number of people who either heard or saw the event was likely exaggerated. Extreme headlines sell news, and news that sells — sells copies of the paper.

The "bystander effect" is the focus of continued research and investigation. Institutions, businesses, and healthcare organizations have incorporated awareness and training on the issue in prevention programs. The recent #MeToo Movement brought the issue back into the spotlight as victims demanded witnesses and bystanders accept personal responsibility to intervene and prevent assault, harassment, and discrimination. Examining the phenomenon and how to effectively incorporate training and awareness requires an appreciation of the complex fabric and matrix of psychological, social, biological, legal, and ethical factors influencing the reactions and behaviors of bystanders.

DEFINING A BYSTANDER VS. AN UPSTANDER

A bystander is an individual who witnesses an event and, although they have the opportunity to intervene or condone, does nothing.[2] The bystander effect is a psychological phenomenon where individuals are less likely to intervene or help due to the ambiguity of the situation, inhibition secondary to the presence of multiple other individuals or witnesses, and the social influence of other people's inaction.[3]

Bystanders may choose not to intervene in an incidence of harassment or discrimination for several reasons, including the following:

1. Fear of retribution.
2. Fear of physical harm.
3. Not knowing or interpreting a situation as discriminatory, harassment, or bias.
4. Social and economic costs to intervention.
5. Not being taken seriously.
6. Not having a social relationship with the victim.
7. Status or perceived power of the perpetrator.
8. Social norms tolerant of discrimination or marginalization.

These bystander behaviors fall into three broad categories: not recognizing help is needed, not knowing exactly how to help, and concern about negative consequences to the self or victim (including harm) from intervening.

The lack of identification or recognition of problematic behavior might be due to cultural norms, personal beliefs, stereotypes, or a lack of awareness of the widespread prevalence of sexual harassment. The bystander may not understand or misinterpret the perpetrator's intent and default to innocence. A bystander may not appreciate the impact of the perpetrated act on a victim. As an example, if a perpetrator makes a sexually suggestive comment, it may be viewed as a joke. It may not be clear to a bystander if an underlying relationship between the perpetrator and the victim makes the joke "acceptable."[4]

An additional challenge is understanding what is acceptable behavior. Recognizing the mismatch in the perceptions of a situation between a person with power and a person without power is essential in knowing and recognizing the difference between harassment and normal collegial interactions. A simple guideline or litmus test is if the following statements are used to absolve a perpetrator and invalidate a victim[4]:

- They didn't mean anything by that.
- Oh, they are harmless.
- They were just joking.
- She is just too sensitive.
- That is just the way he (or she) is.

In all of these statements there is an attempt to reduce the impact of the behavior or what was said. Minimizing the behavior or justifying the behavior is influenced by powerful cultural, psychological, and social factors. This allows these behaviors to continue, and allowing these behaviors to continue reinforces tolerance of unacceptable behaviors.

Not knowing how to help is a significant problem. A bystander may recognize sexual harassment but not know exactly what to do to intervene. Organizations should include guidance and offer training on what to do when someone witnesses harassment.[4]

An effective method for demonstrating how to intervene is to utilize role-play scenarios in a safe setting with no consequences. Participants can play various roles and discuss their actions, behaviors, and emotional consequences.

REFERENCES

1. Vyse S. Kitty Genovese: Revising the Parable of the Bad Samaritan. *Skeptical Inquirer.* July 21, 2016. https://skepticalinquirer.org/exclusive/kitty-genovese-revising-the-parable-of-the-bad-samaritan/.
2. American Psychological Association. *Bystander Intervention Tip Sheet. 2022.* https://www.apa.org/pi/health-equity/bystander-intervention.
3. Jenkins LN, Nickerson AB. Bystander Intervention in Bullying: Role of Social Skills and Gender. *J Early Adolescence.* 2019;39(2):141–166.
4. Aggarwal R, Brenner AM. #Metoo: The Role and Power of Bystanders (aka Us). *Acad Psychiatry.* 2020;44(1):5–10. doi: 10.1007/s40596-019-01173-0

Chapter 55. Physical Exams, Chaperones, and Sensitive Sexual History

EXAMINING PATIENTS and exposing patients' bodies for physical exams and procedures is necessary to provide care or make a diagnosis. Patients often feel vulnerable and embarrassed, and for patients with a history of physical or sexual abuse, the exam can be a trigger for past trauma. As part of their duties for care, all healthcare professionals who perform physical touching or exams need to be sensitive, compassionate, and aware of the patient's needs and emotional state.

Every institution should have a policy regarding sensitive medical exams to protect patients' safety and minimize risks associated with the performance of these exams, according to the American College Health Association (ACHA), the American Medical Association (AMA), the American College of Obstetricians and Gynecologists (ACOG), the American Academy of Pediatrics (AAP), the Association of Women's Health, Obstetric and Neonatal Nurses (AWHONN), and the General Medical Council (GMC) in the United Kingdom.[1] Providing chaperones should be a part of those policies.

Most institutions lack consistency in policy and implementation partly because there is little evidence regarding the impact a chaperone has on patient experience or care outcomes. Despite this, the AAP recommends that a chaperone be mandatory for all adolescent genital, rectal, and breast exams.

The AWHONN supports patients' opting out of chaperone presence during a sensitive exam, and the AMA and ACOG Committee on Ethics endorse offering a chaperone to all patients. Many universities make it mandatory for a chaperone to be present when male-identifying providers care for female-at-birth or female-identified patients.

Most research on the effectiveness of chaperones focuses on provider compliance, documentation, and satisfaction. There remains a paucity of research surveying patient attitudes regarding chaperones. Despite the lack of research on patient attitudes about chaperones, the presence of a chaperone protects the providers, patients, and organizations from false accusations or unwitnessed events.

As much as there may be a power differential between providers and patients, there may also be a power differential between the chaperone and provider. To be effective, chaperones must have the capability and authority to intervene or provide input during an exam without fear of retribution. To protect the integrity and safety of the chaperones, the chaperone should not directly report to the physician or other provider or any direct supervisor of any providers or physicians.

CORE PRINCIPLES FOR POLICY DEVELOPMENT

Healthcare organizations that provide sensitive medical exams should have written policies and procedures that include the following[2]:

- Definition of a sensitive medical exam, near sensitive medical exam, and chaperone.
- Use of chaperones (opt-in, opt-out, and mandatory policies).
- Chaperone training.
- Provider and staff training.
- Patient education on the use and reasons for chaperones during sensitive medical exams.
- Reporting procedures for non-compliance, complaints, or other concerns.
- Risk management related to investigation of complaints, non-compliance, or other concerns.
- Acknowledgment and discussion of power structures that might deter critical feedback

Definition of Sensitive Exams

As of April 2024, HHS requires consent for intimate medical exam procedures. A sensitive exam or procedure includes an exam, evaluation, palpation, physical therapy for, placement of instruments in, or exposure of genitalia, rectum, or breasts. Personal and cultural experiences may define a sensitive exam or procedure differently. For example, partial exposure of undergarments, the groin, and buttocks may not be culturally acceptable for some women or men.

Types of Chaperone Policies

There are three recognized options for chaperone policies.

Opt-out policy: A chaperone is planned and provided for every sensitive exam or procedure and is available for any provider or patient request. A patient has a right to decline a chaperone *after* being educated about the nature of the examination or procedure and the role of the chaperone.

Opt-in policy: A chaperone is not planned but is available upon request by the patient. Signs posted in care areas or clinics offering the option of a chaperone are not adequate, and in some cases, patients may feel uncomfortable asking for a chaperone for a variety of reasons — including the power differential during a medical encounter. For this reason, opt-in policies are discouraged.

Mandatory policy: Chaperones *must* be present for sensitive exams or procedures or the exam or procedure will not be performed. That said, these policies must not impede emergency exams or treatment.

Some institutions may incorporate specific elements of each of these types of policies in the overall policy. As an example, a chaperone should be mandatory for examinations or procedures on minors, patients under sedation, anesthesia, or medications that alter mental status, or patients who lack the capacity to provide informed consent at the time of care .

Policies should respect patients' dignity and rights. Conversely, physicians and other providers should have the right not to perform an exam or procedure if they are not comfortable proceeding without a chaperone present. Extenuating circumstances, emergencies, and other scenarios in which a patient may suffer significant physical harm, morbidity, or mortality unless the exam or procedure is performed should not require a chaperone's presence.

Implementation and Training

Successful implementation of a chaperone program requires training staff who will chaperone sensitive exams and procedures. Some staff may have extensive clinical experience and feel comfortable, while others may have little clinical experience and feel less comfortable and anxious. Comprehensive training with role-playing and discussion should be incorporated into every training program. Role-playing is a safe environment in which to learn how to communicate and interact using real clinical situations without consequences to actual patients.

Outlining the expectations of the chaperone and the components of the exam is crucial. Establishing roles and expectations reduces the impact of the power differential between provider and chaperone and improves communication between the patient, provider, and chaperone. The training should include a culturally sensitive and trauma-informed practice and approach. Additional components are:

1. Ensuring patient comfort.
2. Ensuring patient dignity and privacy for dressing/undressing and appropriate gown or drape positioning.
3. Informing the patient a chaperone will be present (depending on policy).
4. Documenting the presence of chaperone.
5. Positioning the chaperone during the exam to visualize the point of contact of exam or procedure.
6. Reviewing how the chaperone may intervene or stop an exam if they are concerned about patient distress or inappropriate steps during the exam.
7. Reviewing reporting mechanisms for concerns and non-compliance with policy.

Provider training is just as important as chaperone training. Providers should always treat the patient with dignity and respect and uncover sensitive areas just before the exam and immediately cover sensitive areas upon completion of the exam.

Providers should always:

1. Explain to the patient why the exam is necessary.
2. Fully explain to the patient what body area will be examined. If the examination of another sensitive body area is not on the original consent, another consent must be obtained before proceeding.
3. Ask again before the exam if the patient is okay with proceeding.
4. Consider the patient's feelings. Patients with a history of sexual trauma may experience emotional and physical discomfort. Patients may or may not disclose a past history of sexual trauma before the exam. If the patient is uncomfortable for ANY reason, stop the exam and proceed only if the patient feels comfortable.
5. Offer the patient privacy to dress once the exam is complete.

Obtaining consent before a sensitive medical procedure is critical. A Yale-led study revealed nearly 3.5 million Americans received unconsented pelvic or prostate exams.[3] What's more, black patients are four times more likely than white patients to have an exam without consent.

The study revealed that some unconsented exams were medically unnecessary in an academic setting with medical students, residents, and trainees from other programs. While patients were under anesthesia and unconscious, attending physicians taught and allowed the trainees to perform the exam.

Lori Bruce, associate director of Yale's Interdisciplinary Center for Bioethics, who led the landmark study, stated that some of the medical students felt moral distress having done a medically unnecessary exam on a patient who did not give permission for the exam. Patients, too, are negatively affected. Without consent, the exam can have a traumatic impact on the patient.[4]

Case Studies

Janine, a nurse in Arizona, checked into the hospital for stomach surgery in 2017. Before the procedure, she told her physician that she did not want medical students to be directly involved. But after the procedure, Janine said, as the anesthetic wore off, a resident came by to inform her that while conducting a pelvic exam, the resident noticed she had gotten her period. Distressed, she tried to piece together what had happened while she was unconscious. Why had her sexual organs been examined during an abdominal procedure by someone other than her surgeon? Janine had a history of sexual abuse, and this incident brought up bad memories of past events. She was angry and disappointed that she was not informed before undergoing anesthesia.

In another incident, Sarah, a patient in Madison, Wisconsin, said she was given a diagnosis of extreme vulvar sensitivity after a surgery in 2009. She wondered how an operation performed through incisions in her abdomen could have affected her sexual organs. When scheduling another surgical procedure with the University of Wisconsin School of Medicine and hospital system in 2018, she asked to draft her own consent contract. She said the department administrators rebuffed her request. "They told me: Is this a deal breaker for you? If so, you have your surgery somewhere else."

Without question, these two patients felt violated. The new requirements will hopefully prevent these kinds of events from happening to patients.

TAKING A SENSITIVE HISTORY

Family practice physicians and other providers must obtain a patient's sexual history as part of the provision of complete care. Asking patients questions about their sexual history is an emotionally difficult task for new trainees. Using a sensitive, non-judgmental approach makes it easier for the physician and decreases the anxiety or embarrassment a patient may feel.

A patient-centered approach to sexual health includes but is not limited to knowledge about anatomy and function, sexuality, sexual identity, sexual orientation and gender, gender identity, reproductive health and fertility, and, importantly, history of sexual violence or abuse. Some practices, to avoid asking awkward or embarrassing questions in an interview format, ask the questions on an intake form or digital platform.

Some patients may not feel comfortable documenting their own sexual history. A personal, sensitive interview without judgment or bias is the best approach.

Physicians and staff in clinics should make efforts to identify individual implicit bias around sexuality and sexual topics, adverse childhood experiences, and trauma-informed care. Some physicians may benefit from specific training focused on reducing implicit bias or discomfort in discussing sex and sexuality with patients.

The American Association of Sexuality Educators, Counselors, and Therapists offers courses and resources for sexual attitude reassessment. These courses offer a structured group seminar led by a sexual health specialist designed to help participants identify their attitudes and beliefs around sexuality. Physicians, aware of their own discomforts, attitudes, and beliefs, can then incorporate that knowledge into their professional obligations to patients.

REFERENCES

1. American Medical Association. Code of Medical Ethics, Opinion 1.2.4 Use of Chaperones. https://www.ama-assn.org/delivering-care/ethics/use-chaperones.
2. American College Health Association. *Best Practices for Sensitive Exams.* October 2019. https://www.acha.org/wp-content/uploads/2024/06/ACHA_Best_Practices_for_Sensitive_Exams_October2019.pdf.

3. Harrison R. Yale-led Study Spurs Federal Action: HHS Requires Consent for Intimate Medical Procedures. Yale Institution for Social and Policy Studies News. April 2, 2024. https://isps.yale.edu/news/blog/2024/04/yale-led-study-spurs-federal-action-hhs-requires-consent-for-intimate-medical .

4. Seybold SL. Not Just Bodies "Bodies with Vaginas": A Kantian Defense of Pelvic Exam Consent Laws. *Bioethics.* 2022;36(9):940–947.

Chapter 56. Patients Abusing Staff: Organizational Responsibilities

N O WORKPLACE PRESENTS greater personal and professional challenges than the healthcare setting. From patients with diminished capacity to those under the influence of drugs or alcohol, the work environment is dangerous. Abuse and harassment are common.

Given the nuances of the law when applied to the healthcare workplace, courts have held that conduct by a patient who is medically incapable of conforming their conduct to societal norms might not necessarily create a hostile work environment, even if the same behavior by a coworker would. However, this leeway does not immunize healthcare employers who fail to act when allegations of abuse or harassment come to their attention.

CASE STUDIES

In *Landry v. Leesville Rehabilitation Hospital*, Yolanda Landry, a nursing technician, contended her employer knowingly allowed a patient to harass her and then fired her shortly afterward because of her race and in retaliation for reporting the patient's conduct.[1] Landry, who worked the night shift at the rehabilitation facility for patients recovering from traumatic illnesses and injuries, reported a patient who put his hand on her bottom for a few seconds as she helped him get into bed. On a different occasion, the same patient stated she was a "sexy, black beautiful woman." Landry reported these two events and said her employer did nothing in response.

The hospital stated she was fired for walking into the patient's room one evening while he was sleeping and abruptly turning on a light while speaking loudly. These actions startled him awake. There were prior complaints regarding Landry's behavior toward the patient as well. Landry filed a lawsuit contending her employer knowingly allowed the patient to harass her and fired her because of her race and because she reported the patient's conduct.

A federal court in Louisiana granted summary judgment to the hospital, and the United States Court of Appeals for the Fifth Circuit panel affirmed, saying the patient's behavior was not severe or pervasive enough to be sexual harassment under the Title VII standard. Additionally, the court stated that inappropriate sexual conduct is not uncommon, given patients' mental capacity secondary to traumatic brain injuries.

What is interesting in this particular case is the court's stance on what constitutes sexual harassment. The court did not find the harassment was severe and pervasive; there were only two reported events. The court's decision, however, does not absolve an organization's responsibility to prevent harassment.

In a similar case, *Gardner v. CLC of Pascagoula, LLC,* a different panel of Fifth Circuit judges reversed a summary judgment for a nursing home in a 2019 case where the plaintiff, Kymberli Gardner, a certified nursing assistant, alleged a dementia patient repeatedly groped her and even punched her on one occasion.[2]

She complained to her administrator, who allegedly told her to "put [her] big girl panties on and go back to work." The Fifth Circuit found that the patient's behavior was pervasive and the employer's (administrator) response was inappropriate. The case met the conditions and was enough to allow it to go to a jury.

The patient had a long history of violent and sexual behavior toward other patients and staff, including the following:

1. He was transferred from his initial residential wing because he assaulted a bedridden roommate.
2. He repeatedly grabbed numerous female staff in inappropriate areas.
3. He asked for explicit sexual acts on a regular basis and made lewd sexual comments toward female staff. He asked female employees to engage in sexual activity with him "all the time."

Gardner experienced these behaviors from this patient "every day." She and the other employees documented and reported the patient's behaviors to supervisors. His behavior was not a secret to those who ran the facility. The administrators were not always responsive to the complaints. For example, they declined to request a psychiatric evaluation for the patient after he hit his roommate.

Gardner continued to care for the patient under these circumstances, and a final incident led to her termination. Gardner was helping the patient out of bed to attend a therapy session when he attempted to touch her left breast while she was bent over the bed. Gardner tried to move out of the way, and the patient punched the side of her breast. Gardner laid him down and left the room to get help.

Another nursing assistant returned with Gardner, and when they attempted to help the patient get up, he punched Gardner again. Gardner immediately left the room, and the patient tried to grope the other nursing assistant. Gardner sought help from a nurse on duty, and the three of them then transferred the patient to his wheelchair. As Gardner moved to make the bed, the patient punched her a third time. What happened next is what led to her termination.

The nurse claimed Gardner swung her fist over the patient's head and that her arm brushed the top of his head. The nursing assistant claims Gardner went up with her hand as if she were going to hit the patient but didn't strike the patient at all.

As a result of this incident, Gardner refused to care for the patient and requested she be reassigned. The request was denied. She left work and went to an emergency room due to injuries she sustained. She did not return to work for three months and received workers' compensation.

Shortly after returning to work, Gardner was fired. The reasons cited for her firing included insubordination (refusing to care for the patient), violating the patient's rights (swearing in front of him and making a racist comment (she says he treated her poorly because she is not white), and finally, her alleged swing at the patient's head.

Gardner sued, asserting multiple claims under Title VII. The district court sided with the facility and concluded that a hostile workplace did not exist. It stated, "It is not clear to the Court that the harassing comments and attempts to grope and hit are beyond what a person in Gardner's position should expect of patients in a nursing home."

On appeal, the Fifth Circuit Court recognized Gardner endured multiple years of unwanted sexual grabbing and explicit comments. It was, in fact, pervasive and severe. Despite the patient's medical condition (dementia), the organization had a responsibility to protect Gardner. The Court stated, "A jury could conclude that an objectively reasonable caregiver would not expect a patient to grope her daily, injure her so badly she could not work for three months, and have her complaints met with laughter and dismissal by the administration." The Court reversed the entry of summary judgment on Gardner's harassment claim.

PROVIDER SAFETY ALGORITHM

Viglanti and colleagues created an algorithm to guide physicians and medical trainees in balancing their obligation to provide effective and appropriate care with their need to work in a safe and respectful environment.[3] The pivotal question in the algorithm (see Figure 1) for a physician or trainee is: "Do you feel safe?" If a physician feels safe, the patient's behavior needs to be clearly and firmly addressed. If a physician feels unsafe, it is the physician's right to excuse him or herself from the patient as safely and quickly as possible while seeking help.[3]

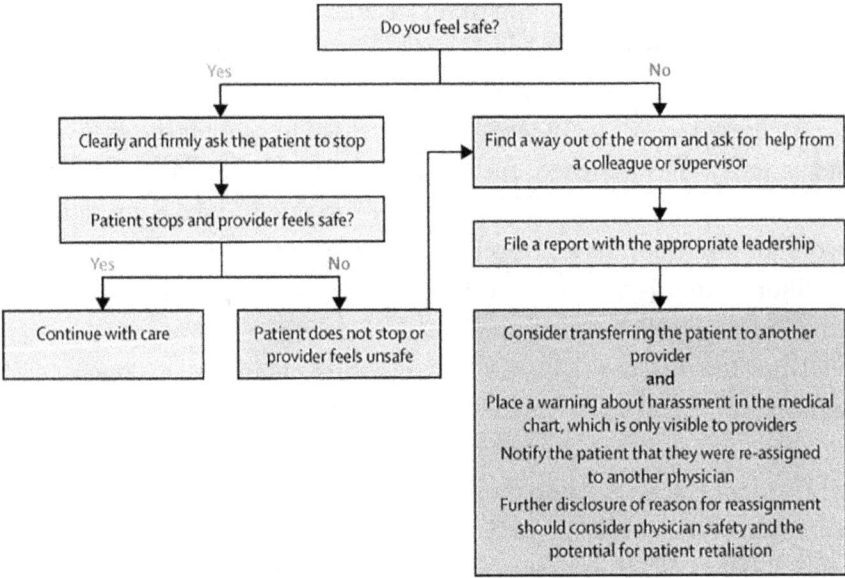

FIGURE 1. Decision-guiding algorithm for physicians who experience patient-initiated sexual harassment and abuse.[3]

Although this algorithm is specifically designed for physicians, the framework is applicable to healthcare providers in a variety of settings regardless of position or title.

TERMINATING A PHYSICIAN-PATIENT RELATIONSHIP

Terminating a physician-patient relationship is sometimes necessary to protect physicians, staff, or other personnel involved in providing care for the patient. It is not as simple as telling the patient he or she is no longer welcome to receive care at the office or practice. Not following local or state laws when terminating a physician-patient relationship is patient abandonment, which is illegal and unethical.

It is beyond the scope of this book to provide a detailed description of the steps necessary to terminate a patient relationship, as laws vary from locality to locality and state to state. If a patient has continually engaged in sexually harassing or inappropriate behaviors despite efforts to communicate to the patient the behavior is unacceptable, terminating the relationship may be the only option.

In the decision-guiding algorithm in Figure 1, transferring care to another provider is an option, and placing warnings in patient charts, electronic medical records, or other means is an effective approach to warn other providers. Another consideration is the mandatory use of chaperones for all future patient encounters. To avoid the many legal and ethical pitfalls inherent in this process, legal counsel is a valuable resource, and terminating the relationship is a last resort.

REFERENCES

1. *Landry v. Leesville Rehabilitation Hospital.* U.S. Court of Appeals, Fifth Circuit, February 7, 2022.
2. Wrigley J. Protecting Employees from Patient Harassment: It's No Laughing Matter. Fisher Phillips Insights., August 1, 2018. www.fisherphillips.com/en/news-insights/protecting-employees-from-patient-harassment-it-s-no-laughing-matter.html.
3. Viglanti EM, Oliverio AL, Meeks LM. Sexual Harassment and Abuse: When the Patient Is the Perpetrator. *Lancet.* 2018;392(10145): 368-369.

Chapter 57. Psychological and Physiological Conditions Affecting Patient Behaviors

PATIENTS WITH ALTERED MENTAL STATUS or impaired mental status secondary to alcohol, drugs, metabolic derangements, or other acute medical conditions affecting their capacity to function are common. With reduced capacity or capability to interpret or respond to their environment, these patients often behave in an irrational, unpredictable, hostile, or threatening manner, depending on the circumstances. Providing care for these patients as a healthcare professional is challenging, taxing, and invokes a strong emotional response. It isn't easy to remain compassionate, objective, and empathic.

Unfortunately, in some healthcare settings, impaired patients or cognitively impaired patients are common: emergency departments, inpatient psychiatry wards, and nursing, memory, and/or long-term care units or homes. Providing daily care for these patients is psychologically and emotionally challenging, and there are risks for bodily harm and injury — especially in the emergency departments.

Organizations must appreciate these unique, high-risk care areas, set expectations, and provide training and support commensurate with the work environment and tasks. Healthcare personnel who choose to work in these high-risk settings, too, need to be fully informed and understand that a negative experience is likely inevitable.

Chapter 58. Changing Culture

CULTURE IS DIFFICULT TO DEFINE because it is created through a complex collection of values, beliefs, and behaviors that define an organization and influence how its members interact. Culture is created through speech and behaviors, not just policy documents or mission statements. Organization leaders have a responsibility to create a positive culture; changing a culture is more difficult, as it takes time and concerted effort.

Many cultural change initiatives fail for various reasons, including poor leadership, inadequate messaging about the change, employee resistance, short-term focus, inadequate planning, and poor execution.

Although leaders are responsible for leading change, a top-down approach rarely works.[1] Empowering and engaging employees in the process is critical. Many mandates and programs for change use blitz communications, town halls, etc. While this type of approach generates enthusiasm, the most important factor to success is understanding change is a process, progress is slow, and setting realistic short-term goals can set up an organization for success.

In January 2019, Francis S. Collins charged a National Institutes of Health working group to examine and offer solutions to reduce sexual harassment in organizations receiving NIH grants and funding. The NIH recognized the continued and pervasive culture of sexual harassment in funded institutions and also acknowledged that Title VII and Title IX protections are not enough to mitigate and reduce sexual harassment. In February 2019, NIH leadership issued a statement, "We can do better. We must do better."[2]

Women are disproportionally affected by sexual harassment in STEM careers, including biomedical research and medicine. As a result, women leave science and medical careers, suffer psychologically from mistreatment, and are not recognized for their contributions and efforts. This, in turn, affects the efficacy of funding research projects supported by the NIH.

To address the systemic problem of sexual harassment, the working group proposed a fundamental restructuring of the research environment and suggested developing new partnerships and dialogue with partner institutions receiving funds. Fundamentally, change requires accomplishing a few key goals:

1. Recognizing and clearly identifying a problem.
2. Measuring, analyzing, and investigating the scope of the problem.
3. Making a call for change on an organizational level.
4. Receiving input from all stakeholders.
5. Creating programs and initiatives.
6. Measuring results and adapting programs as needed.
7. Continuing to perform steps 4 through 7.
8. Recognizing the process takes time, is mutable, and there is no "finish line."
9. Eventually, accomplishing cultural change.

The NIH initiative, broad in scope, faced significant challenges. First, research institutions and medical schools have a local culture. Therefore, the responsibility for creating cultural change requires each institution to oversee individual professional behavior and develop policies and practices fair to all of their unique stakeholders. Despite this challenge, eliminating sexual harassment requires concerted efforts of NIH leadership, institutions, and every individual within the larger ecosystem. Accountability, transparency, equity, and integrity are integral to a just culture.

The NIH recognized five risk factors contributing to sexual harassment in academic science, engineering, and medicine programs[2]:

1. Perceived tolerance for sexual harassment.
2. Male-dominated work settings.
3. Hierarchical power structures.
4. Symbolic compliance with Title VII and Title IX.
5. Uninformed campus or program leadership.

When institutions do not take allegations seriously, personal and professional harm is exacerbated. Psychologists Carly Smith and Jennifer Freyd appropriately call institutional unresponsiveness "institutional betrayal."[3] The psychological effects on victims, including an altered sense of reality and "betrayal blindness," in which the involved parties avoid acknowledging the behaviors can complicate the institutional response to sexual harassment.

Targets of sexual harassment may suffer a "gaslight effect," another form of emotional abuse in which perpetrators and other involved parties make the victims or targets question their own feelings and understanding of the event. Gaslighting is made possible through the cultural and social association of femininity with irrationality and the structural environment and conditions of gender inequality. Sociologist Paige Sweet argues, "*Policies to protect against gaslighting should, therefore, focus on increasing women's institutional credibility and cultural and economic capital.*"[4]

Changing culture within organizations must account for and acknowledge the social and cultural constructs of gender roles, expectations, and perceptions. *Despite recent progress, perceptions and expectations of gender and gender roles are still powerfully influential.* This complicates efforts to create a palpable and significant change in the work environment.

REFERENCES

1. Burnes B. Introduction: Why Does Change Fail, and What Can We Do About It? *J Change Manage.* 2011;11(4): 445–450. doi:10.1080/14697017.2011.630507.

2. Working Group Report to the Advisory Committee to NIH Director. *Changing the Culture to End Sexual Harassment.* National Institutes of Health;2019.

3. Smith CP, Freyd JJ. Institutional Betrayal. *Am Psychol.* 2014;69(6): 575–587. doi: 10.1037/a0037564

4. Stern R. *The Gaslight Effect: How to Spot and Survive the Hidden Manipulation Others Use to Control Your Life.* Harmony; 2007.

Chapter 59. Committees and Organizational Responsibilities

OST HEALTHCARE ORGANIZATIONS HAVE PEER and professional review committees, and depending on the size of the organization, they might have separate committees, one addressing peer review and clinical performance and the other addressing professionalism concerns. Smaller organizations may not have enough resources to separate the two committees, and larger organizations usually have the capacity and resources to create separate sexual harassment or misconduct committees as a sub-committee of the professionalism committee or as a wholly independent committee. In my experience, committees of individuals focused on specific issues are more effective at creating solutions and resolutions.

Committees dedicated to investigating and discussing conduct concerns have several advantages. First, they provide differing perspectives, diffuse responsibility, foster trust in the process, and reduce the burden of one individual taking on the task. Second, committees produce reports that can be presented to medical executive committees and/or the board of directors. This increases the organization's accountability to acknowledge and respond. Third, committee members comprised of personnel from different disciplines and departments demonstrate organizational commitment to taking the issues seriously.

Creating a charter for a new committee that addresses sexual misconduct will set the organization on a path toward improving the culture and work environment. See below for an example of a sexual harassment and misconduct committee. Committees force conversation, and with conversation, which acts as a catalyst for change, change can happen. Organizations have a responsibility to take these issues seriously, and separate committees are an effective approach.

EXHIBIT 1:

Sexual Harassment and Misconduct Committee Charter
Effective Date: [Insert Date]
Review Date: [Insert Date, e.g., Annually]
    1. Purpose and Mission

The Sexual Harassment and Misconduct Committee (the "Committee") is established to promote, foster, and maintain a safe and respectful environment free from sexual harassment for all employees, contractors, volunteers, and any other individuals associated with [Organization Name]. The Committee is responsible for reviewing, advising on, and overseeing the organization's efforts to prevent sexual harassment, address complaints, and support affected individuals.

Mission Statement:

- To ensure a workplace culture that upholds dignity, respect, and equality by:
- Preventing sexual harassment through education and proactive policies.
- Ensuring a confidential, impartial, and thorough process for addressing allegations.
- Promoting accountability and continuous improvement in our organizational practices.

2. Scope

This Charter applies to all employees, management, board members, contractors, interns, volunteers, and any other individuals engaged with [Organization Name]. The Committee's oversight covers all locations, departments, and operational settings.

3. Authority

The Committee is authorized by [Organization Name] to:

- **Review and Recommend Policies**: Evaluate existing policies, procedures, and practices related to sexual harassment and recommend improvements.
- **Investigate Complaints:** Oversee the investigation process for allegations of sexual harassment, ensuring due process and fairness.
- **Advise Leadership:** Provide recommendations to senior management and/or the board regarding disciplinary measures, remedial actions, and policy enhancements.
- **Educate and Train:** Assist in developing training programs and educational initiatives aimed at preventing sexual harassment.
- **Monitor Implementation:** Oversee the implementation of approved policies and the efficacy of training and preventative measures.

4. **Committee Membership**

Composition

- **Chairperson:** Appointed by [Designated Authority, e.g., CEO/ Board of Directors] and responsible for leading the Committee.
- **Members:** A diverse group representing various departments and levels within the organization. Membership should include:
  - At least one Human Resources representative.
  - At least one legal or compliance adviser.
  - Representatives from different employee groups to ensure diversity in perspectives.
  - An external member or consultant (if applicable) to ensure impartiality.

Qualifications

- Demonstrated commitment to fairness, confidentiality, and ethical standards.
- Relevant experience or training in conflict resolution, human resources, legal, or diversity and inclusion practices.
- Ability to handle sensitive information discreetly.

Terms

- Members shall serve a term of [specify duration, e.g., one to two years] with the option for reappointment.
- The Committee may establish subcommittees as needed to address specific tasks or projects.

5. **Roles and Responsibilities**

General Responsibilities

- **Policy Oversight:** Regularly review and update sexual harassment policies and procedures.
- **Complaint Review:** Ensure that complaints of sexual harassment are managed in a timely, impartial, and confidential manner.
- **Investigation Oversight:** Supervise investigations to ensure adherence to legal and organizational guidelines.
- **Support Services:** Provide guidance on support and resources available to affected individuals.
- **Training & Awareness:** Coordinate training sessions and awareness campaigns to educate the workforce on sexual harassment prevention.

- **Record-Keeping:** Maintain secure and confidential records of all complaints, investigations, and outcomes in accordance with legal requirements.

Specific Duties

- **Intake and Assessment:** Develop and oversee protocols for the receipt and initial assessment of complaints.
- **Investigation Coordination:** Collaborate with HR, legal advisors, and external investigators as needed to ensure a thorough investigation process.
- **Reporting:** Provide periodic reports to senior management/board on trends, outcomes, and recommendations while preserving the confidentiality of individuals involved.
- **Monitoring and Evaluation:** Continuously evaluate the effectiveness of sexual harassment policies and training initiatives, recommending adjustments as necessary.
- **Non-Retaliation Assurance:** Ensure that all procedures strictly prohibit retaliation against any individual who reports or participates in an investigation.

6. **Complaint Handling Procedures**
   a. **Receipt of Complaint:**
      - Complaints may be submitted in person, via secure email, or through designated reporting channels.
      - The Committee shall acknowledge receipt within [specify time frame, e.g., 3 business days].
   b. **Preliminary Assessment:**
      - Determine if the complaint falls under the Committee's jurisdiction.
      - If necessary, refer the matter to the appropriate internal or external authority.
   c. **Investigation Process:**
      - Assign an impartial investigator or team.
      - Conduct interviews, gather evidence, and document findings while maintaining confidentiality.
      - Ensure that all parties are treated with fairness and respect throughout the process.

d. **Resolution and Follow-Up:**
  - Based on investigation outcomes, recommend corrective action, disciplinary measures, or other remedial steps.
  - Provide feedback to the complainant and respondent as appropriate, without compromising confidentiality.
  - Monitor the situation to prevent recurrence or retaliation.

e. **Documentation:**
  - Maintain secure records of the complaint, investigation process, findings, and actions taken, subject to applicable privacy laws and organizational policies.

7. **Meetings and Decision-Making**
  - **Frequency:**
  The Committee shall meet at least [specify frequency, e.g., quarterly] and more frequently if urgent issues arise.
  - **Quorum:**
  A quorum, defined as [specify percentage or number, e.g., a majority of members], is required for decision-making.
  - **Decision-Making Process:**
  Decisions shall be made by consensus where possible; if consensus cannot be reached, a majority vote will determine the outcome.
  - **Minutes:**
  Detailed minutes of each meeting shall be recorded and securely stored, with sensitive information redacted as needed to protect confidentiality.

8. **Confidentiality and Data Protection**
  - All Committee members must adhere to strict confidentiality protocols.
  - Information related to complaints and investigations shall only be shared on a need-to-know basis.
  - Records shall be stored securely in compliance with data protection laws and organizational policies.
  - Breaches of confidentiality will be subject to disciplinary action.

9. **Training and Awareness**
  - The Committee is responsible for coordinating with HR and external experts to develop and implement ongoing training programs on sexual harassment prevention and response.

- Training materials shall be reviewed periodically and updated to reflect current legal standards and best practices.
- Participation in training sessions shall be mandatory for all employees, with special training provided for management and Committee members.

10. Monitoring, Evaluation, and Reporting

- The Committee will monitor the implementation of sexual harassment policies and the effectiveness of complaint handling procedures.
- Annual or ad hoc reports summarizing the Committee's activities, trends in complaints, and recommendations for improvement shall be submitted to [Senior Management/Board of Directors].
- Feedback from employees and other stakeholders will be considered for continuous improvement of the policies and practices.

11. Amendments

- This Charter may be amended by a majority vote of the Committee members, subject to approval by [Designated Authority, e.g., CEO/Board of Directors].
- Proposed amendments should be circulated to all Committee members at least [specify time frame, e.g., 30 days] prior to the meeting where the vote will take place.
- Amendments must comply with current laws and organizational policies.

12. Adoption and Implementation

By adopting this Charter, [Organization Name] reaffirms its commitment to a safe and respectful workplace. All employees and stakeholders are expected to cooperate with the Committee and support its initiatives.

Chapter 60. Validated Instruments to Measure Sexual Harassment and Misconduct

I T IS NEARLY IMPOSSIBLE TO MEASURE the effectiveness of a program or establish baseline measurements of behaviors, attitudes, culture, and the work environment without using validated survey tools, instruments, and other means to *objectively* identify the extent of sexually harassing behaviors and discrimination.

Over the last 40 years, several new tools have been used to research and investigate the effects, impacts, antecedents, and consequences of the behaviors. In large organizations, these tools are time-consuming and expensive to administer. Still, considering the high cost of allowing the behaviors (which is difficult to determine), the investment is worth the resources, money, and effort.

Administering a survey assessing these issues raises awareness, holds the organization accountable for responding to issues and instituting change, and validates that it exists. Rather than take the position that a survey puts the organization at risk for bad publicity if the findings suggest a poor climate or high tolerance, I believe the results represent an opportunity to foster change and place the organization on a path toward creating a safe, positive culture.

Of course, the surveys should be conducted anonymously, and the results should be made public. The following is a presentation and discussion of current instruments and survey tools available for organizations. Examples of the available instrument questions and tools are located in the appendix.

Sexual Experiences Questionnaire-Workplace (SEQ-W)[1] (Appendix)
The Sexual Experiences Questionnaire-Workplace assessment is a 17-item measure designed to assess the frequency of sexual harassment that women experience while at work. This measure includes three dimensions of workplace sexual harassment: gender harassment, unwanted sexual attention, and sexual coercion.

Sexual Harassment Attitude Scale (SHAS)[2] (Appendix)
The Sexual Harassment Attitude Scale was developed in 1989 for a study that examined relationships among sexual harassment experiences, perceptions

about harassment (definitions, seriousness ratings, commonness estimates), and attitudes (about both harassment and sex roles) in order to investigate the role of ideology and consciousness in the reporting of sexual harassment experiences.

The SHAS consists of 19 items reflecting attitudes about sexual harassment. The items are rated for agreement on a five-point scale. High scores on the SHAS indicate more acceptance and tolerance of sexual harassment and less agreement with contemporary feminist understandings of its causes.

The SHAS extends the 10-item Tolerance for Sexual Harassment Inventory (TSHI) developed at the University of Rhode Island in 1986 by adding new items to enhance scale reliability while broadening the assessment of respondents' understanding of harassment.

Sexual Harassment Reporting Attitudes Scale (SHRAS)[3] (Appendix)
Many victims do not report concerns and incidents to organizations. Fear of retaliation is a legitimate concern. The SHRAS can be used as a proxy measure for the psychological safety of the organization.

The Organizational Tolerance of Sexual Harassment Inventory (OTSHI)[4]
The Organizational Tolerance of Sexual Harassment Inventory, created in 1996, measures the extent to which respondents perceive that sexually harassing behavior will be associated with negative consequences in their organization. Items are based on two major facets of harassing incidents: the organizational role of the harasser and the type of harassing behavior.

The analysis includes a six-cell design, crossing two harasser roles (supervisor, coworker) with three types of harassing behavior (gender harassment, unwanted sexual attention, and sexual coercion). The six scenarios have three response scales each. Sexual harassment vignettes were written for each of the six cells, depicting either a supervisor or a coworker engaging in one of the three types of harassment behaviors. In each case, the target of the harassing behavior is a female employee.

Following each item, respondents are asked to indicate the probable outcomes if a woman in their department were to complain about such behavior. Specifically, respondents are asked to rate the risk to a woman who complained about different kinds of harassment by different organizational members, what would be the likelihood that she would be taken seriously, and what would be the likely consequences for the supervisor or coworker who had engaged in the harassment behavior.

Comprehensive Sexual Assault Assessment Tool (CSAAT)[5]

The Comprehensive Sexual Assault Assessment Tool was developed to collect data about the victims and offenders in cases of rape and sexual assault that are critical components of victim interviews and crime investigations. The CSAAT provides a systematic guide for victim assessment, evidence documentation, and initial treatment and can be used by healthcare professionals who care for the victims of sexual assault. The tool reflects the major concepts of the Roy Adaptation Model and was designed as a victim evaluation report for clinical and forensic purposes.

The CSAAT can also be used to compile agency statistics, as part of the training for sexual assault nurse examiners, and to collect research data. A case study involving two victims illustrates the importance of evidence collection and use of the Federal Bureau of Investigation's Combined DNA Index System (CODIS) for linking victims by offender DNA.

Sexual Harassing Behavior Questionnaire (SHBQ-X)[6]

This new instrument, created in 2020, evaluates the mental health impact of patients' or clients' sexually harassing behaviors. The construct validity of the 14-item measure was demonstrated by investigating relationships with indicators of care workers' mental health.

This measure provides a useful and sound strategy for assessing sexual harassment from patients or clients and paves the way for the development of a comprehensive theoretical framework for the assessment of sexual harassment. It facilitates future investigations of risk factors for sexual harassment and protective factors, helping healthcare workers cope with sexual harassment from patients or clients.

Development and Validation of an Instrument Measuring Determinants of Bystander Intervention to Prevent Sexual Assault: An Application of the Reasoned Action Approach[7]

This research, published in 2022, investigates the utility and validity of an instrument to measure a reasoned action approach with college students at two universities. The authors note the lack of validated instruments to explore predispositions students have toward engaging in bystander intervention. A seven-factor solution model is proposed as an instrument measuring bystander intervention intention (intentions, instrumental and experiential attitudes, injunctive and descriptive norms, capacity, and autonomy). The authors suggest more research is required to validate a psychometrically tested instrument.

Perceived Organizational Tolerance for Psychological Workplace Harassment (POT) Scale[8]

The perceived organizational tolerance for psychological workplace harassment (POT) scale, introduced by researchers from Spain and Paraguay in 2019, evaluates the level of tolerance, negligence, and connivance that can be shown by an organization when it deals with an inappropriate act occurring within its scope. Tolerance of such acts has been identified as a hindrance when trying to establish an effective and sustainable strategy for the well-being of workers.

A survey that measures the construct was distributed, and 195 employed workers answered. In the first stage of analysis, a scale reduction process was applied to the obtained data using a factor extraction method, and confirmatory factor analysis was performed using structural equation models. The results validated the scale as a model of five factors: Promotion, feedback, ethics, coherence, and training.

These findings indicate that this scale is acceptable as a quantifier of the diligence of the organization when dealing with psychosocial risks at work. This construct is anticipated to be useful for measuring as much research as possible on the behavior of organizations when they deal with negative acts, with the aim of promoting sustainable, healthy working environments.

Likelihood to Sexually Harass (LSH) Scale[9] (Appendix)

The LSH is a 10-item test administered using a variety of scenarios between men and women in which the individual chooses a course of action based on the situation or opportunity presented. The LSH grades responses on the spectrum of Likely (1) and Very Likely (5). Higher LSH scores correlate with a higher probability or inclination to engage in sexual harassment.

This scale is discussed in greater detail in Chapter 29 on psychological profiles of offenders. The scale is provided in the Appendix.

REFERENCES

1. Fitzgerald L F, Gelfand M J, Drasgow F. Measuring Sexual Harassment: Theoretical and Psychometric Advances. *Basic and Applied Social Psychology.* 1995;17(4): 425–445. doi:10.1207/s15324834basp1704_2

2. Mazer D B, Percival E F. *Sexual Harassment Attitude Scale (SHAS)* [Database record]. APA PsycTests. 1989. doi:10.1037/t61661-000

3. Cesario B, Parks-Stamm E, Turgut M. *Sexual Harassment Reporting Attitudes Scale (SHRAS)* [Database record]. APA PsycTests. 2018. doi:10.1037/t69847-000

4. Hulin C L, Fitzgerald L F, Drasgow F. *Organizational Tolerance of Sexual Harassment Inventory (OTSHI)* [Database record]. APA PsycTests. 1996. doi:10.1037/t08852-000

5. Burgess AW, Fawcett J. The Comprehensive Sexual Assault Assessment Tool. *Nurse Pract.* 1996;21(4):66, 71–6, 78 passim. PMID: 8801493.

6. Vincent-Höper S, Adler M, Stein M, Vaupel C, Nienhaus A. Sexually Harassing Behaviors from Patients or Clients and Care Workers' Mental Health: Development and Validation of a Measure. *Int J Environ Res Public Health.* 2020;17(7):2570. doi: 10.3390/ijerph17072570

7. Hackman CL, Rush Griffin SE, Branscum PW, Castle A, Katague M. Development and Validation of an Instrument Measuring Determinants of Bystander Intervention to Prevent Sexual Assault: An Application of the Reasoned Action Approach. *Health Behavior Research;* 5(1). doi:10.4148/2572-1836.1114

8. Perez-Larrazabal J, Lopezdelallave A, Topa G. Organizational Tolerance for Workplace Harassment: Development and Validation of the POT Scale. *Sustainability.* 2019;11(15):4078. doi:10.3390/su11154078

9. Lee K, Gizzarone M, Ashton M C. Personality and the Likelihood to Sexually Harass. *Sex Roles.* 2003;49(1-2): 59–69. doi:10.1023/A:1023961603479

Chapter 61. The Importance of Measuring Program Success and Progress

"Progress is made where progress is measured."
—*Jack LaLanne, fitness guru*

SEXUAL MISCONDUCT, HARASSMENT, AND DISCRIMINATION affect patient safety and quality of delivery of care. The direct impact on patients is easy to quantify and qualify. Without objective measurement through validated surveys or tracking incidents and creating a repository of reports, it is impossible to analyze the efficacy of an organization's efforts. However, it's clear that the overall impact of a toxic environment has a spillover effect; there is less engagement, higher turnover, and greater absenteeism. The cumulative impact of these factors can lead to errors at the bedside.

It takes courage for an organization to face the problems objectively. It takes even more courage to publicly discuss results and openly state the organization accepts systemic factors and responsibilities. Without these efforts, organizations will remain "stuck" and vulnerable.

Some of the cases presented in this book are unquestionably the result of institutional leadership and process failures, and the consequences were compounded over time. An offender allowed to stay employed after numerous complaints is a risk. Not following up after a complaint is made is a failure.

Misconduct, Harassment, and Discrimination in Academic Medicine

"We cannot deliver the best education, medical care, and scientific advancements while harmful, often illegal, behaviors are tolerated—and we need the best of academic medicine in our current environment."— Association of American Medical Colleges, excerpt from Understanding and Addressing Sexual Harassment in Academic Medicine.

∞

Chapter 62. Title IX

"We have to build things that we want to see accomplished, in life and in our country, based on our own personal experiences ... to make sure that others ... do not have to suffer the same discrimination." — Patsy Takemoto Mink, first woman of color and first Asian-American elected to Congress

TITLE IX IS AN EXAMPLE of how the 14th Amendment's Equal Protection Clause has been interpreted over time.

Title IX of the Civil Rights Act was signed into law by President Richard M. Nixon on June 23, 1972. It was the culmination of a long journey that wound its way through all three branches of government when Representative Patsy T. Mink of Hawaii, recognized as the major author and sponsor of the legislation, introduced it in Congress. When she died in 2002, Title IX was renamed the Patsy Mink Equal Opportunity in Education Act. Posthumously, she earned the Congressional Medal of Honor.

Title IX states:

"No person in the United States shall, on the basis of sex, be excluded from the participation in, be denied the benefits of, or be subjected to discrimination under any education program or activity receiving Federal financial assistance."

The original intent of Title IX was to increase women's access to educational and athletic programs. Over time, courts began to recognize that sexual harassment is a form of sex discrimination. Schools were then required to address this issue.

In the late 1980s, a 10th-grade student complained to administrators at her high school that one of the teachers was sexually harassing her throughout the year. The administration did nothing, and the teacher resigned. The case was considered closed, but the student brought action against the school district for failing to take any action.[1]

This case demonstrated that the courts formally interpreted sexual harassment is a form of sexual discrimination and a part of Title IX protection. In 1999, the courts also acknowledged that sexual violence is a form of sexual harassment.[2]

In addition to expanding the behaviors and actions constituting the definition of harassment, the number of programs falling under Title IX expanded in the late 1980s. In 1988, Congress added broad definitions to include "programs or activities and all of the operations of an institution principally engaged in healthcare." With one broad stroke of the pen, academic medical centers (AMCs), not just the medical schools, were responsible for Title IX compliance. Other programs requiring Title IX compliance include all other allied healthcare professional degrees, certificates, or graduate educational endeavors: nursing, pharmacy, dentistry, physical therapy, etc.

The U.S. Department of Health, Education, and Welfare issued the first Title IX regulations in 1975. These first efforts included a relatively simple set of regulations:

1. Disseminate notice of non-discrimination.
2. Designate at least one employee to coordinate Title IX compliance efforts.
3. Adopt and publish grievance procedures.

These guidelines were far simpler in the mid-1970s because the original scope and intention of Title IX was access. The definition of discrimination only included denying access. As mentioned previously, the courts recognized that sexual harassment and violence is a form of discrimination.

In 2011 and 2014, the Department of Education (DOE) issued new guidance stipulating that sexual violence is a form of sexual harassment prohibited under Title IX and providing instructions on how to address this issue. The guidance included details on time frames for completing investigations, standards of proof, and requirements allowing both parties equal access to an appeal and supportive measures.

This new guidance led to a substantial increase in Title IX complaints and litigation. Those subjected to sexual violence claimed institutions were not following guidance, and those disciplined claimed the process was unfair. Indeed, some lawyers and legal scholars criticized the 2011 and 2014 guidance requiring a process that was fundamentally unfair to the accused. In response, in September 2017, the DOE rescinded the 2011 and 2014 guidance, stating that it deprived students of their rights and created confusion among schools and institutions.

Despite the withdrawal of the 2011 and 2014 guidance, complaints and litigation continued to increase. It is important to remember that the #MeToo movement went viral in 2017, and this movement is the predominant reason Title IX complaints increased. In May 2020, the DOE released a 2,000-page document with commentary containing new guidance. Compliance with the new regulations became effective in August, and after they were released, the backlash was immediate.

The 2020 regulations included a new, narrower definition of sexual harassment. Prior to this, the substantive standard for determining whether an individual was sexually harassed was the same for Title IX and Title VII, which prohibits employment discrimination based on race, color, religion, sex, sexual orientation, gender identity, or national origin.

Under the new Title VII regulations, unwelcome sexual conduct is considered sexual harassment when it is "severe *or* pervasive" enough to create a hostile environment for the person or persons being harassed. The new Title IX regulations changed the requirements to meet the standard of sexual harassment. The new regulation stated that the conduct must be "severe *and* pervasive *and* objectively offensive." If conduct met these new requirements, institutions were required to use Title IX processes for the investigation.

If the investigation determined that the conduct did not meet these requirements, the institution would be forced to dismiss the complaint. With this new requirement, determining which standard and process to use increased the complexity and risk for the organization.

Title IX, similar to Title VII, is a mutable, living document subject to change, and as of August 1, 2024, the DOE released a new set of guidelines with some notable new regulations:

1. Expanded definitions of sex discrimination, including sexual orientation, gender identity, and pregnancy.
2. New definitions of sexual harassment, including specific actions that create a hostile work environment. This includes sex-based conduct that, based on the totality of the circumstances, is *subjectively* and *objectively* offensive and so severe or pervasive that it limits or denies an individual's ability to participate in or benefit from your education program activity.
3. Broader scope of potential wrongdoing. This new rule expands the jurisdictional scope of Title IX to cover conduct that affects the program regardless of where it occurs. This includes conduct outside the United States or outside of the educational program or activity.
4. Revised grievance hearings, including increased institutional flexibility and permission to design procedures meeting the needs of the institution. Specifically, live hearings and cross-examination are no longer required. Additionally, there are increased options to create processes for more informal resolutions.
5. Increased privacy rights for all parties.
6. Increased oversight and a new requirement for institutions to monitor programs for sex discrimination. Specifically, a new requirement is creating processes to reduce barriers to reporting.
7. A new requirement for prompt time frames for investigating complaints.
8. Expanded reported requirements. Employees will have greater obligations to notify the Title IX coordinator of known or suspected discrimination or harassment.

9. Increased emphasis on supportive programs. Institutions will be required to offer and provide greater support for complainants throughout the grievance process.

In April 2024, the Biden Administration and DOE finalized new rules stating Title IX also forbids discrimination based on sexual orientation or gender identity. LGBTQ+ students who face discrimination will be entitled to a response from their school under Title IX, and those failed by their schools can seek recourse from the federal government. The continued controversy over allowing transgender athletes protections was specifically left out of the new rules.

REFERENCES

1. *Franklin v Gwinnett County Public Schools*, 503 US (1992).
2. *Soper v. Hoben*, 195 F.3d 845, 855 (6th Cir. 1999).

Chapter 63. Gender and Sexual Harassment and Discrimination in Academic Medicine

"If gender discrimination is allowed, sexual harassment is more likely because there's a continuum of this kind of behavior. Gender discrimination has to be stopped in its track within an organization's culture." — Diana Lautenberger, MAT, Association of American Medical Colleges

IN JULY 2022, the American Association of American Medical Colleges (AAMC) published a landmark report, *Understanding and Addressing Sexual Harassment in Academic Medicine.*[1] The report focuses on medical school faculty educators, physicians, and scientists, an overlooked group in academic medicine. Most research has focused on the experiences of medical students and resident physicians. In the Executive Summary, the authors state[1]:

"Sexual harassment should be seen as one of the critical issues to resolve as part of addressing equity and inclusion writ large. Our attention must be focused on harassment now more than ever, as rates and experiences of harassment may have gone unchecked and unreported for more than two years due to the COVID-19 pandemic. Academic institutions must be bold and brave in eliminating harassment by addressing the foundational and cultural traits at their institutions that continue to allow it to persist, such as tolerance for harmful behavior, acts of retribution, rigid hierarchy, and dominating behavior, often by men."

Complete with data on incidence and prevalence, this report highlights the need for change and offers practical solutions for medical schools to address the problem. To explore faculty experiences of harassment, the authors used a quantitative approach and interviews with leaders about how and why they address harassment on their campuses. The following questions were asked:

- *What is the prevalence of sexual harassment among medical school faculty?*
- *How do faculty perceive their institution's ability to address harassment?*

- *How are institutions creating programs, policies, and practices that focus on preventing sexual harassment and the types of cultures and climates necessary to establish these practices?*

The authors contend that the solution to reducing and eliminating sexual harassment is an institutional responsibility, and it's a recurring theme. Most sexual harassment training programs focus on individuals and individual behaviors as the main focus for prevention. This approach is not effective. In fact, the authors state, *"To understand how to address sexual harassment in academic medicine, we must first understand and bring awareness to the specific environmental, structural, and governance factors that present unique barriers to developing effective solutions."*[1]

In their summary of findings, 34% of women faculty and 22% of faculty overall experienced sexual harassment. The highest rates of harassment were in the departments of anesthesiology and emergency medicine, each at 52.6%. The most frequent sexual harassment behaviors were gender put-downs and the telling of sexist and offensive jokes. Only 54.7% of women who experienced sexual harassment felt safe reporting the behaviors. The report offers detailed and specific strategies for institutions to use innovative, new approaches, which are necessary to create lasting change.

The Accreditation Council for Graduate Medical Education (ACGME) is also committed to the principle that discrimination and harassment are unacceptable and must not be tolerated.[2] The ACGME expects that participants in the greater graduate medical education community will be able to work and study in an atmosphere that discourages discrimination and harassment by colleagues, supervisors, teachers, peers, other staff members, and patients. This principle applies in all areas of graduate medical education, including employment and training.

The ACGME Institutional Requirements include requirements for implementing this principle on a local level. The ACGME also applies this principle to its own staff, to program faculty and staff members, to residents and fellows, to all visitors, invitees, vendors, contractors, consultants, and others who do business with the ACGME via policies contained in its Employee Policy Manual. However, many institutions are failing to create a safe, harassment-free environment.

Arianna Gianakos, assistant professor in the Department of Orthopedic Surgery at the Yale School of Medicine, and others recently published an important systematic review investigating bullying, discrimination, harassment, sexual harassment, and the fear of retaliation during surgical residency training.[3]

The summary report of their findings from 25 studies with nearly 30,000 responses from surgical residents from a variety of surgical specialties is alarming: 37% of residents reported burnout, 33% reported anxiety/depression, and attending surgeons and senior co-residents were identified as the most common perpetrators. In addition, 71% of respondents did not report harassing behaviors. 51% of these respondents did not report the behaviors out of fear of retaliation, and 56% of those who did report the behavior had a negative experience.[3]

A majority of female trainees in surgical residency and fellowship programs do not feel safe or comfortable reporting events. Progress is impossible until trainees can report without fear and have faith and trust in the process.[3]

There remains a paucity of research investigating how these behaviors are reported and managed in order to prevent the perpetuation of a hostile work environment. I suspect that symbolic compliance with policies and the legacy "boys club" mentality that has dominated surgical training for decades is a major culprit. We need to change the lived experience of women in surgical training. We must foster a culture of inclusion with zero tolerance for inappropriate behavior.[4] This problem is pervasive. Studies examining the issue in the EU, US, UK, Australia, Canada, and other nations confirm the existence of a toxic culture for women in surgical training nearly everywhere.[3,5,6]

Yumiko Kadota, a former surgical resident in Australia, recently resigned from her position after being made to work 24 consecutive days on-call. Other trainees in Australian surgical programs describe the demeaning surgical culture as follows:

> "He kept yelling at her with the [whole theatre team]," one participant said. "No you idiot. Don't do it like this'.....they just blamed her for everything, even if it wasn't her fault."

"Ultimately I didn't see more than two choices: kill myself or leave," one former trainee said.

Another trainee told researchers: "Bosses have said to them, to their face, 'I don't think there's any point in me training you because you're going to get married and have kids and then what use are you going to be to this surgical service?'"

Leah Liang says female trainees face myriad different stresses that accumulate — like a tower of blocks that eventually topples, and the reason many interventions fail is because there is a focus on just one of those blocks. I agree. And the elephant in the room is a legacy of a poor culture that is tolerant and accepting of these behaviors. Kadota crashed her car at the end of her last shift and was in the hospital for six weeks.[7]

Academic medicine is culturally engrained, and stereotypical "dominant masculine" traits dominate the environment and are imposed on everyone in the system. It is a major contributor to the prevalence of sexual harassment. Jennifer Berdahl and colleagues refer to this phenomenon as a Masculinity Contest Culture (MCC). Work styles and expectations drive men, especially, to continually "prove" themselves and "behave aggressively, embrace risky behaviors, sexually harass women (or other men), and express homophobic attitudes."[8] This culture impacts many marginalized groups, not just women.

The AAMC, in its report, includes institutional strategies for preventing and addressing sexual harassment:

1. Institute a zero-tolerance policy.
2. Coordinate the approach to the problem.
3. Hold department chairs accountable.
4. Leverage the resources from the parent university if applicable.
5. Hire trained investigators.
6. Centralize and expand the reporting of behaviors.
7. Address less overt yet still harmful behavior through intervening early and often.
8. Use proportionate sanctions.
9. Communicate transparently about harassment incidents.
10. Train beyond compliance.

11. Recognize harassment happens to men, too but women experience it at far higher rates.

Not mentioned specifically, but just as important are mentorships, instituting more flexible options for training, including offering less than full-time training for a longer duration, increasing investments in DEI programs and efforts, and implementing plan-do-study-act (PDSA), an iterative, four-stage problem-solving model used for improving processes or carrying out change. The PDSA approach is widely used in quality improvement efforts (Figure 1).

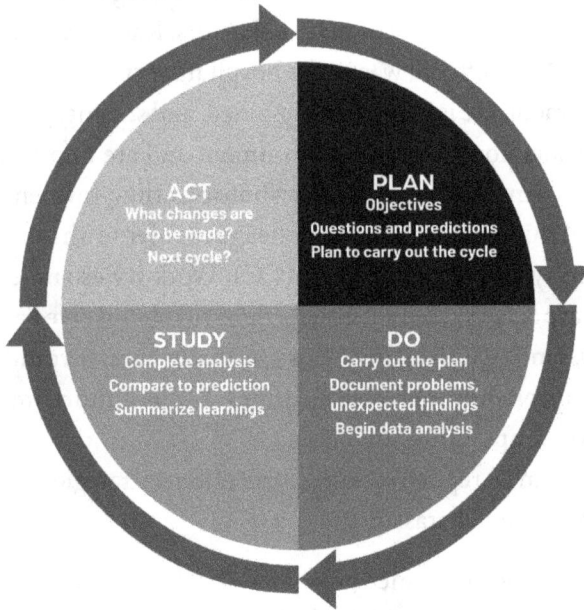

FIGURE 1. Plan-Do-Study-Act Cycle

Plan: A formal intervention cannot be implemented without information. Organizations must assess the current state, identify the top two concerns affecting the organization, and formulate a plan for intervention. This includes seeking feedback from all employees, conducting surveys, and, creating a committee with a formal charter. Communicate with employees, staff, and all stakeholders.

Do: Implement the intervention strategies.

Study: Analyze the effectiveness of the intervention through improvement of key performance indicators (KPIs). As an example, if a KPI is improving the percentage of staff who feel confident and safe reporting an occurrence without retaliation, measure the impact through surveys.

Act: Through analysis of objective and/or subjective and qualitative measures, revise the strategy, formulate a new plan, and continue the cycle.

The PDSA model has been criticized for being too simplistic. Furthermore, varied practices in the use of the PDSA model compromise its effectiveness.[9] An antidote to failure, I believe, is effective leadership, accountability, use of subject matter experts, commitment, communication, and clarity of purpose.

All trainees deserve to train in a safe, respectful, and supportive environment. The irony is the healthcare environment is supposed to be one of healing and compassion and empathy, and those who choose careers in medicine deserve the same treatment as the patients we care for.

I have highlighted the issues in surgery because these programs have traditionally been male-dominated. All specialties, nursing programs, podiatry, dental, and pharmacy programs—anywhere there is a power dynamic and tolerant culture.[10]

CASE STUDY

Becky Cox, a surgical trainee in the NHS in the UK, left surgical training with depression and PTSD after enduring an onslaught of inappropriate sexual harassment and other behaviors. She was determined to become a surgeon and won the Welsh Surgeons Junior Gold Medal prize for research in her first year. She says she quit amid "lots of inappropriate verbal comments, name-calling, being harassed and seniors propositioning themselves on to." She now practices as a GP in Oxford. She and Chelcie Jewitt founded *Surviving in Scrubs* to amplify voices of sexual misconduct within the NHS to create change.[11]

The downstream effects from these experiences result in fewer mentors for newly trained physicians, and with fewer mentors, opportunities for academic advancement and obtaining other leadership roles is substantially more difficult. Medical school deans, department chairs, attendings, and other faculty need to step up and accept responsibility for creating a zero- tolerance environment. It is an international problem that cuts through cultural boundaries.

REFERENCES

1. Lautenberger D, Dandar V, Zhou Y. *Understanding and Addressing Sexual Harassment in Academic Medicine.* Washington, DC: Association of American Medical Colleges; 2022.

2. Accreditation Council for Graduate Medical Education (ACGME). Non-Discrimination Policy. https://www.acgme.org/about/legal/non-discrimination-policy/ .

3. Gianakos A, Freischlag JA, Mercurio AM, Haring RS, LaPorte DM, *et al.* Bullying, Discrimination, Harassment, Sexual Harassment, and the Fear of Retaliation During Surgical Residency Training: A Systematic Review. *World J Surg.* 2022;46(7):1587–1599. doi:10.1007/s00268-021-06432-6

4. Gallagher K, Nayyar A. Sexual Harassment and Women in Surgery: Changing the Lived Experience. *Surgery.* 2021;170(2): 637–638.

5. Ceppa DP, Dolejs SC, Boden N, Phela S, Yost KJ, *et al.* Sexual Harassment and Cardiothoracic Surgery: #UsToo? *Ann Thorac Surg.* 2020;109(4):1283–1288. doi:10.1016/j.athoracsurg.2019.07.009

6. Holzang MN, Koenemann N, Skinner H, Burke J, Smith A, Young A. Discrimination in the Surgical Discipline: An International European Evaluation (DISDAIN). *BJS Open.* 2021;5(3):zrab050. doi:10.1093/bjsopen/zrab050

7. Aubusson K. 'Kill myself or leave': Female Surgeons Reveal Horrifying Conditions. *The Sydney Herald.* February 8, 2019. https://www.smh.com.au/healthcare/kill-myself-or-leave-female-surgeons-reveal-horrifying-conditions-20190208-p50wiy.html.

8. Berdahl JL, Cooper M, Glick P, Livingston RW, Williams JC. Work as a Masculinity Contest. *J Soc Issues.* 2018;74(3):422–448.

9. Taylor MK, McNicholas C, Nicolay C, Darzi A, Bell D, Reed JE. Systematic Review of the Application of the Plan-Do-Study-Act Method to Improve Quality in Healthcare. *BMJ Qual and Saf.* 2014;23(4):290-298. doi.org/10.1136/bmjqs-2013-001862

10. Castner J. Healthy Environments for Women in Academic Nursing: Addressing Sexual Harassment and Gender Discrimination. *OJIN: The Online Journal of Issues in Nursing.* 2019;24(1):5.

11. Dunstan G. Sex Assault Made Me Quit Surgical Training, Says Doctor. *BBC News.* February 1, 2024. http://www.bbc.com/news/articles/c9w4mzjmgk9o.

Chapter 64. Power Differentials in Academic Medicine

"This is just another thing you're going to have to learn how to deal with," the female resident said matter-of-factly. We had just seen a patient who had made lewd comments about our appearance, questioned our qualifications, and called us little girls. It was not the first time one of the authors had encountered sexual harassment. But it was the first time experiencing it in a patient care setting."[1]

POWER DIFFERENTIALS EXIST across all industries, but practicing medicine and training to practice medicine requires an individual to practice, learn, and train in a rigid academic environment with clearly defined roles and expectations based purely on level of training, academic rank, or other formal title.

Within the training environment, freshman students in professional degree programs are the least trained, least knowledgeable, and regardless of other factors influencing their status, the most vulnerable and least powerful. The conditions are ideal for harassment and discrimination. Given these conditions for training, it is paramount to create a safe, harassment-free environment.

Research has consistently demonstrated that institutions and organizations with large power differentials are more likely to be associated with high rates of sexual harassment compared to organizations with smaller power differentials.[1,2] The healthcare environment, and especially the healthcare training environment, is a setting with large power differentials. When power differentials are abused, the negative impact of sexual harassment is greater than if the harassment occurs from an individual with equal or less power.[3]

REFERENCES

1. Ilies R, Hauserman N, Schwochau S, Stibal J. Reported Incidence Rates of Work-Related Sexual Harassment in the United States: Using Meta-Analysis to Explain Reported Rate Disparities. *Personnel Psychology.* 2003;56(3):607–631. doi:10.1111/j.1744-6570.2003.tb00752.x

2. O'Callaghan E, Shepp V, Kirkner A, Lorenz K. Sexual Harassment in the Academy: Harnessing the Growing Labor Movement in Higher Education To Address Sexual

Harassment Against Graduate Workers. *Violence Against Women.* 2022;28(12-13):3266–3288. doi:10.1177/10778012211035793

3. Liang T. Sexual Harassment at Work: Scoping Review of Reviews. *Psychol Res Behav Manag.* 2024 Apr 16;17:1635-1660. doi: 10.2147/PRBM.S455753

Chapter 65. Department Leadership and Attending Physician Responsibilities

LEADERS AND THOSE WITH AUTHORITY are ultimately responsible for the work environment and for establishing cultural norms. Young trainees, especially, need to know department chairs and attending physicians are confident, comfortable, and competent when facing difficult and uncomfortable situations such as harassment or discrimination. Very few academic attendings and department chairs receive formal training on how to recognize and intervene when misconduct or harassment occurs.

Failure to intervene appropriately preserves the status quo. Armani Hawes and Keerthi Gondy from the University of Michigan recently published a paper examining five unique archetypes of leaders who respond inadequately to sexual harassment. More importantly, the authors have created a proposed framework for response strategies.[1] The five archetypes are as follows:

THE AVOIDER

An avoider behaves as if the harassment did not happen:

A female medical student and male attending physician see a male patient in the emergency department presenting with a possible incarcerated inguinal hernia. During the exam, the patient winks at the student and says, "It's been a while since I've had a young girl playing around down there. She wasn't nearly as pretty as you." The student briefly makes eye contact with the attending, who looks uncomfortable but says nothing.

The attending physician may be uncomfortable confronting the patient or addressing the situation directly. Without taking any action, the attending has condoned the patient's behavior.

THE AUTHORITARIAN

Authoritarians fail to acknowledge that sexual harassment is a real problem and believe students should not be offended by patients' statements.

A female medical student sees a patient with lower abdominal pain in a surgery clinic. During her exam alongside the male attending physician,

the patient looks up with a wink and asks, "What else can you do for me?"
The attending laughs and completes the exam for the student. When the
student later tries discussing the incident, the attending tells her that the
patient was obviously joking and that she needs to grow thicker skin if she
wants to make it in surgery.

The attending believes the only problematic aspect of sexual harassment
is the woman's response to it. The student bears both the responsibility
and burden of learning how to manage harassment in an unsupportive
environment.

THE DISMISSER

Dismissers believe that physical assault, such as unwanted touching or
groping, is the most pressing obstacle women face, and only those actions
warrant a response.

As she visits her patients with a resident, a female medical student is asked
by a male patient, "Are you a virgin? Because you sure look like one." The
resident ignores the question and proceeds with taking the history. When
the student tries to discuss the incident with the female attending physician,
the attending responds, "That's just part of the job."

The attending fails to support the student and cites a history of inappropriate behavior as a reason for accepting current inappropriate behavior.
Additionally, the resident, who is a bystander, fails to confront the patient
in the moment. As a result, the student learns that speaking out against
harassment will not be taken seriously.

THE INEFFECTIVE SUPPORTER

Ineffective supporters have a genuine desire to support their team members and condemn sexual harassment, but they could benefit from a more
effective approach.

"You've got a model in your presence," the patient tells the female attending
physician during morning rounds, nodding to the female medical student.
The attending awkwardly chuckles and leaves the room. One week later in
a feedback session, she tells the student, "I spoke to the patient privately to

tell him that he should stop making those inappropriate statements." The patient never changed his behavior.

The attending appreciates the vulnerability of both the student and patient and tries to support them both by addressing the sexual harassment in private. However, she misses the opportunity to address the incident immediately after it occurs, which would have allowed her to demonstrate her support of the student and more effectively change behavior.

THE ENABLER

Enablers fail to recognize sexual harassment and may even contribute to the harassment.

While a female student and resident interview a male patient, he tells the medical student that she should wear a dress because scrubs don't flatter her body type. When the student later mentions this comment to the male attending physician, he chuckles and says, "Well, he's got a point."

This scenario is clearly a sign of multiple failures by the attending physician. First, there was a lack of intervention during the interview by the resident. The attending not only dismisses the concern but tacitly agrees with it. This is not an environment conducive to learning in a psychologically safe manner. The student is unsure how to handle the harassment at this point.

Table 1 provides a framework for responses to sexual harassment attending physicians can use at the bedside and on the wards with patients who sexually harass students and residents. This framework can also be used if an attending physician witnesses medical students or co-residents engaging in harassing behaviors. Calling out an individual, especially a patient who has engaged in misconduct publicly and with witnesses, sends a powerful message that the behavior is unacceptable.[1]

Attending physicians in a clinical role spend many hours with trainees, and they have an opportunity to become role models and mentors. Failure to address misconduct from patients or peers leads to burnout. Some of the physicians who do not feel supported might consider resigning from a career in medicine. We cannot afford to mistreat intelligent, talented, and motivated trainees.

TABLE 1. Framework for response strategies to sexual harassment.

Task	Framework	Example statement
Confront the offender	Immediately address the inappropriate statement or action.	"We need to talk about what you just said."
Name the behavior	Name the offensive behavior and identify it as inappropriate and unacceptable.	"Do not comment on her appearance. That is inappropriate."
Set the expectation	Make it clear to the patient and the team that harassment will not be tolerated to encourage a community of support.	"All members on my team are valued and deserve respect. Comments like that are unacceptable and will not be tolerated."
Support the student	Reinforce to the student that she is a valued member of the team, harassment is not her fault, and that it will never be tolerated.	"I'm sorry you had to experience that. This is not your fault. You are an important member of this team. Are you okay?"
Be proactive	Consider how you can be a stronger ally to female students and keep phrases ready in the back of your mind that you can immediately use in future situations of harassment.	"I will work towards becoming a better ally. How could I have handled that situation better? What can I do better if it happens again?"

DEPARTMENT CHAIRS

Department chairs have a responsibility to set the tone and expectations for department faculty and resident behaviors. Through role modeling and empowering faculty and residents to speak out when harassment occurs and take the claimants seriously is an ethical responsibility. Minimizing and ignoring an occurrence is not optional. There are dozens of cases of department chairs in numerous medical schools who have engaged in sexual misconduct and harassment. These incidents create institutional embarrassment when made public, as people are hungry for the sordid details.

Case Study

Several years ago, I was assigned to perform anesthesia cases for several young women undergoing fertility treatments. The maternal-fetal-medicine (MFM) physician, who was former faculty and chair of MFM medicine at a prominent midwestern university, had booked a series of procedures with monitored anesthesia care — moderate sedation. I had not worked with this surgeon before. One of my partners told me to look him up on the internet.

Before starting the cases for the morning, I privately looked up information regarding the surgeon, and what I found appalled me. The surgeon was forced out of his prior chair position due to inappropriate behaviors with MFM fellows, including showing some of the female MFM fellows sex toys in his office. Other harassing behaviors were also mentioned. He resigned from his former position and had a private practice office as a solo physician. I was not looking forward to working with him.

As I took the first patient back to surgery, I told her I would make her comfortable and keep her asleep during the procedure. I administered propofol to the patient; she quickly lost consciousness, and I assisted her breathing and ventilation with a mask.

Before proceeding, the surgeon asked me if she was awake, and I said, "No, she is not. I administered propofol and she is unconscious." He then blurted, "Well. I need her to be more awake." I quickly replied, "Why do you need the patient to be more awake? Her level of consciousness does not impact your ability to do the procedure safely, and if this was my wife or daughter, I am certain she would not want to be awake for this procedure either."

He replied angrily, "This is how I do things, and my patients are not normally completely asleep." I flippantly replied, "Then why did you request our anesthesia services? I am not comfortable, nor do I think it is in the best interest of the patient for me to allow you to do an intimate procedure on these patients with them semi-conscious and uncomfortable. They are young, healthy, and it is safe for me to mask ventilate while administering propofol." The temperature of the room was starting to hit the boiling point.

I knew there was something "off" about this surgeon from the beginning; his behavior and request for the level of anesthetic was unusual. After the four brief OR cases that were booked, he notified our office I was no longer to be scheduled as the anesthesiologist for his cases. He did me a favor, as I did not want to work with him again, either. Six months later, his privileges were quietly terminated, and he established privileges at another local hospital. His tenure at the other facility was short-lived, too. Approximately one year later, his office was closed, and he no longer practiced in the area.

I suspect there were further incidents of misconduct, and my experience with him was unnerving. In my opinion, he should never have been granted privileges. If his file were up for review today, a hospital would not grant him privileges, given his prior resignation under the former claims from his tenure as a chair and subsequent loss of privileges. Physicians who have relocated many times within a short time period might have clinical or professionalism and conduct concerns. This is why it is important for credentialing and privileging committees to do their due diligence and have the courage to deny privileges.

Case Study

This case was told to me unsolicited when I was discussing the subject matter for this book with a professional colleague I have known for more than 10 years.

Many years ago, as a general surgery resident applying for trauma and surgical critical care fellowships, she was offered an interview at a prominent program with an outstanding national and international reputation. She requested an in-person interview and a site visit. During the interview process with the program director (a male who had been the program director for 25 years), she was asked if she planned on having children during the fellowship. Surprised by this question, she responded with a simple "No."

I asked her how she handled it after she responded, and she shared with me that she remained professional and cordial for the remainder of the interviews and site visits. Soon after the interviews and site visits, she wrote a brief thank-you note to the department chair and program director and informed both that she was withdrawing her application to the program.

I asked her if she considered reporting the question and experience to the ACGME or the department chair regarding the program director's question. She thought about it briefly, but like so many women placed in these particular positions, *her* reputation might become tarnished. She would choose not to attend that program even if offered a fellowship. She said, "It was better for me to just move on and move forward, as there were other great programs I could attend."

Male candidates do not have to endure these experiences. And I suspect this program director asked nearly all female candidates this question. Nothing will likely change until a candidate is willing to stick her neck out. The ACGME does have a formal, anonymous complaint mechanism for current residents and fellows.

In my opinion, to protect the integrity of the interview process, residents and fellow candidates should feel safe enough to anonymously report illegal questions or unprofessional conduct during the interview process. An anonymous complaint about this program director would provide enough evidence for the ACGME to intervene and take appropriate action.

REFERENCE

1. Hawes AM, Gondy K. Sexual Harassment in Medical Education: How We Can Do Better. *J Gen Intern Med.* 2021;36(12):3841–3843. doi: 10.1007/s11606-021-06960-w

Chapter 66. Resident Relationships

[T]he University believes that a sexual or romantic relationship between a teacher and a student, even where consensual and whether or not the student would otherwise be subject to supervision or evaluation by the teacher, is inconsistent with the proper role of the teacher, and should be avoided. The University therefore very strongly discourages such relationships. — Excerpt from the Stanford School of Medicine, Stanford, California, Sexual Harassment Policy

R ELATIONSHIPS AMONG RESIDENT PHYSICIANS are common. The nature of the training environment, power structures, roles and responsibilities, and other factors place unique stresses on the relationship. There are numerous "pitfalls" and potential problems. There are professional and personal risks associated with relationships between residents and/or attending physicians that can jeopardize a young physician's career. Anastasia Climan recently published an excellent summary on *MDLinx,* highlighting the need for residents to navigate dating in residency with caution.[1]

First, she suggests residents familiarize themselves with institutional or human resource policies before committing to a romantic relationship. Every institution has policies and/or codes of conduct regarding intimate relationships at work, including behavioral expectations.

Second, she discourages forming any relationship with a superior (attending, chief resident, etc.) or a co-resident who is married or is in another serious relationship. Infidelity can harm one's professional reputation and career.

Third, keep work separate and maintain professional behavior at work. Airing grievances, openly engaging in conflict or disagreement, having inappropriate discussions, or publicly displaying affection is unacceptable.

Fourth, if the relationship dissolves or sours, both parties have a duty to maintain civility toward each other regardless of how one or both parties feel. Breakups are often messy, and it is difficult to be forced to work with a former romantic partner.

Climan also suggests early disclosure if a relationship develops. Letting an attending physician, program director, or department chair know that there is an intimate relationship with a co-resident is not only professional but can also prevent misinterpretation of events or other issues if there is a problem. The use of social media platforms to share important life events, date nights, etc., is ubiquitous. Residents should exercise caution when posting personal information on social media websites.

In my opinion, there is too much downside risk involved for all parties when a resident decides to proceed with a romantic relationship with an attending or other physician with significant authority. There are potential conflicts of interest, too. Additionally, a relationship with a wide power differential is bound to create gossip and other water cooler talk that is often negative, unflattering, and unprofessional. Unfortunately, due to the double standards between gender roles and expectations for men and women, a woman's reputation can suffer more harm, too.

Case Study

A 29-year-old female internal medicine resident has just been elected as chief resident at a prominent urban program by her peers and other attendings. The program director (PD) is a 41-year-old male who has been married for four years and has two small children.

Part of the onboarding process for the new chief resident is training and discussion with the PD. Late one afternoon, the resident and PD go to his office for further discussion. The following day, the two meet once again, and on the fourth opportunity to meet up, the PD suggests the two go to a local restaurant within walking distance.

Nothing unusual occurs during the meeting at the restaurant. The following week, they meet again at the same restaurant, but this time, they start discussing more personal matters. They agree to meet again the following week, and before discussing anything related to her new chief position, they enjoy drinks and discuss more personal and informal topics. She confides to him that she is developing feelings for him and wishes he was not married. He tells her he has started having some feelings for her as well.

The following week, he calls her and tells her he would like to meet with her on the weekend, as his wife was going to be out of town with the children. That weekend the two have an intimate encounter. The following week, his wife finds his phone on the kitchen counter after it beeps. A new text from the resident pops up on the screen: *"I had a great time over the weekend. I hope we can get together soon."* His wife hands him his phone as he is about to leave for work and asks what is going on with the resident.

He says he has been training the new resident, and they got together over the weekend to discuss her new position and the responsibilities of the position. He says he went out with her and some other residents afterward to hang out at a local gastropub.

When he gets to work, he calls the resident and says what they did was a mistake, and they can only meet in professional settings moving forward. She reluctantly agrees to no longer meet with him outside of work.

This case highlights the slippery slope of meeting and socializing outside of a professional setting. The relationship was brief, and he realized he was making a huge mistake continuing it. He violated professional boundaries when he suggested they go to a local restaurant. With alcohol, people become less inhibited, and the slippery slope can become a full-blown emotional affair that turns physical. Neither one of them had any intent to become emotionally attached to each other, but it happens.

The PD has full responsibility for maintaining professional boundaries in this situation. He has the power and authority in the professional relationship. Here are some questions to consider:

- Do you think the power dynamic in the relationship influenced the resident in her decision to go to the restaurant with the PD the first time? What if she had disagreed and he insisted she go with him?
- What if he threatened to remove her from the position if she did not agree to have sex with him? What recourse would she have?
- What if, after he told her they needed to keep the relationship professional and that it was a mistake, she continued to pursue him and started stalking behaviors?
- What if she threatened to tell his wife about their encounter if he did not continue to see her?

Many scenarios can be discussed using the "what if" approach in this case.

REFERENCE

1. Climan A. Romance During Residency: Is It OK to Date a Co-Resident? *MDLinx.* June 19, 2023. https://www.mdlinx.com/article/romance-during-residency-is-it-ok-to-date-a-co-resident/13SoUya33IjHfNX94DDQS9.

Chapter 67. Medical Student Concerns

T HE TEMPORAL NATURE OF BEING a medical student, especially while on wards and rotations, reduces a medical student's sense of empowerment. Just as a student is comfortable in a new setting with new interns, residents, and attendings, it is time to move on to a new experience. Trust takes time to develop, and two months is not enough time to create a deeper, trusting relationship. Medical students need to feel safe reporting incidents, which is the responsibility of medical schools and training programs.

Medical students do not want to jeopardize their career path and take personal and professional risks if filing a report will do no more than create problems. The same barriers to reporting apply to medical students as well. Furthermore, because of the temporal nature of the experience, medical students may feel it is not worth their time to report. By the time any investigation is complete, which will take weeks or a few months, the student will have moved on to a different clinical setting.

CASE STUDY

A 28-year-old male medical student attends an HIV clinic for two weeks as part of his family practice rotation. The experience is positive, and the student enjoys working with the attending physician. On the last day of the rotation, the attending physician invites the student into his office for a final evaluation and discussion. The student tells the attending physician that the rotation was a challenging experience he thoroughly enjoyed.

The conversation continues, and everything seems to be going well when, all of a sudden, the attending physician starts rifling through a pile of mail on his desk. A bit bewildered, the medical student asks what he was looking for. He continues looking for a few more seconds, finds what he is looking for, and hands it to the medical student. As the student reaches for the paper, he sees it is an advertisement from a local adult store and has images of men in a variety of bondage outfits. There is a coupon for products for the upcoming Folsom Street Fair in San Francisco.

The attending asks the student if he would like to attend the street festival with him this weekend. The medical student instantly realizes what has transpired over a few minutes and politely declines the offer. The attending acknowledges the student's response and tells him to call if he changes his mind.

The attending then tells the student he will be writing a great narrative summary for the rotation, that he deserves honors, and that he should consider family practice as a career. Awkwardly, the student gathers his things, says thank you, and leaves.

Was the attending's behavior sexual harassment?

The medical student in this case study is me. I shared the story with some classmates and never told my clerkship director or anyone else. I certainly did not want to "rock the boat." I realized quite quickly he was asking me out without asking me out. The entire situation was awkward.

In retrospect, this was sexual harassment because he was sharing inappropriate sexually related material with me in a learning environment. Had he not shared the advertisement with me and just asked if I wanted to go to the Folsom Street Fair, a pretty clear line would not have been crossed.

I really did enjoy the rotation. I learned a lot, and he was a great teacher. I never felt intimidated, unsafe, or uncomfortable until the final hour on that last day. I think it is worth bearing in mind my own sexual assault experience did play a part in my staying silent, too. I simply did not want to dredge up old memories.

Putting It All Together: A New Path Forward

"If you don't like the road you're walking, start paving another one." — *Dolly Parton, singer/songwriter*

W E NEED A NEW PATH FORWARD in addressing these problems, and through continued discussion, understanding, and organizational willingness to invest time and resources, new cultures can emerge — cultures imbued with equity, equality, respect, and empathy. It will require a new mindset that the problem cannot be addressed through educational modules alone. As a solution, I propose a robust framework including leadership structures, reporting and training requirements, and training using current quality care improvement models that incorporate andragogy, which is adult learning theory (Figure 1).

Under this proposal, everyone in the organization, including the board of directors and all C-suite executives, participates in the same training. Focused and specialized training would be required for members of the board of directors, C-suite and senior-level executives, human resources leaders, medical staff directors and chairs, and managers and directors. This training would include navigating the reporting process, legal and regulatory compliance education, and instruction on effective interviewing skills. Virtual modules, presentations, and live instruction offered by trained subject matter experts present more thorough, dynamic, and interactive training education with role-playing, small-group work, and feedback.

As of 2018, New York State requires every employer to create a sexual harassment policy and offer *annual* training to all employees using a model policy with minimum standards for training. The New York State Department of Labor, in consultation with the New York State Division of Human Rights, produced a comprehensive model training program unique in its approach. While employers can use other materials for training, the training in New York State must meet these minimum standards. The training must[1]:

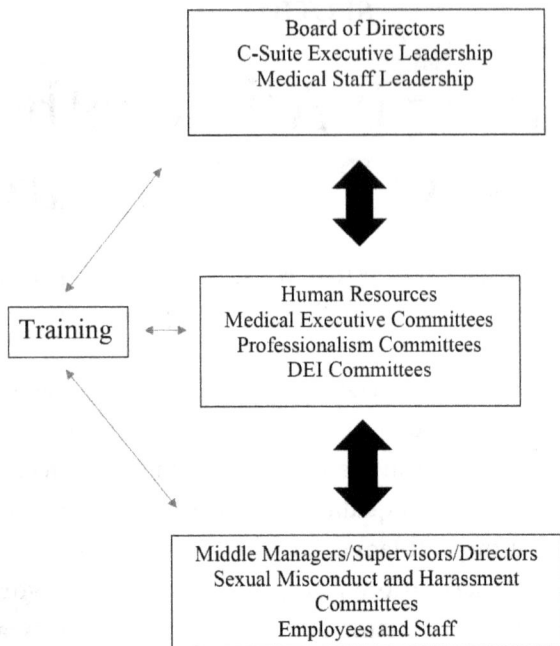

FIGURE 1. Proposed leadership structure and training.

1. Be interactive, meaning it must provide an opportunity for participants to provide feedback. This can be done with an in-person facilitator, an interactive question-and-answer session or forum, or another opportunity for employees to provide feedback on the training.
2. Include an explanation of sexual harassment and definitions of the term.
3. Include examples of *unlawful* sexual harassment.
4. Include information regarding federal and state protections concerning sexual harassment and legal remedies available to targets of sexual harassment.
5. Include information concerning employees' rights of redress and all available forums for adjudicating complaints.
6. Include information addressing conduct by supervisors and additional responsibilities for supervisors.
7. Be offered in both English and an employee's primary language if possible.

The model also includes suggestions for addressing intersectionality and recognizes the training, through case-based modules, may be triggering for some individuals with past histories as victims of harassment, assault, or abuse. The training model handbook from 2023 states:

"If the training is being facilitated in a group (whether in person or virtually), trainers should make clear to those attending that anyone needing to step out briefly on behalf of their mental health may do so…..."

This is *empathic training* in action. It is an effective approach that also reflects the emotional nature of the training, and in my opinion, is the approach we must use to provide more effective training with meaningful impact. The training modules offered use case examples, similar to the format used in this book. I strongly encourage readers to peruse the material offered by New York State. The link is provided in the reference section.

Imagine empathic training in a psychologically safe environment led by competent, confident, compassionate leaders who are role models. This is the goal healthcare organizations should aspire to. Measuring progress using the PDSA and quality effort improvement models incorporated within this framework and a new approach to training will provide *objective* measures of progress. Reporting in huddles and during board meetings will keep people, and therefore, the organization, cognizant and collectively conscious of the efforts. Over time, if this new approach is utilized, I believe the efforts will have a lasting and dramatic impact.

Additional guidance includes the following:

Create and maintain diversity, equity, and inclusion programs. Recent political and social movements calling for an end to DEI efforts in organizations, schools, and businesses are a giant leap in the wrong direction. DEI efforts are making a difference, and the traditional power structures are threatened. Addressing healthcare inequity and inequality requires continued investment in DEI programs.

Standardize investigational processes. Healthcare organizations should incorporate a standardized approach to investigations and consider hiring professional investigators for more challenging or egregious cases.

Create a separate committee and objectively measure the organization's progress. As suggested, organizations should create separate committees with a focus on sexual misconduct, harassment, and discrimination.

As part of its charter, the committee should be responsible for measuring prevalence, incidence, etc., and preparing formal reports to the board of directors annually (minimum).

THE JOINT COMMISSION

When The Joint Commission released *Sentinel Event 40* in 2008, it forced healthcare organizations to formally address unprofessional behavior. Although sexual misconduct and harassment is covered by the new requirement, The Joint Commission should consider a new requirement for organizations to create a separate committee on the issue of sexual misconduct, including surveying staff on the concerns.

Together, these efforts would help healthcare organizations transform the work culture and environment. The new path forward I am proposing is bold, comprehensive, and substantive. We must do more than simply inform healthcare providers — we must empower them to feel safe to report the issues.

REFERENCE

1. New York State. Sexual Harassment Prevention Model Policy and Training. *https://www.ny.gov/combating-sexual-harassment-workplace/sexual-harassment-prevention-model-policy-and-training.*

SECTION 11

Current and Future Research

I N 2023, HUNDREDS OF ARTICLES were published on the subject of
sexual harassment. Topics included policy, interventions, health and
legal consequences, training programs, and prevalence. An emerging area
of focus for research includes examining the issue in other industries and
sectors, specifically non-Western countries. A dearth of research on cultural
influences and incorporating an intersectional perspective remains.

In spring 2024, *Psychology Research and Behavior Management* published
a scoping analysis of reviews exploring workplace sexual harassment. This
paper is the most recent, comprehensive, industry-wide global examination
of sexual harassment in all work settings. Of the 468 articles identified, 22
met the authors' inclusion criteria. Six of the studies focused on employees
in a variety of healthcare settings, from home healthcare workers to nurses
and resident physicians.[1]

Contemporary research emphasizes understanding victim experiences,
including a deeper analysis of the psychological, emotional, and professional impacts of sexual harassment. This is a pivot shift from viewing sexual
harassment as a primarily legal issue.

The review also sheds light on how organizational factors and social
interactions impact the effects of sexual harassment. Sexual harassment in
its various forms is complex and occurs in complex organizational environments and settings.[1] However, it is not surprising that in workplaces where
men dominate the workforce, sexual harassment of women is prevalent.

Women who work in the technology sector, for example, continue to
suffer from not only sexual harassment but also assault and other episodes
of unwanted touching.[2] A frequently touted ethos in the technology world
is that investors fund people, not just ideas. Investors need to get to know
founders, and as entrepreneur Susan Ho, cofounder of travel startup Journy,
states, "Much of that building of camaraderie happens in social settings. It
happens over drinks. It happens over dinner." This environment is especially

complex for female founders, as men control most of the capital; 89% of those making investment decisions at the top 72 firms are male.[2]

Lisa Wang, cofounder of SheWorx, attended the Consumer Electronic Show (CES) in Las Vegas when a pitch meeting went south. She says, "We're sitting at Starbucks, and he grabs my face and tries to make out with me, and I push him back in surprise, and just didn't know what to do, because he continued to try again, and was so aggressive."

Bea Arthur, an entrepreneur for a mental health startup, says, "If a male investor looks at another man, he sees them as an opportunity, a colleague, peer, a mentor. But if you're a female founder, he just sees you as a woman first."[2]

There is a code of silence, too. Ho says, "When you talk about sexual harassment in tech or in any other industry, it's like dropping a nuclear bomb on your career."

Historically, men have dominated the physician workforce, and women comprise the majority of the nursing workforce.

In healthcare, a legacy of harassment continues. Numerous gaps remain in our current understanding of the subject of sexual misconduct, harassment, and discrimination. Several questions are worth further investigation:

- What specific strategies are effective in reducing the prevalence of the behaviors?
- What types of prevention training are most effective?
- Which types of behaviors require a more punitive vs. restorative approach?
- What are the characteristics of women physicians and other female healthcare personnel who engage in misconduct?
- What are the ethical implications of using surveys, tools, and questionnaires to identify individuals who are at higher risk for engaging in misconduct?

Recent developments will hamper continued research, as there is growing backlash against DEI efforts and programs. I suspect abolishment of DEI programs will have short- and long-term negative consequences. Efforts to do more to reduce misconduct and harassment and do it more effectively rely on robust and focused research.

REFERENCES

1. Liang T. Sexual Harassment At Work: Scoping Review of Reviews. *Psychol Res Behav Manag.* 2024;17:1635–1660. doi:10.2147/PRBM.S455753
2. O'Brien S, Segall L. Sexual Harassment in Tech: Women Tell Their Stories. *CNN Tech.* https://money.cnn.com/technology/sexual-harassment-tech.

Social Media and Virtual Harassment

SOCIAL MEDIA PLATFORMS and virtual applications for meetings and other work activities have exploded over the last 20 years, especially since COVID-19 forced employers and healthcare organizations to utilize online meetings and discussions. The work environment's physical "location" has expanded, presenting unique challenges for employers as communication through emails, social media, and online meeting platforms has become ubiquitous in healthcare. It is a brave new world.

In 2021, Pendergrast and colleagues published the results of a survey investigating the prevalence of personal attacks and sexual harassment of physicians on social media. They found that women are more than twice as likely as men to experience online sexual harassment. The most common forms of harassment were receiving inappropriate and sexually suggestive or explicit messages and pornographic images sent without consent.[1] Two physicians in the survey described threats of assault, including a black woman who reported being threatened with rape from white supremacists owing to her civil rights advocacy.

Those who experienced harassment reported emotional distress and fear, leading some participants to limit their online participation in social media. As a result, opportunities for expanding professional networks and participating in some of the professional benefits of having an online presence are limited. This issue is worth further study and investigation.

Physicians and healthcare professionals should also consider how they utilize social media platforms. Publicly posting compromising pictures or making statements or comments of a sexual nature is risky for several reasons. The individual's reputation may suffer harm, and most healthcare organizations and employers now have social media policies prohibiting certain content and material.

Social media policies are written to protect organizations and individuals from reputational harm. For example, a policy may state, "Don't post misleading, offensive, or inappropriate content." *Whether it is images, language, or opinions, ensure that your content aligns with professional healthcare standards.*

Below is a list of guidelines for what I call maintaining social media hygiene:

1. Always set your profile to private and connect only with individuals you are acquainted with or know personally.

2. Consider all posts publicly available, even if your application, web domain, or site settings are private to you and your connections. Remember, connections may screenshot the material and share it without your knowledge.

3. Consider using a fictitious name or abbreviated name on some social media websites.

4. Do not put ANY company information or logos on personal social media. LinkedIn is an exception, as your places of employment and past educational institutions often automatically post their logos when you identify as a former or current employee or alumnus.

5. Do not share co-workers' posts, texts, or emails that contain sensitive or personal information. This includes photographs or other posts that might be considered sexual.

6. Some organizations have explicitly stated they actively monitor social media content from employees. Act accordingly.

7. If you think a post, comment, image, or photo may not be considered professional, DO NOT POST IT. There is a digital trail.

In summary, using social media as a healthcare professional or provider requires individuals to understand the potential pitfalls and ramifications of blurring the boundaries between personal and professional life. Use caution and be mindful of what you post or say. Never publicly discuss patient care or make negative or disparaging comments about co-workers or your employer. It accomplishes nothing and puts you and the organization at risk.

CASE STUDIES

Case 1

Several ICU nurses plan a group trip to a tropical destination in the Caribbean after the holidays. The party of six includes two married couples and another couple who have been dating for eight weeks. While on vacation, one of the men takes a photo of the group with his cellphone . The image is taken from a distance, and one of the women, who is wearing a thong bikini, is facing away from the camera when the picture is taken. Consequently, she looks like she does not have a bikini bottom. He thinks nothing of the photo.

Upon returning from vacation, he selects over 20 photos to upload to his personal social media account. He tags the group members, and the following day, he receives a text from the nurse who had worn the thong bikini. She reported that other nurses at work, including male nurses who were connections on the social media site, began to discuss the picture. By day's end, everyone in the unit and a few other nurses from other units were openly discussing the image.

She asks him to immediately take the image down and confronts him about taking the picture in the first place. He says he was taking "random" pictures of the group and thought nothing of it.

He immediately removes it from his social media account and apologizes to her. The chief nursing officer (CNO) discusses the issue with all unit managers in a huddle that afternoon. The unit and charge nurses and managers send an email reminding everyone about using social media and that sharing any images of employees without consent violates the hospital's social media policy. The nurse accepts his apology, and the issue is resolved.

This particular case is a relatively common occurrence. Social media has blurred the boundaries of keeping our work and personal lives separate. When employees or colleagues work together and also socialize outside of work, there is potential for an event such as this to happen. To avoid problems, ask for permission before posting *any* images. In fact, it is probably best to *never* post any content that includes colleagues unless it is obvious the content won't be offensive.

Case 2

The manager of a large inpatient medical-surgical unit has scheduled a late afternoon virtual meeting with the staff RNs. Two of the nurses log on about

10 minutes before the official start of the meeting; one is a 29-year-old male, and the other is a 27-year-old female. Within a minute of logging on, it becomes obvious to the male nurse that the female nurse has a computer set up in her bedroom, and her pet cat is on the bed behind her.

The male nurse then blurts out, "You have an office in your bedroom. That's the place where the magic happens." She immediately turns red with embarrassment, turns off her camera, and remains silent.

- *Is this sexual harassment or simply an inappropriate comment?*
- *How can she address his behavior? Should she send a private chat to the unit manager during the meeting, informing the unit manager of the event?*
- *What if the unit manager is a 32-year-old male, and the two male nurses frequently socialize outside of work? How will this impact how the female nurse can respond and report the event?*

Case 3

A 38-year-old female dental hygienist has a new patient on her schedule, a 63-year-old male scheduled for a routine cleaning and exam. After some introductions, she begins to clean his teeth. The patient still possesses his cell phone as she begins cleaning his teeth. A few minutes later, he shows the hygienist a picture of a topless woman he finds on the internet and says, "I bet you look like this naked."

She immediately puts her dental instruments on the table and promptly leaves the room, visibly upset. She informs the dentist about the incident, and he walks into the exam room with the office manager, who tells him that his behavior is unacceptable and that he needs to gather his things and leave the office.

- *Does the dentist or hygienist have any legal or ethical obligation to continue to provide care for this patient?*
- *How can an event like this be prevented from happening again?*
- *How can the dentist or other office staff offer support if she needs it?*

The use of social media is a double-edged sword. It is a powerful tool for positive networking and sharing ideas; conversely, it is another format and method for healthcare professionals to be harassed, abused, and threatened.

REFERENCE

1. Pendergrast T. Prevalence of Personal Attacks and Sexual Harassment of Physicians on Social Media. *JAMA Intern Med*. 2021;181(4):550–552. doi:10.1001/jamainternmed .2020.7235

Unique and Challenging Cases

*"You're too sensitive' victims of sexual abuse are told over and over
by those whose reality depends on being insensitive. Most adults
who have been in the victim role cringe when anyone tells them
they are sensitive. In fact, sensitivity is a lovely trait and one to be
cherished in any human being."*— Renee Fredrickson, author

SOME CASES STAND OUT as both challenging and uniquely illustrative of the issues discussed in detail throughout this book. These cases often defy easy categorization, revealing gaps in legal frameworks, ethical dilemmas, and the nuances of human behavior that complicate investigation, justice, and accountability. These cases, with names and other identifying information redacted, are an opportunity for readers to gain a deeper understanding of the systemic and personal dimensions of harassment, equipping us to foster safer, more equitable environments.

CASE STUDIES

Case 1: Resident and student relationship

A third-year internal medicine resident is leading a group of junior residents, an intern, and a medical student on the wards. A couple of weeks into the rotation, a few members of the team decided to go to a local bar and restaurant on a weekend evening.

Over the last week, it became obvious to all team members that the senior resident and medical student were developing a bond beyond that of a resident and student. During the evening out, the resident and medical student both had several alcoholic beverages, so the group decided to take taxis home. The resident and medical student decided to share a cab, as their homes were on the same side of town,

When the cab arrived at the senior resident's home, the resident invited the medical student inside. The student agreed. The resident offered some more alcoholic beverages. The resident and medical student became physically intimate later that night, and the medical student woke up the next morning without any clothes on and little recall of the events from the last half of the evening. The student felt taken advantage of and told the clerkship director.

I purposely omitted the gender of the parties involved to demonstrate the impact of our biases and the potential for incorporating a double standard.

- *As you read this, how do you feel if the resident is male and the medical student is a female?*
- *How do you feel if the resident is a female and the medical student is a male?*
- *What if the resident and medical student are both male or female?*

Before investigating any incidents or conduct, it is important to focus *on the behavior* or *objective facts* and *how the individual feels about the incident.* This reduces the possibility of misinterpreting intentions and ensures the process is fair for all parties. Making any assumptions is a problem.

- *Was consent for any sexual activity possible?*
- *As a program or clerkship director, how would you begin this investigation?*
- *Who would you interview first?*
- *Since this event was unwitnessed, how can the claim be substantiated?*

Case 2: Inappropriate physical contact from a physician to a patient

An 81-year-old female patient confides to her new primary care physician that a male physician inappropriately touched her breast approximately 10 years ago. She says she hesitated to report the event because "He was a nice physician and otherwise treated me well." She feels safe enough to report the incident now because she does not want what happened to her to happen to other patients. The event was not witnessed.

- *What are your legal and ethical obligations in response to this revelation?*
- *Can the patient file a formal complaint with the authorities?*
- *If the physician is still practicing locally, what are the options while investigating this case?*
- *What if the physician is retired or has moved out of state?*

Case 3: Inappropriate conduct from an inebriated patient

A 30-year-old male arrives at the emergency department under the influence of alcohol and marijuana after an altercation at a local bar. The patient requires stitches to his forehead. A female nurse and a young female emergency physician begin to stitch the wound when the patient suddenly grabs the young physician by the buttocks, squeezes, and tells her she is a "hot piece of ass." Taken aback, the nurse and physician promptly leave the room to inform another physician colleague about the incident and state that the physician cannot return to the room to assist the patient. As this is near the end of a 12-hour shift, her colleagues immediately relieved her of her duties.

- *Was this assault? Can the physician press charges?*
- *The next morning, the patient has no recall of the events, as his blood alcohol level was 0.14, and he "blacked out." Does this absolve the patient from his behavior?*
- *This was a witnessed event, as the nurse verified that this incident occurred as described. What if this physician was alone in the room and the incident was not witnessed? How does this change the course of action and investigation?*
- *What steps or processes could have prevented this event from occurring?*

Case 4: Patient stalks a physician

A 35-year-old male psychiatrist accepts a new patient, a 28-year-old woman seeking treatment for depression and anxiety. The patient returns for a follow-up appointment four weeks after her initial appointment. At the end of the day, the physician finds a thank-you card under the windshield wiper on his car, The card is signed by the patient and contains some concerning words: _____ *"Derek, you are the first doctor to really understand who I am and what I am going through. I feel so much better now with you caring for me. I know you are single, and I was wondering if we could go out on a date next week?"*

The stunned physician calls the patient the following day, thanks her for the card, and explains that it is not appropriate for him to have any romantic relationship with a patient. She sounds disappointed after he refuses to meet with her.

At the next appointment four weeks later, the patient arrives in revealing clothing — a marked change from the shirt and jeans she wore at the previous two appointments. Other than the change in dress, the appointment does not seem unusual.

At the end of the day, as the physician leaves the office, he sees the patient in the driver's seat of her car, which she had moved next to his. He quickly walks to get into his own car when the patient rolls down her window and asks him if he is headed home. He does not engage with the patient, gets into his car, and drives home. The physician looks in his rearview mirror and notices her car following his. Concerned, he drives to a local police station.

As he arrives at the police station, the patient quickly drives away . Half an hour later he drives home without any further incident.

- *What should the physician do at this point to address this unusual behavior following the appointment?*

Case 5: Patient-to-patient sexual assault

A 28-year-old female psychiatry patient reports that an older (mid-40s) male patient in the psychiatry ward groped her breasts, tried to kiss her, and exposed his genitals. The female patient wants to press charges against the other patient. The events were not witnessed, but when questioned, the patient admits grabbing the other patient's breasts. Notably, he has other charges pending in the community, and there was another recent allegation from another patient.

- *What are the organization's responsibilities immediately after the patient reports this event?*
- *The perpetrator/patient is homeless and has a diagnosis of uncontrolled schizoaffective disorder. How does this diagnosis impact the investigation?*
- *What can the organization do to prevent another event similar to this from occurring?*

Case 6: Physician witnessing another physician

A male anesthesiologist in his early 40s is scheduled to perform a surgical procedure with a 54-year-old male neurosurgeon on a 65-year-old male patient with acute loss of sensation and weakness in his lower extremities. The anesthesiologist enters the pre-operative area behind a drape in a private bay and logs into the computer to begin his pre-op assessment.

The anesthesiologist hears the surgeon ask the patient if he has any sensation in his private area. The patient, who is somewhat hard of hearing, looks at the surgeon and does not immediately respond to the surgeon's question. The patient has a gown on and is covered in a thin sheet and blanket. The surgeon then proceeds to place his hand on the patient's genitals and asks the patient if he feels it. The patient responds, "Yes." The patient does not look surprised or seem upset.

The anesthesiologist witnesses another inappropriate patient encounter when the surgeon enters a patient's pre-op bay while she is using a bedside commode. He does not excuse himself and proceeds to conduct a history and physical exam and consent the patient for surgery. The pre-operative nurse also witnesses this event and reports.

- *Should the anesthesiologist confront the surgeon privately about this behavior?*
- *If so, why? If not, why not?*
- *There are no witnesses to the event other than the patient. The patient may or may not recall what has occurred at a later date. Should the anesthesiologist report this event?*
- *Why might the anesthesiologist hesitate to report the event?*
- *If the anesthesiologist was a female and recently graduated from residency and the surgeon was a male in his 60s with a long-standing career at the hospital, what risks does the anesthesiologist take in reporting the event if the patient confirms the incident, and the surgeon denies the incident?*
- *What if the patient had been a female instead of a male?*

Case 7: The ogling visitor

A nurse manager in her mid-30s is walking down the hall of the hospital when she hears footsteps behind her and turns around. Another female nurse manager and an older male (mid-60s) are walking behind her. She stops to wait for her colleague to catch up so they can talk about the upcoming meeting. The older male (presumably a visitor) says, "You can keep walking if you want to. I was enjoying the view."

The nurse manager directly confronts him, saying, "Don't tell me what I can or cannot do." Her colleague tells the man it is inappropriate to make comments like that to women. He quickly responds, "Why don't you mind your business. I was not talking to you. I was talking to her."

The man's manner and tone are concerning, so the nurse motions to a security guard at the end of the hall to come over. The security guard arrives, and the nurse quickly tells him about the escalation of the last three minutes. After listening to what transpired, the security guard escorts the visitor out of the building and informs him that due to his threatening nature and tone, he is no longer allowed entry to the hospital.

There is power in groups. Had the nurse manager been alone and security not been so close, confronting the man would have been risky. I am certain most women reading about this case have had similar experiences. Most men have not. This case highlights the pervasive and seemingly unrelenting nature of these behaviors.

- *What if the security guard told the women his behavior and comments were 'no big deal'?*
- *What if the man denied saying he was 'enjoying the view'?*
- *What if the man was in his 40s, sharply and professionally dressed and appeared to be 'important'? Would the security guard treat him differently?*
- *How would you feel if you witnessed this event?*

Case 8: Allied health industry case examples

The following testimonies are from women in the medical device, pharmaceutical, supply, insurance, and other healthcare-related industries. These testimonies are redacted and other specific details have been altered or omitted:

> *At one of the companies I worked with, the owners insisted on hiring an attractive woman for the front desk. They wouldn't hire a good administrative professional with a proven track record if they were over 40 and not attractive to them. Then they would constantly make comments like "Did you notice how cute [name redacted] looks today?" and "Did you see her skirt lift up when she reached for the plates on the top cabinet?"*
>
> *In my first year in the business, a senior vice president at my office got drunk at a holiday party and loudly proclaimed he'd buy me a Porsche if I slept with him. I was buzzed and I loudly told him to go fuck himself. I got a reputation of being the office bitch after that. No one ever messed with me again.*
>
> *I used to sit next to a senior colleague, and one day I asked him a market question that apparently had an obvious answer. He answered me and finished the answer with "okay, you ignorant slut?" Everybody on my team*

heard it, and another senior colleague jokingly asked me not to go to HR. The other senior colleague (not the one who called me a slut) told me it's an SNL (Saturday Night Live) quote. I really don't care. That sucked, and it's one of my most vivid memories of working there to this day.

Besides the hundreds of times men at conferences have asked me who I work for (I own my medical device business) I had a senior (meaning old) advisor call me Baby Doll and ask me if I needed help finding the conference room. I did not.

A supervisor told me, on various occasions, that my chipped nail polish was a sign of an easy woman.

A vice president in my company told a group of women the story of when he and his wife were propositioned to have group sex on her 50th birthday. I also learned that he played a game about "who in the office would rather sleep with him or the other partner."

These comments reflect the contemporary challenges and hostile work environment many women face despite decades of progress. Women in all industries and at all levels of employment, regardless of position, authority, or assignment, can become targets or victims in an instant. In a male-dominated corporate world, women should not have to pay a price to work.

"One of the things I learned was always to question the status quo and not to be afraid to speak up when you do discover something that needs to be said."—Kelly Bayer Rosmarin, business leader

Case 9: Witnessing harassment and misconduct

In 1987, a surgical nurse named Julie Fisher filed a sexual discrimination suit against San Pedro Peninsula Hospital in California. Fisher claimed that a gynecologist she worked with named Barry Tischler contributed to an environment of sexual harassment against women at the hospital. In her lawsuit, Fischer alleged Tischler engaged in sexual insults and inappropriate touching. On one occasion, Fischer claimed Tischler hugged her so tightly that he separated the cartilage in her ribs.

After Fisher complained to hospital management about Tischler's behavior, Tischler wrote her a letter of apology, but no disciplinary action was taken against him. She claimed that following an investigation by the hospital, Tischler continued to engage in harassing behavior with other female hospital employees, including pulling nurses onto his lap, grabbing women from behind, and putting his hands on their breasts, picking them up, and swinging them around. On one occasion, Fisher claimed, he even threw one woman onto a gurney. According to court documents, these actions occurred in hospital hallways, the lunchroom, and the operating room.

The nurse claimed her fellow employees ostracized her after she complained about the doctor's behavior. Fisher said, too, that her husband, also a doctor at the hospital, began seeing a decline in his referrals. The case was considered landmark at the time because Fisher was ultimately allowed to seek damages as a witness to sexual harassment and not as the direct target of harassment.

Before the case went to trial, the California Supreme Court ruled that employees who are not direct targets of sexual harassment could still sue if they can prove the harassment was pervasive enough to create a hostile workspace.

In a decision rendered by the California Court of Appeals, 2nd District, one judge took exception to a lower court's ruling that referred to Tischler's behavior as merely "sophomoric antics." The judge wrote, "Relegating this conduct to such a category is both demeaning and dishonest. Grabbing a woman's breasts, gesturing towards a woman's vaginal area, or even making offensive sexual statements to another is far from being merely sophomoric. It is egregious, hostile conduct which should not be condoned or excused to immaturity."[1]

REFERENCE

1. Robinson B. 10 Crazy Sexual Harassment Cases. Branigan Robertson. October 17, 2016. https://brobertsonlaw.com/10-crazy-sexual-harassment-cases/

SECTION 14

Conclusion

"If you want to change the culture, you will have to start by changing the organization." — Mary Douglas, anthropologist

I HOPE THIS BOOK HAS ENLIGHTENED readers and offered new perspectives. I also hope readers understand the influence and importance of organizational culture and strong leaders who accept responsibility and accountability. Openly discussing this subject is difficult and uncomfortable. It is unsettling and potentially embarrassing, too. It takes courage to embark on change, but having these conversations and creating initiatives and robust programs to reduce sexual misconduct and discrimination is necessary and urgent.

It is impossible to discuss these matters without political, social, religious, personal, and cultural influences adding complexity to the issue. As I boldly stated at the beginning of this book, our humanity and what it means to be human is what bonds us. People have a right to be treated with dignity and respect. Individuals who use their power as a weapon for personal satisfaction or gain through misconduct or harassment must be made aware these behaviors are intolerable and immoral. We all bear responsibility for helping to create change.

Though powerful, transformative, and, at the right time, immensely revolutionary, words fail to transform the world without action. This book is a rallying cry — a call to action and to do more. We are responsible for embracing challenges and summoning the courage to do what is right.

At its core, healthcare is about healing, and most individuals who pursue a career in medicine are driven by noble intentions. We have an ethical duty to change course and treat every person — regardless of who they are — as equals, worthy of respect and dignity in an environment defined by safety, belonging, inclusivity, hope, and healing. The healthcare industry holds a unique mission, and those of us in this field should be at the forefront of efforts to combat sexual violence, misconduct, harassment, and discrimination.

We can do better. We must do better.

Re Vera Lux Est—In truth there is light.

Appendices

∞

Appendix 1. Likelihood to Sexually Harass Scale

On the pages that follow are 10 brief scenarios that describe 10 different interactions between males and females. In each case, you will be asked to imagine that you are the main male character in the scenario. Then, you will be asked to rate how likely you would perform each of several different behaviors in the described social context.

Assume in each scenario that no matter what you choose to do, nothing bad would happen to you due to your action. Try to answer each question as honestly as you can. Your answers will be completely anonymous. No matter what you say on the questionnaire, no one will try to discover your identity.

SCENARIO 1

Imagine that you are an executive in a large corporation. You are 42 years old. Your income is above average for people at your job level. You have had numerous job offers from other companies. You feel very secure in your job. One day your personal secretary decides to quit and you have the task of replacing her.

The personnel department sends several applicants over for you to interview. All seem to be equally qualified for the job. One of the applicants, Michelle S., explains during her interview that she desperately needs the job. She is 23, single, and has been job-hunting for about a month. You find yourself very attracted to her. She looks at you in a way that possibly conveys she is also attracted to you. How likely are you to do the following things in this situation? Indicate your response on a scale of 1–5, with 1 as least likely and 5 as most likely.

1. Would you give her the job over the other applicants?
2. Assuming that you are secure enough in your job that no possible reprisals could happen to you, would you offer her the job in exchange for sexual favors?

3. Assuming that you fear no reprisals on your job, would you ask her to meet you later for dinner to discuss her possible employment?

SCENARIO 2

Imagine that you are the owner and manager of an expensive restaurant. One day, while reviewing the receipts, you discover that one of the waitresses has undercharged several customers. The mistake costs you $100. In talking to some of the other employees, you find that the particular customers involved were friends of the waitress. You call her into your office and ask her to explain her behavior.

The waitress confesses to having intentionally undercharged her friends. She promises never to repeat this dishonest act and tells you she will do anything to keep her job. The waitress, a young divorcee, is someone you have always found particularly attractive. How likely are you to do the following things in this situation?

1. Would you let her keep her job?
2. Would you let her keep her job in exchange for sexual favors?
3. Would you ask her to meet you for dinner after work to discuss the problem?

SCENARIO 3

Imagine that you are the manager of a shipping company. One day, your supervisor asks you to study the possibility of buying several computers for the office. You call several companies that sell computers. A salesperson from company "A" calls you and asks to visit your office. You agree, and the next day, a very attractive woman shows up. She can offer no real reason to buy her company's products over those of the other companies. However, she seems very sexy. How likely are you to do the following things in this situation?

1. Would you recommend her line of computers?
2. Assuming that you are secure enough in your job that no possible reprisals could happen to you, would you agree to recommend her line of computers in exchange for sexual favors?
3. Would you ask her to meet you later for dinner to discuss the choice of computers?

SCENARIO 4

Imagine that you are a Hollywood film director. You are casting a minor role in a film you are planning. The role calls for a particularly stunning actress, one with a lot of sex appeal. How likely are you to do the following things in this situation?

1. Would you give the role to the actress whom you personally found sexiest?
2. Would you give the role to an actress who agreed to have sex with you?
3. Would you ask the actress to whom you were most personally attracted to talk with you about the role over dinner?

SCENARIO 5

Imagine that you are the owner of a modeling agency. Your agency specializes in sexy female models used in television commercials. One of your models, Amy, is a particularly ravishing brunette. You stop her after work one day and ask her to have dinner with you. She coldly declines your offer and tells you that she would like to keep your relationship with her "strictly business." A few months later you find that business is slack, and you have to lay off some of your employees. You can choose to lay off Amy or one of four other women. All are good models, but someone has to go. How likely are you to do the following things in this situation?

1. Would you fire Amy?
2. Assuming that you are unafraid of possible reprisals, would you offer to let Amy keep her job in return for sexual favors?
3. Would you ask Amy to dinner so that you could talk over her future employment?

SCENARIO 6

Imagine you are a 38-year-old college professor teaching in a large midwestern university. You are a full professor with tenure. You are renowned in your field of abnormal psychology and have numerous offers for other jobs.

One day, a female student stops in your office after you return a graded exam to the class. She tells you that her score is one point from an "A" and asks if she can do some extra credit project to raise her score. She tells you that she may not have sufficient grades to get into graduate school without an "A."

Several other students have asked you to do extra credit assignments, and you have declined to let them. This particular woman is a stunning blonde. She sits in the front row of the class every day and always wears short skirts. You find her extremely sexy. How likely are you to do the following things in this situation?

1. Would you let her carry out a project for extra credit (e.g., write a paper)?
2. Assuming that you are very secure in your job and the university has always tolerated professors who make passes at students, would you offer the student a chance to earn extra credit in return for sexual favors?
3. Given the same assumptions as in the question above, would you ask her to join you for dinner to discuss the possible extra credit assignments?

SCENARIO 7

Imagine that you are a junior at a large midwestern university. You just transferred from another school on the East coast. One night at a bar you meet an attractive female student named Rhonda. Rhonda laments to you that she is failing a course in English poetry. She tells you that she has a paper due next week on the poet Shelley, and fears that she will fail since she has not begun to write it.

You remark that you wrote a paper last year on Shelley at your former school. Your paper was given an A+. She asks if you will let her use your paper in her course. She wants to just retype it and put her name on it. How likely are you to do the following things in this situation?

1. Would you let Rhonda use your paper? Would you let Rhonda use your paper in exchange for sexual favors?
2. Would you ask Rhonda to come to your apartment to discuss the matter?

SCENARIO 8

Imagine you are the editor for a major publishing company. It is your job to read new manuscripts of novels and decide whether they are worthy of publication. You receive hundreds of manuscripts per week from aspiring novelists. Most of them are screened by your subordinates and thrown in the trash. You end up accepting about one in a thousand for publication.

One night, you go to a party. There you meet a very attractive woman named Betsy. Betsy tells you that she has written a novel and would like to check into getting it published. This is her first novel. She asks you to read her novel. How likely are you to do the following things in this situation?

1. Would you agree to read Betsy's novel?
2. Would you agree to read Betsy's novel in exchange for sexual favors?
3. Would you ask Betsy to have dinner with you the next night to discuss your reading her novel?

SCENARIO 9

Imagine you are a physician. You go over to the hospital one day to make your rounds, visiting your patients. In looking over the records of one of your patients, you discover that one of the attending nurses on the previous night shift made an error in administering drugs to your patient. She gave the wrong dosage of a drug.

You examine the patient and discover that no harm was done. He seems fine. However, you realize that the ramifications of the error could have been catastrophic under other circumstances.

You pull the files and find out who made the error. It turns out that a new young nurse named Wendy was responsible. You have noticed Wendy in some of your visits to the hospital and have thought of asking her out to dinner. You realize that she could lose her job if you report this incident. How likely are you to do each of the following things?

1. Would you report Wendy to the hospital administration?
2. Assuming that you fear no reprisals, would you tell Wendy in private that you will not report her if she will have sex with you?
3. Assuming that you fear no reprisals, would you ask Wendy to join you for dinner to discuss the incident?

SCENARIO 10

Imagine you are the news director for a local television station. Due to some personnel changes, you have to replace the anchor woman for the evening news. Your policy has always been to promote reporters from within your organization when an anchor vacancy occurs. There are several female reporters from which to choose. All are young, attractive, and qualified for the job. One reporter, Loretta, is someone whom you find very sexy. You initially hired her, giving her a first break in the TV news business. How likely are you to do the following things in this situation?

1. Would you give Loretta the job?
2. Assuming that you fear no reprisals in your job, would you offer Loretta the job in exchange for sexual favors?
3. Assuming that you fear no reprisals in your job, would you ask her to meet you after work for dinner to discuss the job?

Ratings for these items are simply summed to produce an overall LSH score.

Appendix 2. Sexual Experiences Questionnaire-Workplace (SEQ-W)

The Sexual Experiences Questionnaire-Workplace (SEQ-W) is a 17-item measure designed to assess the frequency of sexual harassment that women experience while at work. This measure is a revised version of the Sexual Experiences Questionnaire. It includes three dimensions of workplace sexual harassment: gender harassment, unwanted sexual attention, and sexual coercion.

High Psychometric Score

CATEGORIES

Geographies Tested: United States of America
Populations Included: Female
Age Range: Adults

ITEMS:

Have you ever been in a situation where a supervisor or coworker ...

Subscale: Gender harassment
1. ... told suggestive stories.
2. ... made crude sexual remarks.
3. ... made offensive remarks.
4. ... displayed offensive materials.
5. ... made sexist comments.

Subscale: Unwanted sexual attention
6. ... attempted to discuss sex.
7. ... gave unwanted sexual attention.
8. ... stared, leered at you.
9. ... attempted to establish a sexual relationship.
10. ... repeated requests for drinks, dinner, despite rejection.
11. ... touched you in a way that made you feel uncomfortable.
12. ... attempted to stroke or fondle.

Subscale: Sexual coercion
13. ... subtly bribed you.

14. ... subtly threatened you.
15. ... made it necessary to cooperate to be well treated.
16. ... made you afraid of poor treatment if you didn't cooperate.
17. ... experienced consequences for refusing.

RESPONSE OPTIONS:

Note: The authors of this paper indicate use of a 5-point Likert scale to assess frequency, but they do not provide the scale. We recommend the following 5-point scale to assess frequency:

1 = Never
2 = Rarely
3 = Sometimes
4 = Always
5 = Often

Appendix 3. Sexual Harassment Attitude Scale (SHAS)

The Sexual Harassment Attitude Scale was developed as a research tool to explore psychological factors associated with sexual harassment in educational settings. The questionnaire measures respondents' attitudes regarding responsibility for harassment behaviors, appropriate responses to sexual harassment, and the effects of sexual harassment on victims. Respondents first read two scenarios that depict clear-cut incidents of sexual harassment in a college setting. After each scenario, they indicate to whom they attribute responsibility for the incident. Two questions pertain to victim blame, two to perpetrator blame, and two to no blame. A second set of six questions taps respondents' attitudes about appropriate responses to sexual harassment. Two questions refer to confronting the harassing behavior, two to complying with the harasser, and two to ignoring the harassment. Finally, a set of eight questions measures expectations of the effects of the harassment. Two questions refer to educational effects, and six to emotional effects. All questions have 6-point Likert-type scales except for the questions regarding emotional effects, which have 7-point Likert-type scales.

SCENARIO 1

Suppose that you are attending classes on this campus. After class one day, a professor asks that you come to his office to discuss your grade with him. When you get there, he notes that you barely passed the last exam and are in danger of receiving a D for the course. He then tells you at length how much he enjoys having you in the class, leading up to a dinner invitation. He states that if you "get to know each other better," he might be able to work things out so that you can get a better grade.

The following are several statements about the situation that might help to explain why the above incident occurred. Rate your agreement with each of the following comments. Mark the number on your answer sheet that best describes your feelings. Use the following key:

0 = Strongly disagree
1 = Moderately disagree
2 = Somewhat disagree
3 = Somewhat agree

4 = Moderately agree

5 = Strongly agree

1. The student is probably hoping that getting to know the professor personally will help her get a better grade in the course.
2. The professor probably meant no harm so it should not be taken too seriously.
3. The professor is using his status unfairly to pressure the student into dating him.
4. The professor is responding to normal sexual attraction and cannot really be blamed for his actions in the situation.
5. The professor's actions were unethical and could be harmful to his students.
6. The student is most likely a flirtatious type who enjoys getting special attention from her professors.

The following are a number of statements describing possible ways that you could deal with the situation. Rate your agreement with each of the following statements. Mark the number on your answer sheet that best describes your feelings. Use the following key:

0 = Strongly disagree

1 = Moderately disagree

2 = Somewhat disagree

3 = Somewhat agree

4 = Moderately agree

5 = Strongly agree

7. Change the subject and try to forget about the conversation.
8. Go to dinner with the professor and talk over the problems you are having in the class.
9. Continue to work hard in the class and avoid any individual conversations with the professor.
10. Tell the professor that you are not interested in a personal relationship, and that this should have nothing to do with your grade in the course.
11. See the professor on a social basis if he is interested, as it may help your grade.
12. Go to the department head and tell him/her about the professor's actions.

Below is a set of word pairs that describe how you might feel about this experience. The two feelings in each pair are separated by a 7-point scale. For each word pair, mark the number on your answer sheet that is closest to how you think you or your friend might feel.

13. Insulted	0	1	2	3	4	5	6	Flattered
14. Pleased	0	1	2	3	4	5	6	Angry
15. Comfortable	0	1	2	3	4	5	6	Uncomfortable
16. Relaxed	0	1	2	3	4	5	6	Nervous
17. Intimidated	0	1	2	3	4	5	6	Powerful
18. Embarrassed	0	1	2	3	4	5	6	Proud

SCENARIO 2

Suppose that you are attending this campus. Through the course of the semester you notice that a professor in one of your classes frequently seems to be staring at you. When talking with him after class one day about an upcoming essay exam, he puts his arm around you and touches your hair. He then suggests that you come to his office at the end of the day to discuss the exam further. He adds that if you fail to do so, you will probably not do as well on the exam as expected.

Questions 19–36 are identical to questions 1–18.

Sexual Harassment Reporting Attitudes Scale
Five-point scale
(1=strongly disagree, 5=strongly agree)

1. If someone is being sexually harassed in his or her place of work, then he or she should report it to a supervisor.
2. Reporting workplace sexual harassment is an effective way of stopping the problem.
3. A person who reports workplace sexual harassment is just a tattletale.
4. Reporting workplace sexual harassment creates new problems for everyone.
5. People should not be afraid to report sexual harassment in their places of work.
6. Supervisors have better things to do with their time than deal with reports of sexual harassment.

7. Workplace sexual harassment problems persist, even if people report them.
8. Supervisors need to take reports of workplace sexual harassment very seriously.
9. A person who reports workplace sexual harassment should not be afraid of losing his or her job because of it.
10. In general, reporting workplace sexual harassment does no good.
11. Reporting workplace sexual harassment only makes the problem worse.
12. Reporting sexual harassment creates tension in the workplace.
13. An employee has the right to report workplace sexual harassment to his or her supervisor.
14. All things considered, reporting workplace sexual harassment is a waste of time.
15. People who report workplace sexual harassment risk being looked upon badly by their coworkers.
16. People who report workplace sexual harassment usually end up getting into trouble for it.
17. If I felt that I was being sexually harassed at my place of work, I would report it to a supervisor or other authority figure.

Appendix 4. Sample Title IX
Sexual Harassment Policy

The following policy is adapted from Colorado state law and serves as a template for the creation of a comprehensive Title IX policy. This example is not a legal document and should not be used in part or whole as a template fulfilling the requirements of other state's laws and regulations.

NOTE: Schools are required by federal law to adopt a Title IX policy. Each school should consult with its own lawyer to review this sample policy, and update it as needed per federal law.

1. **PURPOSE:** [THE SCHOOL] aims to provide a safe learning and working environment that is free from sex-based discrimination and sexual harassment for students, employees, and community members. The purpose of these procedures is to ensure prompt and equitable resolution of all such complaints.

   [THE SCHOOL] prohibits sexual harassment under Colorado and federal law, including violations of Title IX of the Education Amendments of 1972 ("Title IX"), Title VII of the Civil Rights Act of 1964, and the Colorado Anti-Discrimination Act. [[THE SCHOOL]]'s prohibition extends to all forms of illegal sexual harassment, including conduct based on sexual stereotypes, sexual orientation, and transgender status. This policy incorporates the changes implemented under the revised Title IX regulations issued by the United States Department of Education that became effective August 14, 2020.

   This policy will be available on [THE SCHOOL]'s website and [FILL IN LOCATIONS such as administrative offices and/or handbooks].

2. **DEFINITIONS:** Unless context requires otherwise:

   Appeals Panel means the persons designated to hear an appeal under this policy. The Appeal Panel shall be two members of the Board not implicated in the Complaint as Respondent or witness, designated by the Board as a whole. The Appeal Panel may include a third person as a non-voting advisor in hearing the appeal, which may be the [THE SCHOOL]]s general counsel, special counsel, or other appropriate person. In no event shall a member of the Appeal Panel or advisor to the appeal panel be the Title IX Coordinator, Investigator, or Decision Maker.

Complainant means a person who is alleged to be the target of conduct that could constitute sexual harassment. "Complainant" includes a possible complainant, such as an individual identified by a third party as a possible victim of sexual harassment.

Decision Maker means the person who assesses the relevant evidence and decides if the burden of proof has been met to determine that a Respondent has engaged in sexual harassment. The Decision Maker shall be the [THE SCHOOL]'s Head of School, unless the Head of School is implicated in the complaint as a Respondent or witness, in which case the Board shall designate an independent Decision Maker. The Decision Maker may not be the Title IX Coordinator or an Investigator. A Decision Maker may not have a conflict of interest in the Title IX matter. A Decision Maker must be trained, as required by federal law.

Education program or activity means the locations, events, or circumstances in which [THE SCHOOL] exercises substantial control over a Respondent and the context in which alleged sexual harassment occurs.

Investigator means a person trained to evaluate objectively the credibility of witnesses, synthesize evidence, and consider the unique circumstances of each situation involved in an alleged act or pattern of sexual harassment. A Title IX Coordinator may act as an Investigator or may delegate that responsibility to a qualified outside investigator. An Investigator may not have a conflict of interest in a matter under investigation. An Investigator must also be trained, as required by federal law.

Title IX Coordinator means a person designated as a Title IX Coordinator of {THE SCHOOL]. Title IX Coordinator may delegate responsibility on a case-by-case basis. [THE SCHOOL] must prominently post to its website and otherwise make known the identity and contact information for the Title IX Coordinator. The Title IX Coordinator must also be trained, as required by federal law. The Title IX Coordinator cannot also act as the Decision Maker.

Parties means the Complainant(s) and Respondent(s) in an individual matter.

Respondent means an individual alleged to have engaged in sexual harassment.

Sexual harassment means conduct —

- of a school director or employee that conditions an aid, benefit or service of [THE SCHOOL], including employment, on participation in unwelcome sexual conduct (that is, *quid pro quo* harassment);
- of a school employee who is engaging in sexual misconduct involving a student;
- that is unwelcome and that a reasonable person would determine is so severe, pervasive, and objectively offensive that it effectively denies a person equal access to employment or to [THE SCHOOL]'s education program and activities; or
- that constitutes sexual violence, dating violence, domestic violence or stalking. See 20 U.S.C. § 1092(F)(6)(A)(v) & 34 U.S.C. § 12291(a)(10).

Supportive Measures means non-disciplinary, non-punitive individualized services designed to restore or preserve equal access to the [THE SCHOOL]'s educational programs and activities (including employment), without unreasonably burdening any other party, and offered without charge. Supportive Measures may include, without limitation, counseling, mentoring, class modification, schedule changes, monitoring, supervision, or restorative justice activities, as deemed appropriate by the Title IX Coordinator.

3. **EMPLOYEE REPORTING OBLIGATION.** All employees are obligated to report any actual knowledge they have that causes them reasonably to believe there has been conduct that constitutes sexual harassment. Parents, students, or others may also make actual knowledge reports. Such reports must be made to the Title IX Coordinator.

4. **RESPONSE TO ACTUAL KNOWLEDGE REPORT.** Upon receiving an actual knowledge report, the Title IX Coordinator shall promptly and confidentially contact the Complainant. The Title IX Coordinator must (a) discuss the availability of Supportive Measures; (b) consider any request for Supportive Measures, (c) inform the Complainant that Supportive Measures are available without regard to whether the Complainant does or does not file a formal complaint;

and (d) explain the process for filing a formal complaint, if applicable. Without regard to whether a formal complaint is filed, the Title IX Coordinator shall complete the form attached as Exhibit 1 for each actual knowledge report.

5. **FORMAL COMPLAINT.** Any person (including a Complainant) may report sexual harassment, in person, by mail, by telephone or by email to the Title IX Coordinator at any time. The report must include the nature of the alleged violation; names of the person(s) responsible for the alleged violation (if known); and any other relevant background information. A Complainant (or their parent or guardian, if appropriate) or the Title IX Coordinator, but not a third-party reporter, may sign a complaint. At the time of a complaint, the Complainant must be participating in or attempting to participate in the [THE SCHOOL]'s education program or activities (including employment). Upon filing of a formal complaint, the Title IX Coordinator shall offer Supportive Measures (if not already offered or provided) to both the Complainant and Respondent. Complainants will be asked to complete the form in Exhibit 2 to this policy. Completion of this form by a complainant is not required to file a complaint.

6. **FAILURE TO OFFER SUPPORTIVE MEASURES.** If supportive measures were not offered in response to a report or a formal complaint, the Title IX Coordinator must document in detail why such failure was reasonable under the circumstances.

7. **INFORMAL RESOLUTION.** If and only if (a) a formal complaint is filed, and (b) the complaint does *not* concern alleged harassment of a student by a School employee, the Parties may voluntarily agree in writing to an alternative form of dispute resolution, such as restorative justice procedures, mediation, fact-finding, or arbitration. Parties may withdraw from such a process at any time before written agreement to a defined process. Agreements to informal resolution that would displace formal investigation (e.g., binding arbitration) require approval of the Title IX Coordinator. Once all Parties have executed a written agreement to an informal resolution, without objection by the Title IX Coordinator, that agreement is binding by its terms. The Title IX Coordinator may disapprove of the use of

alternative dispute resolution for certain complaints, including but not limited to complaints of sexual violence, or refuse to approve certain agreements, including but not limited to those containing onerous terms, and proceed with formal investigation. If informal resolution is attempted and unsuccessful (e.g., a restorative justice process that does not reach the hoped-for resolution), the matter may return to formal investigation.

8. **ADMINISTRATIVE LEAVE, EMERGENCY REMOVAL, SAFETY PLANS.** [THE SCHOOL] may place a Respondent who is an employee on administrative leave while allegations are investigated and resolved. [THE SCHOOL] may remove a Respondent who is a student if removal is necessary to protect the student or another person from an immediate threat to physical health or safety. Removal of a student who is on an IEP or Section 504 plan is subject to compliance with requirements of the Individuals with Disabilities Education Act or Section 504 of the Rehabilitation Act of 1973, as applicable. If a Complainant and Respondent remain in [THE SCHOOL] pending or following investigation the Title IX Coordinator shall determine if a safety plan is advisable and, if so, initiate the process for creating a written safety plan. A decision not to create a safety plan should be documented in writing.

9. **BURDEN OF PROOF.** Respondent is presumed not responsible for sexual harassment. The burden of proof to overcome the presumption is that a violation of the prohibition on sexual harassment is more likely than not; that is, shown by a preponderance of the evidence.

10. **DISMISSAL OF COMPLAINT.** If the Title IX Coordinator determines that the allegations of a formal complaint do not meet the definition of Sexual Harassment (or other prohibitions specific to this policy), *or* did not occur in [THE SCHOOL]'s educational program or activity, *or* did not occur in the United States, the Title IX Coordinator *shall* summarily dismiss the complaint. If the Respondent withdraws from [THE SCHOOL] or terminates employment with [THE SCHOOL], or the Complainant requests withdrawal of the complaint, or other specific circumstances prevent an investigation that permits a determination based on appropriate evidence, the Investigator *may* dismiss the complaint. Regardless of such dismissal,

[THE SCHOOL] may take whatever separate disciplinary or corrective action is appropriate against a Respondent under its student Code of Conduct or under its employment policies and practices. Notice of summary dismissal shall include a statement of the process and bases for an appeal and whether other actions or forms of grievance processing will take place.

11. **FALSE EVIDENCE PROHIBITED.** Complainants, Respondents, and all witnesses are prohibited from making any knowing false statement or providing other evidence known to be false in any investigation. [THE SCHOOL] may take disciplinary or corrective action against a person making false statements or submitting other false evidence. Inconsistencies between evidence and an investigative report or determination of responsibility do not prove a knowing use of false evidence. Discipline for a knowing use of false evidence is not retaliation as otherwise prohibited by this policy.

12. **WRITTEN NOTICE OF FORMAL COMPLAINT.** The Title IX Coordinator will provide written notice to the Complainant and the Respondent of the allegations of a formal complaint and the Title IX grievance process, including any opportunity for informal resolution. The notice must include:

    a. Sufficient detail to permit the Respondent to prepare a response. This includes a description of the conduct alleged, the date and location of the conduct and the names of the Complainant and other involved parties, if any.

    b. A statement that the Respondent is presumed not to be responsible for the conduct and that responsibility will be determined at the conclusion of the process.

    c. A notice of the Complainant's and Respondent's rights to have an attorney or non-attorney advisor.

    d. A statement of the right of the Complainant and Respondent to inspect and review any evidence.

    e. A statement prohibiting providing false statements or evidence.

    If additional allegations arise and require investigation, the Investigator will provide written notice of such additional allegation to the Complainant and Respondent. A sample form of the notice required by this paragraph is Exhibit 3 to this policy.

13. **PRIVILEGED AND IRRELEVANT EVIDENCE.** Evidence that is privileged by law and evidence of sexual predisposition or prior sexual behavior (unless offered to prove either that a person other than Respondent committed the alleged conduct or to prove legally recognized consent) is neither admissible nor relevant in this process.

14. **INVESTIGATIONS.** The Investigator will investigate the allegations in a Formal Complaint. The Investigator may gather evidence by collecting relevant documents and other information, interviewing the parties and witnesses, and/or receiving documents, witness lists, requests to gather documents or other information from the Complainant, Respondent witnesses, or third parties.

15. **EVIDENCE SHARING.** The Investigator will provide the Complainant and Respondent (and advisors, if any) with an equal opportunity to review all evidence directly related to the allegations of the formal complaint. If possible, the evidence will be provided in an electronic format that does not permit downloading or copying. The Parties may submit a written response to the Investigator within [NUMBER] calendar days upon receipt or inspection of the evidence.

16. **NO LIVE HEARING.** [THE SCHOOL] will not conduct live hearings under this Policy.

17. **FINAL INVESTIGATION REPORT.** The Investigator will create an investigative report that fairly summarizes relevant evidence. The Investigator will consider all the relevant evidence discovered during the investigation and consider any written response to the evidence submitted by a Party. The Investigator may need to conduct an additional follow up with witnesses or obtain documentation based on Party responses. The Investigator must provide the report to the Parties and the Decision Maker.

18. **PROPOSED QUESTIONS.** The Decision Maker must afford each Party the opportunity to submit written, relevant questions that a Party wants asked of any Party or witness. The Decision Maker must review the investigative report and the Parties' responses and proposed questions, if any. The Decision Maker shall either exclude questions as irrelevant, with an explanation to the Party proposing the question, or submit the questions for answer and provide each Party with such answers. The Decision Maker shall allow limited follow-up questions

from either Party. The Decision Maker will give the Parties five (5) calendar days to submit relevant questions.

19. **DECISION MAKER DECISION.** The Decision Maker shall determine the question of responsibility. The Decision Maker may not render a decision until at least 10 days after the distribution of the Final Investigation Report. The determination must be based on facts the Decision Maker finds to be more likely than not, and the written decision must include:

   a. A statement of the allegations that may constitute sexual harassment;

   b. A summary of the process followed from receipt of the formal complaint through determination, including notices provided, interviews with parties and witnesses, site visits, and methods used to gather other evidence;

   c. Findings of fact;

   d. Conclusions regarding application of any code of conduct or employment policy and practice to the facts;

   e. A statement of, and rationale for,

      i. the conclusions as to each allegation;

      ii. disciplinary sanctions, if any, on the Respondent; and

      iii. Remedies, if any, designed to restore or preserve the Complainant's equal access to [THE SCHOOL]'s programs and activities (including employment, if applicable).

   f. A statement of the process and bases for appeal. A form for this statement is provided in Exhibit 4 and may accompany the determination of responsibility (as illustrated in Exhibit 4) or be incorporated into that document.

20. **APPEAL.** An appeal may be filed within five calendar days of notice of a determination of responsibility or summary dismissal. The notice should only identify the Party filing the appeal, the decision or dismissal appealed from and which of the three grounds listed in 20(a) through (c) below will be relied upon. An optional form of notice that may be used is provided in Exhibit 5. An appeal shall be filed with the Decision Maker. Appeals will *only* be permitted on the following grounds:

   a. A procedural irregularity affected the outcome of the matter;

b. New evidence not available at the time of the determination of responsibility or summary dismissal that could affect the outcome of the matter; or

c. The Investigator or Decision Maker had a conflict of interest or was biased against a Party or biased against all complainants or all respondents.

21. **APPEAL PROCESS.** The Decision Maker, upon receiving a notice of appeal, shall provide a notice to both Parties (or, in the case of appeal of a summary dismissal, to Complainant) that the appeal has been filed and that each Party has ten calendar days to file a brief written statement supporting or challenging the outcome. A form of such notice is provided in Exhibit 5. The Decision Maker shall also initiate the formation of an Appeals Panel. The Appeals Panel shall be provided with copies of the notice of appeal, statements of the parties challenging or supporting the decision appealed, the formal complaint and, as appropriate, either the summary dismissal or the investigative report and determination of responsibility. Either Party may attach other documents produced during the process to their statement supporting or challenging the outcome. The Appeals Panel shall provide a written decision describing the appeal and the rationale for its decision simultaneously to the Parties.

22. **REMEDIES.** Upon determination that a Complainant was sexually harassed. [THE SCHOOL] may —

a. Offer the Complainant any remedies that will restore or preserve the Complainant's access to [THE SCHOOL]'s educational program and activities (including employment). These may include Supportive Measures or actions similar to supportive measures that have a disciplinary component toward the Respondent. Remedies may be kept confidential as deemed necessary by [THE SCHOOL].

b. Impose any disciplinary sanctions on a Respondent Student, including mandatory participation in counseling services; revocation of extra-curricular privileges (including, but not limited to sports); no-contact orders; schedule changes; short-term or long-term suspension or expulsion, or change of placement as otherwise authorized by law.

c. Impose any disciplinary sanctions on a Respondent employee, including mandatory participation in counseling services, no-contact orders, reassignment; suspension without pay; or termination of employment.

23. **EXTENSIONS OF TIME.** The Title IX Coordinator, Investigator, Decision Maker or Appeals Panel may extend any time limit for good cause shown.

24. **CONFIDENTIALITY.** The identities of persons who made a report of sexual discrimination or harassment, the Complainant, the Respondent, any person reported to have been a perpetrator, and any witness shall not be made public except as provided in the Family Educational Rights and Privacy Act (FERPA), as otherwise provided by law, or as needed for the conduct of any formal investigation or judicial proceeding,

25. **RETALIATION AND INTIMIDATION.** Neither [THE SCHOOL] nor any person may intimidate, threaten, coerce, or discriminate against an individual because such individual has exercised rights under, participated in, or declined to participate in, any proceeding under this policy. Claims of retaliation may be filed under [THE SCHOOL] grievance policy that would be applicable to a claim of sex discrimination (not including sexual harassment) by the person alleging retaliation.

26. **RECORD RETENTION.** All records created of activity under this policy, including, without limitation, training materials, investigative records, alternative dispute resolution records, disciplinary records, supportive measures, decisions, remedies, and appeals, shall be maintained for seven years.

27. **TRAINING.** All School staff and [THE SCHOOL]'s governing board shall receive basic Title IX training that includes, without limitation, the definition of sexual harassment and the obligation of school employees and officials to report suspected sexual harassment to the Coordinator. Any person who will serve as a Title IX Coordinator, Investigator, informal resolution mediator, Decision Maker, or member of an Appeals Panel must have had or receive appropriate advanced training on Title IX — specifically, as applicable and without limitation, on all matters covered in basic training, conducting investigations,

methods of alternative dispute resolution, preparation of investigative reports, preparation of determinations of responsibility, conducting appeals, identification of privileged or irrelevant evidence (including treatment of evidence of prior sexual conduct), impartiality, avoidance of prejudgment, and avoiding use sex stereotypes.

28. **POSTING AND GENERAL NOTIFICATIONS.** [THE SCHOOL] shall place in its student/family and employee handbooks, and post prominently on its website —

    a. The name or title, office address, electronic mail address, and telephone number of the Title IX Coordinator(s).

    b. The availability of the Title IX Coordinator(s) to receive at any time a report of sex discrimination, including any complaint of sexual harassment (whether or not by the person alleged to be the victim).

    c. A statement of [THE SCHOOL] policy to not discriminate on the basis of sex in any education program or activity it operates or in employment.

    d. A copy of or link to this policy and related School policies forbidding and providing procedures for receiving and processing complaints of sex discrimination.

    e. A copy of or link to training materials used by [THE SCHOOL] to comply with paragraph 27, above.

29. **CODE OF CONDUCT.** Nothing in this policy prevents the ordinary application of [THE SCHOOL]'s student Code of Conduct or employment policies and practices to matters or issues other than sexual harassment, provided this is not done in retaliation under this Policy.

30. **POLICY REVIEW.** The Board will review this policy and make appropriate changes, if any, should the Title IX regulation published at 85 Fed. Reg. 30572 (May 19, 2020) be amended, repealed, replaced, or held unlawful in any part in a final and unappealable judgment by a court of competent jurisdiction.

You May Contact [THE SCHOOL]'s Title IX Coordinator at:

_____ **[Name/Office]**

_____ **[Address]**

_____ **[Phone]**

_____ [Fax]

_____ [Email Address]

Persons may report concerns to certain outside agencies.
Office for Civil Rights
United States Department of Education
Cesar E. Chavez Memorial Building
1244 Speer Blvd., Suite 300

EXHIBIT 1

Actual Knowledge Report
(to be completed by the Title IX Coordinator)

1. Date: _____

2. Name of Reporter: _____

3. Name of Complainant: _____

4. Name of Respondent: _____

5. Summary of Report: _____

   _____

   _____

   Attached pages? No   Yes — Number? _____

6. Was the report discussed with Complainant? Yes   No

   Date: _____

7. Was the Complainant:

   Informed of available Supportive Measures, with or without a formal complaint? Yes   No

   Given an explanation of the process for filing a formal complaint? Yes   No

8. Were Supportive Measures requested? Yes   No

9. Will Supportive Measures be provided? Yes   No   If yes, describe:

   _____

   _____

10. If an answer under 6 through 9 above is "No," fully explain why (attach pages if needed):

_____

_____

Attached pages?   No   Yes — Number? _____

11. Formal Complaint filed by/for Complainant? Yes   No

12. Formal Complaint filed by Title IX Coordinator? Yes   No

Signature of Title IX Coordinator _____

Date _____

EXHIBIT 2

Sexual Harassment (Title IX) Complaint Form

Instructions for filling out this form: If you believe that you have been the victim of sexual harassment, please fill out this form and submit it by hand delivery, electronic mail, or U.S. mail to the School's Title IX Coordinator. **You are not required to use this form and may file a complaint by any other reasonable means, orally or in writing.** If the victim of sexual harassment is a minor, the form my be completed and signed by a parent or guardian. A person believed to be a victim of sexual harassment is the "complainant."

If you are reporting sexual harassment you witnessed or know of against another person, please report this to the School's Title IX Coordinator. **Do not use this form.** Please identify for the Title IX Coordinator the victim, the alleged perpetrator; the date, time and place of the conduct; and other factual details. **Under federal law, only an alleged victim (for themselves or, for a minor, through a parent or guardian) or the Title IX Coordinator has the right to file a complaint.**

Please print or type when completing this form. **If needed, attach additional sheets and indicate the number of additional pages below.**

Name of complainant: _____

Parent or guardian (if applicable) _____

Address: _____

Telephone number: _____

Email address: _____

I am an/a: Employee   Student   Parent/Guardian
    Other (_____)

You have the right to be represented by an advisor (who may be an attorney, advocate or someone else) during the complaint process. If you have an advisor, please provide contact information. You may provide this information at a later time.

Name: _____

Address: _____

Telephone number: _____

Email address: _____

A person alleged to have committed sexual harassment is called the "respondent." Please identify the respondent(s) and indicate their relationship to the School.

Employee   Student   Parent/Guardian
    Other (_____)

Please describe the facts and circumstances giving rise to this complaint.

_____

_____

_____

When and where did these events occur? Provide dates, times, and locations, if possible.

_____

Please provide the names of anyone else you believe is a victim of such conduct:

_____

_____

Please provide the names and contact information of anyone who may have witnessed the alleged conduct.

_____

_____

_____

If you have reported this to another person, please state to whom you reported the behavior and provide their contact information (if known).

_____

If you reported to a School employee, please state when, to whom, and what response you received. Please note such a report was not required.

_____

_____

_____

Please list below any evidence that you believe is relevant. This could include audio or visual media, physical objects, online materials, text messages, voicemail messages, screen captures, emails, or any other item. Please include any information in the possession of the School or the Respondent that may be helpful (such as emails, pictures, or video).

_____

_____

_____

Is there any other information you believe would be helpful? For example, if this conduct constituted harassment or misconduct on some other grounds, you may explain that here.

_____

_____

_____

Please explain how this conduct has impacted you. This includes any injuries as well as impacts on your ability to access or benefit from the School's education program or activities or from your employment.

_____

Please describe the outcome or remedy you seek.

_____

_____

_____

Please provide below your physical or digital signature.

Signature: _____

Name (printed): _____

Check one: Complainant   Parent/Guardian   Title IX Coordinator

Date: _____

Notice to Complainant: This document is a legal record requesting a formal investigation. Please keep a copy of this completed form and any supporting documentation for your records.

If your complaint is found not to support a claim of sexual harassment, but would be proper under any other School policy, the School will notify you and proceed to consider your complaint under the proper policy.

EXHIBIT 3

Written Notice of Formal Complaint

[To be promptly prepared and provided by the Title IX Coordinator to the Complainant and Respondent after a formal complaint is filed, if the complaint is not summarily dismissed.]

[School Letterhead]

[Date]

PLEASE TAKE NOTICE THAT, a formal complaint alleging sexual harassment has been filed with the School. [NAME] will be the Investigator during this Title IX grievance process. The Investigator will provide a Final Investigation Report which summarizes the evidence. A Decision Maker will decide the responsibility.

In such complaints, the alleged victim is referred to as the Complainant and the alleged perpetrator is referred to as the Respondent. One purpose of this notice is to ensure that both the Complainant and Respondent are aware of certain rights they may exercise in this process. Another purpose is to allow the Respondent to be prepared to appropriately participate in this process. When a party is a minor, the parent or guardian will be given this notice. The terms "Complainant" and "Respondent" may in some cases refer to a representative of a minor.

NATURE OF REPORT

Complainant: _____

Respondent: _____

Summary of the Complaint:

    Date(s) of conduct: _____

    Location of conduct: _____

    Names of other parties, if any: _____

_____

    Description of the conduct alleged. This is a summary intended to provide sufficient detail to allow the Respondent to prepare a response. (Additional pages may be attached.)

_____

_____

_____

POTENTIAL PROHIBITED CONDUCT

After reviewing the Formal Complaint and the Complainant's request for a formal investigation, the Title IX Coordinator determined it was appropriate to open this matter for a formal investigation consistent with the Title IX Sexual Harassment Policy.

    This report raises the following potential prohibited conduct pursuant to [THE SCHOOL]'s Title IX Sexual Harassment Policy.

    LIST APPLICABLE POLICIES WITH DEFINITIONS

ADVISOR AND SUPPORT PERSON

You have the right to have an advisor of your choice and support person of your choice. The advisor may be an attorney or non-attorney of your choice, at your own expense. The advisor and support person may be present at any meetings or proceedings that are part of the formal resolution process.

The School will communicate with you directly, not through your advisor or support person.

INFORMATIONAL MEETING

You can request a meeting with [THE SCHOOL]'s Title IX Coordinator to review the Title IX Policy for the formal resolution process, to discuss your rights as a [Complainant or Respondent], and to answer any questions that you may have at this point.

As with any portion of the process, you may bring a support person and an advisor with you to this meeting.

BRIEF OVERVIEW OF FORMAL RESOLUTION PROCESS

The Respondent is presumed not to be responsible for the conduct alleged. The Decision Maker will determine responsibility at the initiation of the process. The Investigator will investigate the allegations identified in this Notice.

The Parties have an equal opportunity to identify potential witnesses who have relevant information, including fact and expert witnesses, and other inculpatory and exculpatory evidence to the Investigator, such as documents, communications, photographs, and other evidence, and to suggest questions to be posed by the Investigator to any other parties or witnesses. The Investigator may gather evidence by collecting relevant documents and other information, interviewing the parties and witnesses, and/or receiving documents, witness lists, requests to gather documentation or other information from the parties, witnesses, or third parties. In preparation for the investigation, please preserve any potentially relevant evidence in any format.

The Parties have the right to inspect and review evidence gathered during the investigation. Prior to the conclusion of the investigation, the Investigator will make available to each party and their advisors all evidence obtained as part of the investigation that is directly related to the allegations raised in the Formal Complaint. The parties will have an opportunity to submit a written response, which the Investigator will consider prior to the conclusion of the investigation and the completion of the final investigative report.

Submitting knowingly false statements or evidence is a violation of School policy and will result in disciplinary consequences. Such consequences are not "retaliation." Mere disagreement between the parties, or between a party and a school official investigating or deciding this matter does not, by itself, demonstrate knowing submission of false evidence.

The Investigator will create an investigative report that fairly summarizes relevant evidence. The Parties will have an opportunity to submit relevant questions. The Decision Maker will prepare a decision regarding responsibility.

Please contact me with any questions or concerns.

/s/ Title IX Coordinator

EXHIBIT 4

Notice to Parties Concerning Determination of Responsibility

[This notice is to accompany the transmission of, or be incorporated into, the determination of responsibility to the Complainant and Respondent. The form here is a cover letter.]

[School Letterhead]

[Date]

[Addressee]

Please find attached the determination of responsibility in this matter. This determination can be appealed on one or more of the following three grounds:

- You believe a procedural irregularity affected the outcome of the matter;
- You have new evidence not available as of the date of this decision that could have affected the outcome of this matter; or
- You believe either I was biased, or the Investigator was biased, against you or biased against all persons in your position (that is, all complainants or all respondents).

If you wish to appeal, please send me a notice identifying the ground(s) on which you are appealing. An optional form of notice of appeal is provided in Exhibit 5. If an appeal is filed, I will forward your notice of appeal to an Appeals Panel formed under the School's sexual harassment policy and provide you with a further notice of details of that process.

/s/ [Decision Maker]

EXHIBIT 5

Notice of Appeal

[This illustrates one proper form for filing a notice of appeal. This may be used by a Complainant in response to a summary dismissal or by a Complainant or Respondent in response to a determination of responsibility.]

[Date]

From: [Name and Contact information of party filing the appeal]

To: [Name, Title and contact information of decision maker]

To Whom It May Concern:

I am appealing the (check one)   Summary Dismissal   Determination of Responsibility in this matter dated [date]. I believe (check appropriate boxes and summarize details, if desired):

A procedural irregularity affected the outcome of the matter. Describe (optional): _____

_____

_____

I have new evidence not available as of the date of this decision that could have affected the outcome of this matter. Describe (optional):

_____

_____

The (check as appropriate   Investigator or   Decision Maker was biased against me or biased against all persons in my position. Describe (optional): _____

_____

_____

/s/ [Complainant or Respondent]